The Development of Communication

The Development of Communication

Edited by

Natalie Waterson
School of Oriental and African Studies,
University of London

and

Catherine Snow
Institute for General Linguistics,
University of Amsterdam.

JOHN WILEY & SONS
Chichester · New York · Brisbane · Toronto

Library of Congress Cataloging in Publication Data:

International Child Language Symposium, 3d, London, Eng.,
    1975.
    The development of communication.

    Selected papers of the Symposium held Sept. 3—5, 1975.
    Includes indexes.
    1. Children—Language—Congresses. I. Waterson,
Natalie. II. Snow, Catherine E. III. Title.
P118.15 1975   401'.9   77-27237

ISBN 0 471 99628 9

Printed and bound in Great Britain

Contributors

Martin Atkinson, Dept. of Language and Linguistics, University of Essex, Colchester, Essex, England.

David Barton, at the Dept. of Linguistics, Stanford University, Stanford, California 94705, U.S.A.

Melissa Bowerman, Bureau of Child Research Laboratories, University of Kansas, Lawrence, Kansas 66045, U.S.A.

Anthony W.H. Buffery, Dept. of Psychology, Institute of Psychiatry, London, England.

Anne L. Carter, P.O.Box 5073, Berkeley, California 94705, U.S.A.

Louise J. Cherry, Dept. of Educational Psychology, University of Wisconsin Madison, Madison, Wisconsin 53706, U.S.A.

Ruth Clark, School of Social Studies, Queen Margaret College, Clerwood Terrace, Edinburgh, EH12 8TS.

Jenny Cook-Gumperz, Language Behavior Research Laboratory, University of California, Berkeley, Berkeley, California 94720, U.S.A.

Toni G. Cross, Dept. of Psychology, University of Melbourne, Victoria 3052, Australia.

John B. Delack, The Phonetics Laboratory, Division of Audiology and Speech Sciences, The University of British Columbia, Vancouver, B.C., Canada, V6T 1W5.

Sascha W. Felix, Englisches Seminar der Universität, University of Kiel, Kiel, West Germany.

Linda Ferrier, Eliot Pearson Child Study Dept., Tufts University, Mass., U.S.A.

Adrian J. Fourcin, Dept. of Phonetics and Linguistics, University College, London, London, England.

Patricia J. Fowlow, The Phonetics Laboratory, Division of
Audiology and Speech Sciences, The University of British
Columbia, Vancouver, B.C., Canada, V6T 1W5.

Olga K. Garnica, Dept. of Linguistics, The Ohio State
University, Columbus, Ohio 43210, U.S.A.

Patricia M. Greenfield, Dept. of Psychology, University of
California, Los Angeles, Los Angeles, California 90024,
U.S.A.

Patrick Griffiths, Dept. of Language, University of York,
Heslington, York, England.

John J. Gumperz, Language Behavior Research Laboratory,
University of California, Berkeley, Berkeley,
California 94720, U.S.A.

Bruce Ingham, Dept. of Phonetics and Linguistics, School
of Oriental and African Studies, University of London,
London, England.

David Ingram, Dept. of Linguistics, University of British
Columbia, Vancouver, B.C., Canada V6T 1W5.

Mirjana Jocić, Institut za Lingvistiku, 21,000 Novi Sad,
Bulevar Maršala Tita 16, Yugoslavia.

Willem Kaper, Duits Seminarium van de Universiteit van
Amsterdam, Amsterdam, The Netherlands.

Michael Lewis, Educational Testing Service, Princeton,
New Jersey, U.S.A.

Elena V.M. Lieven, The Psychological Laboratory, University
of Cambridge, Cambridge, England.

Max Miller, Projektgruppe für Psycholinguistik in der Max-
Planck-Gesellschaft, Berg en Dalseweg 79, Nijmegen,
The Netherlands.

Norma M. Ringler, Dept. of Speech Communication, Case
Western Reserve University, Cleveland, Ohio 44106,
U.S.A.

Svenka Savić, Institut za Lingvistiku, 21,000 Novi Sad,
Bulevar Maršala Tita 16, Yugoslavia.

Grace W. Shugar, Psycholinguistics Unit, Institute of
Psychology, Warsaw University, Warsaw, Poland.

Chris Sinha, School of Education Research Unit, Bristol University, Bristol, England.

Magdalena Smoczyńska, Institut Psychologii, Universytet Jagielloński, Krakow, Poland.

Ben Sylvester-Bradley, Dept. of Psychology, University of Edinburgh, Edinburgh, Scotland.

Colwyn Trevarthen, Dept. of Psychology, University of Edinburgh, Edinburgh, Scotland.

Pintip Tuaycharoen, Dept. of Teacher Training, Ministry of Education, Bangkok, Thailand.

Valerie Walkerdine, North East London Polytechnic, Longbridge Road, Dagenham, Essex, England.

Natalie Waterson, Dept. of Phonetics and Linguistics, School of Oriental and African Studies, University of London, London, England.

Bencie Woll, School of Education Research Unit, Bristol University, Bristol, England.

Contents

Page

List of figures, tables and plates

Foreword

This book contains selected papers from the
Third International Child Language Symposium, chaired
by Natalie Waterson at the School of Oriental and
African Studies, University of London, in London,
September 3-5, 1975. At this Symposium the International
Association for the Study of Child Language was incor-
porated with statutes and its officers were elected:

Els Oksaar, University of Hamburg, Germany: President.

Walburga von Raffler-Engel, Vanderbilt University,
Nashville, U.S.A.: Vice-President.

Fred C.C. Peng, International Christian University,
Tokyo, Japan: Secretary.

Terry Myers, University of Edinburgh, Scotland:
Treasurer.

A further fifteen members were elected to serve on the
Executive Committee.

The International Association for the Study of
Child Language originated during a first meeting at the
University of Brno, Czechoslovakia, October 14-16, 1970,
under the chairmanship of Karel Ohnesorg, who also
edited the Proceedings (Colloquium Paedolinguisticum,
Mouton, 1972). At a second meeting, the International
Association for the Study of Child Language was official-
ly organized with Charles A. Ferguson, Stanford Univer-
sity, U.S.A., as President, Walbruga von Raffler-Engel
as Secretary, and Els Oksaar as Treasurer. It also
elected an international committee of vice-presidents:
F. Antinucci (Italy), M. Bullowa (U.S.A.), D. Crystal
(Great Britain), S.H. Herzka (Switzerland), M. Mikeš
(Yugoslavia), T. Slama-Cazacu (Romania) and D.I. Slobin
(U.S.A.). This second meeting, the International Sym-
posium on First Language Acquisition, took place at the
Tuscan Academy of Sciences in Florence, Italy, in
September, 4-6, 1972, and was chaired by W. von Raffler-
Engel. The Proceedings were edited by W. von Raffler-
Engel and Yvan Lebrun (Baby Talk and Infant Speech,
Swets and Zeitlinger, Amsterdam, 1976).

The Association has encouraged international contact and communication by, for example, initiating the establishment of the Journal of Child Language (under the editorship of David Crystal, University of Reading, published by Cambridge University Press) and the Child Language Newsletter (edited by David Ingram, University of British Columbia, published in conjunction with the Linguistics Reporter); also by contributing to the establishment of such projects as the cross-cultural Project in Developmental Kinesics, directed by W. von Raffler-Engel, with its first operating branch chaired by Fred C.C. Peng and sponsored by the Japanese Ministry of Education.

The Symposia of the Association have brought together scholars of child language from Linguistics, Psychology, Paediatrics, Neurology, Speech and Hearing, Early Child Education, Anthropology, and Sociology - from Europe, the Americas, Asia and Africa. From the papers and discussions of this cross-cultural and inter-disciplinary group, a strong trend emerged in Florence to see language as a social phenomenon, with explicit attention drawn for the first time to input factors and to non-verbal communication. That conference signalled the end of the study of language acquisition as if it were a linear development of innate grammatical rules. The full importance of the interactional and pragmatic aspects of language development emerged at the London conference which also saw the first separate sections on pre-speech, kinesics and language disabilities.

The first three gatherings of the Association were mainly invitational. The next meeting will more likely be a congress. It is planned to be held in 1978 in Tokyo, Japan, under the chairmanship of Fred C.C. Peng. This coming conference promises new developments and contributions in all these fields. It may very well be that the trend of the future lies in a pluri-modal approach to language acquisition, how children acquire understanding and production of the auditory as well as the visual rules of conversational interaction. Another trend of the future seems to be the linguist's concern with language pathologies. Interest in pragmatics is not only limited to extra-linguistic factors but includes the observation of natural cases where language has broken down. The co-operation between practitioners and theoreticians may be one of the most fruitful trends of the future in child language studies.

Walburga von Raffler-Engel.

Preface

This volume is based on selected papers, revised and expanded, that were presented at the Third International Child Language Symposium, 3-5 September, 1975, in London. The Symposium was sponsored by the International Association for the Study of Child Language. The Organizing Committee consisted of Natalie Waterson, Chairman; Walburga von Raffler-Engel, Associate Chairman; and Committee members David Bennett, Bruce Ingham and Geoffrey Ivimey. Additional help was given by Margaret Bullowa. There were 12 sections representing a wide range of interests, and 80 papers were given in the form of short research reports. About 200 scholars from 29 different countries attended the Symposium.

The 12 sections and the names of those who chaired them were as follows: Bilingualism, Els Oksaar; Child Sociolinguistics, Susan Ervin-Tripp; Kinesics, Walburga von Raffler-Engel; Language Acquisition and Reading, Ragnhild Söderbergh; Language Acquisition and the Handicapped Child, Geoffrey Ivimey; Language and Cognition, Tatiana Slama-Cazacu; Language Spoken to Children, Catherine E. Snow; Linguistic Universals, Dan I. Slobin; Phonological Development, Charles A. Ferguson; Prespeech, Margaret Bullowa; Semantic Development, Nathan Stemmer; Syntactic Development, Richard Cromer.

There were two invited speakers: Adrian Fourcin and Anthony Buffery. Their papers are included in the volume.

The high cost of publication made it impossible to publish the full proceedings. We are grateful to John Wiley and Sons, Ltd., for agreeing to publish as many as 30 papers, which made it possible to represent those aspects of child language development which created the greatest amount of interest. Selection of papers was a difficult task and we would like to express our gratitude to the section chairmen who gave their advice and recommendations. The selection of only 30 papers meant that several interesting ones could not be included, but these will no doubt appear in print elsewhere in due course.

Within the limits set, we aimed to give an overall representation of what was new and stimulating at the

Symposium, at the same time preserving the international character of the contributions and covering a fair range of language material, as well as including different methodologies such as case studies and experimental manipulation.

The direction in which child language studies have moved in recent years is towards the study of language acquisition within the social context, taking into account the wide range of influences which bear on the child from birth, as well as his influence on those who interact with him. This means that research is no longer neatly compartmentalized. For instance, syntactic development is now mostly studied within the context of language use so that a syntactic study may well overlap with an interactional one. Classifying the contributions under section headings therefore presented something of a problem as several of them could have been placed under more than one heading. However, it is necessary to give some structure to a book in order to make it manageable for the reader, so we grouped the papers in accordance with what seemed to us to be the major emphasis intended by the author. We would not wish, however, to impose our judgement on the reader, and suggest that each paper should be read for its own merits rather than essentially as a contribution to the particular aspect of language acquisition indicated by the section heading under which it is placed.

We owe thanks to many who helped to make this book possible. We are indebted to the authorities of the School of Oriental and African Studies whose generous support enabled the Symposium to be held in London. We thank the authors for responding to our request to expand and revise their ten-minute presentations into fuller papers within a limited time, and all the participants in the Symposium whose comments and questions during the discussions contributed to the final versions of the papers. We acknowledge with pleasure the assistance given to us by the publishers, who provided much helpful guidance during the preparation of the book.

We are also grateful to Vera Williams, who prepared the papers. Her quick and accurate work made it possible to bring the book out sooner than would otherwise have been the case. Our thanks too are due to Bruce Ingham and Marcia Vale who helped in the task of checking the typescript of the book, and to Maria T.H. Singelenberg who assisted in the preparation of the index.

N.W.

C.E.S.

Introduction

The papers collected in this book represent
some of the areas in child language research in which
new and important developments have taken place in
the last five years. Developmental psycholinguistics
has undergone remarkable changes in its theoretical
assumptions, its methodology, and its areas of concentration. Five far-reaching changes in child
language research since 1960 are:

1. Growing interest in the semantic and pragmatic
   components of children's linguistic competence,
   replacing the earlier concentration on syntactic
   competence.

2. Increasing recognition that language is intrinsically communicative and that the acquisition
   of language occurs within and is dependent upon
   a social-communicative context.

3. Growing awareness that language acquisition can
   not be understood without relating it to the
   concurrent cognitive development of the child.

4. A recognition of the importance of perceptual
   processing in language acquisition.

5. A reinterpretation of the nature of the innate
   structures for language acquisition.

The scope of child language studies has thus
broadened considerably and although the emphasis has
changed, this has not resulted in a neglect of the task
of describing the growth of the child's knowledge of
syntax; in fact syntactic acquisition can be better
understood by virtue of being placed in its context of
social interaction, cognitive development, and semantic-
pragmatic acquisition. The shift in emphasis away from
syntactic acquisition has meant that language is no
longer seen as an object of knowledge for the child, a
set of rules which he must discover one by one by
listening carefully to native speakers. Rather,
language is seen as one of several techniques for interacting with other human beings. The communicative
function of language is primary and enables the child
to learn syntactic structure.

The different areas of theoretical interest
are discussed below.

Semantic and pragmatic components. In the early 1960s,
child language researchers, under the influence of what
were new and exciting developments taking place within
theoretical linguistics, concentrated their attention on
the problems faced by children in learning word order and
transformational rules. Children's utterances were analyzed in terms of syntactic rules which were seen as
making their production possible. Such studies were
extremely valuable not only as careful descriptions of
interesting aspects of language acquisition but also because they revealed considerable regularity in the process of syntactic acquisition, both in the individual
child and across children. Unfortunately, the technique
of classifying child utterances in terms of the rules
necessary to produce them fails to capture many important
aspects which can only be understood if the utterance is
studied in its conversational and non-linguistic contexts.
The expression of case relations, for example, or of the
topic-comment distinction, can be identified only by
interpreting the child utterance using information from
preceding utterances and the on-going activities to
determine the child's semantic intent. With full information about context and situation, a start can be made
toward answering such questions as which aspects of a
situation the child chooses to encode in speech, the
rules used for expressing such semantic relations as
agent-action or possessor-possessed, and the syntactic
means used for expressing illocutionary functions such
as demand and inform. A much more complete description
of the young child's knowledge of his language is thus
made possible, and the relationship between syntax,
semantics and pragmatics is made explicit.

The social-communicative nature of language. Emphasis
in both theoretical linguistics and in developmental
psycholinguistics has in the last few years shifted back
to the social-communicative role of language. This
shift has had various consequences for child language
research; it has resulted in

1) Attention to the child's intentions, and to growth in
    the ability to express various kinds of intentions.

2) Attention to the conversational skills which children
    acquire along with the other components of linguistic
    ability.

3) Recognition of the importance of non-verbal communica-
    tion: that language is a rather late step in the de-
    velopment of communicative skills, that communication
    between a child and his caretakers can be established
    long before the first one-word utterance is produced.

Recognition that what and how the child communicates is the true object of language acquisition research has greatly expanded the age range studied. Behaviours of infants as young as 9-10 months can be identified as truly communicative, and a continuum can be seen between those behaviours at 9-10 months and the behaviour of much younger babies.

The emphasis on the child's message has meant that much more attention has been paid to the interactions in which a child engages. Messages are a social construct; they require a sender and a receiver and a set of rules known to both about the form messages can take. The social construction of messages is a process which can be observed in any linguistic interaction, but it is especially clear in the case of a child's interactions with his caretakers. It often happens that only the regular caretakers or companions of a young child are able to interpret his intentions, in other words, that the child is an effective communicator only within a very limited circle. Language acquisition can be seen as the process of learning how to communicate effectively with a wider and wider circle of members of a language community. The range of notions which young children can express is greatly expanded by virtue of the conversational frames provided by interlocutors. In studying children's speech, it has proved very useful to take as the unit of study not just the child or the child's utterances but the caretaker-child dyad and the conversation.

Language and cognitive development. Neither what children talk about nor the way they talk about it can be viewed as purely linguistic phenomena. Development of language is found to be greatly dependent on cognitive development. Between birth and three years, children undergo a dramatic reorganization of the way they see the world. A few aspects of the ability to use language can, on the basis of recent research, be related to milestones of cognitive development - the ability to use tools, to use objects symbolically, to carry out operations like matching and counting. Many more relationships could be sought between specific milestones in linguistic development and the prerequisite cognitive achievements.

Perceptual processing. An aspect of cognition which is of central relevance to linguistic behaviour is information processing. The study of the development of the physiological and psychological functions underlying information processing is indispensable to a full understanding of how the child comprehends speech and how he uses the information about the structure of language available from the speech addressed to him.

The early learning of verbal communication is largely dependent on auditory processing, and auditory processing is therefore of vital importance in language

acquisition. Recent neuropsychological research on the
various asymmetries in cerebral structure and function
and on lateral preferences suggests that their development in man may relate to increasing competence in the
use of complex language codes which in turn depend on
the recognition of auditory stimuli. The fact that the
neonate is found to have a relatively enlarged left-
sided planum temporale provides evidence for innate
structure specialized for speech perception. Babies are
known to be able to discriminate between the human voice
and other sounds very early in life and recent work in
phonetics has shown that the child starts by processing
the lower end of the frequency spectrum and then gradually
discriminates more of the higher frequency range. Studies
on speaker identity, the means by which people recognize
the voice of those they know, have revealed that it is the
fundamental frequency, i.e. the low frequency range of the
individual's voice, that provides the main cue (E. Abberton,
Listener identification of speakers from larynx frequency,
in Speech and Hearing, University College, London, 1974).
It thus seems that young humans, like other young animals,
are biologically endowed to recognize their mother's voice
in early infancy, maybe even from birth, and this may
explain why the child mostly makes use of the low frequency
end of the spectrum in the first stages of language
learning.

Innate structures for language acquisition. Early in the
1960s the view was generally held that the human was born
equipped with considerable (syntactic) information about
the nature of language and that innate factors were of
much greater importance in determining the course of
language acquisition than environmental factors. Now with
the information gained from research into the nature of
speech addressed to children which has revealed that such
speech provides very rich information about the structure
of language, and from growing knowledge about the child's
ability for perceptual processing of the speech signal,
and the link between cognitive development and language
development, there has been a reappraisal of the nature of
innate structures.

It seems that the child is able to acquire the
language of his environment without the aid of innate
linguistic (syntactic) structures but that he has an
innate structure for perceptual processing. He can thus
construct his own language system on the basis of the
linguistic information available to him from the language
his caretakers use in interaction with him.

Perceptual discrimination of the speech signal
has been found, in both experimental and naturalistic
studies, to be a gradual process in children. Longitudinal studies have shown that children can only process
a very limited amount of language in the early stages and
that the amount processed increases as time goes on.

This would appear to be related to the gradual development of asymmetries of cerebral structure and function
as adults are known to have a higher degree of lateralization than children.

Thus it may be said that a picture is emerging
of how the child constructs his own language system.
Environmental factors interact with maturational factors
in the acquisition of language. The growth of perceptual
processing ability and of cognitive skills, as well as
language experience, make their contribution. The
child's linguistic system develops out of a prelinguistic
system of communication, and depends on certain types of
interaction with caretakers. More information is needed
about each of these factors for a fuller understanding of
the language acquisition process. The way child language
studies are now moving, gathering material from several
disciplines and from a wide range of areas presents
greater promise for an understanding of the processes
involved.

Several of the papers in this volume provide
new data on a number of different languages: Dutch,
English, French, German, Persian, Polish, Serbocroatian
and Thai. This should be of interest for cross-cultural
studies of language acquisition. An encouraging aspect
of several of the contributions is the suggestions made
by the authors with regard to the way in which their
research findings might be used to help those with
language disabilities. It is hoped that this volume
will make some contribution in this sphere as well as to
child language studies and linguistic theory.

N.W.

C.E.S.

1
Some Theoretical Considerations

The three papers in this section deal with essential areas of theoretical importance for child language studies which have not received as much attention as they deserve in the past and are only now beginning to be studied intensively.

The paper by Cook-Gumperz and Gumperz represents the new trend of studying child language development within the social context, taking into account the social and pragmatic factors that influence the child's learning. The importance of the non-verbal context is made clear. Such an approach makes it possible to demonstrate the growth of communicative competence empirically. For instance it is shown how interaction between the participants in discourse produces 'code-switching' which marks their changing roles in different situations, such as entering or leaving a game; also the differing status of the participants, for example the way in which the mother, who is not included in the game, is addressed as opposed to the speech style used to the partner within the game. The authors further show how context can be used as a 'framing device' for the 'semantic interpretation of message intent' and demonstrate how it can be treated as part of the interactive process rather than as extra-linguistic background information. It will be seen that many of the papers in the volume describe aspects of language development within this type of social and pragmatic context.

The interpretation of speech involves the processing of non-verbal as well as verbal information; linguistic theories therefore need to take this into account and have to be compatible with what is known of brain structure and function in relation to both verbal and non-verbal skills. Buffery's paper provides an account of recent work on cerebral asymmetries relating to such skills within both an ontogenetic and phylogenetic context. He reviews the neuropsychological aspects of language development and examines the concept of cerebral dominance. The difference in degree of cerebral asymmetry for verbal and spatial function in males and females is described. The finding that females have greater asymmetry, i.e. a more pronounced specialization of the dominant hemisphere for language function than males, suggests a possible explanation for the greater verbal facility of females and the relatively greater vulnerability of males to language disorders. How far this greater verbal fluency of females stems from an innate biological endowment and how far from the differential treatment accorded to them (cf. Cherry and Lewis in section 3) is something that merits further investigation. The development of various asymmetries in cerebral structure and function and of lateral preferences in the course of mammalian evolution is seen to relate to an increasing competence in the use of language codes based on the comprehension of auditory stimuli. The ability to discriminate auditory stimuli is related to an enlarged left-sided planum temporale at birth, suggesting that man is born with a specific structure for the perception of speech.

Fourcin's experimental study forms a link with Buffery's paper. He shows how the perception of speech develops in the infant. An auditory-acoustic type of analysis is proposed as being less adult-biased than conventional phonetic transcription and distinctive feature analysis. Fourcin sees 'normalization', the ability to perceive similarity of structure or pattern, as an essential step in the acquisition of speech. He describes how the infant learns to control vocal fold vibration and what types of sound pattern are the first to be used. The infant is shown to respond to the lower end of the frequency spectrum at the start and an acoustic explanation for the early acquisition of vowels, plosives and nasals and the labial glide, as opposed to other sounds, is given. Fourcin finds a gradual accumulation of speech processing ability. This links up with Waterson's naturalistic study of the acquisition of the phonological system firstly through the perception and production of the auditorily most salient features of the adult model and then the gradual acquisition of the less salient sounds (section 5). Barton's paper on the use of the 'voiced-voiceless' contrast in the discrimination of pairs of words (section 4) may also be seen in relation to Fourcin's study where he considers this phenomenon in both French and English children.

Context in Children's Speech

J. Cook-Gumperz and J.J. Gumperz

CONTEXT AS TOPIC

       To those who study child language, it often
appears that many questions currently of general linguistic interest were first raised in child language studies,
for to study the development of verbal abilities we have
always had to rely to a greater extent than other students
of language on social and contextual information; we have
had to 'fill in' from our own and others' background
experience, both practical and theoretical, in order to map
the limited surface forms of child language onto the wider
framework of the potential linguistic and semantic functions of utterances. In this way child language acquisition has provided a naturally occurring experimental
situation for the study of language material. For example,
the study of speech as intentional speech acts, became of
importance in child language before it surfaced in theoretical linguistics, and the importance of context in the
study of language is now being recognized so that when
after a decade of almost exclusive concentration on syntax
and phonology, scholars of language are now becoming

increasingly aware of the role that context plays in the functioning of language, studies of child language can be seen to have already pointed to the fact that the child's early verbalizations are goal-oriented and governed by an identifiable underlying communicative intent, which for communicative purposes, has mostly to be interpreted from the context of utterances (Bloom, 1973; Halliday, 1975). Studies of mother-child communication from the ethological perspective also show that the child's communicative skills grow out of a complex prelinguistic communicative system which utilizes many different aspects of the ecological situation and nonverbal signs (Richards, 1974). In this paper we shall approach context from a different point of view, we shall try to demonstrate how context is used as a framing device for the semantic interpretation of message intent.

We can already show that assumptions about context play an important part in two kinds of problems. Firstly, in studies of the acquisition of such sociolinguistic phenomena as appropriateness rules, where appropriateness is seen as the selection among a set of options at the levels of phonology, syntax and lexicon, in relation to particular speech functions and extralinguistic factors (Bates, 1974). Examples are: choice of mode of address, acquisition of politeness rules or rules of code or style switching. Secondly, in analyses of the role of contextual factors in the interpretation of speech acts, particularly in those cases where the illocutionary force of utterances is different from their propositional content. Here rules normally take forms such as the following: when a teacher in a classroom makes a negative statement about a practice which a child knows is forbidden, the statement has the force of a request or order. For example: 'We don't sit on tables' is understood as 'Don't sit on this table, or else' (Sinclair and Coultard, 1974).

However, it is in the study of language not only as speech but as conversational communication that the implications of context as an influence on message form, message content and its interpretations becomes most apparent. In the increasing study of conversations all are agreed that a conversation is more than a set of utterances with a single thematic connection. While the initial impetus for the study of conversation was in the social purpose revealed by conversational exchanges (Sacks, 1968/1975), the more recent concerns with conversation analysis have focused primarily on the semantic and pragmatic problems shown by naturally occurring inter-related sets of utterances.

Among child language studies, those by Ervin-Tripp (1975), Keenan (1974), Garvey (1975), Gleason

(1975), Gelman and Shatz (1975) have all focused upon
the understanding of children's developing control of
both conversational competence and a range of increasingly varied speech acts within a conversational, interactive setting.

A recent paper by Keenan and Schiefflin (1975)
sets the tone of this work as predominantly linguistic
while at the same time showing an awareness that contextual features such as non-verbal meanings and setting
influence the participants' linguistic choices. Keenan
and Schiefflin's discussion concentrates upon the linguistic significance of how children are able to introduce and mark new information as discourse topics during
conversational exchanges, and thus how they demonstrate
their competence at initiating and maintaining discourse.
Children's verbalizations are studied with reference to
the production of discourse, where discourse can be described as a coherent body of speech definable in time
and place. As such a definable entity it can therefore
be said to constitute a text, so that context becomes
the extra-linguistic phenomena in which, in a sense, the
text is embedded. As Keenan and Schiefflin point out
the notion of context can be taken as including both the
previous history of the discourse as well as the preceding utterances (in the text) and the immediate social
event of which the verbal interaction is a part, all
features which help to elucidate the child's understanding of the conduct of the discourse.

Although these studies all show an awareness
that children do not merely talk for talk's sake, but
that their talk is closely tied to on-going action, the
analytic concern remains focused on how children demonstrate their ability (competence) to produce and understand increasingly complex speech acts; complex in the
sense of dependent upon an extended chain of implicature
as to their intended effect in the conversational
argument.

What we are suggesting in this paper is that
a notion of context can be developed which can be shown
to be more than a source of background information;
which can be used for more than illuminating ambiguities
in discourse such as unreferenced deixis, or unexplained
shifts of topicalization. Context itself can be taken
to be more than a cluster of already given or constant
social information. The more usual linguistic view of
context raises certain problems for a social definition.
For in all cases the term context serves as a 'label'
for a cluster of extralinguistic or extra-grammatical
factors including: setting, topic, and the social
characteristics of participants such as age, ethnic
identity, education and social class. The reason why
these factors and their inter-relationship are not

specified in more detail is that a social assumption
is made that these factors are (a) known, i.e., that
their perception presents no problem and that speaker,
hearer, and analyst perceive them the same way; and
(b) that their effect is direct, i.e., that if they are
kept constant and if function is constant then both formation and interpretation of the message is predictable.
If, however, context is seen as socially dynamic, that
is, as entering into the information communicated and
perceived by speaker and listener, the focus of concern
shifts from the division between linguistic and extra-
linguistic features. If context is communicated as a
part of the total message from within an ongoing interactive situation, then the assumptions of constancy and
directness of the social information made available may
not always hold; speaker and listener may fail to understand or even mis-communicate. The contextual information does not stand available outside of the linguistic,
that is semantic, process of communication between interactants. Even objects which define settings such as
rooms, furnishings, clothes are subject to interpretation
and have to be taken into account in the semantic choices
of participants.

The process of arriving at a socially active
notion of context moves in the opposite direction from a
linguistic one, not outwards from the linguistic conun-
drum but in from a social definition of the speech situation. The study of discourse as such probably does much
to separate the social interactive purposes of language
from the more specifically linguistic, by assuming the
influence of a similar linguistic phenomenon to be a
constant within a given, or at the least definable, social
space. For from a social perspective it can be shown
that a similarly regarded linguistic feature (e.g., an
indirect request) may have several possible strategic
interpretations or functions within the on-going social
interaction. What we are stressing is that people, including children, talk to achieve certain social goals
or projects, not only to generate discourse, and that
these goals give an interpretative input to the semantic
field.

We suggest that an additional focus of concern
in child language could be on the way in which talk influences and shapes on-going events, how children use
talk to create and act out social activities. This is
not to say that the linguist's concern with the linguistic realization of speech events is too limited, but
that it can be shown that the focus of the analyst's
concerns determines the understanding of what context
constitutes as a theoretical notion. The problem is
essentially a figure-ground one; if the focus of the
analysis shifts to a concern with context as a socially
realized phenomenon, as a part of interactive process,
rather than assuming it to be a parameter or social

given, the notion of context takes on a different relevance and a more substantive character.

COMMUNICATIVE ACTIVITY AS A CONTEXT FRAMING DEVICE

We have suggested that most work with a linguistic focus in the study of conversations has assumed
that contexts can be specified as, at the least, a
cluster of backgrounded social information, which once
known can be used to elucidate any set of linguistic
messages; and secondly, that these features or sources
of information, being extra-linguistic, do not enter
directly into the linguistic process of reasoning. Work
in the conversational analysis of adult speech shows
that neither of these assumptions is justified. It
would be very difficult for example to find any one set
of extra-linguistic factors which could account for the
subtle, often momentary, shifts in speech function and
mood illustrated in work such as Goffman's studies in
Frame Analysis (1975) or to account for the fact that,
as Sacks has shown in his work on puns, the interpretation of any one utterance can change radically as a
result of something else which is said later on in time
(Sacks, 1972).

Our own initial evidence on the operation of
contextual factors in speech comes from work in code
and style switching. The term 'switching' is commonly
used to describe the speaker's selection among clusters
of lexical, prosodic or - in the case of codes -
grammatical options in verbalizing what he wants to
convey. Although such options are semantically equivalent inasmuch as they represent the same 'objective
content', they are associated with certain restricted
classes of communicative activities so that they pass
without notice when their occurrence is expected. When
not expected, however, such selections may be singled
out as inappropriate or lead to inferences which affect
the interpretation of speaker's intent. We thus speak
of such things as lecturing, preaching, announcing or
conversing as distinct types of speech activities.

It can easily be shown that speakers who
share the same communicative background have no difficulty in agreeing on the identification of such activities
even when the details or content of what is said are not
clearly understood, although to describe or characterize
the linguistic knowledge that is involved in such identi-
fications in terms of grammatical or phonological rules
has not been successful. The best that can be done from
a purely linguistic point of view is to rely on statistical counts of key items. These counts, to be sure, do
reveal significant differences in the incidence of
grammatical forms which correlate highly with speakers'
perceptions. Yet they are by their very nature post

<u>facto</u> analyses, which can only be done upon completion
of the act, that is, when the finished text is available.
Therefore, statistical counts do not account for
speakers' ability to categorize speech activities as
they are being produced, that is, to predict, on the
basis of just a few utterances how the one which follows
is to be framed, or to identify and bracket asides and
interjections which do not form part of the overall
frame.

To explain such categorization processes it is
necessary to be much clearer than we have been in relating speakers' perceptive processes to the identification of speech activity. No doubt physical setting
and social background of participants always play an
essential role in the contextualization of talk. When
we see a group of children seated in rows in an enclosure which we identify as a classroom, facing an
adult speaker who is standing behind a desk, we are
fairly safe in assuming that teaching or lecturing is
going on. When the enclosure has the trappings of a
church and the audience consists of adults and the
speaker is standing in front of an altar, the activity
is most probably a church service or preaching. What
we want to point out is that the role of such factors
is never a static one. As Goffman has repeatedly stated,
the mere fact that actors are co-present in an environment does not mean that they are engaged in an interaction. Communication requires involvement and this
involvement is signalled by perceptual cues which must
be actively and continuously monitored in the course of
the interaction.

The recent studies in non-verbal behaviour
vividly illustrate this monitoring process. Scheflen
(1972), in his analysis of psychiatric interview
sessions, shows that such sessions are subdivided, and
to some extent controlled, by systematically changing
arrays of postural configurations of actors <u>vis-à-vis</u>
each other and that these configurations have important
implications for what is communicated.

Kendon (1970) and more recently Erikson <u>et al</u>.
(1973) have demonstrated that conversation is a rhythmic,
cooperative activity involving timing of gestures and
speech and requiring both speaking and listenership
skills. It can be shown that breakdowns in rhythmic
co-ordination can have an important effect on the outcome of an interaction.

What we would like to suggest is that the
linguistic markers of style can be treated from a similar perspective: that is, if instead of looking at
style in statistical terms, we regard speakers and
listeners as constantly monitoring stylistic aspects

of talk as criteria of on-going interaction to produce rhetorical effect, we gain better, more fruitful insights into the role of context in verbal communications.

That speech style affects meaning can easily be shown. Consider the following passage, reconstituted from notes on classroom observations.

Teacher addressing a group of first graders:

1. Now listen everybody.

2. At ten o'clock we'll have assembly. We'll all go out together and go to the auditorium and sit in the first two rows. Mr. Doc, the principal, is going to speak to us. When he comes in, sit quietly and listen carefully.

3. <u>Don't wiggle your legs. Pay attention to what I'm saying.</u>

Part one of the teacher's message, spoken with raised pitch and loud voice is simultaneously a call to attention and an order. In part two the rhythm slows to a measured pace, pitch drops while the volume remains high. These stylistic features, along with certain features of syntax, mark the passage as an announcement. In part three, pitch rises once more, volume increases, rhythm speeds up and <u>don't</u> and <u>attention</u> are stressed, indicating that the teacher is making a side remark addressing a particular child, not the class. Note that in order to understand what is going on here, listeners must be aware of the signalling value that the shifts in rhythm and prosody have in relation to content. Without this information several component sentences are ambiguous. Both the last two phrases of part two, and the two sentences in part three, have the syntactic form of a command. The former, however, being part of an announcement refers to (a) the class as a whole and (b) events in the future, while the sentences in part three are addressed to one individual and require immediate action. Failure to recognize this can result in serious misunderstanding.

In our detailed micro-analysis of conversational exchanges we have distinguished two kinds of relationships of extralinguistic factors to language usage: situational and metaphorical (Blom and Gumperz, 1972). In the situational case there is a direct relationship of usage to extralinguistic factors. In the case of <u>metaphorical usage</u> the speaker's knowledge of rules becomes the basis for further conversational inferences about the meaning of component messages.

To give a trivial example, imagine a mother somewhere in the United States calling her child as follows:

Johnny come here

Johnny come here

John Henry Smith come here.

Most speakers of American English would agree here that the third sentence is more than just a repetition. It is also a slight warning, suggesting that if Johnny does not come, there may be some consequences. What is the basis for such interpretations? One could say that item three represents formal style and that in formal speech a speaker is somehow more serious than in informal speech. But formality itself is a matter of context. We identify certain forms as formal because they are said in highly regulated extralinguistic settings where procedural rules are explicitly stated. Note in our example that the extralinguistic situation remains the same. All we can say is that the full name, John Henry Smith, here is lexically associated with formal activities and that in the absence of any change in extralinguistic factors the choice of form which carries such lexical associations generates the conversational inference of warning.

Systematic analysis of style and code switching in conversation has shown that while it is true that extralinguistic factors constrain language usage, they do not completely determine it (Gumperz, 1975). We suggest that context judgements are in part socio-cognitive judgements and also in part linguistic judgements. For this reason we will talk about processes of contextualization, which build on the speaker's ability to associate certain kinds of linguistic contextualization cues, such as the first name versus full name, or choice of code, style, or pronunciation, with propositional content on the one hand and extralinguistic cues and background expectations on the other. Such associations or co-occurrence expectations among these extralinguistic and linguistic cues lead to meta-semantic judgements, which cause the speaker to categorize what goes on as a social speech activity which can be named in everyday terms as conversation, reading, lecturing, and the like. It is this latter semantic judgement which then feeds back into the interpretation of messages, not the factors directly.

To give another simplified example, the sentence 'You put your hand in there' is interpreted as an instruction if the contextualization process identifies it as part of the activity of instructing, although when the contextualization process suggests conversation, it may count as a statement or perhaps as a request

(Cook-Gumperz, 1975). Similarly, sentences like 'Hey, what's happening', count as greeting when contextualization cues suggest that the rules of American Black rhetoric are being used. If contextualization cues are coded in a way similar to lexico-semantic information, then contextualization itself is a linguistic or meta-linguistic ability and it must be subject to processes and stages of learning as are other types of linguistic learning.

Therefore, in order to study how context enters into speakers' and listeners' judgements and performances in social situations, we have to focus upon how context is realized as a part of the interaction. That is, the focus will be on the social act, or rather upon the social activity, that gets accomplished both through and in conjunction with any specific sequence of talk (Cook-Gumperz, 1976).

We began with the observation that the participants in the activity themselves have a 'notion' (we have left specifically vague what kind of mental/ cognitive construct this represents) of the activity they believe themselves to be engaged in, and they communicate this notion to their partners either as new information or as a check that this information is in fact shared. The notion of the activity then serves as a 'framing device' to limit the degrees of freedom in the search for interpretation of any referential items, any gestural/kinesic schema, i.e., a reference against which participants check their understanding of the speech and social activity taking place before their eyes. Therefore contextual information is both coded as semantic information, and signalled as a part of the interaction by a process we will refer to as contextualization. The signalling of context makes the context available to the participants as a potentially sharable cognitive construct which frames the range of possible interpretations both in terms of the relevance of presuppositions and as guides to further action.

What we are suggesting is that we must know not only the context as a preceding utterance or as the scene in which the activity is taking place, but also the context as perceived by the speaker and listener, in order to make a judgement about the intent and effect of an utterance. What is more, the perceived context becomes a part of the communicative activity itself and is recognized and addressed in times of need such as conversational repair, by the participants themselves.

The perceived context is signalled through contextualization cues across a string of utterances, so that both speaker and listener can potentially share the same interpretative frame, and can use this knowledge strategically to shape the outcome of the interaction.

CHILDREN'S USES OF CONTEXT

The emphasis of this paper so far has been on describing the theoretical armoury useful for talking about context as an achieved and negotiable part of any social interaction; we must now relate these theoretical ideas to the actual practices of children talking, or rather attempt to demonstrate how children use contextualization cues to communicate, or to fail to communicate, about the social activity they are engaged in achieving. Elsewhere we have made the argument that children's talk can be distinguished from that of adults because of differently negotiated uses of context, and that adult-child miscommunication can result from differing views of the ongoing speech activity due to the different uses of contextualization cues (Corsaro and Cook-Gumperz, 1975; Gumperz and Herasimchuck, 1972/75).

Here we will give some examples of how the notion of what activity is taking place unfolds through talk itself without the purposes of the speech activity being formulated or explicitly lexicalized.

1. The following example is a shortened version of a passage analyzed in more detail in Corsaro and Cook-Gumperz (1975). It is based on a videotape recording made by Corsaro in the course of a year-long micro-ethnographic study of nursery school peer group interaction.

C and S are standing at a play table which has some scrap paper and a stapler on it. They are working at stapling together pieces of paper. They have taken over the table from another child who had been using it as a police station and had referred to the table as his police desk. The girls had come to share the table, saying 'We are the teachers'; after a short while the other child left. M, another child, comes along and sits down at the table as the stapling episode begins.

(1) S: (touching table, as M comes up) This is our desk. Nobody can come in our office. (M sits down opposite)

(2) C: (taking no notice of M) No, we show the kids, right.

(3) S: We working.

(4) C: Yea.

(5) S: <u>Nobody can come in</u>. (C and S look at each
          other while C replies)

(6) C: <u>No</u>.

(7) S: <u>Then we ... teaching</u> (as M reaches for the
          stapler)

(8) S: <u>NO</u>. <u>He not can't come in</u>.

(9) C: <u>No, no, we're teachers</u>.

   S's first statement in (1) is spoken in normal
conversational tone. After the first sentence, the
pitch register rises slightly, loudness increases and
rhythm becomes more emphatic to suggest a declarative
announcing tone. C replies by copying this declarative
tone and the same style is maintained, until it is
broken by S's overloud, emphatic '<u>NO</u>' (8). Immediately
afterwards, however, in the next phrase S shifts back
into the previous declarative tone and this tone is
once more copied by C in (9).

   Note how the game develops naturally. There is
no introduction such as '<u>let's play school</u>', no attempt
to formulate the activity verbally by saying '<u>we're
playing teachers</u>', just simple statements such as
'<u>This is our desk</u>' (1), '<u>We working</u>' (3), etc. The fact
that C responds to S's shift from conversational tone
and copies her declarative style is the only signal we
have that the activity of playing teachers has been
agreed upon. The activity, moreover, lasts only as long
as the same prosodic style is maintained. Once it is
recognized what game is being played, this recognition
feeds back into an interpretation of component messages.
For example, the phrase 'no' occurs several times, each
time with different situated meaning. In (2) and (6) it
is simply a response suggesting agreement with S's preceding statement. The loud '<u>NO</u>' (8) marks a stylistic
departure and signals a command addressed to M so that
the meaning is '<u>don't</u>'. While in (9) the return to the
prosody and rhythm of (6) and (7) suggests that '<u>no</u>' is
meant as game talk. Similarly the fact that '<u>nobody can
come in</u>' receives the same prosodic treatment as '<u>we're
teachers</u>' identifies it as game structuring talk, rather
than a command. The teaching game is also built up
through a semantic tie between the use of '<u>our office</u>'
and the statement later on '<u>we teaching</u>', into which
the '<u>Nobody can come in</u>' fits as a statement about
being a teacher in the office. The idea of 'being
teachers' is gradually developed from the two children's
entry into the situation, as they took over the play
table from another child. Earlier and later talk continues with various interruptions to develop the 'being
teacher' theme. In this excerpt it can be seen that

the presence of the other child, M, is brought into the
game cast of characters as a child who is 'naughty'. In
this context 'Nobody can come in' exists as a cue, a
definitional comment, not an order about the play situation. Since the intonation is declarative, it is not
made in immediate response to M who has since the beginning of this sequence, been sitting at the table
drawing. M only enters the game when he reaches for
the stapler: until this point he has been non-
existent for the purposes of this play.

2. This example is taken from a recording of
children's play talk in a London home. Participants
are D, the mother, who made the recording, and two
3½-year old girls, S and L, who regularly play together.
The mother is in the bedroom, sorting out some clothes
in a closet. The children are trying on some of the
clothes the mother has put down.

(1) D: Well you're getting dressed up in all my
         clothes now, are you?

(2) L: (imitating baby talk) natcha natcha, dika
         dika...

(3) D: Wait a minute. This box... I'm stacking
         up to keep, all right?

(4) L: Right.

(5) D: You can play with those things over there.

(6) L: natcha natcha...

(7) D: Leave it alone.

(8) S: sota sota......

(9) L: natcha natcha....

(10) S: No. No.

(11) L: natcha natcha.. Mummy, mummy. That my
         pillow.

(12) D: Wait a minute.

(13) S: No, she doesn't mean you. I mean....

(14) L: natcha natcha.....

(15) S: (to D) I'm putting this for L., out there.

(16) D: All right S....

(17) L: <u>natcha natcha.... What are you doing, mama?</u>

(18) D: <u>I'm still sorting through all these things.</u>

(19) L: <u>No, I mean dattie.</u>

(20) D: <u>You mean S is your mummy.</u>

(21) L: <u>Yea.</u>

L and S are playing mummy and baby. L is doing baby
talk, for the most part using nonsense syllables. On
two occasions however in (11) and (17) she uses her
baby talk to also include content words, '<u>mummy, that
my pillow</u>' and '<u>what are you doing, mama</u>'. The mother,
who has disregarded the baby talk, responds to the content words, perhaps because she is attuned to the call
mummy, even though the voice quality is still that of
baby talk. The children indignantly correct her since
they know that the voice indicates that L is still in
her game character as baby. In this example intonation
and voice quality are the contextualizing features that
distinguish in-character talk.

3.   In this next example, also taken from videotape nursery school data collected by Corsaro, J (a boy)
and M (a girl) had been playing father and mother in the
playhouse earlier in the morning. The game had finished
and they had gone their separate ways to get their morning snack and do other things. When observed, M was
playing with some toy animals, horses, cows, a zebra,
sheep, on a rug. J goes over to M, stands behind her,
while she is kneeling on the rug moving the animals a-
round making them do various things. After standing for
a while he says:

(1) J: <u>Let's go to bed honey, let's go to bed.</u> (this
         remark made in a slightly high pitch has a
         rising contour on each phrase and a slight
         lengthening on the vowel of the two phrase-
         final words)

(2) M: (after a pause) <u>No, I'm playing with these
         animals</u> (normal pitch and rhythm; another
         pause) <u>The animals are going to bed.</u>
         (higher pitch, slower rhythm, the last word
         is lengthened)

     Pause

(3) J: <u>Honey, it's night time, let's go to bed.</u>
         (same pitch and rhythm as the previous
         utterances)

(4)   M: <u>Yes, It's night time, the animals are</u>
              <u>sleepy.</u> (pause) <u>They're all going to bed.</u>
              <u>Horse is going to bed.</u> (M is moving the
              animals around and putting them on their
              sides to make them go to sleep;   copies J's
              pitch and rhythm)

              J stands for some time watching M putting
              the animals to bed;   neither speaks;   then
              J walks away.

Here, J is clearly alluding to the previous game by
adopting the rhythm and prosody of that game, and by
implication asking M to resume the game. M either did
not understand him or chose not to understand him.
Most likely the former, since she uses the suggestion
of J's remarks, but puts them to use in signalling a
game of her own. In other words she is incorporating
J's suggestions as a part of her own play. Since the
game had stopped, the need to restart the game probably
required certain statements of purpose. In this case
use of contextualization cue switch which indexes game
talk and game history is not sufficient and results in
miscommunication. Both children are relying on some
special contextual information signalled through use of
intonation and voice tone, as well as on the semantic
content of the message. M does not immediately tune
into the game talk but gives an answer to the request;
she then uses the information in J's request to build
into her own game, using her own 'game talk' intonation,
a common pattern of intonation that we have observed before in fantasy games. In this sequence both children
are using contextualized information which indexes their
own games, but neither picks up the other's reference
and thus they fail to communicate with each other
(Cook-Gumperz, 1976).

     4.   The final example is similar to the previous
one in that it shows a contextual switch using semantic
choice but this time it is used more successfully. The
switch occurs when the game takes a very different turn
and the context switch seems to signal that the speaker
is ready to accept what the other participant wants.

     Two small girls (aged $3\frac{1}{2}$) are playing in an
upstairs 'sleeping loft'. They are playing 'Mummies
and Daddies'. The game begins to take a turn not liked
by S, she is either fed up or doesn't want to play any-
more. The sequence begins here.

(1)   S: <u>I'm going to go down now.</u>

(2)   L: <u>Aren't you playing?</u>

(3) S: Are you? Are you?

(4) L: Yes, well I'll be quiet if you don't play
         Daddy.

(5) S: Well any rate, I'm just going to go down
         for a minute.

(6) L: And then you'll come back up to help me?

(7) S: Anyway, I'm going to play chalking.

(8) L: Please don't, I'll be dead. Oh, oh please.
         (little whiney voice) Please help me,
         Daddy, please come. Don't you want to
         punch me anymore? PAUSE (S is lingering
         at the top of the stairs, L is on the bed)
         Are you called S? I'm called L I'm not
         playing, I'm taking my slippers off and
         I'm not playing again. I'm just going to
         get down and I'm not playing. I'm called
         L not S or Mummy or Daddy I'm called L not S.

         (The example ends here as S comes down the
         stairs, followed by L and they both get
         involved in having a snack.)

Both intonation, voice tone and semantic switch indicate
a complete change in the game and an acceptance by L
that the game is over but that she is still 'friends'
with S. In fact, although the words don't look like it,
L's tone of voice in the latter part of her long statement is quite placatory, giving support to the idea that
the switch was made so dramatically because L thought
that the game had in some way offended S. S's reference
to 'going to play chalking' (that means to draw on the
chalk board) is really perhaps a way of saying 'I'm
going to do something by myself'. The number of interchanges about ending the game is also unusual for children's play, where games often just come to an end gradually or by some other activity taking their place. L's
shift of context is from 'organizational talk' in normal
tone and 'play talk' in special tone, to the special
ending sequence where both tone and semantics are quite
different from the preceding talk. Since the girls continue to play together, it may be assumed that this
switch of context and tone, although there was no reply,
may have been successful and recognized by S as 'doing
placatory agreement', i.e., as a speech activity signalled both by voice tone and by the shift to redefining
people and out-of-game characters.

        The switch of context through the use of cues,
both semantic and intonational, but not supported by any

formulated comments, is found in both of these examples,
and is very different from what we would expect in
adult-child or adult-adult interactions.

Having shown in these examples semantic and
intonational communication of context as a part of the
unfolding definition of situation, we must ask how it
is, given that there are no explicit or as yet formali-
zable rules for contextualization, that children learn
to do it. We have already suggested that contextualization is a linguistic or meta-linguistic process, and
in this way contextualization cues can be seen as operating at the same level of unconscious awareness as other
linguistic features. We must assume for the moment that
contextualization is learnt as a part of semantic knowledge. Evidence is beginning to be collected that children early in life learn many of the non-verbal postural
communicative skills such as alignment of speaker-
listener's positions, maintenance of gaze, and also turn-
taking and watching for the cues that signal turn
(Stern, 1974). Knowledge, of what we are calling contextualization cues is acquired along with these skills
and used as a part of the total array of signs that the
child relies on to make sense of the linguistic, semantic-syntactic message. The interpretation of messages
between speaker and listener depends upon several modalities or channels of communication. The speaker uses
all of these modalities although emphasizing one or
other modality as the primary carrier of meaning. The
normal daily adult interchange of communication relies
upon a 'balance' of information in all the channels
that meets adult expectation of an 'unmarked' exchange.
More emphasis on gesture, body movement, facial movement (e.g., a wink), or intonational contrast, is a way
of marking special attention to the information carried
in that channel.

Research by Argyle and associates has shown
that adults are so dependent on the normal form of
horizontally monitored information from all channels
that if any alteration is made experimentally, for
example, by restricting the range of one of the interactants' gaze, the normal rhythm of exchange and turn
taking is upset (Argyle, 1975). What we are suggesting
is that while we, as adults, foreground our attention
to the semantic-syntactic channel of information we
rely upon a constantly monitored background of non-
verbal information in all the other available modalities of sight and sound, and on a developed notion of
what constitutes a 'normal array' of information in the
background and the foreground features.

For children, the division between foreground
and background features (see Cook-Gumperz, 1972/75) is
more fluid than for adults, as shown by the fact that

in everyday occurrences children are likely to comment
on 'background' features as part of a normal explanation of a speech event. In children's talk the relationship between the channels of modalities is different, and children appear to regard all the available
information as similarly weighted for the purpose of
making sense of what is being said. At the same time
it appears that children do not share the adults' performance norms which require them to make a statement
in several modalities at once, by movement, by kinesic
gesture, semantic routine, intonation patterns - the
full battery of communicative signalling that adults
use to mark, for example, a leave-taking or the termina-
tion of a neighbourly chat.

The lack of modality redundancy in children's
communication appears to produce sudden shifts of topic
or attention which appear inexplicable to adults. Work
in nursery schools (reported by Corsaro) has shown that
children appear to devote considerable verbal and non-
verbal strategy to getting into play with each other,
whereas leave-taking is a simple, apparently unmarked
phenomenon; games often cease and are similarly re-
entered by previously absent participants with no
verbal formulation of entry or exit. It seems that
once having established a communicative event, as an
activity with a shared history, children do not need
to mark the obvious fact of leaving the scene as a
cessation of activity. The shared activity can often
easily be resumed within a given time period (see
Corsaro and Cook-Gumperz, 1975).

This observation raises the question whether
children in fact rely upon information communicated in
other modalities rather than on the semantic information, or whether different forms or alternations have
differing meanings in child speech. Our examples have
shown that child speech is both more literal and yet at
the same time apparently more indirect than adult
speech. This apparent paradox is the result of the
children's speech being tied more closely to the situation and the meanings depending more upon negotiation
of meaning in the current interaction or in very recent
past encounters. Children often use the utterances
formulaically such as in the 'nobody can come in' example. Since the truth condition of this utterance
did not hold (there was nowhere to come in to, no door-
way or room boundary) the statement related not to
entry into a space but situationally to the definition
of a territory and an idea of the game. At the same
time children do not use the adult technique of 'formulating', saying what the purpose of the talk is in so
many words, but rely upon the purpose becoming clear
from the context of the talk and the ways of contextualizing through a single set of cues. In these

ways the child's talk is both more literal because of
its situational association and more indirect because
seemingly unmarked content utterances are in fact
formulaic statements.

In the case of code-switching, studies have
shown (Genishi, 1975) that children, while using situational switching, presumably have not yet developed
sufficient communicative memory to use subtle metaphorical switching. Children cannot yet take off from
the literal meaning of the speech and disassociate this
meaning from its situation in order to make metaphorical use of semantic linguistic information.

The examples we have used must necessarily be
limited by space in a single paper. In order to examine and build up a strong empirical case for contextualization cues it is necessary to establish the
range of 'normal' unmarked variation in intonation, and
pitch range and other features for individuals and
dyads, before we are able to see the significant
switches and changes. The value and significance of
the semantics of the passages selected as examples,
grows out of the much longer passages and sequences of
interaction in which these were situated.

Our findings reported here are preliminary
but it is hoped sufficient to show some of the possibilities of considering children's speech in context
as a single communicative whole. More systematic investigation is required, but there are both theoretical
and practical consequences for fieldwork from this approach. If it can be shown, as we have tried to do,
that contextualization skills exist then they can tell
us a great deal about how the child acquires social and
cultural rules, for these must operate in a way similar
to contextual frames and information.

REFERENCES

Argyle, M. (1975)   Bodily Communication.   Methuen,
        London.

Bates, E. (1974)   Language and Context: Studies in
        the Acquisition of Pragmatics.   Unpublished
        Ph.D. dissertation. University of Chicago.

Blom, J.P and Gumperz, J. (1972)   The Social Meaning of
        Linguistic Structures.   In J. Gumperz and
        D. Hymes (eds.) Directions in Sociolinguistics.
        Holt, Rinehart and Winston, New York.

Bloom, L. (1973)   One Word at a Time. Mouton, The Hague.

Cook-Gumperz, J. (1972/1975)   The Child as a Practical
    Reasoner. In M. Sanches and B. Blount (eds.)
    The Socio-cultural Dimensions of Language Use.
    Academic Press, New York.

Cook-Gumperz, J. (1975)   Situated Instructions: The
    Language Socialization of School Age Children.
    To be published in S. Ervin-Tripp and C.
    Mitchell-Kernan (eds.) Children's Discourse.
    Academic Press, New York.

Cook-Gumperz, J. (1976)   Game Talk. Unpublished manu-
    script.

Corsaro, W. (1975)   Report on Nurseryschool Inter-
    action. University of Indiana, Bloomington.

Corsaro, W. and Cook-Gumperz, J. (1975)   The Socio-
    ecological Constraints and Language Use.
    University of Indiana, Bloomington and Uni-
    versity of California, Berkeley. Ms.

Erikson, F., et al. (1975)   Inter-ethnic Relations
    in Urban Institutional Settings. Final
    technical report. Project MH8230, MH21460.
    National Institute of Mental Health.

Ervin-Tripp, S. (1974/1976) Wait for Me Rollerskate.
    To be published in S. Ervin-Tripp and C.
    Mitchell-Kernan (eds.) Children's Discourse.
    Academic Press, New York.

Garvey, C. (1975)   Contingent Queries. Johns Hop-
    kins University. Ms.

Gelman, R. and Schatz, M. (1975)   Rule-governed Va-
    riations in Children's Conversation. Uni-
    versity of Pennsylvania. Ms.

Genishi, C.S. (1975)   Rules for Code-switching in
    Young Spanish-English Speakers: An Explo-
    ratory-Study of Language Socialization.
    Unpublished Ph.D. dissertation. University
    of California, Berkeley.

Gleason, J. Berko (1975) 'Say Thank you'. Paper
    presented at Stanford Child Language Sym-
    posium.

Goffman, E. (1975)   Frame Analysis. Harper and Row,
    New York.

Gumperz, J. (1975)   The Sociolinguistic Significance of Conversational Code-Switching. University of California, Berkeley. Ms.

Gumperz, J. and Herasimchuk, E. (1972/1975) The Conversational Analysis of Social Meaning: A Study of Classroom Interaction. In M. Sanches and B. Blount (eds.) The Sociocultural Dimensions of Language Use. Academic Press, New York.

Halliday, M.A.K. (1975)   Learning How to Mean: Explorations in the Development of Language. Arnold, London.

Keenan, E.O. (1974)   Again and Again: The Pragmatics of Imitation in Child Language. To be published in S. Ervin-Tripp and C. Mitchell-Kernan (eds.)\Children's Discourse. Academic Press, New York.

Keenan, E.O. and Schiefflin, B. (1975) Topic as a Discourse Notion: A Study of Topic and the Conversations of Children and Adults. In Charles Li (ed.) Subject and Topic. Academic Press, New York.

Kendon, A. (1970)   Movement Co-ordination in Social Interaction. Psychologica 32. 100-124.

Richards, P.M. (1974) The Integration of the Child into a Social World. Cambridge University Press, Cambridge.

Sacks, H. (1968/1975)   Everyone Has to Lie. In M. Sanches and B. Blount (eds.) The Sociocultural Dimensions of Language Use. Academic Press, New York.

Sacks, H. (1972) An Initial Investigation of the Usability of Conversational Data for Doing Sociology. In D. Sudnow (ed.) Studies in Social Interaction. Free Press, New York.

Scheflen, A.E. (1972)   Communicational Structure. Indiana University Press, Bloomington, Indiana.

Sinclair, J. and Coultard, M. (1974)   Towards an Analysis of Discourse: The English Used by Teachers and Pupils. Oxford University Press, England.

Stern, D.N. (1974)   Mother and Infant at play: the
        Dyadic Interaction involving Facial, Vocal
        and Gaze Behaviours.   In   M. Lewis and L.
        Rosenblum (eds.) The Effect of the Infant
        on the Caregiver. 1.   187-213.   The Origin
        of Behaviour Series. Wiley, New York.

Neuropsychological Aspects of Language Development: An Essay on Celebral Dominance

A.W.H. Buffery

> "In summary, the why of hemisphere specialization still eludes us, but we shall come closer to an answer if we perfect our understanding of the what, the how and the whence. Perhaps it is a personal bias if I express the belief that much more can still be learned in the last of these areas, the evolutionary and ontogenetic aspects; wherever we see differentiated living structures, we understand them much better if we can show by what stages their differentiation has come about"
>
> From "Why Two Brains?" by H-L Teuber (1974)

The term 'cerebral dominance' is not commonly used to refer to the human brain's general lateral asymmetry of functional topography but rather to denote the usually left-sided cerebral hemisphere's specific commitment to language function.[1]   Since language is only one of many higher cognitive skills and since there is evidence

*The author wishes to express his gratitude to Miss Christine Robson for her assistance in the preparation of this paper.

25

that its lateralization is a relative rather than an absolute phenomenon (Joynt and Goldstein, 1975; Zangwill, 1967) and can even occur laterally reversed (reviewed by Roberts, 1969) it would be more appropriate and less misleading to adopt the term 'cerebral predominance' and use it only within the context of a specified laterality for a particular skill (Buffery, 1974); 'left cerebral predominance for verbal skill' and 'right cerebral predominance for spatial skill' being examples of the most probable 'brainedness' in an individual (Buffery, 1967, 1968). The idiosyncratic nature of 'brainedness' is clear from measurements showing that the degree of cerebral asymmetry of function varies from task to task as well as from person to person (Buffery, 1976). The term 'cerebral dominance' therefore is not only confusing it is simplistic. Neurologists, neurosurgeons, neuropsychiatrists and neuropsychologists would make more accurate diagnoses and prognoses and provide more appropriate treatment for brain-damaged patients if they abandoned the term and concept of 'cerebral dominance' and became more concerned with the investigation of the nature of an individual's cerebral functional topography and the monitoring of the idiosyncracies of the ongoing reorganization required of a brain to restore and/or compensate for damaged functions and/or structures (Buffery, 1977).

Some lateral asymmetries of function have been noted in the brains of animals other than primates. Webster (1972) found that in 'split-brain' cats the cerebral hemisphere ipsilateral to the preferred paw was superior in solving certain visual discrimination problems, and Nottebohm (1971, 1972) found that in the adult chaffinch the 'full song' was mediated by the left hypoglossal nerves. However, the present paper is more concerned with the development and significance of hemispheric asymmetry in the primate brain and, in particular, with the usually left cerebral predominance for verbal skill in the human brain (for reviews see Berlucchi, 1974; Dimond, 1972; Dimond and Beaumont, 1974; Gazzaniga, 1970; Kinsbourne and Smith, 1974; Liberman, 1974; Milner, 1971, 1974; Ornstein, 1972; Sperry, 1974; Sperry, Gazzaniga and Bogan, 1969; White, 1969, and Zangwill, 1976).

Phylogenetically, lateral asymmetries of cerebral function and structure in the primate brain emerge in parallel with a growth in the complexity of communicative skill and with the capacity to acquire more sophisticated language codes. The communicative skill of the rhesus monkey through gesture and vocalization (Hinde and Rowell, 1962; Rowell and Hinde, 1962) is subserved by a brain in which functional but not structural asymmetries have been observed (Dewson, Burlingame, Kizer, Dewson, Kenney and Pribram, 1975; Hamilton, Tieman and Farrell, 1974). The capacity of the chimpanzee to

acquire more sophisticated language codes, such as
speech sounds (Hayes and Hayes, 1951), sign language
(Gardner and Gardner, 1969) and symbols (Premack, 1970,
1971) is subserved by a brain in which structural asymmetries have been observed (LeMay and Geschwind, 1975;
Yeni-Komshian and Benson, 1976) but in which functional
asymmetries, though probable, have yet to be investigated.

Ontogenetically, in humans, there is some
evidence that less marked hemispheric asymmetry of
function is associated with less competence in certain
verbal skills such as reading (see Taylor, 1962 and
Taylor and Kimura cited by Kimura, 1967 and the reviews
by Satz, 1976, and others in Knights and Bakker, 1976)
and speech (Springer and Eisenson, 1977). What could
be the advantage of a more unilateral cerebral mediation
of verbal skills? It has been suggested (Buffery and
Gray, 1972 : 144) that the nature of the timing and patterning of the neural activity necessary to subserve
language functions efficiently, with their demand for
rapid associations and serial ordering, would benefit
from being mediated by specialized cerebral structures
of a clearly lateralized and localized character. There
is now evidence (reviewed by Geschwind, 1974) that one
such specialized cerebral structure is the planum temporale (usually of the left cerebral hemisphere) which
lies between the sulcus of Heschl and the posterior end
of the Sylvian fossa, see Figures 1a and 1b. Heschl's
gyrus includes the primary auditory cortex which receives
the major outflow of the medial geniculate body, and the
major speech areas lie in the banks of the Sylvian fissure and its borders - Broca's area (concerned with language expression) lying in the posterior portion of the
left third frontal gyrus which forms the frontal operculum and Wernicke's area (concerned with language comprehension) lying in the lower bank in the posterior part
of the left superior temporal gyrus which forms part of
the temporal operculum. Heschl's gyrus is not found in
monkeys but becomes prominent in higher primates and is
most pronounced in man. Connolly (1950) points out that
no true homologue of the Sylvian fissure exists in the
brains of non-primate mammals. Heschl's gyrus crosses
the upper surface of the temporal lobe in an anterior
direction and on reaching the Sylvian fissure joins the
superior temporal gyrus. There is a deep sulcus behind
this gyrus, the sulcus of Heschl. Between the sulcus of
Heschl and the posterior end of the Sylvian fossa lies
the planum temporale.

Connolly (1950) cites several studies, e.g.
Cunningham (1892), that demonstrated a longer Sylvian
fissure in the left cerebral hemisphere than in the
right. Pfeifer (1936) found the left gyrus of Heschl
was usually angled forward more sharply than the right

28

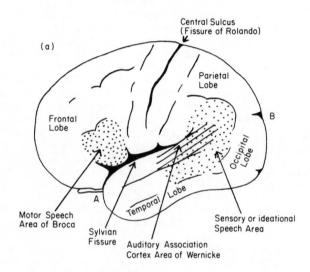

(a)

Central Sulcus
(Fissure of Rolando)

Parietal
Lobe

Frontal
Lobe

B

Occipital
Lobe

Temporal Lobe

A

Motor Speech
Area of Broca

Sylvian
Fissure

Auditory Association
Cortex Area of Wernicke

Sensory or ideational
Speech Area

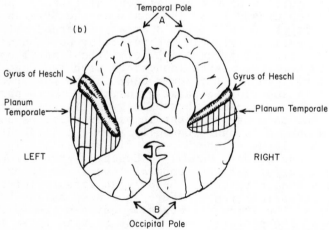

Temporal Pole

A

(b)

Gyrus of Heschl

Gyrus of Heschl

Planum
Temporale

Planum Temporale

LEFT

RIGHT

B

Occipital Pole

Fig. 1a.   Human brain: left cerebral hemisphere

Fig. 1b.   Human brain: cross section A ↔ B

and that as a result the planum temporale was larger in the left cerebral hemisphere. Similar lateral asymmetries for the Sylvian fissure and the gyrus of Heschl were found by Geschwind and Levitsky (1968), Teszner (1972), Wada (1969), Wada, Clarke and Hamm (1975) and Von Economo and Horn (1930), all confirming that the planum temporale of the left cerebral hemisphere is usually larger than that of the right. The prediction that such a cerebral hemispheric structural asymmetry of the human brain would be present at birth and that the degree of structural asymmetry would be greater within the female brain than within the male (Buffery, 1970, 1971a, b, c, d) was made in the context of an evolutionary hypothesis of human sex differences in non-sexual behaviour (Gray and Buffery, 1970). This was elaborated in later papers concerned with endocrinological (Gray, 1971), neurological (Gray and Buffery, 1971) and neuropsychological (Buffery and Gray, 1972) bases. The prediction (Buffery and Gray, 1972 : 146) found support from a modest study by Witelson and Pallie (1973) of 16 adult and 14 infant brains (the latter with ages ranging from one day to the third postnatal month); the tendency for the left planum temporale to be more developed than the right was more marked in female than male babies. Wada, Clarke and Hamm (1975) in a major investigation confirmed the presence of the relative enlargement of the left planum temporale with 100 adult and 100 infant brains (the latter with ages ranging from the eighteenth gestational week to the eighteenth postnatal month); the main sex difference to emerge being that a greater number of female adults showed reversed structural asymmetry, i.e. the right planum temporale larger than the left. This sex difference finds an interesting parallel in a study by Buffery (1976) of 100 females and 100 males in which a greater number of female adults showed reversed function-al asymmetry as measured by a verbal task presented tachistoscopically to the left or right cerebral hemisphere via the contralateral visual hemifield.

The implications of sex differences in the structural and functional cerebral hemispheric asymmetries of the human brain for a neuropsychological explanation of the reported female superiority in certain verbal skills and male superiority in certain spatial skills were considered by Buffery and Gray in 1972. In brief it was then argued that greater cerebral predominance for language function was beneficial to verbal skill and more characteristic of the female human brain, whereas less cerebral predominance for non-verbal function was beneficial to spatial skill and more characteristic of the male human brain. Thus the general prediction arising from their theory was as follows. Under normal 'in the round' conditions the female brain would tend to be more efficient than the male for subserving certain verbal skills (reviewed by Broverman, Klaiber, Kobayashi and Vogel, 1968; Garai and Scheinfeld, 1968; Hutt, 1972a, b, c; Maccoby, 1966),e.g. verbal reasoning (Guilford, 1959, 1967) and verbal fluency (Tyler, 1965), whilst the male brain would tend to be more efficient than the female for subserving certain spatial skills (reviewed as above),e.g. rotary pursuit (Ammons, Alprin and Ammons, 1965), aiming (Connolly, Brown and Bassett, 1968), orientation-type visuo-motor tasks (Keogh, 1971, 1972), perceptual field independence (Witkin, Dyk, Faterson, Goodenough and Karp, 1962), and maze learning (Yule, Berger, Butler, Newham and Tizard, 1969). Under more constrained conditions where one cerebral hemisphere is tested at a time,(for instance a) with auditory input by 'dichotic listening' (Broadbent, 1954; Kimura, 1961, 1963, 1967; Milner, 1962), b) with visual input by 'tachistoscopic exposure' to either hemifield (Bryden and Rainey, 1963; Kimura, 1966; Mishkin and Forgays, 1952), or c) with tactile or proprioceptive input by 'dichotomous' or 'conflict' tasks to the limbs (Buffery, 1970, 1971d; Lukianowicz, 1970, 1971, 1974)) assuming the more usual laterality of cerebral predominance for verbal and spatial skills, the female left cerebral hemisphere was predicted to be more efficient than the female right cerebral hemisphere or than either of the male brain's cerebral hemispheres, for subserving certain verbal skills, e.g. dichotic recognition of spoken digits at 5 years of age (Kimura, 1967), and the audio-visual cross-modal matching of spoken with written words (Buffery, 1971a; Buffery and Gray, 1972) and of drawings with their spoken names (Buffery, 1976) from 5 to 8 years of age. Under similar conditions the female right cerebral hemisphere was predicted to be more efficient than the female left cerebral hemisphere, or than either of the male brain's cerebral hemispheres, for subserving certain spatial skills, e.g. left hand superiority in the 'Conflict Drawing Test' (Buffery, 1970, 1971d; Buffery and Gray, 1972) from 3 to 11 years of age.

Since 1972 there has been a considerable amount of experimental data collected for and against the Buffery and Gray 'cerebral asymmetry' theory of sex differences in cognitive development - evidence at least of its heuristic value. In particular, data against their hypothesis that spatial and other non-verbal functions are more bilaterally represented in the male brain have been abundant and impressive,e.g., Witelson (1976). However, Hutt (1972c) and several authors in Lloyd and Archer (1976) criticize the Buffery and Gray theory without fully understanding the argument and without reference to the neuroanatomical data. More telling and certainly more constructive criticisms are made by Marshall (1973) and by Fairweather (1976), the latter providing by far the best review of sex differences in cognition yet to appear in the literature and compulsory reading along with the Maccoby and Jacklin (1976) magnum opus. Nevertheless, it is difficult to reconcile Fairweather's (1976) final sentence, which concerns the future of psychological research into sex differences, i.e., 'Studies within the normal population, predicted on the assumption that discriminations are useful, can only be regarded as tempting sexism' with his own, as then unpublished, paper (Fairweather and Butterworth, 1977) entitled: 'The WPPSI at four years: A sex difference in Verbal-Performance discrepancies.'

Laterality of limb preference has been studied in a variety of animals including mice (Collins, 1968, 1969, 1970), rats (Peterson, 1934), cats (Cole, 1955) and monkeys (Warren, Abplanalp and Warren, 1967). The majority of individual primates exhibit clear hand preferences (e.g., monkey: Cole, 1957; Ettlinger and Moffett, 1964; Gautrin and Ettlinger, 1970; chimpanzee: Finch, 1941; and mountain gorilla: Schaller, 1963), but these are usually distributed equally between the left and right limbs rather than being biased towards a dextrality subserved by a contralateral cerebral hemisphere that is predominant for language function.
        Although some functional asymmetries have been observed for the cerebral hemispheres in animals other than man, there has been little investigation of the possible relationship of these to limb preference (but see Lehman, 1970). In man, however, the relationship of varieties of lateral preference and dominance (e.g., hand, eye, ear and foot), have been used as indirect predictors for the cerebral lateralization of verbal and spatial skill, and, in turn through this tenuous connection, as 'explanations' for patterns of cognitive deficit e.g., the undesirability of crossed or non-congruent lateral preferences and of incomplete or mixed cerebral dominance for the normal development of certain verbal skills (Orton, 1928, 1929, 1937, 1939 and 1966; Delacato, 1959, 1963 and 1967, both reviewed critically by Myers and Hammill, 1969). Buffery (1976) presented Easy to Verbalize (EV) and Difficult to Verbalize (DV) visual stimuli tachistoscopically to the left or right hemifield and found that 200 University students (100 female and 100 male from 18 to 25 years of age) exhibited a wide variety in the degree of lateral congruity and noncongruity for their preferred hand, dominant eye and cerebral predominance for verbal and spatial function. Crossed laterality of preferred hand to dominant eye was found in 40% of the women and 52% of the men, whilst only 52% of the women and 38% of the men had a lateral congruence of preferred hand with dominant eye subserved by a contralateral cerebral hemisphere predominant for verbal skill as measured by the EV task (Buffery, 1976, Figure 8: 200). The finding of such inconsistencies of lateral preference and cerebral asymmetry in a highly

intelligent adult population is incompatible with the
hypotheses of Orton and of Delacato which suggest that
crossed laterality and incomplete cerebral dominance
impair intellectual development (see also McBurney and
Dunn, 1976). Although the degree and laterality of
cerebral predominance for verbal and spatial skill may
well influence cognitive growth, the technical advances
that have permitted its more direct assessment have
shown that the indirect method of predicting 'brainedness' from observed lateral preferences is both inaccurate and misleading (Satz, 1976). If there is a link
between laterality and cognition, it lies in 'brainedness' and 'brainedness' itself should be measured
(Bryden, 1965; Satz, 1976; Satz, Achenback and Fennel,
1967). Buffery did find a higher incidence of more unilateral 'Verbal Brainedness (VB) in females (84%) than
in males (65%) and a higher incidence of more bilateral
'Spatial Brainedness' (SB) in males (43%) than in females (24%), and that these patterns of 'brainedness'
correlated respectively with a superior performance in
the EV tasks by the females and in the DV tasks by the
males (Buffery, 1976, Figure 10: 201). This sex difference in the performance of EV and DV tasks, and perhaps also in other verbal and spatial tasks, reflects a
sex difference in the incidence of the various degrees
of asymmetry of cerebral lateralization for verbal and
spatial function rather than a sex difference in performance levels per se.

        Having consideration for both the neuroanato-
mical and neuropsychological evidence the general conclusion of Buffery and Gray (1972) may still have
utility:

        'Sex differences in the development of the
human brain's functional topography can, therefore,
explain the female's superiority in linguistic skill
and the male's superiority in spatial skill. But these
sex differences in functional topography, we have suggested, depend upon sex differences in structural topography.'   (Buffery and Gray 1972: 144-145).

        What is the relationship of the various cer-
ebral asymmetries and lateral preferences in animals
other than man to those observed in humans? It has
been suggested (Webster, 1972) that since the carnivore
and primate neocortex have evolved independently (Diamond
and Hall, 1969), the relationship is, at best, analogous. Nevertheless there is certainly adaptive value
in the evolution of an asymmetric nervous system for
both carnivores and primates (Corballis and Beale, 1970;
Trevarthen, 1974; Tschirgi, 1958). In Africa there is
evidence from the Pliocene Epoch of over 2 million years
ago that Australopithecus, an ape-like ancestor of Homo
sapiens, was usually right handed (Dart, 1949) and had

cerebral asymmetry,i.e. a larger left parieto-occipital region of the skull (Gundara and Zivanovic, 1968). In the 30 thousand year old La Chapelle aux Saints skull of Neanderthal man LeMay and Culebras (1972) found the right Sylvian fissure's imprint in the skull to be angled upwards more sharply than the left (see also Beaumont, 1975, on handedness, and Levy, 1975, on the psychobiological implications of bilateral asymmetry - both in Dimond and Beaumont, 1975).

In summary, the phylogeny and ontogeny of the various asymmetries in cerebral structure and function and of lateral preferences may relate to a growing competence in the use of more complex language codes - ones usually based upon the comprehension of auditory stimuli. The presence of a relatively enlarged left-sided planum temporale at birth in man provides support for the suggestion by Buffery and Gray (1972: 136) that the human brain is 'pre-wired' for speech perception and that the planum temporale of usually the left cerebral hemisphere is a necessary structural component of a 'linguistic device', such as that described by Studdert-Kennedy and Shankweiler (1970), for the extraction of linguistic features from other auditory parameters of the speech signal. Further, such structural asymmetries of the human brain could initiate the functional asymmetries which in turn contribute to the differential patterning of intellectual development of males and females (Buffery, 1971d).

Such data and hypotheses provide a biological balance to the more environmental explanations of language development. In the human brain the interaction of an innate lateralized (usually left-sided) neural structure specialized for speech perception with an appropriate auditory input is seen as a necessary condition for the establishment of various cerebral asymmetries of function (Buffery and Gray, 1972: 147). Evidence from a study by McKeever, Hoemann, Florian and Van Deventer (1976) supports this view for they found less clearly lateralized cerebral predominance for the processing of visual-verbal information in deaf subjects! (see also similar studies by Lewis and Whatley, 1975 and by Lukianowicz, in press). The lateralization of cerebral predominance for the processing of auditory-verbal information is, however, predicted to be normal in blind subjects by the present author.

Neuropsychological aspects of language development have been reviewed and the concept of 'cerebral dominance' reconsidered. Recent neuroanatomical and psychological data suggest a sex difference in both the rate of emergence (Taylor, 1969) and eventual degree (Buffery, 1976) of the cerebral asymmetry for verbal and spatial function which is initiated by an innate sex

difference in the cerebral asymmetry of a 'speech perception' structure (Buffery, 1971d). Such ontogenetic differences are phylogenetic consequences of the
differential effects of the interaction between the
sexes' division of labour in reproductive behaviour and
the development of increasingly more complex vocalized
language codes (Gray and Buffery, 1972). Such sex differences in the cerebral asymmetries of structure and
function can contribute to explanations of the normal
patterning of intellectual development in males and females and of the relative vulnerability of males to language disorders (e.g. specific reading retardation, Yule
and Rutter, 1976; see also reviews of these issues in
Knights and Bakker, 1976). These sex differences also
have implications for the strategies of teaching language skills, in particular that of reading (Bakker,
Teunissen and Bosch, 1976; Coltheart, Hull and Slater,
1975). Further, the apparatus and techniques used for
assessing cerebral predominance can be modified to become therapeutic aids for those suffering from a variety
of sensory or motor loss; for accelerating recovery
from brain damage and for reorganizing cerebral functional topography (Buffery, 1977). Neuropsychology is well
placed to stimulate and mediate the application of relevant findings from what Bever in 1970 termed 'The integrated study of language behaviour' to the problems of
language disorders. Let us hope that the next decade
witnesses just that.

Notes.

1.   See Head (1926) for a consideration of the claims
      of Dax (1836) and of Broca (1864) for being the
      initiator of the concept of cerebral asymmetry
      for language function, and Jackson (1874) on the
      duality of the brain in volume 2 of his selected
      works edited by Taylor (1932), and also Zangwill
      (1960) on cerebral dominance, and Young (1970) on
      19th Century ideas of brain function.

REFERENCES

Ammons, R.B., Alprin, S.I. and Ammons, C.H. (1965)
      Rotary Pursuit Performance as related to Sex
      and Age of Pre-adult Subjects. Journal of
      Experimental Psychology 49. 127-133.

Bakker, D.J., Teunissen, J. and Bosch, J. (1976)
      Development of Laterality-Reading Patterns.
      In R.M. Knights and D.J. Bakker (eds.) The
      Neuropsychology of Learning Disorders: Theore-
      tical Approaches. University Press, Baltimore.

Beaumont, J.G. (1974) Handedness and Hemisphere Function. In S.J. Dimond and J.G. Beaumont (eds.) Hemisphere Function in the Human Brain. Elek Science, London.

Benton, A.L. (1965) The Problem of Cerebral Dominance. Canadian Psychologist 6. 332-348.

Berlucchi, G. (1974) Cerebral Dominance and Inter-Hemispheric Communication in Normal Man. In F.O. Schmitt and F.G. Worden (eds.) The Neurosciences: 3rd Study Program, M.I.T. Press, Cambridge, U.S.A.

Bever, T.G. (1971) The Integrated Study of Language Behaviour. In J. Morton (ed.) Biological and Social Factors in Psycholinguistics. Logos Press, London.

Broadbent, D.E. (1954) The Role of Auditory Localization in Attention and Memory Span. Journal of Experimental Psychology 47. 191-196.

Bryden, M.P. (1965) Tachistoscopic Recognition, Handedness, and Cerebral Dominance. Neuropsychologia 3. 1-8.

Bryden, M.P. and Rainey C.A. (1963) Left-right Differences in Tachistoscopic Recognition. Journal of Experimental Psychology 66. 568-571.

Buffery, A.W.H. (1967) Delayed Paired Comparison of Verbal or Non-verbal Stimuli Presented Tachistoscopically to the Right or Left Visual Hemifield. Paper read at the July meeting of the Experimental Psychology Society, Oxford.

Buffery, A.W.H. (1968) Evidence for the Asymmetrical Lateralization of Cerebral Function. Bulletin of the British Psychological Society 21. 29.

Buffery, A.W.H. (1970) Sex Differences in the Development of Hand Preference, Cerebral Dominance for Speech and Cognitive Skill. Bulletin of the British Psychological Society 23. 233.

Buffery, A.W.H. (1971a) An automated Technique for the Study of the Development of Cerebral Mechanisms subserving Linguistic Skill. Proceedings of the Royal Society of Medicine 64. 919-922.

Buffery, A.W.H. (1971b) Sex Differences in Cerebral Dominance for Speech: A Theoretical Contribution towards a Neuropsychology of Intellectual Development. Bulletin of the British Psychological Society 24. 53.

36

Buffery, A.W.H. (1971c)   Sex Differences in the Development of Cognitive Skills. Bulletin of
the British Psychological Society 24. 242-
243.

Buffery, A.W.H. (1971d)   Sex Differences in the Development of Hemispheric Asymmetry of Function in the Human Brain. Brain Research 31.
364-365.

Buffery, A.W.H. (1974)   Asymmetrical Lateralization of
Cerebral Functions and the Effects of Unila-
teral Brain Surgery in Epileptic Patients. In
S.J. Dimond and J.G. Beaumont (eds.) Hemi-
sphere Function in the Human Brain. Elek
Science, London.

Buffery, A.W.H. (1976)   Sex Differences in the Neuro-
Psychological Development of Verbal and
Spatial Skills. In R. Knights and D.J. Bakker
(eds.) The Neuropsychology of Learning Dis-
orders: Theoretical Approaches. University
Park Press.

Buffery, A.W.H. (1977)   Clinical Neuropsychology: A
Review and Preview. In S.J. Rachman (ed.)
Advances in Medical Psychology. Pergamon
Press, Oxford.

Buffery, A.W.H. and Gray, J.A. (1972)   Sex Differences
in the Development of Spatial and Linguistic
Skills. In C. Ounsted and D.C. Taylor (eds.)
Gender Differences: Their Ontogeny and Significance. Churchill Livingstone, Edinburgh.

Cole, J. (1955)   Paw Preference in Cats related to Hand
Preference in Animals and Man. Journal of
Comparative and Physiological Psychology 48.
137-140.

Cole, J. (1957)   Laterality in the Use of the Hand,
Foot and Eye in Monkeys. Journal of Comparative and Physiological Psychology 50. 296-299.

Collins, R.L. (1968)   On the Inheritance of Handedness:
I. Laterality in Inbred Mice. Journal of
Heredity 59. 9-12.

Collins, R.L. (1969)   On the Inheritance of Handedness:
II. Selection for Sinistrality in Mice.
Journal of Heredity 60. 117-119.

Collins, R.L. (1970)   The Sound of One Paw Clapping: An
Investigation into the Origin of Left Handedness. In G. Lindzey and D.D. Thiessen (eds.)

Contributions to Behaviour-Genetic Analysis: The Mouse as Prototype. Appleton-Century-Crofts, New York.

Coltheart, M., Hull, E. and Slater D. (1975) Sex Differences in Imagery and Reading. Nature 253. 438-440.

Connolly, C.J. (1950) External Morphology of the Primate Brain. Charles C. Thomas, Springfield, Illinois.

Connolly, K., Brown K. and Bassett, E. (1968) Developmental Changes in some Components of a Motor Skill. British Journal of Psychology 59. 305-314.

Corballis, M.C. and Beale, I.L. (1970) Bilateral Symmetry and Behavior. Psychological Review 77. 451-464.

Cunningham, D.J. (1892) Contribution to the Surface Anatomy of the Cerebral Hemispheres. Cunningham Memoirs. No. VII. Royal Irish Academy, Dublin.

Dart, R. (1949) The Predatory Implemental Technique of Australopithecus. American Journal of Physical Anthropology 7. 1-38.

Delacato, C.H. (1959) The Treatment and Prevention of Reading Problems. Charles C. Thomas, Springfield, Illinois.

Delacato, C.H. (1963) The Diagnosis and Treatment of Speech and Reading Problems. 6th Edition. Charles C. Thomas, Springfield, Illinois.

Delacato, C.H. (1967) Neurological Organization and Reading. 2nd Edition. Charles C. Thomas, Springfield, Illinois.

Dewson III, J.H., Burlingame, A., Kizer, K., Dewson, S., Kenney, P. and Pribram, K.H. (1975) Hemispheric Asymmetry of Auditory Function in Monkey. Journal of the Acoustical Society of America 58. (Suppl.1) S66.

Diamond, I.T. and Hall, W.C. (1969) Evolution of Neocortex. Science, N.Y. 164. 251-262.

Dimond, S.J. (1972) The Double Brain. Churchill Livingstone, Edinburgh.

38

Dimond, S.J. and Beaumont, J.G. (eds.) (1974) Hemisphere Function in the Human Brain. Elek
Science, London.

Ettlinger, G. and Moffett, A (1964) Lateral Preferences in the Monkey. Nature 204. 606.

Fairweather, H. (1976) Sex Differences in Cognition.
Cognition 4. 231-280.

Fairweather, H. and Butterworth, G. (1977) The
WPPSI at Four Years: A Sex Difference in
Verbal-Performance Discrepancies. British
Journal of Educational Psychology 47. 85-90.

Finch, G. (1941) Chimpanzee Handedness. Science, N.Y.
94. 117-118.

Gardner, R.A. and Gardner, B.T. (1969) Teaching Sign
Language to a Chimpanzee. Science, N.Y. 165.
664-672.

Gautrin, D. and Ettlinger, G. (1970). Lateral Preferences in the Monkey. Cortex 6. 287-292.

Gazzaniga, M.S. (1970) The Bisected Brain. Appleton-
Century-Crofts, New York.

Geschwind, N. (1974) The Anatomical Basis of Hemispheric Differentiation. In S.J. Dimond and
J.G. Beaumont (eds.) Hemisphere Function in
the Human Brain. Elek Science, London.

Geschwind, N. and Levitsky, W. (1968) Human Brain:
Left-right Asymmetries in Temporal Speech
Region. Science, N.Y. 161. 186-187.

Gray, J.A. (1971) Sex Differences in Emotional Behaviour in Mammals including Man: Endocrine
Bases. Acta Psychologica 35. 29-46.

Gray, J.A. and Buffery, A.W.H. (1970) The Neural
Bases of Sex Differences in Nonsexual Behaviour in Animals and Man: A Review and
an Evolutionary Hypothesis. Brain Research
24. 556.

Gray, J.A. and Buffery, A.W.H. (1971) Sex Differences
in Emotional and Cognitive Behaviour in
Mammals including Man: Adaptive and Neural
Bases. Acta Psychologica 35. 89-111.

Guilford, J.P. (1959) Three Faces of Intellect. American Psychologist 14. 469-479.

Guilford, J.P. (1967)   The Nature of Human Intelligence.
McGraw Hill, New York.

Gundara, N. and Zivanovic, S. (1968)   Asymmetry in East
African Skulls. American Journal of Physical
Anthropology 28. 331-338.

Hamilton, C.R., Tieman, S.B. and Farrell, W.S. (1974)
Cerebral Dominance in Monkeys? Neuropsychologia 12. 193-197.

Hayes, K.J. and Hayes, C. (1951)   The Intellectual Development of a House-raised Chimpanzee. Proceedings of the American Philosophical Society
95. 105-110.

Head, H. (1926)   Aphasia and Kindred Disorders of
Speech. 2 Volumes. Cambridge University
Press, Cambridge.

Hinde, R.A. and Rowell, T.E. (1962)   Communication by
Postures and Facial Expressions in the Rhesus
Monkey (Macaca Mulatta). Proceedings of the
Zoological Society of London   138. 1-21.

Hutt, C. (1972a)   Sexual Dimorphism: Its Significance
in Human Development. In F.J. Mönks, W.W.
Hartup and J. de Wit (eds.) Determinants of
Behavioral Development. Academic Press,
London.

Hutt, C. (1972b)   Neuroendocrinological, Behavioural
and Intellectual Aspects of Sexual Differentiation in Human Development. In C. Ounsted
and R.C. Taylor (eds.) Gender Differences:
Their Ontogeny and Significance. Churchill
Livingstone, Edinburgh.

Hutt, C. (1972c)   Males and Females. Penguin Books,
Harmondsworth, Middx., England.

Jackson, H.J. (1874)   On the Duality of the Brain.
Medical Press 1. 19. Reprinted in J. Taylor
(ed.) Selected Writings of John Hughlings
Jackson. Volume 2. Hodder and Stoughton,
London (1932).

Joynt, R.J. and Goldstein, M.N. (1975) Minor Cerebral
Hemisphere. In W.J. Friedlander (ed.)
Advances in Neurology. Volume 7. Current
Reviews of Higher Nervous System Dysfunction.
Raven Press, New York.

Keogh, B.K. (1971)   Pattern Copying under Three Conditions of an Expanded Spatial Field. Developmental Psychology 4. 25-31.

Keogh, B.K. (1972) Preschool Children's Performance on Measures of Spatial Organization, Lateral Preference and Lateral Usage. Perceptual and Motor Skills 34. 299-302.

Kimura, D. (1961) Cerebral Dominance and the Perception of Verbal Stimuli. Canadian Journal of Psychology 15. 166-171.

Kimura, D. (1963a) Speech Lateralization in Young Children as Determined by an Auditory Test. Journal of Comparative and Physiological Psychology 56. 899-902.

Kimura, D. (1963b) A Note on Cerebral Dominance in Hearing. Acta Oto-Laryngologica 56. 617-618.

Kimura, D. (1966) Dual Functional Asymmetry of the Brain in Visual Perception. Neuropsychologia 4. 275-285.

Kimura, D. (1967) Functional Asymmetry of the Brain in Dichotic Listening. Cortex 3. 163-178.

Kinsbourne, M. and Smith, W.L. (eds.) (1974) Hemispheric Disconnection and Cerebral Function. Charles C. Thomas, Springfield, Illinois.

Knights, R.M. and Bakker, D.J. (eds.) (1976) The Neuropsychology of Learning Disorders: Theoretical Approaches. University Park Press, Baltimore.

Lehman, R.A.W. (1970) Hand Preference and Cerebral Predominance in 24 Rhesus Monkeys. Journal of Neurological Sciences 10. 185-192.

Le May, M. and Culebras, A. (1972) Human Brain: Morphological Differences in the Hemispheres Demonstrable by Carotid Anteriography. New England Journal of Medicine 287. 168-170.

Le May, M. and Geschwind, N. (1975) Hemispheric Differences in the Brains of Great Apes. Brain Behavior and Evolution 11. 48-52.

Levy, J. (1975) Psychobiological Implications of Bilateral Asymmetry. In S.J. Dimond and J.G. Beaumont (eds.) Hemisphere Function in the Human Brain. Elek Science, London.

Lewis, S.M. and Whatley, M.A. (1975) The Ontogeny of Hemispheric Dominance for Language in Hearing Impaired Children. Unpublished special

study for the Diploma in the Education of
Deaf and Partially Hearing Children. Institute of Education, University of London.

Liberman, A.M. (1974) The Specialization of the Lan-
guage Hemisphere. In F.O. Schmitt and F.G.
Worden (eds.) The Neurosciences 3rd Study
Program. M.I.T. Press, Cambridge, U.S.A.

Lloyd, B. and Archer, J. (eds.) (1976) Exploring
Sex Differences. Academic Press, London.

Lukianowicz, M.S. (1970) Temporary Regression in the
Development of some Cognitive and Linguistic
Skills. Paper read in January to the Depart-
ment of Psychology, University College of
Swansea.

Lukianowicz, M.S. (1971) Sex Differences in the Development and Interaction of Verbal and Con-
servation-type Skills. Bulletin of the
British Psychological Society 24. 242.

Lukianowicz, M.S. (1974) Age and Sex Differences in
the Development and interaction of Some Verbal
and Conservation Skills. Unpublished Ph.D.
thesis, University of Cambridge.

Lukianowicz, M.S. (in press) Sex Differences in
Verbal Skills and their Relationship to Hand
and Ear Preference in the Deaf Child.

Maccoby, E.E. and Jacklin, C.N. (eds.) (1975) The
Psychology of Sex Differences. Oxford University Press, London.

Marshall, J.C. (1973) Some Problems and Paradoxes
associated with Recent Accounts of Hemispheric Specialization. Neuropsychologia 11.
463-470.

McBurney, A.K. and Dunn, H.G. (1976) Handedness,
Footedness, Eyedness: A Prospective Study
with Special Reference to the Development
of Speech and Language Skills. In R.M. Knight
and D.J. Bakker (eds.) The Neuropsychology of
Learning Disorders: Theoretical Approaches.
University Park Press, Baltimore.

McKeever, W.F., Hoemann, H.W., Florian, V.A. and Van Deventer, A.D. (1976) Evidence of Minimal Cerebral
Asymmetries for the Processing of English Words
and American Sign-Language in the Congenitally
Deaf. Neuropsychologia 14. 413-423.

42

Milner, B. (1962)   Laterality Effects in Audition. In
V.B. Mountcastle (ed.) Interhemispheric Rela-
tions and Cerebral Dominance. John Hopkins
Press, Baltimore.

Milner, B. (1971)   Interhemispheric Differences in the
Localization of Psychological Processes in
Man. In A. Summerfield (ed.) Cognitive Psycho-
logy. British Medical Bulletin   27.   272-277.

Milner, B. (1974)   Hemispheric Specialization: Scope and
Limits. In F.O. Schmitt and F.G. Worden (eds.)
The Neurosciences 3rd Study Program. M.I.T.
Press, Cambridge, U.S.A.

Milner, B. and Taylor, L. (1972)   Right Hemisphere
Superiority in Tactile Pattern-recognition
after Cerebral Commissurotomy: Evidence for
Non-Verbal Memory. Neuropsychologia   10.
1-15.

Mishkin, M. and Forgays, D.G. (1952)   Word Recognition
as a Function of Retinal Locus. Journal of
Experimental Psychology   43.   43-48.

Myers, P.I. and Hammill, D.D. (1969) Methods for Learning Disorders. Wiley, New York.

Nottebohm, F. (1971) Neural Lateralization of Vocal
Control in a Passerine Bird. I. Song. Journal of Experimental Zoology   177.   229-262.

Nottebohm, F. (1972) Neural Lateralization of Vocal
Control in a Passerine Bird. II. Subsong,
Calls, and a Theory of Vocal Learning.
Journal of Experimental Zoology   179. 35-50.

Ornstein, R. (1972)   The Psychology of Consciousness.
W.H. Freeman, San Francisco.

Orton, S.T. (1928)   Specific Reading Disability -
Strephosymbolia. Journal of the American Medical Association (JAMA) 90. 1095-1099.

Orton, S.T. (1929)   The Sight Reading Method of Teaching Reading as a Source of Reading Disability.
Journal of Educational Psychology   20.
135-143.

Orton, S.T. (1937)   Reading, Writing and Speech Problems in Children. Norton, New York.

Orton, S.T. (1939)   A Neurological Explanation of the
Reading Disability. Educational Record   20.
(Suppl. 12). 58-68.

Orton, S.T. (1966)   "Word-Blindness" in School Child-
ren and Other Papers on Strephosymbolia
(Specific Language Disability-Dyslexia).
The Orton Society Inc., Pomfret, Connecticut.

Peterson, G.M. (1934)   Mechanisms of Handedness in the
Rat. Comparative Psychology Monographs   9.
No.6.

Pfeifer, R.A. (1936)   Pathologie der Hörstrahlung und
der corticalen Hörsphäre. In O. Bumke and
O. Foerster (eds.) Handbuch der Neurologie.
Volume VI. Springer, Berlin.

Premack, D. (1970)   A Functional Analysis of Language.
Journal of the Experimental Analysis of Behaviour   14.   107-125.

Premack, D. (1971)   Language in the Chimpanzee.
Science, N.Y.   172.   808-822.

Roberts, L. (1969)   Aphasia, Apraxia and Agnosia in
Abnormal States of Cerebral Dominance.   In
P.J. Vinken and G.W. Bruyn (eds.) Handbook
of Clinical Neurology. Volume 4. North-
Holland Publishing Company, Amsterdam.

Rowell, T.E. and Hinde, R.A. (1962)   Vocal Communica-
tion by the Rhesus Monkey (Macaca Mulatta).
Proceedings of the Zoological Society of
London   138.   279-294.

Satz, P. (1976)   Cerebral Dominance and Reading Disability: An Old Problem Revised.   In R.M.
Knights and D.J. Bakker (eds.)   The Neuropsychology of Learning Disorders: Theoretical
Approaches.   University Park Press, Baltimore.

Satz, P., Achenback, K. and Fennel, E. (1967)   Correlations between Assessed Manual Laterality and
Predicted Speech Laterality in the Normal Population. Neuropsychologia   5.   295-310.

Schaller, G.B. (1963)   The Mountain Gorilla.   University of Chicago Press, Chicago.

Semmes, J. (1968)   Hemispheric Specialization: Possible Clue to Mechanisms. Neuropsychologia
6.   11-26.

Sperry, R.W. (1974)   Lateral Specialization in the Sur-
gically Separate Hemispheres.   In F.O. Schmitt
and F.G. Worden (eds.) The Neurosciences 3rd
Study Program.   M.I.T. Press, Cambridge, U.S.A.

Sperry, R.W., Gazzaniga, M.S and Bogan, J.E. (1969)
Interhemispheric Relationships: The Neocor-
tical Commissures; Syndromes of Hemisphere
Disconnection. In P.J. Vinken and G.W. Bruyn
(eds.) Handbook of Clinical Neurology. Volume
4. North-Holland Publishing Company, Amsterdam.

Springer, S.P. and Eisenson, J. (1977) Hemispheric
Specialization for Speech in Language-disor-
dered Children. Neuropsychologia 15.
287-293.

Taylor, D.C. (1969) Differential Rates of Cerebral Ma-
turation between Sexes and between Hemispheres.
Lancet ii. 140-142.

Taylor, L.B. (1962) Perception of Digits Presented to
Right and Left Ears in Children with Reading
Difficulties. Paper read at the meeting of
the Canadian Psychological Association, Hamilton.

Teuber, H-L. (1974) Why Two Brains? In F.O. Schmitt
and F.G. Worden (eds.) The Neurosciences 3rd
Study Program. M.I.T. Press, Cambridge, U.S.A.

Tesner, D. (1972) Étude Anatomique de l'Asymétrie
Droite-gauche du Planum Temporale sur 100
Cerveaux d'Adultes. Doctoral thesis. Univer-
sity of Paris.

Trevarthen, C.B. (1974) Cerebral Embryology and the
Split Brain. In M. Kinsbourne and W.L. Smith
(eds.) Hemispheric Disconnection and Cerebral
Function. Charles C. Thomas, Springfield,
Illinois.

Tschirgi, K.D. (1958) Spatial Perception and the Central Nervous System Symmetry. Archives de
Neuro-Psiquiatria 16. 364-366.

Tyler, L. (1965) The Psychology of Human Differences.
3rd Edition. Appleton-Century-Crofts, New
York.

Von Economo, C. and Horn, L. (1930) Uber Windungs-
relief, Masse und Rindenarchitektonik der
Supratemporalfläche. Zeitschrift für die
Gesamte Neurologie und Psychiatrie 130.
678-757.

Wada, J.A. (1969) Interhemispheric Sharing and Shift
of Cerebral Speech Function. Excerpta Medica
International Congress Series 193. 296-297.

Wada, J.A., Clarke, R. and Hamm, A. (1975) Cerebral Hemispheric Asymmetry in Humans. Archives of Neurology 32. 239-246.

Warren, J.M., Ablanalp, J.M. and Warren, H.B. (1967) The Development of Handedness in Cats and Rhesus Monkeys. In H.W. Stevenson, E.H. Hess and H.L. Rheingold (eds.) Early Behavior: Comparative and Developmental Approaches. Wiley, New York.

Webster, W.G. (1972) Functional Asymmetry between the Cerebral Hemispheres of the Cat. Neuro-psychologia 10. 75-87.

White, M.J. (1969) Laterality Differences in Perception: A Review. Psychological Bulletin 72. 387-405.

Witelson, S.F. (1974) Hemispheric Specialization for Linguistic and Non-Linguistic Tactual Perception using a Dichotomous Stimulation Technique. Cortex 10. 3-17.

Witelson, S.F. (1976) Sex and the Single Hemisphere: Specialization of the Right Hemisphere for Spatial Processing. Science, N.Y. 193. 425-427.

Witelson, S.F. and Paillie, W. (1973) Left Hemisphere Specialization for Language in the Newborn: Neuroanatomical Evidence of Asymmetry. Brain 96. 641-646.

Witkins, M.A., Dyk, R.B., Faterson, H.F., Goodenough, D.R. and Karp, S.A. (1962) Psychological Differentiation. Wiley, New York.

Yeni-Komshian, G.H. and Benson, D.A. (1976) Anatomical Study of Cerebral Asymmetry in the Temporal Lobe of Humans, Chimpanzees, and Rhesus Monkeys. Science, N.Y. 192. 387-389.

Young, R.M. (1970) Mind, Brain and Adaptation in the Nineteenth Century. Clarendon Press, Oxford.

Yule, W., Berger, M., Butler, S., Newham, V. and Tizard, J. (1969) The WPPSI: An Empirical Evaluation with a British Sample. British Journal of Educational Psychology 39. 1-13.

Yule, W. and Rutter, M. (1976) Epidemiology and Social Implications of Specific Reading Retardation. In R.M. Knights and D.J. Bakker (eds.) The Neuropsychology of Learning Disorders: Theoretical Approaches. University Park Press, Baltimore.

Zangwill, O.L. (1960)   Cerebral Dominance and its Relation to Psychological Function.   Oliver and Boyd, Edinburgh.

Zangwill, O.L. (1967)   Speech and the Minor Hemisphere. Acta Neurologica et Psychiatrica Belgica   67. 1013-1020.

Zangwill, O.L. (1976)   Thought and the Brain.   British Journal of Educational Psychology   67. 301-314.

An additional important article has been published since the writing of this paper which deals with philosophical, psychological and physiological aspects of language development in primates. This is given below:

Limber, J. (1977)   Language in Child and Chimp?   In American Psychologist, April.   280-295.

Acoustic Patterns and Speech Acquisition

A. J. Fourcin

By far the greater part of the work at present in progress in the field of speech acquisition
depends on two related descriptive tools. The first
comes directly from classical phonetics and makes use
of place, manner and voice descriptors and a traditional transcription. These investigations attempt to define the sound contrasts of speech qualitatively, both
in production and perception, in what are primarily productive, articulatory, terms. The second method of
description uses a particular set of distinctive features (Chomsky and Halle, 1968) which are based on subsets of these phonetic, articulatory, dimensions. These
distinctive features are intended to facilitate the definition of phonological contrasts.

This contribution is concerned with a complementary description of some of the aspects of speech
acquisition in strictly quantifiable acoustic terms.
The acoustic form of speech can be given a direct auditory as well as an articulatory interpretation and this
makes it possible to arrive at a realistic appreciation
of what elements in a speech sound sequence are likely
to be dominant in sensory terms and how these elements
must be processed - in normalization for example when
listening to a small as opposed to a large vocal tract -
so that physically different acoustic stimuli can have a
common phonetic identity.

48

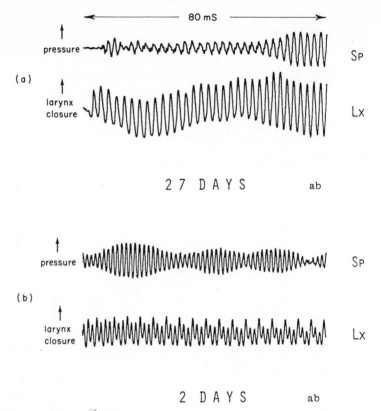

Fig. 1. Cry development

The two pairs of waveforms shown have been taken from a
developmental study of one child during the first six
weeks after birth (I am grateful to Anne-Britte Parker for
making the recordings and to Simona Bennett for her co-
operation). In each pair of traces, Sp refers to the
acoustic pressure and Lx indicates the output of an
electro-laryngograph, simultaneously recorded on an ordinary two channel tape recorder. Laryngeal vibration in
the first weeks after birth is not always well defined,
and this is shown by the irregularity of Lx in 1(b). The
Sp waveform shape, however, is determined primarily by the
first formant frequency and the relative inadequacy of
larynx excitation is responsible only for a small amplitude. When the child has increased his voicing skill and
his cry has greater amplitude, his larynx vibration is
necessarily more regular and his vocal tract movement
necessarily more precise. This is shown clearly in the
onset waveforms of 1(a).

It is important to note that the application of the simple
auditory feedback criterion of loudness can guide quite
complex productive skills.

The use of a phonetic transcription necessarily limits the adult investigator and may lead him to assign importance to aspects of a child's speech which are of little contrastive significance to the child himself. The use of quantitative acoustic-auditory descriptors is beginning to reveal aspects of both productive and perceptual processing which could not otherwise have been guessed at. A first example of this, below, is drawn from a study of baby cries (see figure 1). This is followed by a discussion of normalization (see figures 3, 4 and 5). Normalization depends on an ability to perceive similarity of structure - or pattern - and a general indication of the way in which pattern perception may contribute to speech development is given in the discussion relating to figures 6, 7 and 8. The stimuli and data of figures 9, 10 and 11 relate to a particular acoustic study of the way in which English and French children develop their ability to perceive elements of what is phonetically described as the voiced-voiceless distinction.

Acoustic patterns not only provide a means for describing speech events but also for the assessment of auditory dysfunction, using synthetic speech, and the correction of inadequate production using pattern displays. This work depends on the possibility of referring to normal acquisition and this is briefly discussed finally.

CRY DEVELOPMENT

The waveforms in the top half of Figure 1 have been recorded from the cry of a 27-day-old baby. Sp refers to the acoustic pressure waveform and Lx designates the synchronously recorded output of an electro-laryngograph (Fourcin, 1974). During normal voicing in both adult and child the vocal folds vibrate regularly, successive closures occur with a quite well-defined periodicity and the maximum glottal opening and greatest degree of vocal fold contact during closure typically vary little from cycle to cycle. The Lx waveform shows this clearly since it is determined primarily by the nature of vocal fold contact during closure and it can be seen in Figure 1(a) that this 27-day-old baby has the type of closure sequence which, in its regularity, corresponds to normal vibration. The frequency of vocal fold vibration , Fx, is markedly higher than that normally found for child and adult (see Figure 3) and starts in this example at about 400 Hz, falling to 340 Hz. Fx determines the fundamental frequency of voiced sounds and is the primary physical correlate of their pitch.

The Sp waveform also has some mature features. This can best be seen when the two waveforms in Figure 1(a) are interpreted jointly. The Lx waveform starts before there is an appreciable Sp pressure. This results

from the baby's breathstream initiating vocal fold
vibration before the release of a vocal tract articulatory closure. Prior to this release both nasal
and oral branches of the vocal tract have been held
closed, and a controlled oral release has then taken
place relatively slowly during the 60 mS interval
following the initiation of vocal fold vibration. This
sequence of combined laryngeal control and vocal tract
gestures is typical in general form - although not in
detail - of an initial voiced plosive consonant-vowel
combination; it is an essential basis for later contrastive speech productive ability.

The pair of acoustic pressure and vocal fold
closure waveforms shown in Figure 1(b) have been recorded
from the same baby at the age of 2 days. The Sp waveform
has a dominant frequency of about 690 Hz and a smoothly
fluctuating amplitude which varies as a result of the
baby's uncoordinated control of his vocal tract shape.
These rapid vocal tract changes - the first two peaks
are separated by 30 mS, the second pair by 18 mS - make
it very difficult to interpret the formant patterns of
the corresponding spectrograms and add to the obstacles
which are ordinarily in the way of a spectrographic interpretation of vocal fold excitation. The synchronously recorded Lx waveform is easy to interpret, however.
It shows a vocal fold vibration which is quite atypical
of the normal mature form. In the adult this regularly
repeated sequence of doublets or triplets of decreasing
amplitude of closure is found in some of the samples of
phonation for unilateral vocal fold palsy (Fourcin, 1974).
When the folds are asymmetrically tensed their natural
frequencies of vibration may be quite different and they
will not act in unison. This can result in a vocal fold
version of acoustic beats. A sequence of vocal fold
beats will be reset by the relatively violent closure
which occurs when the phasing of the folds returns to
that of normal vibration. Normally phased vocal fold
vibration occurs when the two folds have symmetrical
movements; it puts all the acoustic energy into the
basic harmonic spectrum and has a greater sound producing
efficiency than that of this irregular vibration. The Lx
waveform of Figure 1(b) in consequence indicates an asymmetric tensioning of the baby's vocal folds which will be
associated with a weak cry of ill-defined voice pitch.

The triplet sequences of closure which are
shown here have a frequency of about 230 Hz whilst the
intrinsic vocal fold frequency is about 690 Hz. This
difference, if it is substantiated by other work, could
account for the paradoxical developmental increase in
pitch of the neonate cry which has been observed to occur
for some babies in the first month after birth and partially explain the relative weakness of the cry in this
period. An increase in regularity of vocal fold vibration improves the pitch definition and loudness of the

cry and both of these features are, in principle, readily capable of mediation by the baby's hearing mechanism. In this case, loudness and pitch are directly related. He can, in consequence, use loudness as a feedback control which will improve his cry in quite detailed aspects of its laryngeal excitation. The uncoordinated control of his vocal tract will also reduce the signalling effectiveness of his cry and can similarly be improved by attention only to the auditory feature of loudness. This factor of auditory feedback must also be of primary consequence in the development of the sound productive skills shown in Figure 2.

IMPORTANCE OF LOW FREQUENCY ENERGY

The essential factor which distinguishes speech sounds from all others which may be produced by the vocal tract, is that they are used contrastively. The basis of contrast is provided by pattern diffference and Figure 2 gives an example of the first type of sound pattern which is used by a baby in a controlled way.

A sequence of a falling tone, level tone and slightly rising tone is produced by the baby. This is reinforced by the mother and immediately repeated by the infant.

In order for the baby of Figure 2 to respond to his mother's utterances and to repeat his own he must be able to make use of at least some aspects of the pitch variations both of her voice and of his own. There is strong empirical evidence that pitch is mediated in the human adult as the result of two distinct types of acoustic signal processing. First and more classically in terms of the place theory, by the positions along the length of the basilar membrane of regions of maximum movement (Newby, 1972). Second, by the transmission along the eighth nerve of time structure information about the acoustic stimulus. When, like the majority of voiced vowels, the acoustic stimulation is a complex waveform with a well-marked period then the frequencies of the fundamental and its harmonics will operate the first pitch mediating mechanism and the periodic waveform irregularities will contribute to triggering the second (Fourcin, 1970). The new-born child has a nearly adult size tympanum and a well formed cochlea (Northern and Downs, 1974). Although a considerable amount of growth dependent development remains to be accomplished, once the middle ear is fluid-free some mechanical cochlear response to acoustic stimulation is to be expected at least at the lower end of the frequency spectrum, since the acoustic impedance match of the immature ear to air may improve as frequency diminishes. Weir (1976) has examined the results of direct experimental assessments of the auditory frequency sensitivity of the neonate.

Her analysis gives credence to the earlier conclusions
that stimulation frequencies below 500 Hz and square
rather than sine waveforms are most effective in pro-
voking startles in neonates. Although this practical
demonstration of the relative effectiveness of low frequency, temporally well defined, acoustic stimulation
requires further experimental support; three other
factors make it seem possible that the low frequency
end of the acoustic spectrum is most important not only
to the neonate but also to the young child. The first of
these additional factors comes from the preferential
masking of high frequency energy by low in hearing;
this is a classic result using pure tone stimuli (Wegel
and Lane, 1924) and occurs also with voiced formants
(Nye, Nearey and Rand, 1974); it appears to result
partly from the hydromechanical response of the cochlear partition and is likely to occur in the neonate
cochlea as well as in the adult.

The second of these factors arises from a
hypothesis (Salus and Salus, 1974) concerning the
child's neurophysiological development. The process
of myelination is known to influence the high frequency
transmission characteristics of nerve fibres and if
myelination is incomplete this might (although not according to a strict place theory of hearing) reduce
hearing ability for higher frequencies. Finally, and
most certainly, the nature of voiced speech sounds is
such that ordinarily there is always greater energy at
the fundamental frequency than elsewhere and the first
formant ordinarily is greater in amplitude than all
others. This physical spectral bias would in consequence act to direct auditory attention to these components of speech.

FIRST INTERACTIVE COMMUNICATION

Figure 3 illustrates the quantitative nature
of the baby's task when he interacts with the other
members of his family solely on the basis of voice
pitch. In order to produce the same pattern of change
as his father when the father produces a simple falling
[ɑ], or to be reinforced when the father imitates the
baby's [ɑ], the baby must, as in Figure 2, be capable
of pattern rather than absolute imitation. This imitative interaction with the father is likely to be facilitated by a previous extension of the interaction
with the baby's mother. Since her normal range of larynx frequencies is already considerably below that of
the baby, any successful use of ordinary voice by the
mother, in responding to or in eliciting a corresponding response from the baby will contribute to the baby's
ability to abstract pattern form. In this way, simple
intonation forms produced by parents or siblings can be
treated as being perceptually the same and the first
step can be made towards the solution of the general

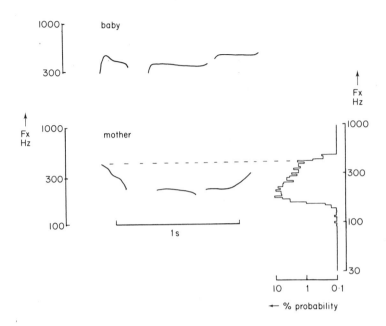

Fig. 2.   Voice pitch interaction

The top part of this figure shows the voice frequency contours, Fx, of a particular sequence produced by a 4 week old baby in the company of its
mother.   Immediately below these three tones are
the three voiced segments ([ɑ]) produced by the
mother in response to her child.   The mother has
repeated her baby's sequence with constraints
coming partly from the phonology of English and
partly, perhaps, from her desire to tune the
physical nature of her voice to that of the baby:
her fall+rise sequence is a typical English intonation form but is here displaced into an atypical
high pitch range.   The distribution on the right
hand side of the figure shows the range, and probabilities of occurrence, of the voice frequencies
in the mother's expressive speaking voice.   Her
first fall, in this example, starts at a frequency
which is at the top extreme of her range.   In normal speech this high to mid fall would not occur.
Its production here enables her to reduce the
complexity of the baby's matching task.

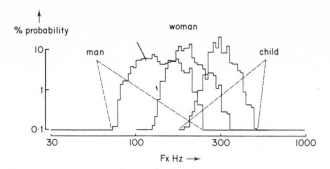

Fig. 3.   Environmental voice frequency ranges

Three superimposed voice frequency, Fx, distributions are
shown.   They have been obtained from three-minute samples
of laryngograph waveforms separately recorded by normal
man, woman and child speakers.   Each speaker produces his
intonation forms within these physical confines and the
developing child must learn to recognise Fx patterns as
being identical although their absolute ranges may, as
here, be markedly different.

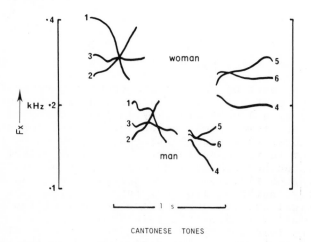

CANTONESE TONES

Fig. 4.   Cantonese tones

In terms of fundamental frequency structuring, Cantonese
has six main tones.   The choice of tone by a speaker
determines the lexical value of a word.   The main pattern
relations between the tones - in a given accent - are
fixed from one speaker to another and the developing
child must learn these relations, and ignore absolute
physical differences, in order to perceive and produce
lexical tonal contrasts.   In the tonal language environment this normalization will be basic to a child's first
phonological skills.

problem of acoustic pattern identification. This perceptual congruence is the basis of phonetic identity and it involves a hypothetical processing level which is often referred to as normalization (Fourcin, 1971; 1975). For the child who is born in a tone language environment we must expect that ease of pitch pattern normalization will provide a first introduction to phonological contrast since contrasting fundamental frequency patterns can be used lexically. At first the contrasts are likely to be crude and oppositions which are the least pitch confusable will precede those which have similar levels and contours. The fundamental frequency basis of lexical tone contrast is shown in Figure 4 for two Cantonese speakers. If, in a tone language environment, the baby's mother restricts her use of articulatory contrast and relies only on the simple pitch distinction which can be based on these Fx contours, we can expect that the first stages of phonetic discrimination will be easier than if the spectral envelope contrasts of non-tonal languages are used.

English babies in their first year can make communicative use of voice pitch changes (Ricks, 1975; Lewis, 1968) and it has been commonly observed that at the babbling stage the English child uses English pitch forms. Tone does not have a simple lexical significance in English, however, and the first lexical contrasts depend not on the excitation of the vocal tract but on the spectral envelope of its output. The normalization process must now make use of more complex physical information. Figure 5 shows the average formant frequencies of English vowels produced by young English adult males and, below, the particular values for a four-year-old child. Just as for Cantonese tones, the overall patterning for the two phonetic sets of contrasts is the same although the physical size of the speech sources is markedly different. Although it is generally agreed (Anthony and McIsaacs, 1970; Sheridan, 1948; Fry, 1966) that the English vowel system is fully acquired long before the consonant system, little is known concerning the pattern of confusions which arises in the early stages of acquisition. In terms only of the first spectral peak, F1, [i] and [u] are most distinct from [æ, ʌ, ɑ] and it seems probable that in the very early stages on the basis of purely auditory information [i] will be highly confusable with [u], as is the case for the deaf child with little high frequency hearing (Fourcin, 1976). Contrasts due to nasalization, which is associated with primarily low frequency spectral features, will not present an especial perceptual difficulty in early development. Increasing skill in the interpretation of the acoustic signal will enable the position of F2 to disambiguate F1 information for all the vowels. The diphthongs, which are characterized by relatively slow spectral changes, will also be differentiated by this extra spectral information.

Consonant contrasts are all carried by a combination of spectral and relatively rapid temporal differences. The shorter duration of their distinctive elements introduces a variety of difficulties. First, they are more easily masked by external acoustic events since their transient nature reduces the redundancy which is associated with repetition. Second, in the nature of speech production, variability from utterance to utterance, even for a single speaker, is unavoidable and this makes the individual token less well-defined. Third, the sensory processing is handicapped by additional masking, both forward and backward (Elliot, 1971), in time. For example, the initial burst in a voiceless plosive-vowel combination could, in forward masking, reduce the perceptibility of the F2 transition; and in backward masking, the same transition could be masked by the relatively high voice energy in the F2 of the vocalic part. Fourth, the nature of the transitions which characterize consonants will necessarily vary as a function of their context so that their defining patterns and the normalizing processes which are necessary for their retrieval are inevitably more complex than is the case for tone and vowel distinctions. Little has been done to elucidate the perceptual mechanisms which operate at this crucial stage of speech processing (Verbrugge et al., 1976) but the experiments which have been performed (Fourcin, 1968) show very large changes in the interpretation by child and adult subjects of identical consonantal stimuli purely as a function of the subjects' inference of the characteristics of the speech sound source. When a child produces a phonetically acceptable consonant-vowel combination he is necessarily using normalization processing either in order to monitor his output or to set up the original reference from adult models. His processing may not, however, be as complete as that employed by a competent adult. At first, the needs of a limited set of phonological oppositions may be served only by attention to F1 and nasal formant transitions. At a later stage, as greater auditory skill is acquired, both F1 and F2 pattern elements could be used and, subsequently, F3 and the fricative formant transitions could be employed in perception and normalization to provide the basis for an essentially complete speech sound inventory. These acoustic auditory pattern considerations do not explicitly include the articulatory constraints which determine ease of production and govern coarticulation and assimilation but their examination in isolation reveals an aspect of speech development which may prove to be of equal consequence. The child who cannot perceive the relations between the acoustic pattern elements of speech is shut out from ordinary communication.

NORMAL CONSONANT DEVELOPMENT

The way in which speech productive skill is acquired by the normally communicating child in an English speaking environment has been studied by a number of investigators both in Britain (for example:

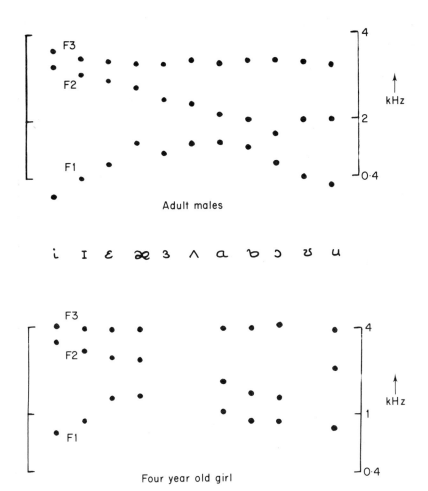

Fig. 5.　English vowel formant frequencies

In English, phonological oppositions are
carried by vocal tract rather than vocal fold
features and tonal differences are of minor
lexical importance.

Formant frequencies provide the primary
acoustic information which enables an auditory
assessment of these vocal tract differences to
be made and, once more, the listener must
allow for physical differences between speech
sources in his appraisal of pattern forms.
Vowel formant patterns are simpler than consonantal and their essential independence of
source is illustrated here.

58

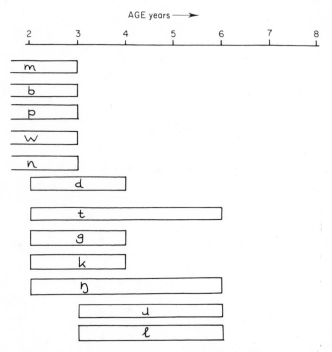

Fig. 6.   Consonant acquisition

This summary of English consonant developmental studies is based on a con-
venient representation introduced by
Sander (1972).   The left-hand bar for
each closed box corresponds to the age
at which 50% of the children studied
use the sound (ideally this should be
a contrastive use);   the right hand bar
corresponds to the 90% age.   Initial,
medial and final position occurrences
have been averaged.   /h/ has been
omitted;   grouping follows phonetic
class.

Sheridan, 1948; Morley, 1957; Fry, 1966; Waterson, this volume; Anthony, Bogle, Ingram and McIsaacs, 1971) and in the U.S.A. (for example: Templin, 1957; Poole, 1934; Wellman, 1931; Menuyk, 1972). A classic phonetic transcription of the material has been employed in all cases and the adult investigators have, of course, applied adult criteria in their categorization of the children's utterances. Although little has been reported in respect of vowel development, each study has yielded results with regard to consonant acquisition and overall there is a useful, and interesting, consensus of opinion. Sander (1972) has summarized some of the American work (Wellman and Templin) and his graphical representation is basic to Figure 6. All workers both in Britain and the U.S.A. find that the voiced and voiceless fricatives and affricates occur towards the end of development and are ahead only of cluster production. [h] is an exception to this rule; in the U.S.A. this is found to occur very early but in the U.K. it is amongst the last observed. The later stages have been omitted from figure 6 since the ordering of acquisition within the fricative class as a whole is not well defined - at least in published reports. The plosives and nasal continuants not only precede the fricatives but also have a fairly well-defined order within themselves. Labials tend to occur before alveolars and these tend to be used contrastively before velars. /w/ occurs with the labials but /l/ and /r/ follow the velars. Only an incomplete definition and only a partial understanding of the factors which lead to this developmental ordering are available at present. Four obvious sources of influence are: speech sound environment; use in communication; ease of production; ease of perception. To an important extent these four appear to fall into two pairs, since the use of speech in the child's environment will be directed towards communication with him and we can expect that early sounds must be readily produced and perceived.

The pressure of sound environment for an English speaking family arises partly from the mere frequency of occurrence of sound types and their contrastive use. The probability of occurrence of sounds in English (Denes, 1963) has been combined in Figure 7 with their median age appearance, using the data on which Figure 6 is based. [t], [n], [d] and [s] are by far the most frequently occurring sounds and their minimal pairs (contrasts such as day-say) also occur most often.

It is significant that these alveolar contrasts are so much more frequent in English speech since, even if subsequent work shows that they are not so common in the environment of baby and young child, this result will indicate an important modification of normal speaking habit. The sounds [m], [w], [b], [p] which occur so early

are of far lower frequency of occurrence. This fact
of early acquisition is not explained in terms of normal environmental pressure on communicative convenience.
There is no simple correspondence between the acquisition orders of Figure 6 and the ocurrence probability of
Figure 7.

      In early production consonants occur most fre-
quently in initial rather than in final position. For
the voiced plosive consonants this requires a moderate
degree of coordination between laryngeal and vocal tract
controls to be exerted by the speaker. The speaker's
soft palate must be raised so that an oral pressure increase can be established, the vocal folds approximated
to their position for free vibration and then the airstream can be initiated. No fine adjustment is needed
and the baby's early sucking and crying abilities are
directly applicable to this speech skill. For the production of [m] the control sequence is simpler since the
closure is maintained instead of being released rapidly
as for [b]. [w] is obtained by using the controls for
[b] but associating them with a much slower movement and
an incomplete vocal tract closure. These bilabials are
the simplest consonants in productive terms and their
simplicity may well have a bearing on their early appearance in the young child's speech. An important difficulty arises in the case of the voiceless bilabial [p],
which requires a much greater degree of productive skill
in the simultaneous control of vocal tract and vocal
folds so that oral pressure is built up and released before the onset of vocal fold vibration (Stevens, 1971 ;
Kewley-Port and Preston, 1974). In spite of this considerable additional complexity [p] occurs before the
productively simpler [d]. When the potential ease of
perception of these different consonants' acoustic patterns is considered a complementary explanation is found
which goes some way towards resolving this dilemma.

For initial [b] the burst of acoustic energy which accompanies the release of articulatory closure occurs essentially together with the voicing excitation of the formants. F1, as for all initial voiced plosive consonants,
starts from a low value and increases quite rapidly to
its value for the accompanying vowel. This pattern of
change in F1 is a primary acoustic trait for this consonant class. F2 also increases to the vowel value, from
a lower frequency which, when taken in conjunction with
the set of F1 and F2 frequencies characteristic of the
particular speaker, can be found from an inferable locus
- a concept given its first quantitative definition in
work at the Haskins Laboratories (Delattre, et al.,
1955). This pattern of change in F2 can be regarded as
a secondary trait, of relevance only for distinguishing
[b] from [d] and [g]. If a young child has a greater facility for the processing of low rather than high fre-

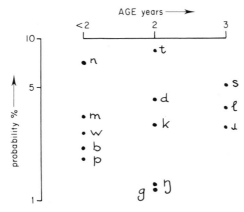

Fig. 7. Probability of consonant
occurrence in the normal
speaking environment,
against age of (50%)
acquisition

/t/, /n/, /s/, /d/ occur most frequently in adult speech and provide the most
common minimal contrasts (Denes, 1963).
This functional pressure does not
appear to influence age of acquisition
since it can be seen that these and
other probable occurrences in developed speech are not necessarily amongst
those which are earliest acquired. At
present it seems more likely that relative ease of perceptibility is more
important in early development than
phonological pressure.

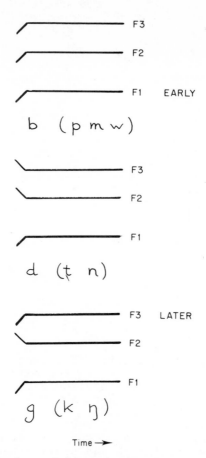

Fig. 8. Schematic Formant-Time
         Patterns

The early development of bilabial
consonants may be influenced both by
visibility and auditory clarity.
Simplicity of consonant acoustic
patterning in general, however,
appears to be related to ease of
acquisition. It may prove to be of
considerable significance that the
alveolar and velar patterns are acquired later, not merely because of
their relative lack of visual cues
but also because of their relative
acoustic pattern complexity.

(These consonant patterns could be
associated with a front open vowel
produced by the child of Fig. 5.)

quency information in a stimulus having several formant peaks, then he is more likely to be able to perceive formant patterns which have F2 in the low end of
the frequency spectrum than in the high.

In Figure 8 the formant patterning for initial
[b] is drawn in a highly schematized way but it is clear
that the F2 for [b] will be less masked than that for
either [d] or [g]. This greater sensory clarity of the
[b] pattern may be important in the early stages of
speech perception in enabling the contrasts between [b],
[m] and [w] to be established primarily on the basis of
F1 changes in time and secondarily with the aid of F2
as a source of reinforcement. Production of these sounds
will then be facilitated by the auditory feedback made
possible by a simple set of pattern references which require little cognitive elaboration for their successful
application to a wide range of speech sources of different vocal tract dimensions. In this way, at this
first level (Fourcin, 1971; Lisker and Abramson, 1964)
and first developmental stage of speech processing, normalization can be established as the joint result of
perception and associated production.

For initial [d] the formant patterning in Figure 8 shows a falling transition for both F2 and F3 and,
as greater auditory skill is acquired this reinforcing
F2-F3 alveolar fall may be contrasted with the reinforcing bilabial rise in F2-F3 which typifies [b]. This is
a much simpler opposition in acoustic pattern terms than
that between [b] and [g] or [d] and [g], since F2 and F3
for velars tend to move in opposite directions. From a
purely auditory-acoustic pattern point of view this makes
it quite likely that [d] and its associated nasal [n]
will be next employed contrastively with each other and
with the previously acquired bilabials.

For initial [p], although the skilled adult
may make use of more than a dozen different acoustic
traits, the very young child is likely only to be influenced by the most evident pattern change. Following
the release burst for [p] there is typically an interval
in which no voicing occurs and only aspiration excites
the speaker's vocal tract. The aspiration gives relatively less energy to F1 than to F2 and F3 compared with
vocal fold excitation, and the F2, and possibly the reinforcing F3, transitions may be utilisable by the child
as a secondary trait. The gross trait of lack of initial voicing dominates for [p], [t] and [k] and is a
primary characteristic. At the beginning of speech acquisition when attention is directed essentially to the
F1 region the voicing gap provides a simple way of including [p] in the family of contrasting bilabials. With
increasing auditory skill the secondary F2-F3 information can be utilized and, depending on individual cir-
cumstance and vowel environment, the difference in burst

frequency, which exists between bilabial and alveolar initial plosives, may be utilized.

In acoustic pattern terms initial [k] is most confusable with initial [t] (and this confusion will be greatest for a high F2 front close vowel environment). With the increasing auditory skill, which comes with the gradual approach to speech maturity, however, the more complex F2-F3 patterns from the velars will be resolved and the family of velar contrasts will be added more consistently to the alveolars and bilabials.

This brief discussion of the possible relevance of acoustic pattern forms to the ordering of speech sound acquisition has concentrated on only the most obvious facts. It is evident, however, that the correspondence between the ordering implied by the pattern sequence of Figure 8 and that of Figure 6 is far greater than that implied by the occurrence probability structure of Figure 7.

It is not possible using either the standard techniques of transcriptive phonetic analysis or distinctive feature categories (Chomsky and Halle, 1968) to examine the way in which children's speech development is influenced by these acoustic pattern forms. It is feasible, however, to use processes of acoustic analysis to measure the evolution of productive skill and to use speech synthesis techniques to assess children's ability to perceive acoustic pattern differences which have speech significance. Both of these methods have been employed in this department (University College, London) for normal children and for the deaf child (Martin and Fourcin, in press). The first results of this work indicate that the stages of speech development and the influence of auditory disability are better understood when acoustic pattern description is allied with phonetic analysis. The phonetician necessarily applies an analysis which reflects his ability to hear whole pattern forms, he is intrinsically unable as the result of his training to attend to the pattern elements which may dominate a child's perception of particular contrasts and which give rise to such phonetically strange contrasts in the young child's speech repertoire. The following example is concerned with what phonetically is termed the 'voiced-voiceless' contrast.

PATTERN PERCEPTUAL DEVELOPMENT

The acoustic pattern forms corresponding to a particular example of this voiced-voiceless contrast are shown in Figure 9. The voiceless extreme (V-) is on the right, the voiced (V+) is at the lower left. Acoustically, a large number of factors underlie this simple phonetic opposition (e.g. for V+, an initial

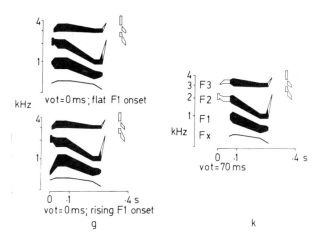

Fig. 9.   Synthetic pattern extremes for
          [g] and [k]

These patterns are particular examples
of stimuli which can be used in a controlled way to examine a listener's
ability to make contrastive use of particular components in speech. The left-
hand patterns represent 'goat' , the
right-hand pattern 'coat' . The flat F1
onset stimuli cannot be produced naturally but it proves to be an acoustic
pattern feature which can be employed
perceptually in speech sound discrimination by the deaf - to infer lack of
initial voicing; 'k' labels are then
given both to these flat F1 stimuli as
well as those of the form shown on the
right.

In the next two figures, average responses to these rising F1 transition
stimuli are shown by squares, the
crosses represent responses to flat F1
and large voice onset time delays.

66

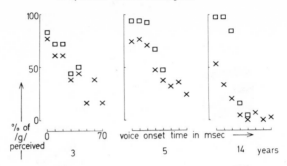

RESPONSES OF ENGLISH CHILDREN
to synthetic stimuli (coat/goat)

Fig. 10.   Voice-voiceless perception by English children

The ability to discriminate between initial /g/ and /k/
is only acquired, on average, gradually. At first the
pattern features which are most obvious guide the child's
labelling and, for the three year-old children, there is
little distinction between formant shapes, only the degree
of periodic excitation is of real importance. With
increasing age there is increasing skill both in labelling
and in the ability to reject non speech-like patterning,
the cross stimuli are not, in consequence, often put in
the /g/ category.

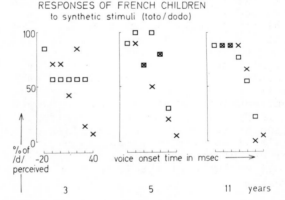

RESPONSES OF FRENCH CHILDREN
to synthetic stimuli (toto/dodo)

Fig. 11.   Voice-voicless perception by French children

French does not rely on the presence or absence of
aspiration, and the associated delay in voicing onset, to
provide a basis for the voiced-voiceless distinction. Pre-
voicing, before release, characterizes the voiced sounds.
This provides a quite different perceptual bias, as compared with English, and the French children of all ages
are not markedly influenced by Fl shape but are progressively more skilled in using the onset timing of periodic
excitation.

upward step in Fx; a rising Fl, a lower intensity
burst which occurs close to the onset of voicing; and
for V- an initial turbulent excitation following the
burst which is often described as a delay in voicing,
an initial downward fall in Fx with an initial breathy
excitation, an effective initial absence of Fl and an
initially greater burst intensity). Other factors can
be listed particularly as a function of vocalic environment but only two of all those possible are explicitly
dealt with in the figure. The first arises from the delay in voicing - this is called voice onset time, VOT
(Lisker and Abramson, 1964). The second arises from the
normally rising Fl for V+. In the top part of the figure a flat Fl is shown for V+; this is not a naturally
produceable pattern form but for the deaf listener with
high frequency loss it can be used to elicit a V- response (Martin and Fourcin, in press). This type of
listener cannot respond to patterning associated with
the burst and can only contrast Fl pattern forms.

In Figure 10,(Simon, 1976), the rising Fl stimulus responses are shown by squares and for the 14-year-
old children it can be seen these stimuli evoke a sharp
categorical response. The average responses to the flat
Fl stimuli in the same VOT range are shown by crosses,
these are not well categorized. The 3-year-old children, however, categorize both of these stimulus types in
essentially the same way, they are responsive to VOT and
do not make any special use of the rising Fl information.
This is not the case for the 5 year-old children who are
in an intermediate state of development. These results
show how two acoustic traits can be used differently as
perceptual development proceeds. The learning is gradual and it can be easily interpreted in terms of acoustic pattern salience but not at all in classic phonetic
or distinctive feature terms. In consequence a child
could make consistent contrasts which are not under-
standable with normal analytic techniques.

In Figure 11 (Simon, 1976), the results are
shown from the same type of experiment performed with
French children. The speech environment of these children does not employ the post-burst turbulence used in
English and the presence of a rising Fl is not a useful
contrastive trait. This is reflected in the uniformity
of response by the 11-year-old children to both rising
and flat Fl stimuli. The same similarity of response is
found with the 5-year-old children. It is evident from
these two language different experiments that response
is influenced by the models afforded by the speaking environment and that categorization skill may be acquired
quite slowly. The greatest future value of speech pattern tests may come, however, from the quantitative information which they provide concerning individual ability and development - both normal and handicapped.

DISCUSSION

The work which has been described has all
been concerned with a study of various aspects of
speech communication, as opposed to mere discrimination. It appears quite likely that the acoustic-
auditory description, and definition, of prominent
aspects of speech sound combinations will be of real
help in understanding the increase in skill which is
basic to the developmental process underlying the progression from the first cry to the complete mastery of
phonological oppositions.

At each stage of development prominent acoustic traits will be used by the individual listener both
in assessing his own production and that of other
speakers. His processing of other source outputs will
depend on his ability to normalize, and his ability to
use sounds contrastively will depend on his ability to
categorize. Rules of acoustic pattern processing are
needed for both of these aspects of perception and, in
due course, we must be able to formulate grammatical
systems for these pattern relations both to understand
the process of speech acquisition more fully and to be
able more adequately to describe normal adult usage. An
outstanding apparent anomaly exists, however. Work,
especially by Eimas (1975) has shown that the very young
infant can discriminate speech sounds in ways which appear to reflect an innate predisposition to categorization. The discriminations, however, are sensory rather
than phonetic.

The work described here shows only a gradual
accumulation of speech processing ability. The experiments that Eimas has performed depend on the baby's
sensory ability to discriminate between sound patterns
presented in sequence. Later on it seems likely, from
the present discussion, that a ready ability to normalize on the basis of only a little prior experience will
also be found. It does not follow, however, that the
ability to categorize speech sounds contrastively, so
that communication ability is achieved in a particular
language environment, can be innate. This is a higher
skill which must be learnt from experience, and which
could well in part depend on an innate auditory ability
to process prominent acoustic pattern traits.

We must expect, for example, that the categorization of VOT differences will partly depend simply
on the peripheral hearing mechanism's response to transient stimulation (a 20-30 mS minimum stimulus duration
is required for accurate pitch assessment and this corresponds to the VOT labelling transition). In consequence, elementary VOT discrimination will be possible
for all animals having similar cochlear characteristics.

Similarly, the critical band response characteristics of the cochlea will make a major contribution to the sensory evaluation of formant energy concentrations and, in consequence, partly determine the ability to detect formant transitions, by both man and animal. These are innately determined characteristics. Normalization and phoneme categorization abilities will be acquired from experience, however. This first without difficulty, by animals as well as infants, since only elementary pattern processing is needed. The second with increasing difficulty as the degree of pattern complexity becomes greater (e.g. in going from labials to velars).

A practical application of speech pattern descriptors is beginning to be made in the remediation of speech productive disability (Fourcin, 1974; Abberton and Fourcin, 1975) and in the assessment of hearing for speech (Fourcin, 1976). It seems possible that future work based on the acoustic analysis of speech, in terms which are of auditory significance, will be a major source of knowledge of both normal speech development and of means for its encouragement.

REFERENCES

Abberton, E.R.M. and Fourcin, A.J. (1975)   Visual Feedback and the Acquisition of Intonation. In E.H. Lenneberg and E. Lenneberg (eds.) Foundations of Language Development. Academic Press, New York.

Anthony, N. and McIsaacs, M.W. (1970)   Notes on Patterns of Development found by using the Qualitative Phonetic Assessment Sheet of the Edinburgh Articulation Test. British Journal of Disorders of Communication 5. 148-164.

Anthony, N., Bogle, D., Ingram, T.T.S. and McIsaacs, M.W. (1971)   Edinburgh Articulation Test. E.S. Livingstone. Edinburgh and London.

Chomsky, N. and Halle, M. (1968)   The Sound Pattern of English. Harper and Row, New York.

Delattre, P.C., et al. (1955)   Acoustic Loci and Transitional Cues for Consonants. Journal of the Acoustical Society of America 27. 769-773.

Denes, P.B. (1963)   On the Statistics of Spoken English. Journal of the Acoustical Society of America 35. 892-904.

Eimas, P.D. (1975) Speech Perception in Early Infancy. In L.B. Cohen and P. Salapatek (eds.) Infant Perception. Academic Press, New York.

Elliot, L.L. (1971) Backward and Forward Masking. Audiology 10. 65-76.

Fourcin, A.J. (1968) Speech Source Inference. Institute of Electrical and Electronic Engineers. AU-16. 65-67.

Fourcin, A.J. (1970) Central Pitch and Auditory Lateralization. In R. Plomp and G.F. Smoorenburg (eds.) Frequency Analysis and Periodicity Detection in Hearing. A.W. Sijthoff, Leiden, The Netherlands.

Fourcin, A.J. (1971) Perceptual Mechanisms at the First Level of Speech Processing. In A. Rignault (ed.) Proceedings of the VII International Congress of Phonetic Sciences. Mouton, Lattay: Paris.

Fourcin, A.J. (1974) Laryngographic Examination of Vocal Fold Vibration. In B. Wyke (ed.) Ventilatory and Phonatory Control Systems. Oxford University Press, London.

Fourcin, A.J. (1975) Speech Perception in the Absence of Speech Productive Ability. In N. O'Connor (ed.) Language, Cognitive Deficits, and Retardation. Butterworths, London.

Fourcin, A.J. (1976) Speech Pattern Tests for Deaf Children. In S.D.G. Stephens (ed.) Disorders of Auditory Function II. Academic Press, New York.

Fry, D.B. (1966) The Development of the Phonological System in the Normal and Deaf Child. In F. Smith and G.A. Miller (eds.) The Genesis of Language. M.I.T. Press, Camb., Mass.

Kewley-Port, D. and Preston, M.S. (1974) Early Apical Stop Production: Voice Onset Time Analysis. Journal of Phonetics 2. 195-210.

Lewis, M.M. (1968) Infant Speech. Routledge and Kegan Paul, London.

Lisker, L. and Abramson, A.S. (1964) A Cross-language Study of Voicing in Initial Stops. Word 20. 384-422.

71

Martin,M.C. and Fourcin, A.J. (in press) Synthetic
    Speech Tests with Deaf Children. British
    Journal of Audiology.

Menyuk, P. (1972) The Development of Speech.
    Bobbs-Merril,Studies in Communicative
    Disorders (Library of Congress, ref. 74-
    173981).

Morley, M. (1957) The Development and Disorders of
    Speech in Childhood. Livingstone, Edinburgh.

Newby, H.A. (1972) Audiology. Appleton-Century-
    Crofts, New York.

Northern, J. and Downs, M. (1974) Hearing in Child-
    ren. Williams and Wilkins, Baltimore.

Nye, P.W., Nearey, T.M. and Rand, T.C. (1974)
    Dichotic Release from Masking: Further
    Results from Studies with Synthetic Speech
    Stimuli. Haskins Laboratories. Status
    Report on Speech Research   37/38   123-138.

Poole, I. (1934) Genetic Development of Articulation
    of Consonant Sounds in Speech. Elementary
    English Review 11. 159-161.

Ricks, D. (1975) Vocal Communication in Pre-Verbal
    Normal and Autistic Children. In N. O'Connor
    (ed.) Language, Cognitive Deficits and Re-
    tardation. Butterworths, London.

Salus, P.H. and Salus, M.W. (1974) Developmental
    Neurophysiology and Phonological Acquisition
    Order. Language 50. 151-160.

Sander, E.K. (1972) When are Speech Sounds Learned?
    Journal of Speech and Hearing Disorders
    37. 55-63.

Sheridan, M.D. (1948) The Child's Hearing for Speech.
    Methuen, London.

Simon, C. (1976) A Developmental Study of Acoustic
    Pattern Production and Perception in Voiced-
    Voiceless Oppositions. Ph.D. thesis for the
    University of London.

Stevens, K.N. (1971) Aerodynamic and Acoustic Events
    at the Release of Stop and Fricative Con-
    sonants. Journal of the Acoustical Society
    of America 50 139.

Templin, M. (1957)   Certain Language Skills in Children. University of Minnesota Press, Minneapolis.

Verbrugge, R.R. et al. (1976)   What Information enables a Listener to Map a Talker's Vowel Space? Journal of the Acoustical Society of America 60. 198-212.

Wegel, R.L. and Lane, C.E. (1924)   The Auditory Masking of One Pure Tone by Another and its Probable Relation to the Dynamics of the Inner Ear. Physical Review 23. 266-285.

Weir, C.G. (1976)   Auditory Frequency Sensitivity in the Neonate: a Signal Detection Analysis. Journal of Experimental Child Psychology 21. 219-225.

Wellman, B. et al. (1931)   Speech Sounds of Young Children. University of Iowa Studies in Child Welfare 5. 1-82.

2
From non-verbal Communication to Language

One of the fields which at the 1975 Symposium
showed a minor explosion of research interest was that of
the development of communicative competence in the period
before true language acquisition. Two kinds of research
relevant to this theme were presented: 1) studies of
the development of vocalization from the early period
through babbling and into the period when one-word utterances begin to be produced, and 2) studies of mother-child
interaction during the prespeech period. Of the papers
presented in this section, those by Delack and Fowlow
and by Carter fall primarily into the first category, and
those by Sylvester-Bradley and Trevarthen and by Garnica
into the second, while the paper by Tuaycharoen presents
information both about the development of child vocalizations and of adult responses to the infant. The papers
are arranged according to the ages of the children
studied. Sylvester-Bradley and Trevarthen describe the
way mothers and infants respond to one another, how they
establish communication, when the infant is only a few
months old. Delack and Fowlow present data on the nature
of infant vocalizations and the situations within which
infants vocalize, covering the age range from one month
to twelve. They find a difference of patterning in the
progress of males and females. Buffery (section 1) and
Cherry and Lewis (section 3) are also concerned with sex
differences. Tuaycharoen describes the development of
vocalizations in a baby exposed to a tone-language, Thai,

and adults' responses to the infant's babbling. Carter
discusses how a child's first words develop out of his
vocalizations in the prespeech period, on the basis of a
case history of one child. Garnica analyzes how mothers
make the meaning of their utterances clear even to children without any productive language ability, by the use
of gestures.

The papers in this section all present evidence
in support of the notion that the first stages in language
acquisition are already advanced stages in the development
of vocalization and communicative ability.

Baby Talk as an Adaptation to the Infant's Communication

B. Sylvester - Bradley and C. Trevarthen

This paper is a discussion of films and video-tapes taken of one baby girl, Sarah, between the ages of 8 and 20 weeks, with her caucasian, primiparous, middle-class mother. At approximately weekly intervals the mother visited our laboratory where she was asked to chat with Sarah while we filmed from another room. Twelve sessions yielded, on average, 4 minutes 39 seconds of film (see Trevarthen 1977, for procedural details).

With this small corpus of data we wish to illustrate the necessary preconditions for discussing a mother's baby talk as an adaptation to her infant's communication. Two subsidiary issues are involved: first, the ways in which the mother's baby talk changes in relation to her infant's behaviour, and secondly, in what sense these changes constitute adaptations to a growing communication.

*This research was supported by an M.R.C. Studentship and S.S.R.C. Grant No.HR 2263 'Prespeech in Communication of Infants with Adults'.

CHANGES OF BABY TALK IN RELATION TO THE INFANT'S BEHAVIOUR

We observed striking changes in both Sarah's behaviour and her mother's baby talk. In the first few weeks of the study both mother and child interacted with animation, Sarah displaying many of the behaviours we associate with sociability (e.g., smiling and eye-contact). By 14 weeks, however, the mother-infant interaction no longer seemed so successful. As noted in some other studies (e.g., Polak, Emde and Spitz, 1964), there was a marked decline in the proportion of each session for which Sarah would look positively (without crying) at her mother, and there was also a marked decline in the proportion of time Sarah spent smiling (see Figure 1). However, as in Ambrose's (1963) study, these drops in our indicators of interactional success were followed at around 17 weeks by second peaks. (N.B. These indicators are not homogeneous. For example, the final decline in eye-contact to the level found at 18, 19 and 20 weeks, differs from the first decline at 12, 13 and 14 weeks in that it represents less Sarah's purely looking away from her mother, e.g., just to stare at the floor, the ceiling or her hands, than looking away to examine the rest of the room.)

Here we have a conspicuous change in Sarah's behaviour, and it is clear in our analysis that her mother's baby talk showed a concurrent change. Although we do not want to claim any direct causal relations between the indices we happen to have measured, it is true to say that, as Sarah began to grow less sociable, there was an increase in the verbal density of her mother's baby talk (syllables/sec. of Standard English), and, furthermore, it was only when the baby talk showed a definite decrease in density that Sarah's positive regard and smiling recovered. These changes in verbal density were also associated with an overall increase in the proportion of utterances which were contentless.

Our use of the terms 'verbal', 'non-verbal' and 'contentless' is as follows. An utterance is deemed verbal if it is made up of Standard English words, otherwise it is deemed non-verbal. An utterance is registered as contentless when the verbal information it might convey is subordinated to the effect of its constituent physical sounds. Thus non-verbal utterances, such as imitations of Sarah's babbles, are automatically contentless, but verbal utterances are only contentless when their stressing and intonation undergo a marked alteration, as in verses, chants or songs (cf. Snow, 1975). This means that the approximately inverse relationship between changes in verbal density and changes in the proportion per session of contentless utterances shown in Figure 2 is by no means a necessary artefact of our method. The level of verbal

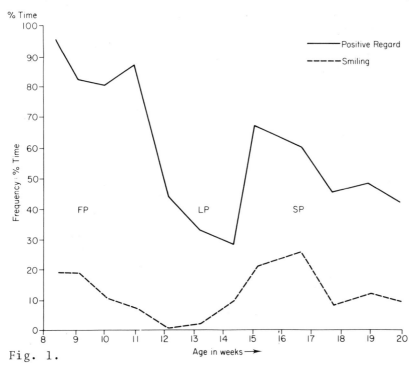

Fig. 1.

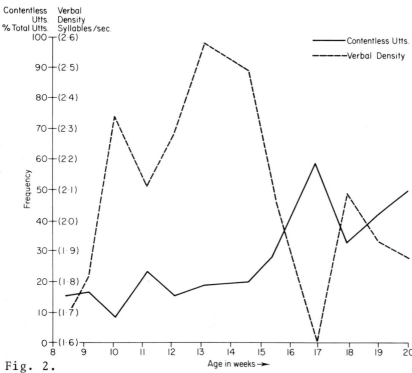

Fig. 2.

density at the end of our study is at least partly due
to an increase in those utterances which are verbal but
contentless (i.e., 14.8% of contentless utterances are
verbal up to 15 weeks whereas from 16 to 20 weeks, the
proportion is 38.6%).

We will discuss the significance of these various changes of the mother's baby talk and her infant's
behaviour in the last section, after we have outlined the
philosophical basis for our approach to them as communicative.

THE PHILOSOPHY UNDERLYING OUR RESEARCH INTO MOTHER-INFANT COMMUNICATION

It is difficult to judge if and when infant
behaviour is communicative. This problem stems from
the traditional idea that communication is fundamentally a process of 'knowing' or 'getting to know' in which
one entity, the knower or subject, gains awareness of
another, the thing known or object; an idea which
leads to the more general problem of whether or not we
can know other minds. To the empiricist, who accepts
(irrationally, in Hume's view) that external objects
can be known, the idea that 'behind' the appearance of
some such objects (people) there hides a knowing subject (an essence or Being) is irrational and Romantic.
Thus, in psychological treatments of communication, the
behaviouristic empiricist approach permits no analysis
of behaviour as meaningful and directly opposes the
more Romantic, psychoanalytic approach in which it is
contended that all behaviour is meaningful. The limited
practical use of both approaches for the scientific
study of communication is rooted in the subject-object
dualism.

To dispose of this philosophic opposition
between subject and object is a primary prerequisite for
the study of communication. The resolution has been
achieved in philosophy by placing the opposition in the
living context of what we will call a 'field': 'immediate
flux of life', James (1904), the 'practical human sense
activity' of Marx (1845), or Wittgenstein's (1958)
'forms of life'. The ideas of 'subjectivity' and 'consciousness', the terms 'subject' and 'object', have
ceased to be dignified with epistemological primacy in
human research. They are the products of a philosophical language and no language can be superimposed on the
field of social life, something which embraces and is
infinitely more subtle than language itself. As do all
words, philosophical jargon has value but only insofar
as there are forms of social life in which it plays a
useful part. It follows that an understanding of social
affairs is the precondition for an understanding of
language and indeed, of philosophy, rather than vice
versa! Any understanding of social life must originate

in a knowledge of other minds which is taken for granted
as inherent in the society of men. Thus, any student of
social affairs must acknowledge from the start, both
a priori, methodologically and in fact, observationally,
that man is endowed with an intuitive understanding of
his fellows. The main problem facing us in this approach
to the study of social behaviour is the status of the
individual. If we argue, with Macmurray (1961), that
the original form of knowledge is knowledge of others,
how can we come to know ourselves? As Nietzsche concludes, this is the question we are least able to answer
('Jeder ist sich selber der Fernste', Nietzsche, 1887,
sect. 335).

What we are saying is that the sense of 'communication' will be discovered in terms of the nature
and articulation of what now appears as a field of
social forms. The investigation of this field is difficult because of the investigator's participation in
it - implicating him in polarizing the field, however
hard he does or does not try to detach himself as an
observer. Thus, to analyse social relations as if
they were divided from oneself is to adopt an uncriti-
cal position. But as yet, no way has been found to
analyze them usefully as a part of one's personal life.
This difficulty dogs the study of mothers and infants
even where it is least apparent. For illustration, we
will examine the 'pragmatic' approach to the study of
mother-infant communication taken by those psychologists who accept the philosophy of, among others,
Peirce, James, Dewey, Mead, Searle and Grice (e.g.,
Bruner, 1975; Shotter, 1975).

As an example we will take one of Grice's
(1957) criteria for meaningful communication, that
'the speaker must intend to produce a certain effect
in his listener'. This criterion poses the problem of
establishing the infant's intention. For instance,
Sarah's mother often commented on her daughter's behaviour around 14 weeks as if it were a rejection (e.g.,
Are you just gonna ignore me?, You've got the pip with
me, haven't you?) which was directed specifically at
her (e.g., It's just me you don't want to talk to,
isn't it?), particularly as the decrease in Sarah's
sociability was less noticeable when she was with other
adults (cf. Fitzgerald, 1968; and Caldwell, 1965, in
Schaffer, 1971, who found similar strange preferences
at 3 months). But did Sarah intend to reject her
mother? We cannot ask her as we would ask an adult,
and to posit a non-verbal procedure for the verification of intention is to accept that actions embody intentions in the absence of any conscious acknowledgement, a position akin to Freud's notion of 'unconscious ideas' and subject to the problems of Roman-
ticisim (see below).

Nevertheless, Bruner (1975) in his paper 'The Ontogenesis of Speech Acts', outlines just this sort of procedure. He asserts that intentional behaviour has measurable features which can be used for 'inferring that children "have" intentions'; for example, 'anticipation of an outcome of an act', 'a stop-order defined by an end-state', 'appropriate means for the achievement of an end-state', and so on. In this vein, we might argue that, because Sarah's rejection was active (she would refuse her mother's attentions despite her mother's repeated attempts to re-establish contact, e.g., calling out Hello!, Sarah!, etc., putting her head in Sarah's line of regard, and even tugging Sarah's head round to face her), it was intended. But such a designation of the 'end-state' of Sarah's behaviour as a rejection must still ultimately depend on the more or less covert assumption of an ideal form of communication within which some logic of human relationship is supposedly working, a form conceptualized in psychoanalysis, for instance, as culminating in the 'prise de conscience' or 'passage into the Full Word' (Lacan, 1956).

If the analysis were to stop at this point, with the use of criteria, its conclusions would at best be condemned to relativity; they would be less the product of real discoveries in the field of social relations than of some position, political, moralistic or religious, which had been adopted by the investigator. For example, Shotter concludes, near the beginning of his article on mother-infant interaction (1975), that the goal of personal development (and therefore developmental psychology) is 'to act deliberately rather than spontaneously'. To adopt this kind of dogmatic position is to reinstitute the dualism between the appearance and the underlying 'essence' of development, dividing the analyst as by divine right from his subjects. Indeed, it is to assume psychological knowledge which we do not have and of a type we would be mistaken to seek.

The weakness of the pragmatic analysis of communication lies in its ignorance of origin: on the one hand, the psychological origins of communication (e.g., of the illocutionary force), and on the other, the origins of the analyst's position vis-à-vis his investigation (i.e., his view of social relations). Either way a consideration of origins leads back to the field of social relations. For the truth of the investigation depends first, on the psychological processes which allow the investigator to make real discoveries in his involvement with others as a natural, historical individual, and secondly, on the possibility of representing those discoveries in a language which others can understand and, as a corollary, in whose terms he can comprehend his own position in the field of human relations. What saves such discoveries from relativism is that they are a product of the investigator's personal life, which is for him absolute. The individuality expressed in a finding about humans is to the researcher a gain in self-knowledge, to others it is his originality. That knowledge about our fellows can only be gained within a personal context is thus not a drawback to social research, but its precondition and its only true worth. This personal approach is therefore essential to any research into human relations, the vexing difficulty of which should not be glossed over.

Our research into communication between mother and infant must begin with the delineation and description of the social forms in which we perceive them to participate: it is in terms of the nature and articulation of these forms that we will come to understand the psychological processes underlying mother-infant communication. That is why we emphasize a descriptive approach (Trevarthen, 1977).

Our argument that Sarah takes part in social forms of life runs as follows. The majority of English speakers distinguish certain patterns of life as 'social' (e.g., arguing, chatting, joking) and these patterns incorporate certain behaviours. In analysing our films of Sarah supposedly chatting with her mother, we recorded many of the social behaviours accepted as important in 'chatting' between adults (often in diverse cultures, see, e.g., Eibl-Eibesfeldt, 1970; Ekman, 1973): facial expressions such as smiling, frowning, and surprise, vocalizations, crying, laughing, patterned eye-contact, spontaneous and reciprocal eye-brow flashing, gesture-like arm-movements and some speech-like lip and tongue-movements (see Trevarthen, 1977), imitation of and a degree of bodily synchrony with the mother (see Plate 1). Moreover, we found that Sarah showed these behaviours specifically in the context of 'chatting'; the frequency of these behaviours while chatting was much greater than their frequency while attempting to grasp a suspended wooden ball (e.g., at 9 weeks the chatting : reaching ratios were % regard 81 : 85, number of eyebrow flashes 17 : 5, number of tongue protrusions 61 : 8, number of mouth openings 51 : 16, number of vocalizations 6 : 0, number of frowns 8 : 0, number of smiles 16 : 0, see Sylvester-Bradley, in preparation). Sarah exhibited not only social behaviours but also a basic distinction between social and asocial contexts. We conclude that this distinction is of great psychological significance and in this cannot agree with many statements to the contrary in the developmental literature (e.g., Schaffer, 1971: 1, 31). Trevarthen (1976, 1977) incorporates the idea of an inherent aptitude for perceiving persons as partners in communication and for

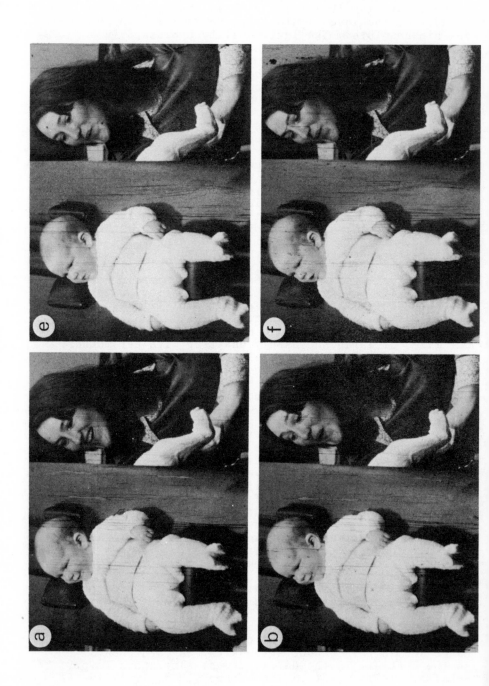

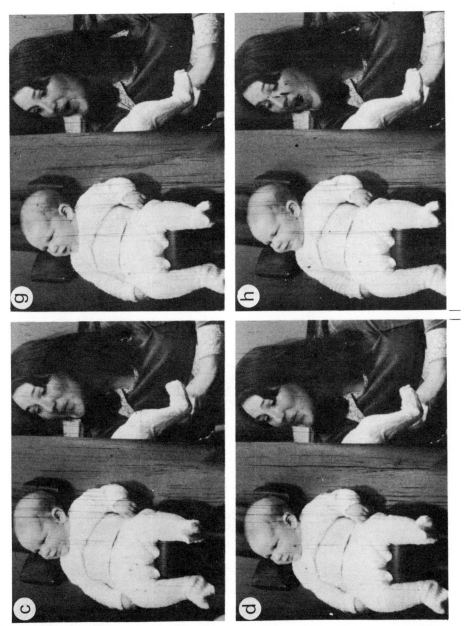

PLATE I.

expressing communicatively, into the term 'inter-
subjectivity' which both describes the nature of
communication and presumably reflects some specific
but unknown structure of the brain, with which the
infant is born.

We will now proceed with a more detailed
discussion of those changes in Sarah's behaviour and
her mother's baby talk outlined above in terms of a
description of the social patterns in which Sarah and
her mother took part. In this way we hope to establish
not so much the presence or absence of their communication as the forms in which it is constituted.

FORMS OF ADAPTATION

Conversational Form.   Baby talk is social behaviour and social behaviour must involve mutual adaptation at some level of description. At the most superficial level, baby talk sounds like half a conversation (Snow, 1975). And further, if one describes the
interchange as a conversation, one finds that the
mother's baby talk adapts to the infant's acts. For
example, subtle movements of Sarah's head, although
often ignored, are often picked up as formal contributions to a conversation. At eight weeks, three
slight, alternating head-movements by Sarah produced
an emphatic head-shake in her mother accompanied by
an abrupt change from a succession of positive statements and questions to a negative statement: You're
looking very pensive, aren't you? You're looking very
pensive. Mmm. What are you doing? (Sarah's head
moves laterally.) You don't want to smile (with emphatic head-shake). No. etc. The mother, in treating Sarah's behaviour as communicative, lends this
episode the form of conversational turn-taking. But
to say that the mother is holding a conversation with
Sarah is in fact absurd: the interaction may be conversational but it is not a conversation. In the
first place, there is no exchange of ideas, and secondly , even adult conversation cannot be adequately
characterized by a simple transcription of what is
spoken. An analysis of baby talk as a conversation
is misplaced because it exaggerates the baby's conscious achievement and it totally neglects baby talk's
intersubjective origins.

At another level, a primary origin of mother-
child interaction is the mother's responsibility for
satisfying her child's physiological needs. This responsibility, however, is not obviously reflected in our
mother's baby talk. She did not assume dominance,
scarcely referring to herself at all (only 9.0% of all
pronominal subjects were 'I'; 76.8% were 'you'; and
only 2.7% of all her utterances referred to her own
feelings or intentions and these were often playful,

e.g., 'I'll bite your little hand off; 23.5% referred to the infant's psychical state). Neither did
she exercise much authority; only 2.9% of her utterances were imperative and these too were often playful (e.g., You let me go! when Sarah was holding her
hair). Thus in the main, baby talk is not an accompaniment to the management of physiological needs. These
needs may be mentioned (e.g., You a bit hot, eh?, or
You wanna drink?) but only amongst all the other varied
references to Sarah, her body, her clothes and her general psychical state , which make up 84.3% of all the
references in our corpus of baby talk. The mother
appears to be playing a passive, receptive role in
which she continually interprets back to Sarah Sarah's
immediate state, her moods (e.g., You're giving me the
cold shoulder), her facial expressions (e.g., You're
not looking very happy), and her actions (e.g., You've
got your hand in the air) as they happen. Thus, in
the first two weeks of our study, 83.8% of all verbs
used were in the present tense (overall proportion:
69.8%). In these early sessions this receptive role
was particularly apparent. We wish to distinguish it
as the defining characteristic of a social form we
will call 'mirroring'.

Mirroring. Mirroring is a strategy used in
psychotherapy (see, for example, the transcriptions
in Axline, 1947) which is particularly useful in early
stages of treatment for establishing the therapist's
emotional understanding of a patient, and also for
developing the patient's consciousness of his own
actions. It is a strategy demanding an attitude of
mind which Freud (1912) described as the 'fundamental
rule of psychoanalysis', namely, that the analyst
'must adjust himself to the patient as a telephone receiver is adjusted to the transmitting microphone ...
so (his) unconscious is able, from the derivatives of
the unconscious which are communicated to him, to reconstruct that unconscious, which has determined the
patient's free associations' (cf. the infant's actions).
This is an excellent description of the attitude of
mind evinced by the mother, who appears in the role of
an unconsciously skilled analyst. Furthermore, it is
clear that the mother has a symbolic key or programme
of categories for experience (as does the analyst: he
uses the 'Freudian' or 'Jungian' system), a key which
is partly idiosyncratic and partly cultural and which
leads to a very selective construction of her baby's
actions. This key operates obviously in the verbal
sphere (in the adjectives used, e.g., 'grumpy',
'cheeky','pensive'), but also programmes the non-
verbal sphere of the interaction (as the movement
mirrored as a 'head-shake' for 'No' reported above,
p. 84.

86

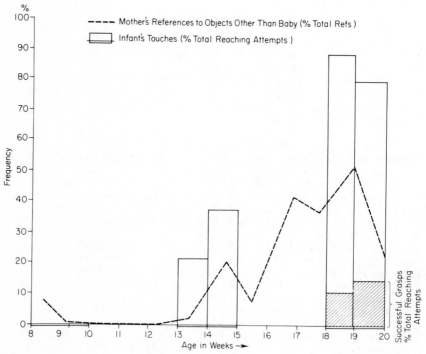

Fig. 3.

Although a mother's mirroring may just sound as if she is talking to herself it is not a wholly verbal activity, in fact verbal mirroring appears to be sometimes a substitute for and sometimes a projection of a non-verbal interactive process into the verbal sphere. As far as the infant can recognize her own actions in the mirroring of her mother (and this ability would be no more than a reorganization of the imitative process which Sarah sometimes demonstrates, see Plate 1; cf. Maratos, 1973) it is the non-verbal modes of mirroring which must be primary. These modes are both visual (see Plate 1) and vocal. Thus for example, a cry may be mirrored concurrently by the mother in terms of amplitude, intonation and phrasing; it might also be repeated after Sarah had stopped crying. The spheres of verbal and non-verbal mirroring may thus unite, a verbal interpretation being delivered in the form of the non-verbal sound it is mirroring (e.g., the mother says You're crying!; mirroring the cry in terms of amplitude and pitch). However, non-verbal and verbal mirroring do not always harmonize; they may conflict. For example, a long sequence of visually mirrored mouth movements (see Plate 1) finished abruptly when one of Sarah's movements was interpreted verbally as a yawn (i.e. Howowowowo (non-verbal mirroring of Sarah's mouth movements which culminate with a pseudo-yawn) Tt! Are you very bored?).

As Sarah grows older, her mother mirrors different things. In fact, mirroring is a social form ideally suited to incorporate the infant's changes of interest and development of ability. For example, Sarah's ability to touch and grasp objects showed a marked improvement during the study (Figure 3). This new ability and the associated interest in the outside world is reflected in the mother's baby talk by a large overall increase in the proportion of references to bodies other than Sarah's (i.e., her clothes, her mother, her toys and other objects around the room, see Figure 3b). Thus mirroring remains an important pattern throughout the study and indeed into adulthood when speakers and listeners often complete each other's unfinished sentences, demonstrating the degree of their mutual understanding (see, for example, Ferguson, 1975, on 'silent interruptions' and 'predictive monitoring').

It is in terms of what 'mirroring' offers to the infant that we may begin to understand the changes outlined in the second section of this paper. These changes lead the communication to other forms of interaction. It is clear that the mother is concerned at Sarah's increasingly antisocial behaviour at three months (see her comments, page 79). Her response to this behaviour is first to mirror it verbally (e.g., You're telling me off, aren't you?' You're not gonna have a chat today. Are you bored with Mummy; talk

all the time). Thus the correlation between the rise
in verbal density of baby talk and the fall in Sarah's
sociability can be seen as a part of the social form of
mirroring. However, the recovery in Sarah's positive
regard and smiling seems to be associated with a decrease rather than this increase in verbal density (cf.
Figures 1 and 2). We contend that this decrease reflects the rising importance of an alternative social
form to mirroring, best exemplified in games.

  Playful Form. The rise of the game-playing is
indicated by the overall increase of contentless utterances in baby talk (see Figure 2a). Although this increase partly reflects the increasing number of Sarah's
vocalizations - because vocalizations are usually imitated - one major contribution to it is the increasing
number of rhythmically repeated verbal utterances (see
page 78) for example, You're gonna play a game with
me — you're goin to play a game. Goin to play a game.
Goin to play a game. Hey! Hey! Hey! Goin to play
a game. In chanting and dancing games like this, in
their rhythm and music, the verbal and non-verbal
spheres are integrated in a new way. Games have a
regular structure which lasts several seconds, and
this structure is always accentuated vocally by the
mother, and often by the baby too. Thus, a phase of
action, which often has its own vocally stressed beat
(e.g., butting Sarah in the stomach, worrying her fin-
gers) is inevitably followed by a pause during which
the mother looks at her baby and smiles, laughs or
calls out. If the baby expresses enjoyment at this
point, by happy animation or a call, the game will be
renewed, often in a slightly altered form.

     We believe that this playful social form
differs from mirroring in that it requires the mutual
understanding and confidence which mirroring is
adapted to foster. Mirroring is receptive while play
is more assertive; thus, borrowing from Grice's termi-
nology in the citation above, we would say that early
on, the mother was developing her comprehension of the
various 'effects' Sarah 'intended' to produce in her,
passively letting her have her say, while in the later
stage, the mother has gauged Sarah and can thus more
actively have a say too. To do so, she has had to
change her language into a form more compatible with
Sarah's embryonic understanding and expectations. Thus,
by the end of our study, the interaction between Sarah
and her mother seemed as successful as at the beginning
but in a different way and at a higher plane of complexity. Not only had Sarah's abilities and interests
grown and changed, objects becoming more important, but
the emergence of the playful form of social interaction
had involved transformation of Sarah's social behaviours
as well as her mother's baby talk.

In summary, we see the most fruitful way of understanding the complex variations in Sarah's behaviour from 8 to 20 weeks and in her mother's baby talk to be as manifestations of a developing relationship. The growth of joint enterprise fostered in the forms of mirroring and play would seem to prepare naturally for more complex enterprises later, in which the growth of Sarah's understanding, both of people and of things, will take place in a predominantly social world.

CONCLUSION

In this paper we have discussed baby talk as part and illustration of the mutual interactive adaptation between mother and child. 'Adaptation' is here less a biological than a psychological term: an infant's rejection of its mother would be strictly maladaptive in evolutionary terms were it not taking place within a psychological realm with its own systems of control and laws of growth. In our terms, an adaptation is a social form in which both mother and child share through their inherent similarities. Such similarities are not only the basis of mother-child interaction but also of the investigator's understanding of their communication. Although this shared core at the heart of each social form may vary in the complexity and content of its expression, it persists through life: while knowledge develops, the fundamental forms of sociability stay the same. For example, the onset of language is a cognitive milestone with enormous consequences in the pragmatics of communication, but is it an interactive milestone? We think our work shows that it is not. Sarah's linguistic skills will be employed within pre-existing forms of interaction just as was her new interest and ability with objects.

Although the main form stays the same, the student of interactive development is faced with a process of change. We must withstand the temptation to call this change progress because the formulation of development as progress destroys any curiosity for the actual nature of change. For this reason we have not considered the development we observed as a necessary progression of social forms; those forms were observed to a lesser or greater extent throughout our study and will continue to recur (see Trevarthen, 1976, for further discussion). A child does not disregard her mother for the last time at the age of fifteen weeks! Neither were the changes we recorded unidirectional. But then, in our view, social change does not gain sense from its place in a chronological progression but from the position of the individual concerned within the field of social relations at the time of change and the investigator's perception of that position.

What we have tried to demonstrate in this paper is less a theory of social development than a necessary orientation to our subject-matter. Thus, if our approach appears tautologous because we assume sociability in studying the baby, it is with good reason; because, as Samuel Beckett has remarked a tautology is the expression of a relation. The practical value of that relation, as the tautologous theory of biological evolution by 'survival of the fittest' shows, is the opening of new fields of description to procedures of scientific verification. The aim of our argument then has been to illustrate the necessity and productivity of describing baby talk as an adaptation to the infant's communication within the field of social relations.

REFERENCES

Ambrose, J.A. (1963)   The Concept of a Critical Period in the Development of Social Responsiveness.   In B.M. Foss (ed.) Determinants of Infant Behaviour II.   Methuen, London.

Axline, V.M. (1947)   Play Therapy.   Ballantine Books, New York.

Bruner, J.S. (1975)   The Ontogenesis of Speech Acts. Journal of Child Language   2. 1-19.

Eibl-Eibesfeldt, I. (1970)   Ethology: The Biology of Behaviour.   Holt, Rinehart and Winston, New York.

Ekman, P. (1973)   Cross-cultural Studies.   In P. Ekman (ed.) Darwin and Facial Expression: a Century of Research in Review.   Academic Press, New York.

Ferguson, N.H. (1975)   Interruptions: Speaker-switch Nonfluency in Spontaneous Conversations. Ph.D Thesis, Edinburgh University.

Fitzgerald, H.E. (1968)   Autonomic Pupillary Reflex Activity during Early Infancy and its Relations to Social and Nonsocial Stimuli. Journal of Experimental Child Psychology 6.   470-482.

Freud, S. (1912)   Recommendations for Physicians practising Psycho-analysis. In J. Strachey (ed.) (1958) Freud, Standard Edition (24 vols.) Vol. XII. Hogarth Press, London.

Grice, H.P. (1957)   Meaning.   In P.F. Strawson (ed.)
Philosophical Logic (1967), Oxford University Press, London.

James, W. (1904)   Does Consciousness Exist?   In
Essays in Radical Empiricism (1912) Long-
mans, New York.

Lacan, J. (1956)   The Function of Language in Psycho-
analysis.   In A. Wilden (ed.) The Language
of the Self (1968).   Johns Hopkins Press,
Baltimore.

MacMurray, J. (1961)   Persons in Relation.   Faber
and Faber, London.

Maratos, O. (1973)   The Origin and Development of
Imitation in the First Six Months of Life.
Ph.D. Thesis, University of Geneva.

Marx, K. (1845)   Theses on Feuerback.   In T.B. Botto-
more and M. Rubel (eds.) Karl Marx: Selected
Writings in Sociology and Social Philosophy
(1956).   Penguin Books, Harmondsworth,
Middx., England.

Nietzsche, F. (1887)   Die Fröhliche Wissenschaft.
Trans. with commentary by W. Kaufmann as
The Gay Science.   Vintage Books (Random Ho.),
New York.

Polak, R.R., Emde, R.N. and Spitz, R.A. (1964)   The
Smiling Response II: Visual Discrimination
and the Onset of Depth Perception.   Journal
of Nervous and Mental Diseases 139 (5),
407-15.

Schaffer, H.R. (1971)   The Growth of Sociability.
Penguin Books, Harmondsworth, Middx., England.

Shotter, J. (1975)   Methodological Issues in the
Micro-analytic Study of Mother-Infant Interaction. Department of Psychology, University
of Nottingham. (To be revised and published
as The Cultural Context of Communication.
In A. Lock (ed.) (1977) Action, Gesture and
Symbol. Academic Press, London).

Snow, C.E. (1975)   The Development of Conversation
between Mothers and Babies. Pragmatics
Microfiche, 1, 6.

Sylvester-Bradley, B. (In preparation)   Qualitative
Differences in Infant Behaviour with People
and with Things. Department of Psychology,
University of Edinburgh.

Trevarthen, C.B. (1976, in press) Basic Patterns of Psychogenetic Change in Infancy. To be published in H. Nathan (ed.) Proceedings of the O.E.C.D. Conference on Dips in Learning, St. Paul de Verie, March, 1975.

Trevarthen, C.B. (1977, in press). Descriptive Analyses of Infant Communicative Behaviour. In H.R. Schaffer (ed.) Studies in Mother-Infant Interaction: The Loch Lomond Symposium. Academic Press, London.

Wittgenstein, L. (1958) Philosophical Investigations. Blackwell, Oxford.

The Ontogenesis of Differential Vocalization: Development of Prosodic Contrastivity During the First Year of Life

J. B. Delack and P. J. Fowlow

The relationship between the infant's early vocal behaviour and subsequent linguistic (qua communicative) speech development has been generally a matter of speculation, largely based upon anecdotal corroboration, despite the voluminous literature on the subject. Consequently, it is of interest to be able to characterize the natural history of such vocalizations in reasonably objective terms. Such a programme is currently being carried out (cf. Delack, 1974 for details), some of the results of which constitute the present report. In particular, we shall be concerned with tracing certain aspects of vocal differentiation in infants over the course of the first year of life, concentrating on the description and development of non-segmental phenomena.

*The research reported herein was supported in part by the Department of National Health and Welfare (Canada), under Federal Public Health Project No. 609-7-324 and Medical Research Council Grant No. MA-5369. The authors would like to take this opportunity to thank those who contributed most substantially to this project: Judith Davis for data collection and collation; John Nicol for computer programming; and Dale Stevenson for computer programming, graphic illustration, data analysis and interpretation.

93

94

Comprising a large part of the extant research
on early prosodic development are firmly buttressed descriptions of differentiated crying behaviour ostensibly
evoked by endogenous stimuli and becoming expressive of
different internal states (such as hunger, pain and
pleasure; cf. Wasz-Höckert, Lind,Vuorenkoski, Partancu,
and Valanne, 1968), as well as of the morphological and
functional relatedness of cry and non-cry vocalizations
(Wolff, 1969). Instances of differential vocalization
to objects and people have likewise been alluded to in
the literature; but such studies have not been systematic,nor has the phenomenon been adequately pursued by
empirical investigation (cf. Crystal, 1973a, 1973b;
Lieberman, 1967). In this paper we shall concentrate
on the infant's utterances vis-à-vis maternal vocalizations, as well as to objects in his/her environment,
by recourse to description in terms of various acoustic
parameters, such as fundamental frequency (F_0), its contours and within-utterance range, and duration.

METHOD

Selected for inclusion in this study were 19
normal, healthy, full-term, and first-born infants (7
female, 12 male), all of whom were being reared in an
exclusively monolingual English home environment, where
all data were collected - utilizing high quality equip-
ment (Nagra IV-D tape recorders, AKG D202E dynamic
microphones, Ampex 434 low-noise tape recorded at 19.05
cm/s) - at biweekly intervals from one month to approximately one year of age. For details of the data
collection, including biographical information, cf.
Delack (1974); the subjects' families were distributed
over the socioeconomic spectrum and the home environ-
ments were stable and stimulating throughout the course
of this study. At three-month intervals the infants'
mental and motor capabilities were assessed by means of
the Bayley Scales of Infant Development (Bayley, 1969);
these periodic assessments indicated that our subjects
developed normally. In this regard, our attempts to use
the derivative scores as an alternative metric to chronological age by which to evaluate developmental trends
have not as yet yielded meaningful results; i.e., using
the gross scores versus age did not significantly
improve predictive power.

With respect to the vocalization data, in
excess of 11,000 utterances were examined; the utterances had been collected from 10 infants (4 female, 6
male) over the period of one full year, and from the
remaining subjects during the first half year. These
data constitute the spontaneous or reactive utterances
of the infants under a variety of maximally normal home
routines. The vocalizations singled out for analytic
purposes were those produced when the infants were
alone (S), when 'conversing' with the mother (SM) or

with another adult (SOP), and when alone in the presence
of various objects. The latter contexts were ultimately
categorized   according to the sensory modalities by
which the objects would be primarily, or at least most
likely, apprehended:

SV   (Visual: Mobiles, pictures, etc.),

SAV   (Auditory + Visual: music boxes, radios, etc.),

STV   (Tactile + Visual: stuffed toys, blankets,
          etc.), and

SATV   (Auditory + Tactile + Visual: rattles, bells,
          keys, etc.).

These data have been analyzed spectrographical-
ly for certain acoustic features. The information thus
obtained was then subjected to statistical analysis, in
order to obtain the trends of and the probable relationships among the established variables.

RESULTS AND DISCUSSION

Figures 1-4 graphically present our findings
with respect to F_0, duration and range, as well as two
indices based on these acoustic parameters, and are displayed according to the independent variables of age,
context, and subject. Solid lines represent the averaged data in terms of the given dimensions; dashed
lines are curves predicted on the basis of an additive
model utilizing a multiple classification analysis (MCA;
cf. Andrews, Morgan and Sonquist, 1967), which displays
the main effects of a given predictor (or independent
variable). The better the fit of the two curves, the
more likely it is that the observable trends can be accounted for by the given predictor; if they demonstrate
a poor fit, it will be due in large measure to an interaction component based on either one or both of the
other predictors. Our confidence in the validity of the
additive model assumed by MCA is strengthened by the
fact that subsets of the data in these dimensions follow
the same trends.

Figures 1-3 demonstrate the intersubject
variability with respect to F_0, duration and a range. The
contextual distributions show that females pattern rather
differently from males for all three parameters in
the object categories, which also evince a poor fit in
terms of the MCA additive model; in addition to a possible interaction component (as noted above), inapplica-
bility of the additive model may be due to the somewhat
arbitrary nature of the classifications, as well as to
small numbers of observations, particularly in the SAV
category.

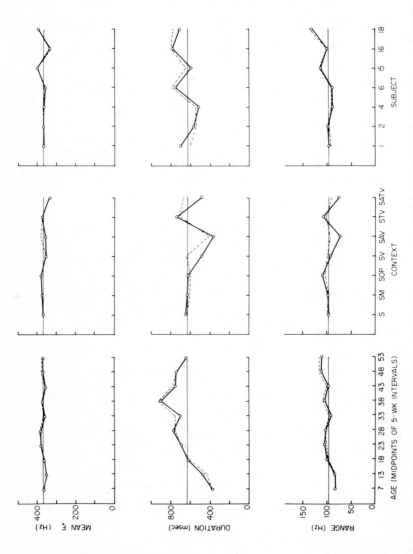

Fig. 1. Females (N=7): Means of F₀, duration, and within-utterance range (4,540 vocalizations). Solid lines represent the averaged data; dashed lines are predicted curves based on the MCA additive model; horizontal lines correspond to the overall means.

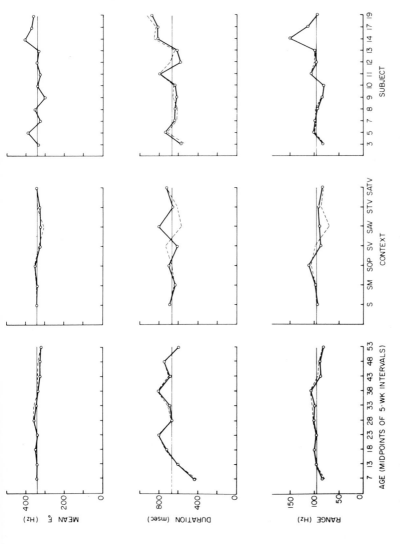

Fig. 2. Males (N=12): Means of F_0, duration, and within-utterance range (6,828 vocalizations). Solid lines represent the averaged data; dashed lines are predicted curves based on the MCA additive model; horizontal lines correspond to the overall means.

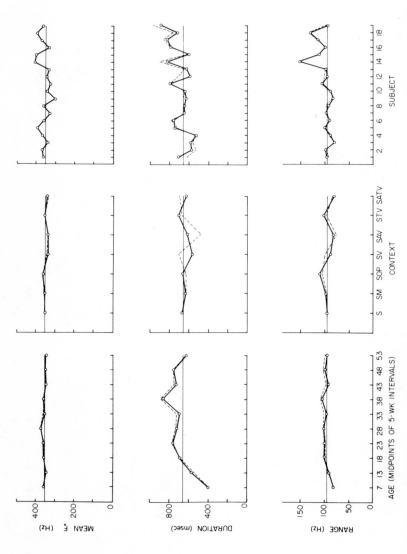

Fig. 3. All subjects (N=19): Means of Fo, duration, and within-utterance range (11,368 vocalizations). Solid lines represent the averaged data; dashed lines are predicted curves based on the MCA additive model; Horizontal lines correspond to the overall means.

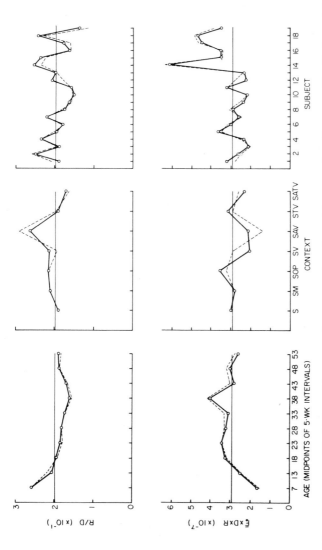

Fig. 4. All subjects (N=19): Means of range to duration and of mean F_O X duration X range. Solid lines represent the averaged data; dashed lines are predicted curves based on the MCA additive model; horizontal lines correspond to the overall means.

The mean F_0 remains fairly stable at 355 Hz
over the first year of life, with females generally ex-
hibiting a higher F_0 throughout this period (25 ± 20 Hz).
The males, however, drop to 325 Hz by the end of the
first year. Differential trends by sex are also found
with respect to duration and range. In general, there
is a mean 50% increase in duration over the first year.
For both sexes, range increases by about 20% (from 85
Hz) up to the age of six months and continues to rise
to 110 Hz for females, but drops back to 80 Hz for males
by the end of the first year.

In Figure 4, the ratio of range to duration
illustrates their nonlinear relationship over time, indicating that they are only partially independent; however, it is not apparent that the trend is strictly a
function of age. Another index of vocal development,
arbitrarily specified as mean F_0 X Duration X Range,
dramatically exhibits the peaking behaviour seen in the
individual graphs at 5-6 months and 9 months, the minor
peak at 11 months becoming less outstanding. Range and
duration are both constrained by contour, as suggested
by Figure 5, which displays the status of the contours
across three age groups. The developmental changes are
minimal and all in the expected directions (cf. Figures
1-3).

The disparity between males and females in
trends of F_0 development may be due to variables not
examined here, such as greater maternal restrictiveness
vis-à-vis females (cf. Lewis and Freedle, 1973), the
disposition of mothers to respond imitatively to their
female infants (cf. Moss, 1967), and, towards the end
of the first year, the propensity of the infant for more
effective 'role-playing' or imitation of adult models
(cf. Lieberman, 1967; Lewis, 1951; Piaget and Inhelder,
1966). Moreover, the peaking behaviour observable in
Figures 1-4 may be correlated with the advent of corti-
cal control and organization of vocal output, as suggested by Bever (1961) and Tonkova-Yampol'skaya (1969).
Furthermore, descent and growth of the larynx, as well
as the concomitant readjustment of the supralaryngeal
vocal tract and its growth may be of import here (cf.
Kirchner, 1970; Wind, 1970). These peaks thus appear
to correspond to, or at least coincide with, several
physiological and (as mentioned above) psychological
milestones in the latter half of the first year of life.
For amplification of these issues and more detailed discussion of Figures 1-4, cf. Delack (1975).

Figure 6 demonstrates the essentially identical distribution of contours for both males and females.
The rise-fall pattern is not only the most predominant,
but also exhibits the most notable changes with respect
to age (Figure 7), increasing from 40% to 55% during the

first year. The other contours do not appreciably alter
their distributions over time.

A similar pattern exists in the percentage
distribution of contexts (Figure 6). The main difference
between males and females involves the category SM, and
to a lesser extent STV; this may be due to differential
modes of maternal interaction inter alia (cf. Lewis and
Freedle, 1973; Moss, 1967). An intensive investigation
of this phenomenon is now in progress.

Figure 8 reveals the developmental findings in
terms of contextual vocalizations. Taken together, these
distributional frequencies provide a measure of the infant's interests over the first year of life. The peaks
found in the graphs may be due in part to our data collection procedures, which required sampling the occurrence
of vocalizations rather than the lack of them during any
given recording session. Such a qualification, however,
does not impair the reliability or validity of our study;
on the contrary, such observations merely reconfirm the
developmental significance of psychological and environmental variables.

The S category increases in frequency with
age, with rather gross excursions at 4-6 months and at 9
months; during these periods the infants were more apt
to vocalize when alone than otherwise. The SM context
evinces a complementary decrease, without corresponding
deviations, except at the beginning and end of the study;
here, the subjects tended to spend more time with their
mothers. The other person category, SOP, exhibits a
rather random and hence unremarkable distribution. On
the other hand, a few interesting trends are apparent
in the object contexts.

The context SV peaks strongly between 3-4
months and again between 9-10 months. This is largely
due in the first instance to life in the crib, where
most of the collected utterances were directed to mobiles; in the latter case, the high incidence is likely a reflection of the infant's interest in his/her sur-
roundings, since many of the later sessions included sequences of the infant's gesturing or vocalizing at a
distant object, whereupon the mother would respond by
naming or describing the object. All such objects were
included in the SV category, because they were not noise-
makers and the child generally did not touch them.

The relative frequency increase of the STV
category from the outset to its peak at about six months,
as well as a similarly high frequency of occurrence
during the first half year in the context SATV, can be
attributed to the presence of toys in the crib and play-
pen, where the infant spent much of the time. The SAV
context played little role in this study.

102

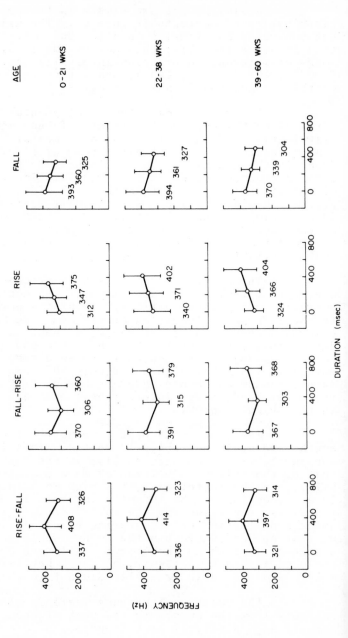

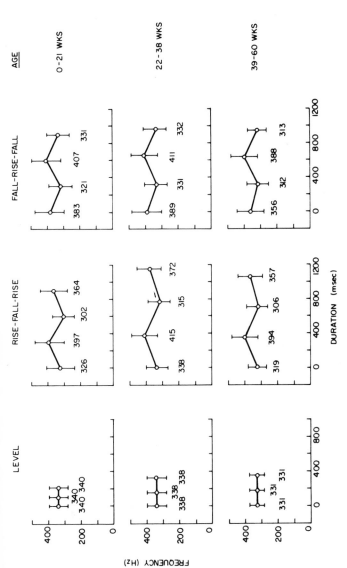

Fig. 5. Contours and their developmental status in three age categories for all subjects.

104

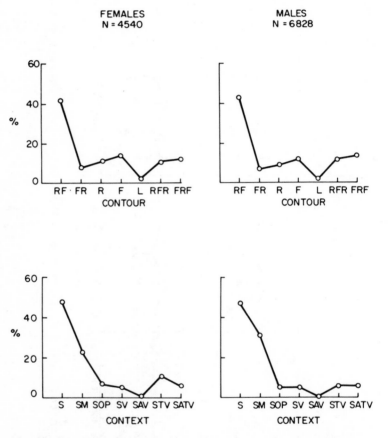

Fig. 6. Percentage distribution of vocalizations by contour and context for females and males.

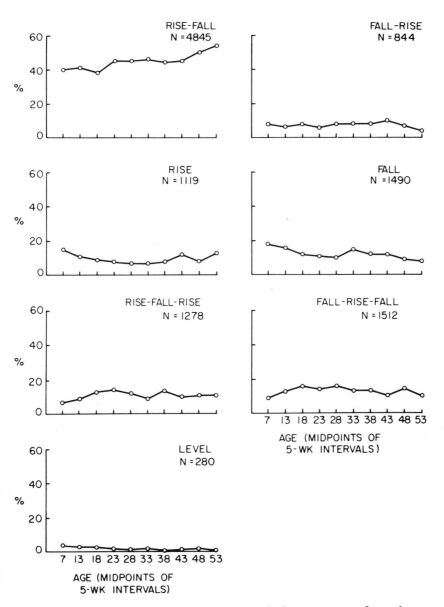

Fig. 7.   Developmental trend of frequency of each
contour for all subjects.

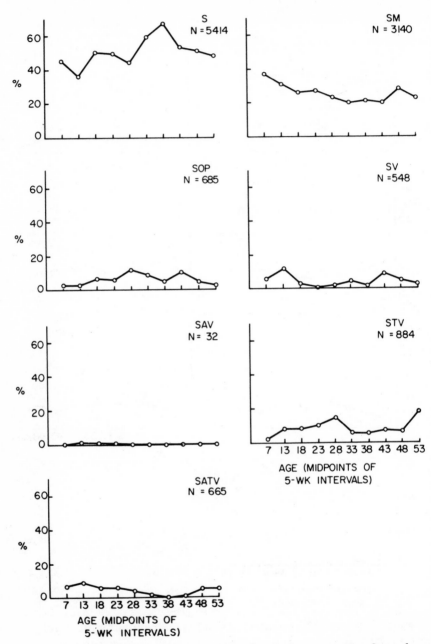

Fig. 8. Developmental trend of frequency of each context for all subjects.

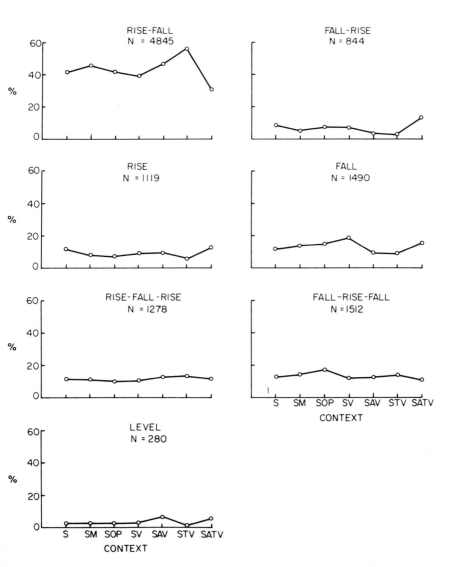

Fig. 9.   Percentage distribution of contours by context
for all subjects.

The distribution of contours by context is illustrated in Figure 9, which combines and reinterprets the data presented in Figure 6. While the frequencies remain much the same across the contexts, detailed inspection of the distributions reveals differences sufficient to warrant a classification on the basis of contour expectancy. Although statistical evaluation finds that only the contour distributions of the SAV, STV and SATV categories differ significantly from the mean, examination of relatively substantial deviations from the mean (as an index of distributional anomaly) indicates that each context may be described by a unique constellation of contours, in terms of their greatest deviations (both positive and/or negative). Any predictive power achieved should not be overrated, however, since some of it may be due to analytic artifacts (such as contextual categorization procedures).

In the following list, reference is made exclusively and in order of magnitude, to contours whose frequency of occurence is substantially above (= positive) or below (= negative) the mean for a given context.

CONTEXT	CONTOUR	
	Positive	Negative
S	Fall-Rise, Rise	Rise-Fall
SM	Rise-Fall	Fall-Rise, Rise
SOP	Fall-Rise-Fall, Fall	Rise, Rise-Fall-Rise
SV	Fall	Rise-Fall
SAV	Rise-Fall, Level	Fall-Rise, Fall
STV	Rise-Fall	Fall-Rise, Rise, Fall
SATV	Fall-Rise, Rise, Fall, Level	Rise-Fall, Fall-Rise-Fall

It is interesting to note that the distributions of contour in the S and SM contexts are complementary when examined on such an index. By the same token, S and SATV exhibit virtually the same patterning, albeit with more variation in the latter, with (relatively speaking) most vocalizations rising in their terminal portion. In all other cases, falling contours predominate on the positive end of the scale.

It should be remarked that although contours are construed here as complex composites of more basic features, they are not uniquely determined by these; in fact, the converse could be true. In any event, the observed differences in contour distributions (even if more than artifactual) cannot be attributed solely to concomitant fluctuations in variables such as F_0, duration and range. Moreover, from either the cognitive psychological or physiological point of view, we do not know whether the infant is manipulating contours, their associated features, or other variables which have not been examined. A meaningful interpretation of our findings must, therefore, await future specification.

We feel, however, that the findings of our study document a very real, albeit circumscribed, capacity on the part of the infant for vocally differentiating environmental events, one of the basic components in the development of communicative competence. In general we hold that there exists sufficient evidence to refute the parochial view that linguistic acquisition can only be relevantly discussed when the child's segmental phonetic output begins to resemble that of the adult standard; in other words, we support the hypothesis of continuity from babbling to speech. We are hopeful that our research will help to fill the gap of 'ignorance about the fundamental development of prosodic contrastivity in children' (Crystal, 1973a: 33) and, more importantly, will ultimately provide a fund of information on infant vocalization whose essence will find its proper niche in the overall characterization of the development of communicative function.

REFERENCES

Andrews, F.M., Morgan, J.N. and Sonquist, J.A. (1967) Multiple Classification Analysis. University of Michigan Institute of Social Research, Ann Arbor, Michigan.

Bayley, N. (1969)   Bayley Scales of Infant Development. The Psychological Corporation, New York.

Bever, T.G. (1961)   Pre-linguistic Behaviour. Unpublished honors thesis, cited in D.McNeill, The Acquisition of Language. Harper and Row, New York.

Crystal, D. (1973a)   Linguistic Mythology and the First Year of Life. British Journal of Disorders of Communication 8. 29-36.

Crystal, D. (1973b)   Non-segmental Phonology in Language Acquisition: A Review of the Issues. Lingua 32. 1-45.

110

Delack, J.B. (1974) Prelinguistic Infant Vocalizations and the Ontogenesis of Sound-meaning Correlations. Bulletin d'Audiophonologie 4 (No. 6, Supplémentaire; Prélangage II: Prélangage de l'homme). 479-499.

Delack, J.B. (1975) Prosodic Features of Infant Speech: The First Year of Life. Paper presented at the Eighth International Congress of Phonetic Sciences, Leeds, England, 17-23 August.

Kirchner, J.A. (ed.) (1970) Pressman and Kelemen's Physiology of the Larynx, Revised Edition. American Academy of Ophthalmology and Otolaryngology, Rochester, Minnesota.

Lewis, M.M. (1951) Infant Speech: A Study in the Beginnings of Language, 2nd Edition. Routledge and Kegan Paul, London.

Lewis, M. and Freedle, R. (1973) Mother-infant Dyad: The Cradle of Meaning. In P. Pliner, L. Krames, and T. Alloway (eds.) Communication and Affect. Academic Press, New York.

Lieberman, P. (1967) Intonation, Perception, and Language. M.I.T. Press, Cambridge, Mass.

Moss, H.A. (1967) Sex, Age, and State as Determinants of Mother-infant Interaction. Merrill-Palmer Quarterly 13. 19-36.

Piaget, J. and Inhelder, B. (1966) La Psychologie de l'Enfant. Presses Universitaires de France, Paris.

Tonkova-Yampol'skaya, R.V. (1969) Development of Speech Intonation in Infants during the First Two Years of Life. Soviet Psychology 7. 48-54.

Wasz-Höckert, O., Lind, J., Vuorenkoski, V., Partanen T. and Valanne, E. (1968) The Infant Cry: A Spectrographic and Auditory Analysis. Spastics International Medical Publications, Lavenham. William Heinemann Medical Books.

Wind, J. (1970) On the Phylogeny and the Ontogeny of the Human Larynx. Wolters-Noordhoff, Groningen.

Wolff, P. (1969) The Natural History of Crying and Other Vocalizations in Early Infancy. In B.M. Foss (ed.) Determinants of Infant Behaviour IV. Methuen, London.

The Babbling of a Thai Baby: Echoes and Responses to the Sounds made by Adults

P. Tuaycharoen

Wherever human beings live together they seek a means of communicating with each other. Infants are no exception. Starting from a very early stage, they show their need for communication with people around them: they vocalize, listen, and watch. The study of child language development will provide a natural picture of human speech development if the child's social interaction is taken into consideration.

This paper is part of a longitudinal study on the speech development of a Thai baby boy 3-18 months old. The analysis is based on the first few samples of the data, collected daily by tape recorder when the baby was 3-5½ months old. The recordings were made in a natural home situation at the times the baby vocalized, either on his own or in interaction with adults. The vocalizations were transcribed by using the IPA symbols to show the areas of sound quality. It has to be noted that the values of these symbols do not have precisely the same qualities as when used to represent the sounds of adult speech. In this paper some of the diacritics which would have given greater detail are omitted as the finer detail is not relevant to the discussion.

The purpose of the longitudinal study is to give a picture of how speech emerges from early vocalization. An account of phonetic and phonological development, and of adult-baby interaction is to be given. It has been found that by the age of 18 months some phonetic features as well as phonological structures which characterize the conventional language have been acquired. As Thai is one of the tone languages spoken in South East Asia, the development of the use of pitch in general and of lexical tones in particular is one of the main interests of the longitudinal study. The terms 'pitch' and 'tone' are used in the following way: pitch is related to the frequency with which the vocal cords of the speaker open and close during the utterance (cf. Abercrombie, 1967:27); tone is related to the functional distinction carried by the pitch of each lexical item in the language. The acquisition of glottalization and of aspiration will also be examined. In Thai, glottalization of the syllable with a plosive ending or with a short vowel is a common feature, and voiceless aspirated and unaspirated plosives are separate functional units.

This paper is centrally concerned with performance in relation to contexts of situation. This does not mean that the innate capacity for language and cognitive development are not considered important. The writer believes that the relationship between language and cognitive development is necessary to account for the sequence of development in language acquisition (cf. Menyuk, 1971; Bloom, 1975), and that the acquisition of language takes place through the child's social interaction with others (Snow, 1977). However, the psychological processes of language acquisition are not the concern of this paper. The main focus of the paper is on echoes and responses of the baby to the sounds made by adults, and on adult language addressed to the baby.

THE BABY'S VOCALIZATIONS

As background, a general picture of the baby's vocalizations at the age between 3-5½ months will be given first. The vocalizations during this period are divided into 3 stages on the basis of phonetic changes, i.e. there is progress in the acquisition of phonetic features in each stage. The 3 stages are: Stage I (0;3-0;3.22), Stage II (0;3.23-0;4.19), Stage III (0;4.20-0;5.15). Age is given in months and days.

Stage I. At this stage the baby's vocalizations were 'fluid', consisting mostly of vowel-like sounds which varied from open to close and from close to open in various sequences; there was also variation from front to central and back. The sounds produced by the baby were neither closely lip-rounded nor widely spread. Sometimes there were long nasalized stretches; sometimes oral. (A stretch is an utterance followed by a short pause). Nasalization occurred both when the baby was in a happy and an unhappy state.

The vocalizations, which were mainly made with
an open passage of the airstream (vowel-like sounds),
were sometimes interrupted by strictures of close approximation and of complete closure (consonant-like sounds).
At the early period of this stage, consonant-like sounds
with which the vowels were interspersed were labial,
velar, and glottal fricatives, e.g. [βʉ], [ɣɯ], [hɨ],
and those with stricture of complete closure made at the
velar and glottal places, e.g. [ɛkh], [ʔaːg]. Syllables
with velar closure were heard in particular when the
baby was in a happy state. Glottal constriction and
breathy articulation, e.g. [ʔɨ], [hɨ], were consistent
features in the baby's vocalizations. These features
have also been found in a study of the vocalizations of
babies in an English-speaking environment (Stark, Rose
and McLagen, 1975).

Voicing generally continued throughout the sequence of utterance, but there were sometimes pauses of
silence and sometimes the voicing was interrupted by
breathy articulation. There was also variation in loudness and in pitch. Loudness was most often associated
with diphthongization or long duration of vowel, and
with prolongation of pitch level or pitch movement.
Within a stretch, the pitch varied among any of the
following: low, mid, or high level, falling, rising,
and rising-falling. Variation in pitch made rhythmic
groups; the change of pitch direction was unpredictable.
However, it was noticeable that at the end of almost
every stretch, the pitch level appeared to be lowered
or there was a change of pitch direction, i.e. falling
or rising. The observation of lowering or the changing
of pitch direction seems to be in agreement with
Lieberman's study of intonation signals observed in the
cries of newborn infants (Lieberman, 1967).

In the later period of this stage, vowels were
also interspersed with strictures made at the lips,
e.g. [w] [m] [p] [b] [p̄p̄p̄] [b̄b̄b̄] ([p̄p̄p̄] and [b̄b̄b̄] represent labial trills); at the alveolar place, e.g.
[n̩] [l̩]; at the palatal place, e.g.[ʒ] [j]; and at the
velar place, e.g. [ŋ]. However, they were articulated
vaguely and imprecisely. There were also labial and
palatal glides from one syllable to the next.

Examples of the baby's general vocalizations
are given below:

Early Stage I.   Here the baby is vocalizing on
his own; his mother is talking softly to a visitor.

| ʔɨ̃ | ɨ̃:ɨ̃ɛ̃:ɛ̃| ɛ̃:ɣ̃ʉ | ɨ ɯ: |ɛɔʉᵍɛ̃:ɯ| ɨ|pause| hɛɯ: | pause |
| - | ╱ ╲ | ‾ | ‾ ╲ | ╱ ‾ ‾ ‾ ╱| | ‾ ╲ | |

Later Stage I.   Here the baby is vocalizing
loudly on his own in a noisy situation. Loudness increases.

ḷɛːˡḷɛ ḷɛə| |əʲ ʒɯ ːwɨd aˡʒaː ʔɛːḷəi ʔɨ | ɛḷəi ɛḷəiˡʒɛːəːi |
╱ _ ╱ |- ‾ - -╱ ╲ ╲ _ | ╲ ╲ ╲ ╲ ⌐╲ |

(The vertical lines indicate the boundaries of a stretch
of utterance; the straight and curved lines underneath
the transcription represent pitch contours.)

Stage II.   In addition to the sounds produced in
Stage I, vowels in Stage II became more clearly distinguished. Diphthongization of front vowels: half
close, half open, and open, to close front unrounded and
close back rounded appeared to be produced more frequently, e.g. [ei] [ai] [eu] [ɛu] [au]. In the later period
of this stage [o] and [ɔ] occurred.

The consonant-like sounds appeared to have increased in that complete closure made at the alveolar
place, [t̪] [d̪], was more frequent, and they sometimes occurred with liquid, [ḷ] [r],release. There was also
oral-oral and nasal-oral homorganic articulation.
Strictures of complete closure, however, were not
strongly articulated.

In the later period of this stage, screeching
vocalizations were often produced with a combination of
normal pitch register and high pitch register. The
screeching appeared regularly from this time onwards.
The use of pitch and nasalization was similar to that
described in Stage I.

Stage III.   The baby's vocalizations developed
from mainly 'free-onset' (i.e. those with strictures of
open approximation and close approximation) to mainly
'checked-onset' (i.e. those with stricture of complete
closure). This stage may thus be the starting point for
the acquisition of plosives and affricates; they were
strongly articulated and repetitively produced. The
strictures of these plosives were made at the lips, alveolar and palatal places, the same places where the
fricatives were produced. Most stretches began with an
open vowel followed by relatively long duration of
closure and then release again of open vowel quality.
The release was strongly accented. It is interesting
that the pitch of this type of vocalization was less
variable, and the same pattern of pitch was used repetitively for a long period of time, e.g.

a aḍḍʑɛ a:idʑɛ	aḍʑɛ aḍʑɛ:	ḍʑɛ	aḍḍʑɛ	aḍ:ḍʑɛ	a:ḍ:ḷɛ	ad:ŋa
-- ⌣ ＼ ⌣	- ⌣ -＼	⌒	- ⌣	-⌒	⌣	⌒

(high pitch -->) (normal pitch --------------------------->)

(The dot at the start of the straight or curved line represents syllable accentuation; [:] following a consonant
symbol represents duration of held contact.)

It was noticeable that in this stage when the
checked-onset type was produced, only front vowels - half
close, half open, and open - were used, but when the
free-onset type was produced back vowels as well as
front vowels were heard.

Nasalization, which had appeared randomly
either with free-onset or with checked-onset in previous
stages, was now produced mainly in connection with free-
onset vocalizations and disappeared when the checked-onset vocalizations were produced.

THE BABY'S RESPONSES TO ADULT SPEECH

The echoes and responses of the baby to the
sounds made by adults in his environment are considered
below. As mentioned earlier, the data for this study
were collected in a natural home situation. Sounds in
the environment, in addition to speech sounds, seemed
to play an important role in the baby's vocalizations.
In the house, there were a number of things which
created noise and attracted the baby's attention, such
as a cuckoo-clock, a telephone, a radio, etc. Furthermore, the adults who were around always drew his attention to such objects and often repeated the sounds in
onomatopoeic form. In a home situation, the baby also
paid attention of his own accord to the sounds made a-
round him, e.g. cuckoo-clock striking, adults talking to
each other, and the mention of his name. In the example
below, the baby was vocalizing on his own while the
adults were talking to each other, but when he was addressed directly, he made an immediate response.

Stage I. In this sample the mother is talking to
a visitor; the baby has been vocalizing on his own for
some time; then his mother turns to address him,
using sounds from his repertoire. The baby echoes what
his mother produces.

Visitor			Baby				
ki: dʉən lɛu ha			hᵻ	ɣʉ ɣʉ	ɣʉ:	pause	
_ _ ⌣ ⌣			-	- ⌣	＼		
'How old is the baby?'			ʉ: ɣʉg ʉ		pause	ei	
			⌣ ＼			＼	

Mother   Baby

| saːm kha | | ʉ? ʉː | εː ɣʉ ɣʉ ε^khə | pause |

'Three.' ('months'
          understood)

Visitor

| mai khɔi rɔːŋ   thau rai | | ɣɯ ɣʉːː | ɣɯ ɣ   ɣɯɣ ɣεː | pause |

'Doesn't often cry,
does he?'

Mother

| kha mai khɔi rɔːŋ |

'No, he doesn't.'

Mother

| khui si luk khui pai |

'Come on talk, baby.'

| ɣɯː | ɣɯ ɣɯː | aɣɯː | | ɣʉː ɣʉg | ɣʉː ɣʉg ɣʉː | hɨ |

| ʔəkhap | | ɣʉg ɣʉː hʉ | ɣʉː ε^ʔkh | pause |

(The adult's conversation is transcribed according to
the colloquial style. When the pitch contours are shown,
the tone marks are omitted. It has to be noted that in
some words the pitch contours differ from the expected
pitch of the actual lexical tones.)

What the mother was saying directly to the baby, in the last utterance of the above example, is not within the adult phonological system (except the last two syllables, |ʔəkhap̂| , which are a question particle and a polite word), but she was using the sounds in the baby's repertoire. The mother had heard the baby making these sounds before while she was talking to the visitor; she then used them in addressing the baby. The result was that he responded to her sounds, producing sounds very similar to hers.

It is tempting to believe that the expression |yʉ: yʉg| , and some others within this range, originated as the echoing of the cuckoo-clock heard by the baby from the time he was born. He, then, fitted these sounds, especially the pitch, into his repertoire, and practised saying them, sometimes when he was on his own. Once he heard these sounds directly expressed to him, he made the responses immediately, matching them. Similar echoing of a cuckoo-clock by an English girl aged seven to eight months has been reported to the writer by the child's mother. (Personal communication from Mrs. O. Harding, School of Oriental and African Studies, University of London.)

Falling pitch in the adult's speech seemed to be the most salient feature for the baby, as it is the one to which he responded most consistently. As the baby's linguistic ability increased, other features from the model were responded to. Examples of response to falling pitch are given below.

Stage I. The grandmother and the baby are having a 'dialogue'.

Grandmother | Baby

| arai ə luk | bɔk arai ə luk a | | ɛ ɯ: |

'What, baby? What are (you)*
telling (grandma)*, baby?'

| lu:k bɔk arai khap lu:k pui | | ʔe ɣ ɯ: |

'What are you telling (grandma),
baby?'

| ɔ: bɔk arai ə luk | | ʔ ɯ: ʔ ɯ:: |

'Yes, what are (you) telling
(grandma), baby?'

118

| Grandmother | Baby |

| auɯ: ə lu:k | | yɯ: |laughter.
| ‾ ⟍ ‾ ⟍ | | ⟍ |

'Is it ayɯ: , baby?'

* The omission of the subject or the object of a sentence is common in the colloquial style of the Thai language.

       Stage II.   During this dialogue, the father was sweeping the floor; the baby was on his mother's lap. When he saw his father, he began to vocalize to draw his father's attention.

| Father | Baby |

| ʲɛ: ?ɛ::: |
| ⟋   ‾‾⟍ |

| liək phɔ: ə luk hm | | hɛ: ?ɯ : ɯ |
| ⟍   ⟍ ‾ ⟍ ⟋ | | ⟋   ⟍ ‾ |

'Calling Daddy, baby?'

| phɔ: kwa:t   ba:n | | aŋl̩   ma:ŋ̍ |
| ⟍   —   ⟍ | | —   ⟍ |

'Daddy is sweeping the floor.'

       In the 'conversation' above, the baby initiated the dialogue by saying |ʲɛ: ?ɛ:::|, which the father interpreted as [ˏphɔ:], 'father' on the basis of the auditorily salient features (cf. Waterson, 1971) namely, falling pitch and the broad degree of openness of vowel – that is half-open vowel quality, and possibly the closed onset. He claimed that the baby was calling [ˏphɔ:], 'father'. The baby responded using three different levels of pitch, but the falling one seemed to be the most distinct, i.e. accompanied by loudness. His father went on talking to him loudly with special emphasis on the last syllable of the utterance, i.e. [ˏba:n] ([ˏba:n] usually means 'house', but it means 'floor' in this context). As a consequence, the baby responded loudly to the whole of the last syllable producing |aṇḷ ma:n|. What the baby seemed to perceive from that syllable is labiality, nasality, pitch, loudness, vowel length and vowel quality, and syllable structure, i.e. CVC, e.g. [ba:n] compared with [ma:n]. He may, of course, have perceived oral onset but not been able to make a contrast of oral onset with nasal ending (cf. Waterson, 1976).

At Stage III when plosives and affricates appeared to be consistently produced, the adult seemed to adapt his/her speech by producing utterances with plosive or affricate onset. The expression [ʈɕa: ʋtɕa] (each is used as a polite particle in Thai), sometimes produced with variation in pitch, was used frequently in addressing the baby because of its similarity to some syllables produced by him. The baby responded to such an expression similarly. In the following example, the baby was with his grandmother; he was vocalizing while investigating his toy bottle. His grandmother repeated what she recognized as his attempts.

| Grandmother | Baby |

|hadʐə hadĵ|

hp------→

|tɕa: tɕa | tɕa: tɕa| |ɖrɛ: ɖrɨ | ɖrɨ ɨɖrɨ|a::u a::u |

*
hp-----→np--→ hp-→np--→

|wa:: | ap pppɛ| hap pppa|

|ɔ: atɕa | tɕa tɕa: lɛu ə luk|

'Yes, ⁻atɕa. Did (you) say ⁻tɕa ‚tɕa:, baby?'

|tɕaʔ tɕa: ə luk | tɕaʔ tɕa: |

'Is it ⁻tɕa ‚tɕa:, baby?'

|tɕa: tɕa | |hɛ::: |ʔa:ɖ: ɖʐə | aɖ:dʐa: e:i |
laughter   laughter

120

| Grandmother | Baby |

luk pui pui khui keŋ   laughter

\ ⟋ ⟋ ⌐ _

'Baby Pui Pui** is very chatty.'

a:d dʑa   a: a::ə^d dʑa

* hp = high pitch register; np = normal pitch register.

** reduplication of the baby's name.

In adult-baby interaction, even in the very early stages, there is evidence that the baby was learning to participate in a conversation-like situation. He listened to the sounds, watched the face of the interlocutor, created his responses on the basis of what was most salient for him, and paused to await the adult's response. This shows that both participants share a conversational role, enabling turn-taking to occur. A careful study of mother-baby interaction has been reported by Snow (1975). The writer agrees with her important statement that 'the growth of turn-taking skills in these two children (her subjects), and the process of language acquisition which is dependent upon and inextricably linked with that growth, were possible only because their mothers had from the beginning a strong conception of their babies as social beings with needs, intentions, and interest in human adults. Without that set of beliefs, the mothers would never have started so early treating their babies in a way so well designed to induct them into the conventions of social intercourse'.

Apart from some imitations of the sounds in the baby's repertoire, most of the adults' speech addressed to the baby in conversation-like situations at 3-5½ months was conventional and meaningful, but there were some features showing an adaptation of the conventional form. Such phonetic features, which are found throughout the data, are the lengthening and reduction of vowel length, the prolongation of pitch, the use of high pitch register, the use of interrogatives, and the repetition of expression. These features have also been found to be typical in language addressed to young children in other languages (Ferguson, 1964; Garnica, 1977; Rūķe-Draviņa, 1977; Snow, 1975).

With reference to the use of high pitch register, what is striking in the present study is the

use of high pitch register by men. The baby's father
and other male visitors when directly addressing the
baby, used very high pitch.

For example, Y., a male visitor, stops and
talks to the baby who is producing a 'protest cry' and
then turns to speak to the baby's grandmother.

                    Y   Baby

(very high pitch)

| e:: | lɔ:ŋ jai leu | ɛ::: ɤ̠i: ɛ::: ɤ̠i: | Baby stops
| — | •— | —   — | crying and
| | — | | watches

'Ey, what are (you) crying for?'

(very high pitch)

| pai thiəu mai kha: | (palatal clicks)
| —   ＼   —   — |
'Want to go out?'

(very high pitch)

| ɤ:::i ɤ:::i | (palatal clicks) | gru::: gru::: |
(very high pitch)

| he: he: | (claps hands) | he::: |
| —   — | | —— |

Y. turns and talks to the baby's grandmother using normal
pitch register; then addresses the baby again.

(very high pitch)

| gru:::: |

(Utterances without translations are meaningless sounds
made to draw the baby's attention.)

When transcribing the tape, the writer did not
realize at first that it was a man speaking until he
spoke to the baby's grandmother using his normal pitch.
It was not only the high pitch which caused him to sound
like a female, but also his use of a female politeness
particle, [⁻kha] (with additional length), in the second
utterance. The use of female politeness particles to
babies. is common in some families. In general in talking

to a young boy, adults use a male politeness particle, and a female politeness particle to a young girl, in order to teach the correct politeness formulae to children.

The use of interrogatives and repetition of expressions are common in this study. Examples of this can be seen in the 'dialogue' between the grandmother and the baby from Stage I.

As in some other tone languages, the tones in Thai are governed by phonological rules. The lengthening and shortening of vowel length in some words in this study violate these rules. The words commonly used with such modifications are sentence-ending particles, for example, the politeness particle for men, [‾khrap], and the word [ˎlu:k] which is used as a second person form of address, meaning 'baby'.

The prolongation of vowel length in the particle [‾khrap] is found consistently, e.g. [‾kha:p] or [‾kha::p]. The absence of [r] in the initial cluster is a common feature of colloquial Thai. This word is conventionally produced in a form with a short vowel and a high lexical tone. The reduction of vowel length is found in the word [ˎlu:k] which has a form with a long vowel and falling lexical tone. In this study it is used varying in form with [ˎluk], [-luk], and [_luk], i.e., short vowel with falling, mid, or low pitch. These modifications break the conventional rules of the phonological structures of the language, which are given below:

Some phonological rules of Thai words.

Checked syllable   ($C_1\breve{V} C_2$ C_2 = Stop, $\bar{V}$ = long vowel,

$\breve{V}$ = short vowel.)

$C_1\breve{V} C_2$ ——— $\begin{cases} \text{high tone:} & [‾khrap] \text{ 'polite word for men'} \\ \text{low tone:} & [\_khap] \text{ 'to drive'} \end{cases}$

$C_1\bar{V} C_2$ ——— $\begin{cases} \text{falling tone:} & [ˎkhra:p] \text{ 'a stain'} \\ \text{low tone:} & [\_kha:t] \text{ 'to be torn'} \end{cases}$

In Thai, a checked syllable, a syllable with a stop ending and a short vowel, occurs only with a low or a high tone. A checked syllable with a long vowel has a low tone or a falling one.

Modified forms used by adults in language addressed

to children.

Conventional		Modified
[¯khrap]	———————	{[¯kha:p] {[¯kha::p]
[˅lu:k]	———————	⎰[˅luk] {[-luk] ⎱[ˍluk]

(IPA tone marks are used here.)

These modifications are linguistically ex-
plicable. In Thai, the sentence-ending particle may
be produced with difference in pitch from its lexical
tone (cf. Henderson, 1970: 44-50). The word [¯khrap]
is an ending particle by nature. The word [˅lu:k] is
a noun meaning 'offspring', but it is used in the language addressed to children as a subject, as an object
of a sentence, or as a second person form of address.
As a subject and an object, the tone is never varied;
as an address form it is used in the same way as an
ending particle, so it can be termed a 'vocative particle'. Variation in pitch for the so-called vocative
particle is possible.

The modifications of forms found in this
study are systematic in that the change of pitch is
constrained by the lexico-semantic restriction of the
word. That is to say, the same form can be used with
a different pitch only if it does not have a meaning
contrast in other contexts, for example, [¯kha:p]
[¯kha::p] for [¯khrap]. As long as the pitch is high
they are acceptable and have the semantic interpretation of a polite form. However, the following are not
possible as forms for [¯khrap] even though they are
admissible in terms of phonological rules:

[ˍkhap] 'to drive', [˅kha:p] 'to mouth',
[˅khra:p] 'a stain'. These are excluded because they
are meaningful in other contexts.

[˅luk], [¯luk], [ˍluk], for [˅lu:k] as a vocative particle, are semantically admissible in this
context since

[˅luk] never occurs in other contexts

[¯luk] never occurs in other contexts

124

[_luk] never occurs by itself in the language except as the first syllable
of a disyllabic word, e.g., [_luk
_lik] 'naughty'.

The form [‾luk], i.e. with high tone, can never be used
as a modified form of the vocative particle since it is
meaningful as a verb, meaning 'to rise' or 'to get up'.

CONCLUSION

Within the first few months of life, the increase in complexity in the range of vocalizations is
very considerable.

At the stage studied, 3-5½ months, it is not
possible to assume that the functional use of pitch,
i.e. tones, has been acquired, as may have been expected
from a baby in a tone language environment. The writer
had a chance to listen to a recording of the babbling
of an English boy of the same age as the subject of
this study and found that the variation of pitch and
some other features, e.g. glottal constriction and
breathy articulation, were very similar.

The study of the later stages not dealt with
in this paper, from 5½ months to 18 months, supports
the hypotheses presented by others who have worked on
babbling (Gilbert, 1974; Delack and Fowlow, this
volume; Oller, Wieman, Doyle and Ross, 1976) that there
is continuity from babbling to speech. Furthermore,
the evidence collected confirms Waterson's theory
(Waterson, 1971) that the child pays attention and responds to the most salient features of the utterance at
first, and that the closeness to the adult model increases as the child's linguistic ability and cognitive
knowledge gradually develop and he is able to take the
less salient features into account.

Abercrombie, D. (1967)   Elements of General Phonetics.
Edinburgh University Press, Edinburgh.

Bloom, L. (1975, second printing)   One Word at a Time.
Mouton, The Hague.

Ferguson, C.A. (1964)   Baby Talk in Six Languages.
American Anthropologist 66. No.6 Part 2.
103-114.

Garnica, O.K. (1977) Some Prosodic and Para-
linguistic Features of Speech directed to
Young Children. In C.E. Snow and C.A. Fer-
guson (eds.) Talking to Children: Language
Input and Acquisition. Cambridge University
Press, Cambridge.

Gilbert, J.H. (1974) On Babbling: Some Physiologi-
cal Observations. Papers and Reports on
Child Language Development 8. Stanford
University. 42-49.

Henderson, E.J.A. (1970) Prosodies in Siamese: A
Study in Synthesis. In F.R. Palmer (ed.)
Prosodic Analysis. Cambridge University Press,
Cambridge.

Lieberman, P. (1967) Intonation, Perception, and
Language. M.I.T. Press, Cambridge, Mass.

Menyuk, P. (1971) The Acquisition and Development of
Language. Prentice Hall, Englewood Cliffs,
New Jersey.

Oller, D.K., Wieman, L.A., Doyle, W.J., and Ross, C.
(1976) Infant Babbling and Speech.
Journal of Child Language 3. 1-11.

Ruķe-Draviņa, V. (1977) Modifications of Speech
addressed to Young Children in Latvian. In
C.E. Snow and C.A. Ferguson (eds.) Talking
to Children: Language Input and Acquisition.
Cambridge University Press, Cambridge.

Snow, C.E. (1977) Mothers' Speech Research:
From Input to Interaction. In C.E. Snow, and
C.A. Ferguson (eds.) Talking to Children:
Language Input and Acquisition. Cambridge
University Press, Cambridge.

Snow, C.E. (1975) The Development of Conversation
between Mothers and Babies. Pragmatics
Microfiche. 1.6 A2.

Stark, R.E., Rose, S.N. and McLagen, M. (1975)
Features of Infant Sounds: The First Eight
Weeks of Life. Journal of Child Language 2.

Waterson, N. (1971) Child Phonology: A Prosodic
View. Journal of Linguistics 7.

Waterson, N. (1976) Perception and Production in the
Acquisition of Phonology. In W. von Raffler-
Engel and Y. Lebrun (eds.) Baby Talk and
Infant Speech. Swets and Zeitlinger,
Amsterdam.

The Development of Systematic Vocalizations prior to words A Case Study

A.L.Carter

The first uttered words of an infant's native tongue are the focus of numerous recent investigations (Bloom, 1973; Clark, 1973; Dore, 1973; Nelson, 1973; Ingram, 1974; Greenfield and Smith, 1976; Bowerman, this volume). However, most researchers have looked at these single word utterances from the perspective of later language development; only a few, such as Halliday (1970, 1973), have recently looked at the possibility of systematic vocalizations immediately antecedent to words.

There is no a priori reason why some of the infant's preverbal vocalizations could not be systematic, i.e., composed of sounds highly correlated with intentions and/or situations. This possibility in fact seems to have been the basis for treatment of infant vocalizations by Preyer (1882), Stumpf (1900), Wundt (1900), Meumann (1902), Guillaume (1927), Stern (1928), Grégoire (1939), Leopold (1949), Lewis (1936), and Werner and Kaplan (1963), who dealt with this difficult topic in different ways, often obtaining remarkable insights. However the infant's early diffuseness of sound and meaning, stemming from lack of articulatory and acoustic precision and the vagueness of cognitive categories, renders it virtually impossible in most cases to reliably confirm the existence of sound-meaning regularity. One's

*Support for this research came from MSF doctoral dissertation improvement grant #1-444036-21221, and NIMH grant #MH 25356-01.

ignorance of the extent to which the cognitive-pheno-
menological world of the infant matches that of the
adult often precludes knowing what features, real or
imagined, of the situation or the infant's internal
state elicit a given vocalization. Uncertainty of the
extent to which the sound produced corresponds to the
sound intended, constrains one equally in assigning
utterance significance.

This handicap can be overcome only with additional information, such as other cues provided by the
infant or the situation, upon which judgements of intentionality can be made. The observer in situ may find it
difficult to survey and evaluate all sources of information because his impressions must be gleaned in a single
moment. Videotapes however provide a means of circum-
venting this problem through potentially unlimited repeated observations. It was through the support of re-
viewable videotaped incidents that it was possible to
confirm systematic and reliable discriminative cues to
the intentionality of one second-year infant's pre-verbal
vocalizations, in his gestures. On this basis a system
of sound-significance relations was established.

The infant, named David, participated in a
series of 10 one-hour videotaped play sessions, which
covered his second year at fairly regular intervals. The
resultant 10 videotapes and their narrative and coded
transcriptions constitute the source of the present observations. David's gestures in the period 12-16 months
were frequent, salient, and almost always accompanied
by a vocalization immediately before, during, or after
production. Further, certain of his gestures were exclusively tied to certain sounds. For example, when requesting an object via a reach, the phonetic shape of the
associated utterance was the highly predictable m + V
(Carter, 1975b);[1] when reaching for an object from, or
proferring an object to, someone else, co-occurring
h-initial sounds were equally predictable (Carter, 1975a);
and likewise for acts of drawing attention to objects
(pointing and showing) and the alveolar (1 and d) sounds
(Carter, in press).[2] Exhaustive examination of his
gestures in this four-month interval revealed eight categories of communicative behaviour, each usually composed
of a specified gesture together with a uniquely co-
occurring vocalization, and each having a unique goal,
the criterion for each category.[3] More detailed frequencies, conditions of occurrence, and the overall attributes of each of these composite behaviours, or
communicative sensorimotor schemata, have been presented
in a previous report (Carter, 1974). For present purposes Table 1 lists, in simplified form, each schema's
gesture, sound, goal, and simultaneous and total frequency of occurrence, with the grand total accounting for
91% of his gestural or vocal communications in the first
four play sessions.

Focusing on the vocalizations reveals eight categories of sound, each associated only with a particular gesture or gesture set with a recognizable goal, and each, it may therefore be inferred, related to the significance of the gesture. Thus, for example, m-initial sounds tended to be uttered in situations in which an object was being b-initial sounds when an object was being rejected (its disappearance being requested); voiced h-initial, when a transfer was being requested; l-initial, when drawing attention to an object; and n-initial, in disliked situations.

Similar categories of significance have been observed in studies of other infants between the ages of roughly 9 and 24 months. For the Request Object category (defined by object reach and m-initial vocalization), Bates (1974) mentioned an Italian infant's request for an object via the vocalization 'mm, a word-like signal with no referential value'. Jespersen (1964) described a 19-month-old Danish child 'who was accustomed to express his longings in general by help of a long m... while at the same time stretching out his hand toward the particular thing he longed for'. For the Attention to Object category, pointing plus alveolar sounds have been observed in second-year infants by Stern and Stern (1928), Leopold (1949), Grégoire (1939), and Bullowa (1967). The Attention to Self utterances of [ma], [mam], [mama], [mamɪy], etc., all resembling baby talk variants of the name for the mother, have been observed in the second year by Leopold (1949), Guillaume (1927), and Grégoire (1939), to name a few. Request Transfer was observed as a goal category by Antinucci and Parisi (1973), who reported the production of the same vocalization by a 14-month-old Italian infant when either giving or taking an object; and in Leopold's study of English-German bilingual infants, the h-initial utterances [hm] and [hɪ] were produced in the second year when handing or reaching for objects. The category Dislike-Rejection was observed for Leopold's Hildegarde, in a detailed description of her second-year production of mono- and di-syllabic nasals, accompanied by headshakes and manifestations of negative affect (Leopold, 1949). Grégoire described the connection between nasals and negative feeling in his son in detail.

With regard to the Disappearance hand motions and b-initial utterances, both were produced by Leopold's Hildegarde at 1;11 in response to thunder. Scupin's (1910) son Bubi produced [ba--sss] at 1;3½, glossed by Scupin as 'gone! fly'. And finally the PSR (breathy 'oh', 'ah', 'hi', 'ha', etc.) vocalizations were produced by infants in the studies of Grégoire (1939) and Lewis (1936), with the earliest observed instances beginning around the end of the first year.

TABLE 1. Simplified Description of David's Eight
Communicative Schemata in the Period 12-16
months.

Schema	Gesture	Sound
1. Request Object (RO)	reach to object	m-initial
2. Attention to Object (AO)	point, hold out	alveolar l-initial d-initial
3. Attention to Self (AS)	sound of vocalization	phonetic variants of 'David' 'Mommy'
4. Request Transfer (RT)	reach to person	h-initial (constricted & minimally aspirated)
5. Dislike (Disl)	prolonged, falling intonation	nasalized, especially n-initial
6. Disappearance (Disa)	waving hands, slapping	b-initial
7. Rejection (Rej)	negative head-shake	[ʔʌ̃ʔʌ̃]
8. Pleasure-Surprise-Recognition (PSR)	(smile)	flowing or breathy h sounds, especially oh, ah, hi, ha

Note: Frequencies, representing simultaneous and total
(both simultaneous and non-simultaneous) instances
of each gesture vocalization pair, were derived
from four videotapes of play behaviour, recorded
at approximately one-month intervals. The total
length of videotaped data from which these frequencies were obtained came to less than three
hours. (The sound track of each of the four tapes
was less than the full hour in length.)

Goal	# Instances (1st 4 play sessions: 1;0.15 -1;4)	
	Simultaneous	Total
Get receiver's help in obtaining object	298	342
Draw receiver's attention to object	245	334
Draw receiver's attention to self	142	142
Obtain object from, or give to, receiver	94	135
Get receiver's help in changing situation	82	82
Get receiver's help in removing object	4	32
Same as for Dislike (above)	3	20
Express pleasure	--	20

The significance of vowel sounds seems to vary greatly over the first year; [ʔa] for example is often the first non-crying sound reported. Its significance is not definable for a while, although it is sometimes early viewed as requesting attention. Later in the year it is commonly used to express both positive and negative affect. Von Raffler-Engel (1972) described the use at eight months of [i] to indicate a desired object, [u] as a sign of disapproval, and [U]'as an expression of in-quiring marvel' at a new object. None of these sounds is clearly related to David's second year sounds. And for that matter, a quick survey of the literature reveals no consistently inferred significance for any of his sounds, vowel or consonant, even in second year infants.

Is it possible that the eight sound classes were actually words in disguise: i.e., that each had a unique goal word in the adult language? In David's case, studies of his later linguistic development suggest that the answer is 'no' for almost all categories, though phonetic targeting on 'David' and 'Mommy' was implied in Attention to Self vocalizations. Months later, words were indeed found to evolve from these earlier vocaliza-tions, but usually through a very indirect chain of de-velopments, best characterized as a process of assimila-tion to the pre-existing sound structures on the basis of both semantic relatedness and phonetic similarity. Thus, David's Request Object m + V later developed into the phonetically and semantically related 'more', signal-ling request for another object, and 'mine', signalling request to maintain (rather than to obtain) possession of an object (cf. Carter, 1975b). H-initial utterances pro-duced both the words 'here', which incidentally only later acquired locative significance, and 'have', which though often used by adults in Request Transfer situa-tions, has additional components of meaning (cf. Carter, 1975a). And the alveolars l and d produced 'look', 'that', 'there', 'this', 'these', and 'the' (Carter, in press). However, the adult meanings of 'more' and 'mine' are essentially mutually exclusive, as is the case for 'here' and 'have', and some of the Attention to Object derivatives. It is unlikely that David could have in-tended a combination of such divergent adult meanings in the earlier vocalizations, since he had not acquired their separate meanings, nor even apparently attained a sufficient reduction in egocentrism in the first 19 months' 'Copernican revolution' (cf. Piaget and Inhelder, 1969:13) to be capable of acquiring them. Analysis under-lying these observations, presented in Carter (1974, 1975a 1975b, in press) involved the inference, based on the significance of co-occurring gestures, that his sensori-motor vocalizations, centered on his own wishes and at-titudes. Moreover, being tied to his own movements, these vocalizations were apparently not conceptually autonomous enough to be semantically referential, but were still little more than pragmatic markers.

At the same time, analysis of their phonetic properties revealed that many vocalizations sounded, except for a common initial consonant, distinctly unlike the words they ultimately engendered. Even members of a given meaning-equivalent class were often unrelated as to sound, except in the initial consonant segment. Hence there was, in effect, a potentially unlimited number and range of 'allomorphs' of any sensorimotor 'morpheme'. In sum, both their properties of meaning and of sound argue against their being conventional words from the outset.

Where could such non-word vocalizations have come from, if not from words? Since the observations only began at 12 months, I can only conjecture. From the broadest possible perspective, there are only three alternative sources: environmental, naturalistic, and an interactive combination of the two. Without trying to reach any conclusions, possibilities under each alternative will be considered.

1. Environmental. The sounds of words frequently produced by his mother in specific early situations such as nursing might have determined the outlines of sounds a child would associate with gestures of want. If this should be generally true, though it might be stressed that the writer has no data as yet on larger populations, in Romance and Germanic languages Request Object sounds might have high probability of being m-initial, based on sounds of words such as 'milk', 'mama', etc. (note in this regard the Guillaume and Bates references above), and in other languages, would be similarly determined. In support of this possibility, recently the writer observed a bilingual Indian mother carrying her infant, who said that her child produced d-initial sounds, similar to and including [duwda] whenever reaching for an object. In Hindi, which was the language she spoke to her child, this same sound (she said) means 'milk'. However, although some of the observations above as well as this anecdote form a set of supporting observations, only after early communication of many other infants has been detailed, hopefully in studies beginning soon after birth so as to allow the mother's early speech to her child to be recorded, can any such generalized statements concerning environmental influence have real validity.

2. Naturalistic. Even though in other studies a wide variety of significances has been inferred for any one of David's sounds, at the same time a noticeably large number of same or similar significances has been reported for each, even cross-linguistically (cf. previous examples). Apparently this impression is shared by a number of language scholars, whose opinions are cited here as provisional support for the naturalistic position.

First, with regard to the Request Object 'm', Leopold (1949) observed that 'm' sounds were associated with like, want, or request for food in many languages. He gave as sources Wundt, Compayre, Preyer, C. Franke, Darwin, Taine, Heinicke, and Fritz Schultz. Jespersen (1964) stated that 'in many countries it has been observed that very early a child uses a long m (without a vowel) as a sign that it wants something', and argued that the origin of this sound-significance relation was the use of labial muscles in sucking.

In regard to Attention to Object alveolar sounds, Stern and Stern (1928), in agreement with Wundt (1900), Buhler (1934), and Tischler (1957) concerning the cross-linguistic deictic use of dentals (included in our broad alveolar or alveolar ridge articulation category), suggested that dentals function deictively because of their 'outwardly-directed' character.

The Attention to Self 'mama' and variants can also be seen in many languages. Jespersen (1964) argued that it derived from the same nursing roots as the object requesting m.

The b-initial Disappearance morpheme has been less noticed in other studies, consonant with its fewer instances in David's case. A suggestive observation was provided by Stern, however, in the comment that infant sounds connected with bed and sleep (undoubtedly associated with disappearance, cf. Piaget, 1954) in many languages are b sounds: e.g. the English 'bye-bye', German 'baba', Russian 'beibei', and Malay 'bobo'. Despite some evidence of cross-linguistic applicability, a naturalistic basis for this sound-significance relation has not to the writer's knowledge been hypothesized.

The Dislike and Rejection schemata are described in Jespersen's (1964:131) observation that the nasal is used by fretful infants in so many different countries because it is only the gesture of '"turning up one's nose" made audible'.

Finally, the PSR 'oh', observed by Darwin (1904) throughout the world, was considered by him to be simply a reflexive reaction to being surprised, which would certainly give this vocalization a naturalistic basis.

3. <u>Interaction between Naturalistic and Environmental Influences</u>. The suggestion in this collection of observations that some of the sound-significance relations found for David may be language-independent is provocative. However, infant studies produce so many other contrary sound-significance relations, such as that in the Hindi example above, that a naturalistic origin cannot be the whole story. At most the result of naturalistic

influences would be a strong tendency toward certain relationships which both the infant's experiences and
other behavioural tendencies could support or diminish.
Of the three possibilities, therefore, an interactive
origin for David's system of prelinguistic sounds seems
the most likely. However, in keeping with Halliday's
(1973) conclusion from his own case study that there is
'no obvious source for the great majority of the child's
(pre-verbal) expressions', it is presently impossible to
make any stronger statement concerning the origins of
David's systematic vocalizations.

In summary, David produced between 12 and 16
months a set of vocalizations related in a general way
to like and dislike of objects, and like and dislike
of situations. These sounds were perhaps influenced by
the sounds he typically heard in early life situations,
but for most of them there is no evidence of an underlying adult goal word. During the period studied he
appeared to have developed his own system of sound and
significance relations, which would form the basic
structures underlying his later acquisition of words,
but which, on the basis of available evidence, were not
words themselves.

Notes.

1. Particular segments are used as cover terms to
    describe phonetic categories, and are intended to
    include differences such as degree of voicing that
    often could not be discriminated in the tapes.

2. The term alveolar is used to indicate articulation
    made at or in the general area of the alveolar
    ridge, and is intended to be sufficiently loose to
    include sounds which would correspond to well-
    defined alveolar and dental articulations in the
    adult language.

3. Inter-judge reliability obtained for characteriza-
    tion of schemata in the first four play sessions
    has been assessed at 93%. This and all related
    obtained reliability measures for the coding cate-
    gories of utterance transcription, gesture,
    gesture-vocalization time relationship, gesture
    contour, object of regard, receiver, location of
    sender and gestural object are presented and dis-
    cussed in Carter (1974).

REFERENCES

Antinucci, F. and Parisi, D. (1973)   Early Language
    Acquisition: A Model and some Data. In C.A.
    Ferguson and D.I. Slobin (eds.) Studies of
    Child Language Development. Holt, Rinehart
    and Winston, New York.

Bates, E. (1974)   Language and Context: Studies in
    the Acquisition of Pragmatics. Doctoral
    dissertation, University of Chicago.

Bloom, L. (1973)   One Word at a Time. Mouton, The
    Hague.

Buhler, K. (1934)   Sprach Theorie. Fischer, Jena.

Bullowa, M. (1967)   The Start of the Language Process.
    Paper presented at the Tenth International
    Congress of Linguistics, Bucharest.

Carter, A. (1974)   The Development of Communication in
    the Sensorimotor Period: A Case Study.
    Doctoral dissertation, University of California,
    Berkeley.

Carter, A. (1975a)   The Transformation of Sensorimotor
    Morphemes into Words: A Case Study of the De-
    velopment of 'Here' and 'There'. Papers and
    Reports on Child Language Development 10. Stan-
    ford University. 31-47.

Carter, A. (1975b)   The Transformation of Sensori-
    motor Morphemes into Words: A Case Study of
    the Development of 'More' and 'Mine'.
    Journal of Child Language 2. 233-250.

Carter, A. (In press)   Learning to Point with Words:
    the Structural Evolution of Attention-
    directing Communication in the Second Year. In
    A. Lock (ed.) Action, Gesture and Symbol: The
    Emergence of Language. Academic Press, London.

Clark, E. (1973)   How Children Describe Time and Order.
    In C.A. Ferguson and D.I. Slobin (eds.) Studies
    of Child Language Development. Holt, Rinehart
    and Winston, New York.

Darwin, C. (1904)   The Expression of the Emotions in
    Man and Animals. John Murray, London (first
    published 1872).

Dore, J. (1973)   The Development of Speech Acts.
    Doctoral dissertation, City University of New
    York.

Greenfield, P. and Smith, J. (1976)   The Structure of
Communication in Early Language Development.
Academic Press, New York.

Grégoire, A. (1939)   L'Apprentissage du Langage: Les
Deux Premières Années. Bibliothèque de la
Faculté de Philosophie et Lettres de l'Univer-
sité de Liège.

Guillaume, P. (1927)   Les Débuts de la Phrase dans le
Langage de l'Enfant. Journal de Psychologie
24.1-25.

Halliday, M.A.K. (1970)   Language Structure and Language Function. In J. Lyons (ed.) New Horizons in Linguistics. Penguin Books, Baltimore.

Halliday, M.A.K. (1973)   Early Language Learning: A
Sociolinguistic Approach. Paper presented for
IXth International Congress of Anthropological
and Ethnological Science, Chicago, August and
September.

Ingram, D. (1974)   Stages in the Development of One-
word Sentences. Paper presented to the
Stanford Child Language Forum, Stanford,
California, April.

Jesperson, O. (1964)   Language, Its Nature, Development
and Origin. Norton, New York. (Originally
published in 1922 by Holt, Rinehart and
Winston.)

Leopold, W. (1949)   Speech Development of a Bilingual
Child: A Linguist's Record. III (Grammar and
General Problems in the First Two Years).
Northwestern University Press, Evanston,
Illinois.

Lewis, M.M. (1936)   Infant Speech: A Study of the
Beginnings of Language. Harcourt, Brace, New
York.

Meumann, E. (1902)   Die Entstehung der ersten ver-
gleichenden Grammatik der Bantusprachen.
Englemann, Leipzig.

Nelson, K. (1973)   Structure and Strategy in Learning
to Talk. Monographs of the Society for Research in Child Development, 38. No. 149.

Piaget, J. (1954)   The Construction of Reality in the
Child. Ballantine, New York.

Piaget, J. and Inhelder, B. (1969)   The Psychology of
    the Child. Trans. by H. Weaver. Basic Books,
    New York.

Preyer, W. (1882)   Die Seele des Kindes. Grieben,
    Liepzig.

Scupin, E. and Scupin, G. (1910)   Bubi im vierten bis
    sechsten Lebensjahr. Grieben, Liepzig.

Stern, C. and Stern, W. (1928)   Die Kindesprache.
    Barth, Leipzig. First edition, 1907.

Stumpf, C. (1900)   Eigenartige sprachliche Entwicklung
    eines Kindes. Zeitschrift für Pädagogische
    Psychologie und Pathologie 3, 6.420-447.

Tischler, H. (1957)   Schreien, Lallen und erstes
    Sprechen in der Entwicklung des Säuglinges.
    Zeitschrift für Psychologie 160. 209-263.

von Raffler-Engel, W. (1972)   The Relationship of In-
    tonation to the First Vowel Articulation in
    Infants. Acta Universitatis Carolinae-Philo-
    logica 1. Phonetica Pragensia III. 197-202.

Werner, H. and Kaplan, B. (1963)   Symbol Formation.
    Wiley, New York.

Wundt, W. (1900)   Voelkerpsychologie, I. Die Sprache.
    Englemann, Leipzig.

Non-verbal Concomitants of Language Input to Children

O. K. Garnica

Recently there has been increasing interest in the hypothesis that the verbal environment in which language is acquired by the young child may play a significant role in the language learning process itself. Numerous studies have shown that speech directed to the language learning child differs in systematic ways from speech directed to adolescents and adults (Snow, 1977; Garnica, 1975, 1977). It is suggested that the speech the young child hears, characterized by short and simple sentences, multiple repetitions, prosodic modifications, etc., may be useful to the child in developing an understanding of the precise relationship between meaning and linguistic expression within his language.

To date discussions have focused on the strictly verbal aspects of adult-child communication. The child, however, has a wider range of input available to him. In communicative situations, particularly conversational exchanges, the nonverbal aspects of the face-to-face interaction, e.g. gestures, may be an important source of cues to the speaker's intention. These features of the child's communicative environment have thus far not been studied.

In this paper I analyze one aspect of nonverbal behaviour concomitant with verbalizations produced by

---

*The research is supported by a grant from the Graduate School of The Ohio State University through its Small Grants Program. I would like to thank Louise Cherry, Grace Shugar, and Catherine Snow for their comments on an earlier version of this paper.

mothers interacting with their young children. The purpose is to examine the frequency and type of non-verbal cues accompanying verbalizations directed to the young child and to observe how these cues vary with the response of the child as well as with his linguistic sophistication. The paper is part of a larger study designed to specify the informational sources, clues to meaning, available to the child as he proceeds to learn language (Garnica, forthcoming).

METHOD

The data examined in this paper is based on videotaped recordings of nine mother-child dyads. Three of the children were one-year-olds (18 mths., 18 mths., 20 mths.), another three were two-year-olds (26 mths., 31 mths., 32 mths.) and the remaining three were three-year-olds (38 mths., 40 mths., 42 mths.).[1] The mother-child dyads were videotaped for fifteen minutes through a one-way mirror while they were engaged in an unstructured play situation in a room well-equipped with books, puzzles and various toys. The nature of these interactions can be characterized in Goffman's (1963) terms as 'focused interaction', 'instances of two or more participants in a situation joining each other openly in maintaining a single focus of cognitive and visual attention -- what is sensed as a single mutual activity' (1963:89).

The speech and concomitant nonverbal behaviour of both members of the dyad were transcribed. Speech was transcribed into ordinary orthography except for unintelligible utterances produced by the child. These were transcribed phonetically. The nonverbal behaviours were recorded using a system developed for the larger study.[2] Due to space limitations, the nonverbal portions of the examples are presented in this paper in the form of summary statements.

REQUESTS FOR ACTION

In this paper I discuss the gestures concomitant with one type of illocutionary act - the request for action (Searle, 1969). The request for action (henceforth, RA) is one of a more general set of speech acts whereby one person attempts to influence the behaviour (or attitude) of another. Specifically in the RA a speaker conveys to an addressee that he (the speaker) wishes the other (the addressee) to perform an act. The RA can be in direct or indirect form. In this paper only direct requests are considered. Indirect requests, including the children's responses, are considered elsewhere (Garnica, ms.). The speech produced by the mother was scanned for direct request forms.

The imperative form utterances were subjected
to the simple test established by Garvey (1975), i.e.
the imperative is prefaced with a performative tag (I request, I command, I order you to) and judged for appropriateness in the particular context of the utterance.
A total of 192 imperative utterances passed this test.
The episodes which contained these utterances were then
analysed.

NONVERBAL ACTIONS ACCOMPANYING REQUESTS FOR ACTION

Requests for action were directed approximately as frequently to all the children in the sample. The
frequency and explicitness, however, of the mother's concomitant gestures varied with the age and responsiveness
of the child. This can be seen quite clearly by comparing the following two examples from a one-year-old child
and a three-year-old child:

(1)   One-year old child.

General context: Child and mother sitting on floor.
Child puts small wooden toy dolls into a toy car which
is located between him and his mother.

VERBAL	NONVERBAL
Mother: Oh boy! That's terrific. Very good!	Mother claps hands.
Can you push the car?	Mother points to car as she says 'car'.
Push the car.	Mother touches car and gives it a tap. Car moves slight-ly. Child watches, then looks to other side of room.
K____. Watch.	Mother pushes car, turning it around so it is now in front of child and facing away from him. Child watches entire action of sequence.
Vroom. Vroom. Vroom. Vroom. (sound of car engine)	Mother pushes car in four jerky motions and returns it to the starting point.
Push the car.	Mother leans over and looks directly into the child's face.
Vroom. Vroom. Vroom. Push the car?	No accompanying action by mother. Mother looks direct-ly at child. Child picks up another toy and examines it.

<u>Push the car.</u>	Mother pushes car in direction away from child and returns it to starting position.
<u>Vroom. Vroom. Vroom.</u> <u>Vroom.</u>	Mother pushes car in four jerky motions and returns it to start position. Child picks up a toy and examines it.
<u>You want to look at</u> <u>that? Okay.</u> (pause)	Mother looks at toys in child's hand.
<u>Push the car.</u>	Mother pushes car.

(2) Three-year-old child.

General context: Mother and child sitting on floor next to one another examining a puzzle which has pieces shaped like various vehicles (bus, ambulance, car, van, etc.). Each vehicle piece can be removed from board. Underneath each piece is a picture of the inside compartment of the vehicle.

<u>VERBAL</u>	<u>NONVERBAL</u>
Mother: <u>Let's look at</u> <u>this puzzle.</u>	Mother places puzzle in front of child.
Child: <u>Puzzle. That's</u> <u>a puzzle. Puzzle.</u>	
Mother: <u>Yes, Where's</u> <u>the bus? Where's</u> <u>the bus at? Can you</u> <u>pick up the bus?</u> <u>Pick up the bus.</u> <u>Pick up the bus.</u>	Child looking at different parts of the puzzle.
Child: <u>Why?</u>	Child looks at mother.
Mother: <u>Let me see</u> <u>that bus. I want</u> <u>to see the bus up</u> <u>close. Pick up</u> <u>the bus.</u> <u>Oh. Look at the</u> <u>people on the bus.</u> <u>Can you pick up the</u> <u>bus? Pick up the</u> <u>bus.</u>	Mother points to pictured person on the bus.
Child: <u>There.</u>	Child picks up bus piece and holds it up in front of mother's face.
Mother: <u>Oh! Very good!</u>	

These examples are representative of the data.
Although both children received a large number of verbal
renditions of the RA, the mother of the one-year-old
presents many more nonverbal cues as to what is requested
of the child. She quite explicitly models the action
requested on six different occasions, i.e. puts the toy
car into motion as she repeats the RA. This modelling
begins almost immediately after the RA is verbally
introduced.

The mother of the three-year-old refrains from
any overt related gestural behaviours until the RA has
been repeated many times. Even then, she only points
to the object of the RA (rather than picking up the object). Her pointing gesture accompanies the utterance
'Look at the people on the bus'. She does not model the
action requested nor does she indicate the object of the
RA in conjunction with the direct request 'Pick up the
bus'. The use of such more subtle or covert nonverbal
cues to meaning is the predominant behaviour in mother-
child pairs involving three-year-olds. In fact there
was only one case of a mother of a three-year-old performing the requested action simultaneously uttering the
RA. The modelling occurred at the end of a long sequence
of verbal renditions of the RA a sequence not unlike the
one in the three-year-old example given above.

There were two major types of adult nonverbal behaviour accompanying RAs. One type involves the manipulation of an object (usually one of the toys). The other type
only involves the two interactants. The first type is the
most common accounting for almost all the RAs noted. For
RAs involving objects the adults exhibited two classes of
gestures: (a) pointing to the object(s) referred to in the
RA, and (b) manipulating the object(s) referred to in the
RA. In the case where the adult points to the object(s) referred to in a RA, the gesture may occur simultaneously
with the production of the word for the object in question
or nonsimultaneously:

(3)   Two-year-old.

General context: Toy car and small dolls.

VERBAL	NONVERBAL
Mother: Put the people in the car.	Mother points to the two toy dolls when saying 'people' and to car when saying 'car'.

(4)   One-year-old.

General context: Toy car and small dolls.

VERBAL	NONVERBAL
Mother: Push the car.	Mother points to car.

In the case where the adult manipulates an object or objects referred to in the RA, the gesture may also occur simultaneously or nonsimultaneously. Here, however, we see an added dimension. The adult performs the complete action or only some part of the action sequence. Examples of complete and partial actions in the simultaneous category are given below:

(5)   One-year-old: complete action.

General context: Toy car and small dolls.

VERBAL	NONVERBAL
Mother: Push the car.	Mother pushes toy car.

(6)   Two-year-old: partial action.

General context: Child searching for pieces of puzzle.

VERBAL	NONVERBAL
Mother: Tip it (box) upside down.	Mother tips box half way and returns it to the upright position.
Maybe we will find the piece.	Child turns box with puzzle pieces upside down and all the pieces fall out.

Examples of complete and partial actions also occurred in the case of the nonsimultaneous category:

(7)   One-year-old: complete action.

General context: Toy doll and toy chair.

VERBAL	NONVERBAL
Mother: Look.	Mother puts doll in chair and takes doll out. Child watches. Mother points to doll.
Mother: Can you do it? Put the boy in the chair.	

(8)   Two-year-old: partial action.

General context: Toy merry-go-round which has two slots for riders.

VERBAL	NONVERBAL

Adult puts merry-go-round in front of child. Positions two toy dolls around perimeter of merry-go-round.

Mother: Put the people in the merry-go-round and give them a ride.

The second major type of adult nonverbal behaviour accompanying RA's did not include objects but rather consisted of the adult herself performing the requested action as in (9) below or of the adult physically manipulating the child into complying with the RA.

(9) Two-year-old.

General context: Child searching for missing piece of puzzle.

VERBAL	NONVERBAL
Mother: Look in the box and see if you can find it.	Mother leans over child's shoulder, facing the box referred to.

(10) One-year old.

General context: Mother introducing new activity to child.

VERBAL	NONVERBAL
Mother: Come sit next to me.	Mother holds child under his arms and moves child next to her.

The behaviour in (9) appeared consistently in all the episodes with the two- and three-year olds. The behaviour exhibited in (10), i.e., actually physically handling the child, was restricted to the episodes with the one-year-olds. The other mothers used verbal means ('Come sit here and see what toys I have') often combined with nonverbal features (e.g. Mother holds up toy with one hand and pats place on floor where she wants child to sit).

CONCLUDING REMARKS

From the analysis of the mother-child interactions, we conclude that the adult adopts certain nonverbal strategies such as modelling, pointing, etc., as an adjustment to the child's limited understanding

of the meaning being conveyed in the utterances directed to him. Further investigation is necessary to determine whether these and other strategies produce a sufficiently rich environment which provides the child
with specific information which could be used for testing his/her linguistic hypotheses. The lines of inquiry
we are pursuing include a detailed analysis of the sequential patterns established on the adult-child interaction unit which includes RAs (direct and indirect),
an examination of other types of speech acts and their
concomitant nonverbal aspects, and an analysis of the
effect of the type of child response (or lack of it)
on the patterning of the mother's nonverbal behaviour.
With this type of information we can better assess the
contribution of aspects of the total communicative environment to the language development of the child.

Notes.

1.   The videotapes were selected for analysis randomly
      from a set of ten such pairs for each of the three
      age groups. This material forms the data base of
      the analysis presented in Garnica (ms., forth-
      coming).

2.   Various parts of this system are still being re-
      vised and supplemented. The fully developed no-
      tation will appear in Garnica (forthcoming).

REFERENCES

Garnica, O.K. (1975)   Some Prosodic Characteristics of
      Speech to Young Children. Ph.D. dissertation,
      Stanford University.

Garnica, O.K. (1977)   Some Prosodic and Paralinguis-
      tic Features of Speech Directed to Young
      Children. In C.E. Snow and C.A. Ferguson (eds.)
      Talking to Children: Language Input and
      Acquisition. Cambridge University Press,
      Cambridge.

Garnica, O.K. (ms.)   Nonverbal Concomitants of Language
      Input to Children II: Indirect requests.

Garnica, O.K. (Forthcoming)   Adult-child Discourse: the
      Communicative Environment of the Language
      Learning Child.

Garvey, C. (1975)   Requests and Responses in Children's Speech.   Journal of Child Language   2.
41-63.

Goffman, E. (1963)   Behavior in Public Places.   Free
Press, New York.

Searle, J.R. (1969)   Speech Acts: An Essay in the
Philosophy of Language.   Cambridge University
Press, Cambridge.

Snow, C.E.   (1977)   Mother's Speech Research: from
Input to Interaction.   In C.E. Snow and C.A.
Ferguson (eds.)   Talking to Children: Language
Input and Acquisition.   Cambridge University
Press, Cambridge.

3
Interaction in Language Acquisition

A great many papers presented at the London Symposium included a discussion of the speech addressed to children as an important factor influencing the course of language acquisition. The papers by Sylvester-Bradley and Trevarthen, Tuaycharoen, and Garnica in the previous section, as well as those by Ferrier, Kaper, Smoczyńska, and Woll in section 4, also Greenfield, and Miller in section 5, are all concerned with the role of parent-child interaction and the speech addressed to children in language acquisition. The papers in this section, however, deal most centrally with this issue, and demonstrate the wide variety of research issues which arise within the small field of parent-child interaction.

The paper by Jocić is perhaps the most classic example of research on the nature of the speech addressed to children. It is a careful description of the speech register used with children in Serbocroatian, a language never before studied in this way. Both Savić and Shugar

also present descriptions of the speech addressed to
children, Savić for Serbocroatian and Shugar for Polish,
but in both cases it is considered in relation to the
speech produced by the child. Savić relates the kinds of
questions asked by parents to the acquisition of questions
and Shugar describes how mothers interweave their own
utterances with the child utterances to produce relatively
complicated texts, to which the child contributes as a
conversational partner. Lieven emphasizes the interaction
al influences on the nature of the speech addressed to
children - that the child to a large extent creates his ow
linguistic environment. Cherry and Lewis analyze the
nature of interactions with boys as opposed to girls, and
find that certain conversation-maintaining devices are use
more often to girls than to boys. Ringler introduces a
novel independent variable - the amount of contact between
mother and baby in the immediate postnatal period - and
finds that this has a large effect on many parameters of
the maternal speech one and two years later. Cross
analyzes which of the various kinds of modification in
speech addressed to children have an effect on rate of
language acquisition. She presents evidence that language
acquisition is most facilitated by the semantic relevance
of maternal utterances to preceding child utterances.

The theme which should be borne in mind as the
following papers are read is that speech is addressed to
children in the course of conversations with them, conversations whose primary aim is communication, not the
imparting of information about the structure of language.
Nonetheless, these communicative interactions do provide
the information on the basis of which the child learns
language.

A Longitudinal Study of Mothers' Language

N. Ringler

What caretakers happen to do when they talk
with children has potentially important implications
for how children's language develops. The emphasis in
studies of the language acquisition process in the
1970's has been on the kind of linguistic environment
mothers provide for their children and on mother-child
interaction. This is quite a shift in emphasis from
the 1960's, when the stimulus-response paradigm, which
viewed adult speech as a model for the child to imitate,
predominated, and from the view that language is a
species-specific behavioural pattern which the human
nervous system is pre-programmed to learn, and that only
a minimum of language input is thus necessary for normal
linguistic development (Lenneberg, 1967; McNeill, 1966).
Caretakers' speech is now viewed as the most important
source of speech input to the child in his environment,
and the mother is seen as supplying a rich sample of
language, determining the child's responses by her intentions as speaker, and interpreting the child's
language by acting as provider, expander, and idealizer
of utterances while interacting with the child (Bruner,
1975). Cross-sectional studies began to investigate the
structure of maternal linguistic input to children by
comparing mothers' speech to their children with speech
to other adults. Results from these studies (Broen,
1972; Phillips, 1973; Remick, 1971; Snow, 1972) suggested that maternal language to children is simplified,
redundant, and restricted in vocabulary, and that

151

length of utterance and syntactic complexity of maternal speech increase with age of child.   These
studies dealt exclusively with middle class parents,
and none observed mothers and children longitudinally.

The longitudinal study presented here ex-
plores some aspects of the question of relationship
between maternal input to the early language learners
and acquisition of language, investigating the questions:

1.   Does nursery language used with the child
     change after he begins to talk?

2.   Is there reason to believe that a child's
     speech is influenced by or influences the
     mother's speech?

In other words, in what sense is there a causal influence of the child's linguistic environment on his
development and use of language, and in what sense is
there a causal influence of his linguistic maturity on
his linguistic environment?

The subjects were ten lower class black
mothers, speakers of urban language, all of whom had
their first-born full-term babies at University Hos-
pitals in the summer of 1970 and who were part of a
larger study of the effects of infant exposure on
mother attachment in 28 mother-child pairs (Kennell,
Jerauld, Wolfe, Chesler, Kreger, McAlpine, Steffa,
and Claks, 1972;   Klaus, Jerauld, Kreger, and Kennell, 1972).   Five mother-child pairs were randomly
selected from each of the two groups of 14 mothers in
the larger study;   the control group mothers had the
usual hospital exposure to their babies after birth,
and the experimental group mothers had 16 additional
hours of contact one hour after birth and during the
next three days, to determine whether hospital procedures affected subsequent maternal behaviour.
Significant differences were found between the two
groups in how they addressed their two-year-olds
(Ringler, 1973;   Ringler, Jarvella, Kennell, Navojosky
and Klaus, 1975).   The experimenter was unaware of
which group the mother-child dyad were in during all
testing and analysis.   Of the sample of ten, six were
mothers of girls and four were mothers of boys.

All the mothers returned to University Hospital in the summer of 1971 (Time I) and again in the
summer of 1972 (Time II), as well as the summers of
1973, 1974, and 1975.   Each time they participated in
a one and one-half hour session including five different observation situations in the same controlled
laboratory setting.

I.   Interview (parent, examiner, and child)

II.   Free Play Period (mother and child alone)

III. Formal Testing Period (mother and child,
      and psychologist)

IV.   Physical Examination of the Baby (mother,
      child, examiner)

V.   Ice Cream Sequence (mother and child alone)

Out of this fairly extensive programme of protocols 10
hours of observation were analyzed.

Tape recordings were made in each situation
at each time. Simultaneously, transcriptions of
dialogue and notes as to non-verbal behaviour and the
context in which the speech was produced were also
made.

Findings will be presented from the interview, adult to adult speech (A-A), and the free play
session, adult to child speech (A-C), at Time I, when
the babies were 10-13 months old, and Time II, when the
babies were 22-25 months old and had in most cases begun producing utterances of two words or more.

Utterances and their constituents were classified according to a number of linguistic criteria,
yielding measures of rate, length, complexity, function
of sentences, syntax, and semantics. A two-by-two analysis of variance with repeated measures was used for
each of the dependent variables; the factors were
Hearer (A-A, A-C) and Times (Time I, 12 months; Time II,
24 months). Post hoc F tests were used to determine the
significance of differences between the means of particular cells.

First, results concerning the amount of
speech used will be discussed. Rate, which reflects
the amount of speech a child hears per unit of time,
was restricted in A-C speech as compared to A-A speech.
Mean rate in A-A speech was 61 words per minute, versus
34 words per minute in A-C speech, with slower speech
to the one-year-old than to the two-year old. There was
a 300% increase in the amount of speech from age one to
age two. This increased amount of speech may indicate
that the mothers were sensitive to the child's increased
processing ability and increased comprehension. Perhaps
it reflects the mothers' awareness of the child's increased demand and need for a rich language environment
as he grows older, and of his growing ability to grasp
the meaning of syntactically complex utterances.

Mean length of utterance (MLU), widely used as a measure of language development, was much shorter in A-C speech. A-A utterances were twice as long as A-C utterances (7.8 words versus 3.0). Significantly longer utterances were addressed to the older child; MLU to the two-year-old was above three words, compared to less than two words to the one-year-old child.

About 70% of all utterances at both times with both listeners were complete sentences. There were not, as expected, more complete and grammatical sentences in A-C speech and more non-sentences in A-A speech, as hypothesized by Chomsky (1967) and Lenneberg (1967). More sentence fragments (utterances isolated by pauses not related to a sentence boundary) and more elliptical utterances (incomplete but correct utterances, e.g., 'Yes' in answer to a question) were addressed to the younger child. These accounted for one utterance in three at one year and only one in five at two years. These results suggest increasing parental sensitivity to the child's need to have English sentences modelled in the correct, complete form. In addition, more simple (single-clause) sentences were addressed to the child than to the adult; 84% of utterances in A-A speech were multiclause sentences, compared to 63% in A-C speech. No significant difference was found between Times I and II in incidence of multiclause sentences.

The following results were obtained concerning the functions and the reference of the mothers' sentences. The form of sentences was taken as indicating their function (for example, declaratives were assumed to function as statements, imperatives as commands, and interrogatives as questions). The most frequent category used in A-C speech was commands, which accounted for about 60% of the sentences at each age. Recent studies by Nelson (1973) and Holzman (1974) indicate that the use of commands by parents affects the cognitive development of children. These results support the finding of Williams and Naremore (1969), Robinson (1972) and Lawton (1968) that lower class speakers use more propositional speech (statements) in A-A speech and a more directive style (imperatives) in A-C speech. Most of the commands were at least overtly affirmative ones. From age one to age two the relative frequency of statements used in A-C speech decreased and the relative frequency of questions increased. Very few statements, only about 13% of all sentences, were produced in A-C speech when the child was two years old. Similarly, the number of utterances repeated in A-C speech within a sample dropped substantially between age one and age two.

More content words, i.e. high information words such as nouns, verbs, adjectives, and adverbs,

were used in A-C speech, and more to the younger child
than to the older child. Fewer function words, i.e.
prepositions, conjunctions, articles, and demonstratives,
small words which may signal a meaning difference and
indicate more complex grammatical structure, were produced in A-C speech than A-A speech (14% versus 25%),
with more to the older child than to the younger (23%
versus 8%). Twice as many auxiliary verbs were addressed to the adult as to the child (8% versus 4%).
As reflected in these measures, syntax in A-A speech
was more complex than in A-C speech. The increased use
of function words in speech to older children suggests
that the children were increasingly able to process and
comprehend complex syntactic constructions.

Over 80% of nouns used with children were concrete nouns and referred to objects within the speech
environment. English-speaking children seem first to
learn names for things having a characteristic size and
shape, and parents have been reported to use tangible
referents and correlated visual forms in their speech
to children (Brown and Hanlon, 1970). There was an interesting increase in use of direct objects as the
child grew older, while incidence of subjects decreased.
Influence on the adult's speech by the child is suggested by the fact that more noun phrase objects were
used in A-A speech when more were used in A-C speech,
and they decreased in A-A speech as in A-C speech as
the child grew older. Far more locative noun phrases
and adverbs of place were used in A-C speech than adverbs of time and temporal noun phrases. If time language develops largely out of spatial language, as
Clark (1971) has suggested, this is precisely the order
of frequency we might expect in an environment sensitive to the child's capabilities. In our A-A samples
time vocabulary was relatively more frequent than space
vocabulary; this may, however, have been partly an
artifact of the interview. The analysis of later
samples of A-C speech will give a better determination
of trends of this kind. Of the verbs addressed to the
children, 83% were action verbs at Time I and 78% at
Time II, compared to 59% action verbs in A-A speech.
Considerably more animal and human movement was described in A-C speech. Less variety, measured by the
type-token ratio (TTR) (the ratio of the number of
different words (types) in a sample to the total
number of words in the sample (tokens)) was found in
A-C speech, with an increase in A-A and A-C speech
when the child was two-years-old.

In summary, rate of speech was found to be
significantly slower to the child and to increase as
the child grew older. Shorter utterances were addressed to the child, and length of utterances increased with age. Speech to the child was simpler,
with more single-clause sentences, main clauses, more

content words and fewer function words. Complexity increased over time. Grammatical complexity and use of
complete utterances to the child increased over time.
There were more imperatives, affirmatives, and questions
addressed to the child. Repetitions decreased with age.
Speech to the child was more concrete, with more noun
actors, and adverbs of place to the child than to the
adult, but more noun objects and adverbs of time to the
older than to the younger child. There were significantly more action words addressed to the child and
less variety of vocabulary. The parent's speech to
other adults seemed influenced by the child, as there
was a decrease in concreteness and in the use of adverbs of place in A-A speech at time II. Richness of
vocabulary (TTR) was greater in A-A speech, and also
increased between Time I and Time II.

Results suggest that mothers' speech to
children is much different from that to an adult inter-
viewer, that the language used with children changed
after they began to talk, and that the children's speech
was probably influenced by and influenced the mother's
speech.

In an attempt to observe any specific effects
of mothers' speech on their children's language maturity we compared the mothers' speech to their children
at two with the children's speech and language comprehension at five.

When the children were five, they again returned to the hospital with their mothers. In addition
to the one and one-half hour follow-up session consisting of the five different observation situations, the
children were given two tests of intelligence and two
tests of linguistic functioning. Recent studies have
indicated maternal influence on children's language,
but this influence has not been demonstrated after the
child was two years old (Nelson, 1973; Holzman, 1974).
Our test was designed to help determine whether the way
a mother talked to her child at two years influenced
his language at five years.

Results indicated that several dimensions of
a mother's speech to her child at two were significantly related to the speech and language comprehension of
the child at five as measured by the Stanford Binet
form L-M, the Peabody Picture vocabulary test, and the
Northwest Syntax Screening Test.

The number of words per proposition used by
the mothers when their children were two was significantly related to the five-year-old's comprehension of
vocabulary and of phrases with four critical elements
(e.g. 'dog standing and cat sitting'). Mothers who

used more adjectives had children who understood more
phrases with four critical elements and had greater
expressive ability. Number of content words addressed
to the child at two correlated negatively with expressive ability at five. These correlations were significant at p < .01. Use of content words tended to be
negatively correlated with ability in the use of two and
four critical elements. This may suggest that content
words are too concrete, that the child needs to hear
functional classification and association discussed.
The use of imperatives to the child at two showed a negative correlation with the child's MLU (p < .05), and
non-significant negative correlations with the use of
two and four critical elements as well as with I.Q.
scores at five. The use of questions to the child at
two was correlated positively, though non-significant-
ly, with higher Binet I.Q. scores, and with higher
scores in the use of two critical elements and expressive ability. These results indicate that the way
a mother addresses her two-year-old may have lasting
effects on the speech and language development of the
child as measured by standardized tests at five.

REFERENCES

Broen, P.A. (1972)   The Verbal Environment of the
        Language-Learning Child. American Speech
        and Hearing Association Monograph. No.17,
        December.

Brown, R. and Hanlon, C. (1970)   Derivational Comple-
        xity and Order of Acquisition in Child Speech.
        In J.R. Hayes (ed.) Cognition and the De-
        velopment of Language. Wiley, New York.

Bruner, J. (1975)   The Ontogenesis of Speech Acts.
        Journal of Child Language 2. 1-21.

Chomsky, N. (1967)   The Formal Nature of Language.
        In E.H. Lenneberg (ed.) Biological Foundations
        of Language. Wiley, New York.

Clark, H. (1971)   Space, Time, Semantics, and the
        Child. Presented at the Conference of De-
        velopmental Psycholinguistics. State Uni-
        versity of New York at Buffalo, August.

Holzman, M. (1974)   The Verbal Environment Provided by
        Mothers for their Very Young Children.
        Merrill-Palmer Quarterly 20. 31-42.

158

Kennell, J. Jerauld, R., Wolfe, H., Chesler, D., Kreger, N., McAlpine, W., Steffa, M. and Claks, M. (1974) Maternal Behavior at One Year after Early and Extended Post-partum Contact. Developmental Medicine and Clinical Neurology 16. 172-179.

Klaus, M., Jerauld, R., Kreger, N., Kennell, J. (1972) Maternal Attachment: Importance of the First Post-partum Days. New England Journal of Medicine 286. 460-463.

Lawton, S. (1968) Social Class, Language, and Education. Wiley, New York.

Lenneberg, E. (1967) Biological Foundations of Language. Wiley, New York.

McNeill, D. (1966) The Creation of Language. Discovery 27. 34-35.

Nelson, K. (1973) Structure and Strategy in Learning to Talk. Society for Research in Child Development Monographs 38. No.149.

Phillips, J. (1973) Syntax and Vocabulary of Mothers' Speech to Young Children: Age and Sex Comparisons. Child Development 44. 182-185.

Remick, H. (1971) The Maternal Environment of Language Acquisition. Unpublished doctoral dissertation, University of California at Davis.

Ringler, N. (1973) Mothers' Language to their Children and to Adults over Time. Unpublished doctoral dissertation, Case Western Reserve University.

Ringler, N., Jarvella, R., Kennell, J., Navojosky, B. and Klaus, M. (1975) Mother-to-child Speech at 2 Years - Effects of Early Postnatal Contact. The Journal of Pediatrics 86. 141-144.

Robinson, W. (1972) Language and Social Behavior. Penguin Books, Baltimore.

Snow, C. (1972) Mothers' Speech to Children Learning Language. Child Development 43. 549-565.

Williams, F. and Naremore, R. (1969) On the Functional Analysis of Social Class Differences in Modes of Speech. Speech Monographs (Speech Association of America) 36.

Adaptation in Adult Speech during Communication with Children

M. Jocić

The bases for adaptation in adult speech to
a child, especially within the family circle, are the
emotional relation between the child and the adult,
their different cognitive and experiential capacities,
and the need to succeed in communication with the child.
These three factors cause general adaptations, as well
as modifications specific to speech, in adults communicating with children aged six months to four years.
Adult speech adaptations will be treated as part of the
process of adult interpretation of child utterances,
which is an indispensible element of successful adult-
child communication (see Jocić, 1975; see also Vasić,
1976 for a discussion of speech modifications of elder
children speaking to younger children).

Not all the types of adaptation in adult
speech will be discussed here, only some syntactic and
morpho-semantic adaptations encountered in the speech
of 10 Serbocroatian-speaking adults while communicating
with children. Data for this paper were taken from
diaries of four individual children (age 0;6 to 4;0) and
three pairs of twins (age 1;3 to 3;0). The diaries were
compiled on the basis of longitudinal observation and
notation, or recording, during two-hour weekly sessions,
of the speech development and behaviour of the children
and the adults who communicated with them most frequently.
The sessions were conducted in a family atmosphere. It

should be noted that the adult subjects were of high
socio-cultural background. This is important since
the social and cultural level of the adult affects the
type of speech adaptation and its quality. For example,
none of our adult subjects made vocal, phonetic modifications in their speech. However, several individuals
who came into contact with the children only occasionally,
two from the village and one from the town, but all three
without any formal education, did make modifications of
a phonetic nature, even though they did not know about
the speech behaviour of the children they were addressing,
i.e., whether the children pronounced words 'correctly'
or not.

SYNTACTIC MODIFICATION

Adults modify their speech depending on their
estimate of children's cognitive and verbal capacity.
They do this, on the one hand, so that the child should
understand them better, and on the other, because they
are influenced by the child's speech.

Some of the types of syntactic modification in
the speech addressed to children by the adult subjects
will be presented below:

In Referring to Persons, Names are used instead of
Personal Pronouns, and the Corresponding Verb Suffix is
Eliminated. This phenomenon is very frequent in the
adult subjects. All personal pronouns in the singular
are replaced by either the child's name (Vladan, Sara,
Tanja...) or by designation persons, such as a child,
mother, father, aunt, grandmother. This phenomenon
lasts throughout the observed period, and even after the
child is four years old. By that time he has already
acquired the personal pronoun system and the system of
finite verbal forms of standard Serbocroatian. As the
child grows older, this adaptation becomes emotionally
coloured and almost a mannerism indicating intimacy
between the adult and the child, as can be seen from
the examples that follow. These are given in the following manner: the adult utterance is given first, with
the modified forms underlined, (a); a translation follows, (b); the correct adult utterance is given third,
with the adult equivalent of the modified form underlined, (c); a translation of the correct adult utterance is given fourth, (d).

| Adult | Child |

(1) (The child is crying because his pacifier has fallen.
    The mother calms him.)

a. Sad će mama dati dudu.   dudu

Adult	Child

b. 'Now <u>mummy</u> will give   'The pacifier'
    you the pacifier'.

c. Sad ću ti <u>ja</u> dati cuclu.

d. 'Now <u>I</u> will give you the
    pacifier'.

(2) (The girl is trying unsuccessfully to blow up a
     rubber bunny. She shows it to her aunt, who takes
     it and blows it up.)

a. Neće <u>dete</u> da duva, <u>teta</u> će.   nećem, neće

b. 'Baby won't blow, <u>aunty</u>   'blow, blow'
    will'.

c. Nećeš <u>ti</u> da duvaš, <u>ja</u> ću.

d. '<u>You</u> won't blow, <u>I</u> will'.

(3) (The mother is putting the child's shoes on.)

a. Koliko <u>ima</u> <u>Vlada</u> cipela?   de (dve)

b. 'How many shoes <u>has</u> <u>Vlada</u>?'   'two'

c. Koliko <u>ti</u> <u>imaš</u> cipela?

d. 'How many shoes <u>have</u> <u>you</u> got?'

(4) (The aunt is sending the child to the mother,
     telling him that his mother will give him milk.)

a. <u>Mama</u> <u>će</u> ti dati mleko.

b. '<u>Mummy</u> <u>will</u> give you milk'.

c. <u>Ona</u> <u>će</u> dati mleko.

d. '<u>She</u> <u>will</u> give you milk'.

(5) (The mother spreads her arms and calls the child
     to her.)

a. Dodji da <u>mama</u> tebe poljubi.

b. 'Come let <u>mummy</u> kiss you'.

c. Dodji da <u>te</u> poljubim.

d. 'Come let <u>me</u> kiss you'.

162

(6) (The mother is preparing the child's dinner.)

a. Hoće <u>dete</u> jesti?   neće (neću)

b. 'Does my <u>child</u> want   'No, I don't'
   to eat?'

c. Hoćeš da jedeš?

d. 'Do you want to eat?'

The Grammatical Subject is Often 'We', which
Includes Mother and Child Together. This Adaptation
has been Observed Only with Female Relations who are
Emotionally Close to a Child. It indicates the high
degree of identification of the adult with the child
during intimate interaction. The child is at first
completely dependent on the adult, and later partly so.
The adult therefore carries out a large number of
actions for the child. This could be one of the reasons
for this grammatical adaptation. Like the previous one,
this adaptation continues to appear in adult speech
after the child is four years old. Examples included:

           Adult   Child

(1) (The mother prepares to breast-feed the child.)

a. <u>Hoćemo</u> sikiti?

b. '<u>Shall</u> we suck?'

c. Hoćeš da sisaš?

d. 'Do you want to suck?'

c. Hoćeš da ti dam da sisaš?

d. 'Do you want me to let
   you suck?'

(2) (The girl stepped into some mud and got her shoes
     dirty.)

a. Idemo da <u>presvučemo</u> cipele.

b. 'Let's go change our shoes.'

c. Idemo da obuješ druge cipele.

d. 'Let's go put your other shoes
   on.'

c. Idemo da ti obujem druge cipele.

d. 'Let's go and I'll put
    your other shoes on.'

(3) The mother carries the child to the bathroom.)

a. Hoćemo se kupati?

b. 'Shall we have a bath?'

c. Hoćeš se kupati?

d. 'Do you want to have a bath?'

c. Hoću li te kupati?

d. 'Shall I give you a bath?'

Omission of the Copula Form of To Be (Jesam). This
type of adaptation includes the omission of the verb
copula to be in the third person singular je in the
present tense, in the nominal predicate, and in the past
tense. This is more frequent at an early age, when the
child starts to identify objects, persons and phenomena.
At a later age, after three years, this adaptation is
assimilated to a similar phenomenon which is characteristic of colloquial speech of Serbocroatian-speaking adults,
the so-called past tense without the auxiliary verb.

Adult	Child

(1) (The girl has brought a teddy-bear and gives it to
      her mother.)

a. To meda , hvala Tanja.

b. 'That teddy-bear, thank
    you Tanja.'

c. To je meda...

d. 'That's a teddy-bear...'

(2) (The girl complains that she no longer has the
      bandage she had been wearing on her leg because
      she had hurt it.)

a. Pa ne treba više, prošla   Nemam zavoj
    noga.

b. 'You don't need it any-   'I don't have a bandage'
    more, leg well.'

c. ...prošla je noga.

d. '...your leg is well.'

(3)   (The aunt is showing the younger sister how her
      elder sister Nataša has combed the doll's hair.)

a.   Vidi kako je lepa beba.
     Nataša očešljala malu bebu.

b.   'See how nice the baby is.
     Nataša combed the little
     baby.'

c.   ...Nataša je očešljala...

d.   '...Nataša has combed...'

Omission of the Particles Li and Da, and the
Interrogative Da Li.

          Adult   Child

(1)   (The mother is setting the table for dinner.)

a.   Može Vlada da jede?

b.   'Can Vlada eat?'

c.   Može li Vlada da jede?

d.   'Can Vlada eat?'

c.   Možeš li da jedeš?

c.   Da li možeš da jedeš?

d.   'Can you eat?'

(2)   (Mother is addressing the child.)

a.   'Oće Ivan večerati?

b.   'Does Ivan want to eat dinner?'

c.   Hoće li Ivan večerati?

d.   'Does Ivan want to eat dinner?'

c.   Hoćeš li večerati?

c.   Da li hoćeš da večeraš?

d.   'Do you want to eat dinner?'

(3)   (The mother addresses her son in a tender voice.)

a.   Voli Vlada svoju mamu?

b.   'Does Vlada love his mummy?'

c. Voli li Vlada svoju mamu?

d. 'Does Vlada love his mummy?'

c. Voliš li ti svoju mamu?/mene/

c. Da li voliš svoju mamu?/mene/

d. 'Do you love your mummy?/me/'

> The use of the interrogative da li is very rare in the speech of all our adult subjects. The reason for this probably lies in its low frequency in colloquial speech. The omission of da li is frequently combined with the use of names rather than personal pronouns.

Specific Types of Imperatives

Adult	Child

(1) (The child wants to throw a piece of bread on the floor.)

a. Ne baciti!

c. Ne bacaj!

c. Nemoj baciti!

b./d. 'Don't throw!'

(2) (The child is crying very hard and his mother wants to make him stop.)

a. No, no, ne plakati!

c. Ne plači!

c. Nemoj plakati!

b./d. 'Don't cry!'

> A special type of imperative, negation no (ne) plus infinitive, plus exclamatory intonation, appears most frequently when the child is little.

> At a very early age, another type of imperative is used: a modified lexeme plus exclamatory intonation. These imperatives incorporate the lexeme kaka, which belongs to the lexical inventory used by Serbocroatian-speaking adults for communicating with children. Kaka signifies something dirty, ugly, something that should not be touched, eaten or done.

<table>
<tr><td>Adult</td><td>Child</td></tr>
</table>

(3) (The child picks his pacifier off the floor and
     wants to put it back in his mouth. His mother re-
     acts to this.)

a. Kaka to!

c. Ostavi to, to je prljavo!

b./d. 'Leave that, it's
       dirty!'

(4) (The child wants to put a ballpoint pen in his mouth.)

a. Pi, kaka!

c. Ne stavljaj to u usta, prlja-
    vo je!

b./d. 'Don't put that in your
       mouth, it's dirty!'

(5) (The child has put his hand into an ash-tray full of
     cigarette butts. His grandmother is reacting to
     this.)

a. Kaka!

c. Ostavi(ne diraj) to je
    prljavo!

b./d. 'Leave that alone (don't
       touch that) it's dirty!'

      Adaptations in Word Order.   In standard Serbocroa-
tian the attribute comes before and not after the noun.
There are instances of consistent change in the standard
Serbocroatian word order when addressing children.

Adult	Child

(1) (In his toy-chest the child has found a picture-book
     and he asks his mother who bought it.)

a. Mama tvoja   Ko je ovo kupio?

b. 'Mummy your'.   'Who bought this?'

c. Tvoja mama.

d. 'Your mummy'.

c. Ja sam kupila.

d. 'I bought it'.

(2)   (The aunt asks the younger child who is alone with
        her in the room.)

a.   Gde je sestra tvoja?

b.   'Where is sister your?'

c.   Gde je tvoja sestra?

d.   'Where is your sister?'

(3)   (The adult is showing the child a picture of a small
        baby in a book.)

a.   Vidi, beba mala.

b.   'Look, a baby small'.

c.   Vidi, mala beba.

d.   'Look, a small baby'.

          This type of modified word order appears in a
number of emotionally coloured adults' utterances addressed to the child: when the adult is particularly pleased
with the child, when he praises the child. Such examples
are: Decko moj lepi 'Little boy my lovely' instead of
Moj lepi dečko 'My lovely little boy'; Veliki moj dečko
'Big my boy' instead of Moj veliki dečko 'My big boy';
Luče moje belo 'Doll my white' instead of Moje belo luče
'My white doll'; Mače moje malo 'Kitten my little' instead
of Moje malo mače 'My little kitten'; Sunce milo moje
'Little sunshine dear my' instead of Moje milo sunce 'My
dear little sunshine; Sunce milo majkino 'Little sunshine dear mother's' instead of Milo majkino sunce 'Dear
mother's little sunshine'. This type of adaptation continues to be used, particularly in emotional utterances
addressed by parents to children, regardless of the age
of the children.

          Adaptations in Asking Questions.

          Adult   Child

(1)   (The mother wants to praise the child for picking
        all his toys up from the floor.)

a.   Ko sluša mamu?

b.   'Who listens to mummy?'

(2)   (The mother brings home her son who has had a hair-
        cut; the grandmother asks:)

a. Ko se ošišao?

b. 'Who has had a haircut?'

(3) (The mother addresses the child tenderly.)

a. Koga majka voli?

b. 'Whom does mother love?'

(4) (The mother takes the child into a store to buy him a toy car.)

a. Kome će majka kupiti auto?

b. 'Who is going to get a car?'

(5) (The mother pets the child.)

a. Koje je mamina lepa glava?

b. 'Which is mummy's pretty head?'

(6) (The mother kisses the child's eye.)

a. Gde je mamino oko?

b. 'Where's mummy's eye?'

(7) (The mother plays with the child's feet after giving him a bath.)

a. Čije su ovo nožice?

b. 'Whose little feet are these?'

The essence of this type of adaptation is that the adult is not really asking a question. He knows the answer already. He asks these questions for purely emotional reasons. It is a pleasure for him to hear the answer from the child, since the question concerns his relationship with the child. It is the mother who most often asks such questions. This type of adaptation also becomes a mannerism in adults close to children and it is found during the entire observation period.

Simplicity. Authors who have written about syntactic modifications in adults' speech addressed to very young children have emphasized that adults' sentences are shorter, less complex, that there are fewer causal and relative clauses, and that there is no passive. This is also true of the Serbocroatian speech sample. In addition to this, adults restrict the use of verb forms for denoting time to the present and past tense. For a more quantified approach to this phenomenon in adult

speech, it is necessary to determine the frequency of
these categories in everyday adult colloquial speech.
A very impressionistic view suggests that these categories are rare in everyday adult to adult speech in Serbocroatian. Of course the topics about which adults usually communicate with children must also be borne in mind.
Due to the cognitive level of the child, all child topics
are modified and limited, and so they call for a simpler
manner of expression.

MORPHO-SEMANTIC MODIFICATION

Within the scope of morpho-semantic adaptation,
the writer has found, like many other authors who have
studied adults' speech addressed to children in various
languages, a large number of diminutives (prstić 'little
finger'; krevetić little bed'; nonica 'little pot';
mišić 'little mouse'; glavica 'little head'; Tanjuša,
Šarica, Vladica), and hypocoristics (majka/mama, 'mother/
mummy'; seka/sestra, 'little sister/sister'; lane 'little
deer'; luče 'little doll'; sunce 'little sunshine';
dušo 'dear'; pile 'chick'; mače 'kitten'; meda 'teddy-
bear'; zeka 'little rabbit'; kuca 'puppy').

Lexical adaptations in adult speech also include
the occurrence of a large number of modified lexemes of
a universal kind. For instance, no, no, 'don't touch, you
musn't do that, you're not being good'; opa, 'get up,
jump'; pec! 'it's hot, don't touch it'; pa-pa, a form of
leave taking, 'to go, to go away'; dje-dje, 'horse';
tu-tu, ti-ti, di-di, 'automobile'; vau-vau, 'puppy, dog';
papati, 'to eat'; duda, 'pacifier'; nona, nosa, 'chamber
pot'; ziza, 'light bulb, fire, source of light'.

The adult subjects also imitated and used
lexemes which each individual child created and which
other adults, outside the family circle, did not understand until they were explained to them. For example:
lololo, 'tongue'; tutau, 'cock'; za-za, 'water, drink';
ga-ga, 'chocolate'; pokolo, 'everything's broken down,
broken'; ea, 'pencil'; daga, 'pencil, paper, station-
ery'; jao, 'to fall down, to hit, to wreck'; zzzz,
'vacuum cleaner'.

A very characteristic type of lexeme adaptation
which occurs in adults' speech under the influence of
child speech, and which is then carried over to adult-
adult communication, is the phenomenon of addressing
particular people in the child's environment by the name
the child uses for them. There are two variations of
this type of adaptation:

(a) influenced by the child's speech, adults from his
closer or wider circle start to call his mother mama, his

father tata, his grandmother baba, his grandfather deda, his aunt tetka or teta and so on, although these forms of address do not denote kinship but rather indirect identification with the child.

(b) adults accept and begin to use permanently the name of a person from the child's circle in the child's modified form, which originated from his inability to pronounce the full name. In this way, a particular individual acquires and retains a new name in the family circle and outside it. For instance, Jelka becomes Eka, Djole becomes Dota, Nada becomes Dada.

As a result of adult speech adaptation initiated with children, the spontaneous use of hypocoristics, diminutives and phrases of the inverted word order type sine moj, dete moje, mali moj, mili moj, dušo moja, srce moje lepo appears in adults' communication with other adults.

CONCLUSION

When adults communicate with a small child they adapt their speech to the child's communicative competence in accordance with how they interpret a child's utterance. Adaptation in adults' communication with a child is deter-mined by the emotional tie with the child, the unequal cognitive and experiential capacities of the adult and the child, and the need to achieve successful communication between the adult and the child.

Speech adaptation in an adult's communication with the child results from (a) an attempt to communicate with the child more successfully and become more firmly bound to him; (b) the effect of continual care for and communication with the child. The stronger the emotional tie between the adult and the child, and the more the adult cares for the child, the more frequent are the ob-served types of grammatical adaptation.

Several types of syntactic and morpho-semantic adaptation have been found in the speech of the adult subjects: the use of nouns instead of personal pronouns and finite verbal forms, the use of the first person plural instead of the first and second person singular (present tense), the omission of the verb copula jesam, the omission of the particles li and da and the inter-rogative expression da li, the use of specific types of imperatives, adaptation in word order, and adaptation in asking questions. Some syntactic adaptations in regard to sentence structure and the use of tenses also occur, but it was not possible to discuss these fully in this paper.

The morpho-semantic adaptations included the use of a large number of diminutives and hypocoristics, the use of a large number of modified lexemes of a universal type, the use of lexemes created by the individual child which became part of the familiar code in the family circle, and adaptation in addressing particular individuals. It should be noted that some types of adaptation in adults' speech remained in constant use and can be found in adult-adult communication.

REFERENCES

Jocić, M. (1975)   Adult Interpretations of Child Utterances: Their Function in Adult-child Verbal Communication. Psyhologia Wychowawcza, No.4, Tom XVIII (XXXII). Krakow.

Vasić, V. (1976)   The Verbal Interaction between the Older and the Younger Child in the Micro-environment. Language in Social Context. Proceedings of the conference 'Language and Society', Beograd.

Conversations between Mothers and Young Children: Individual Differences and their Possible Implication for the Study of Language Learning

E.V.M. Lieven

This paper will focus on some perhaps obvious but in my opinion somewhat neglected, features of language development in children. Firstly, mothers and children have conversations. Secondly, mother-child pairs differ markedly in how they talk to each other. Thirdly, children have effects on mothers as well as the other way round.

One of the most striking features in the protocols of children's speech which many investigators have been struggling with over the years is that, with very few exceptions, they are conversations, usually between the mother and child, sometimes with other adults or children, (Ryan, 1974 ;   Keenan and Klein, 1974;   Bates, 1975).

We depend on their being conversations for many aspects of our analysis.   For one thing it would often be impossible to interpret what the child was saying at all if

*The study reported in this paper was supported by a grant for training in research methods from the Medical Research Council, London, England.

I am more than grateful to Joanna Ryan for supervising me for the research on which this paper is based, to Catherine Snow and Gerald Gazdar for their criticism and encouragement and to John McShane for help in the final stages.

it were not that the response to him or her almost always
clarifies his or her previous utterance. Many of the
suggestions that have been made as to the possible helpful
ness of various aspects of adults' speech to children have
implicitly involved the fact that the mother and child are
having a conversation. For instance the whole debate
about the possible usefulness of expansions and extensions
(Brown and Bellugi, 1964; Brown, Cazden and Bellugi, 1969
Cross, this volume) is premised on the finding that many o
the mothers studied responded to their children's utteranc
with an expanded version of what the child had just said.
The educative potential of such interchanges in which the
child may, of course, respond in turn to the mother's
expansion, is clear. This implies that the mother and
child are involved in reciprocal verbal interchange, in
turn-taking in conversation. Another example: considerable discussion has centred around the very high proportion of questions in adults' speech to young children
relative to their normal speech, (Remick, 1972; Sachs,
Brown and Salerno, 1976). Questions, at least in speech
among adults, presuppose answers and are, according to
Sachs, Schegloff and Jefferson (1974), a device for en-
suring continued turn-taking in conversation.

If it is the case then, that certain features of
the adults' speech to the child are both important to
language learning and dependent on conversation-like
interactions between adult and child, it would be interest
ing to re-examine protocols in terms of the conversationa\
skills of the participants. Catherine Snow (1975) has
argued that the interactions between the two children in
her study and their mothers gave the impression, at 18
months, of being 'proper' conversations. This was in par\
due to the mothers' effectiveness in keeping the conversation going despite the inadequacies of the children (i.\
interrupting, failing to answer) but also because the
children were reasonably adequate turn-takers by this age
although in other respects their language was not particularly advanced. Looking at conversations between these
mothers and their children from 3 to 18 months, she showe\
how the mothers treated their children as partners from a
very early age and how initially they would accept almost
anything (e.g. a burp) as constituting the baby's turn.
As the children grew older, the mothers became more stringent in their criterion of what was an acceptable utteran\
on the part of the child, although they were still willin\
to accept 'almost any conversational opening on the part
of the child and to fill in for the child whenever necessary' (Snow, 1975).

In analyzing the data from two of the children
whose language development was being studied, a very mark\
degree of individual difference both between the two children's speech and between that of the two mothers to them
became obvious. On looking more closely, it was clear
that the child-mother pairs were also very different in

terms of the conversational skills described by Snow. One child-mother pair conformed to Snow's description of conversational interaction between the two pairs in her study when the children were 18 months old, but the other mother-child pair in my study appeared to be interacting very differently and, at least on the surface, not to be having conversations at all.

Data to illustrate these points is taken from a study of these two mother-child pairs over a six-month period for each child. The children were seen in their homes with their mothers. Recordings were made at approximately fortnightly intervals but the data presented here are taken from sessions when only the mother, child and investigator were present.

The investigator behaved, and seemed to be treated, as a familiar visitor by both mothers and children. One child (Beth) was 20 months at the start of the study and the other (Kate) was 18 months. Beth was second-born with a brother who was two years older. Kate was first-born. Both mothers spent all day at home with the children at the time of this study and both fathers had professional occupations. Tape recordings were made with a Uher 2000 Report L and sessions lasted 45 minutes. Summary descriptions of the sessions are presented in Table 1.

THE CHILDREN'S SPEECH

In terms of MLU (measured in words), the children were not very different. At 20 months, Beth's MLU was 1.16 and Kate's was 1.10. By approximately 25 months, Beth's MLU had increased to 1.76 and Kate's to 1.98. Kate therefore appears to be only slightly ahead of Beth at 25 months. In other respects however the children did differ very markedly.

Beth was at least twice as repetitive as Kate in all sessions. Beth said a small number of words over and over again in both her single-word and multiple-word utterances. In all sessions the words mummy, look, there and Sebastian (Beth's brother) were the most frequently used. Her multiple-word utterances gave the appearance of lacking word order rules. For instance, in the session at 25.0 there were nine occurrences of Sebastian there, four of there Sebastian, two of there Sebastian there and one of Sebastian, Sebastian there Sebastian, to say nothing of there Sebastian mummy, mummy there Sebastian etc., etc. To make matters more confusing, Sebastian was not present at the time and Beth was not pointing to one of his possessions or at pictures in a book. These and nearly all of her utterances were made in a high-pitched excited tone and appeared to be attempts to attract her mother's attention.

176

TABLE 1.   Summary description of sessions

Session	Age (Months, weeks)	MLU	Total number of comprehensible utterances	Type/ Token ratio	Comprehensible utterances minute
Kate					
1	18.2	1.07	65	.59	1.7
2	19.1	1.10	66	.66	4.3
3	20.3	1.14	195	.46	6.4
4	22.3	1.54	201	.44	7.8
5	24.3	1.98	263	.46	6.9
Beth					
1	20.0	1.16	72	.33	2.8
2	22.1	1.22	163	.26	5.2
3	24.0	1.30	163	.26	5.3
4	25.1	1.76	170	.27	9.3
5	26.1	2.23	342	.12	9.3

A comprehensible utterance was defined
as an utterance containing only one or
more lexical items of English but including items which the child used idiosyncratically but systematically as
lexical items if these were agreed to
be such by the mother and the investigator.

The children's spontaneous multiple-word utterances were analyzed into semantic-syntactic categories based largely on those used by Bloom, Hood and Lightbown (1974). Categories were defined as follows:

Notice. Utterances that called attention to the existence of an object and included a notice verb such as 'see' or 'look' or the form 'hello' (changed from 'hi' in Bloom's definition) as in hello spoon. e.g. look mummy.[1]

Locative Action. Utterances that made reference to movement that had the goal of affecting an object by changing its location in space. e.g. hand off, stick it there, go on self.

Existence. Utterances that made reference only to the fact of an object in the environment as the child either touched, looked or pointed to it. e.g. there moon, there hand there.

Recurrence. Utterances that made reference to the reappearance of an object or another instance of an object or event. e.g. more mummy, more car bang.

Attribution. Utterances that made reference to properties of objects with respect to a) the inherent state of the object e.g. hot fire; b) a specification of the object which could distinguish it from others in its class e.g. red bird; c) quantity of objects e.g. two shoes.

Possession. Utterances that made reference to objects within the domains of different persons e.g. mine car, frogs dinner.

State. Utterances that specify an internal state that was transitory and referred to animate objects e.g. I want biscuit, lion hungry.

These definitions are simplified from Bloom et al. (1974) with my own examples added from the children's speech. It should be emphasized that it is always necessary to know the context in which an utterance occurs before it is possible to assign it to a particular category. It proved easier to assign Kate's utterances to these categories than those of Beth. In the case of Beth, the illocutionary force of the utterance seemed considerably more relevant for an analysis of her utterances than did an analysis based on semantic relations. This is not, of course, a claim to the effect that a pragmatic analysis is mutually exclusive of a semantic analysis. On the

contrary, the question is whether some children express
the illocutionary force of their utterance in part by
using generative semantic relations while others may
succeed well in conveying illocutionary force by combining words in a way that does not imply the possession of
a small set of linguistically expressible semantic relations. Only those categories to which the assignment of
Beth's utterances was relatively unproblematic are include
for analysis here.

Figure 1 shows the percentage of utterance type
falling into each of the above categories in sessions 2-5
Percentages are of total number of spontaneous multiple-
word utterances in each session. As very few multiple-wo
utterances occurred in session 1 for either child, they
have not been included.

Beth produced relatively more utterances which
fall into the categories of 'notice', 'existence' and 'recurrence' while relatively few, if any of Kate's utterances fall into these categories. Kate's utterances fall
relatively more often into the categories of 'locative
action' or 'attribution'. Even in those categories into
which approximately similar percentages of the two children's utterances fall, i.e. 'possession' and 'state', the
utterances themselves were of a somewhat different type.
There were only two possessors in Beth's utterances: her
self (represented by 'my' or 'mine') and Sebastian. A mucl
greater number of people and animals were treated as
possessors by Kate. Similarly all Beth's 'state' utterances contained the verb 'want' and appeared to refer to
herself, while Kate, as well as talking about wanting
things, also discussed the hunger of the lion, the fact
that she liked the lollies and so on.

These two children appeared to be using languag
for different ends. Kate talked slowly and coherently
about things happening around her and objects in her
environment while Beth devoted more time to using her
speech to try and engage her mother's interest. These
characteristics relate to features of the mothers' own
speech to their children.

THE MOTHERS' SPEECH

The speech of both mothers to their children
showed many of the features which by now have become
familiar (cf. Snow, 1977).   In comparison with their
speech to the investigator in the same sessions, the MLUs
of the mothers' speech were much lower to their children.
The MLU to the children, measured in morphemes for sessio

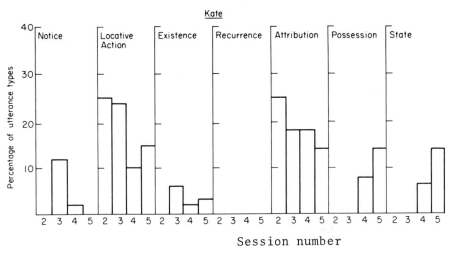

Total number of utterances per session:
    Session 2 = 4;   Session 3 = 17
    Session 4 =51;   Session 5 = 98.

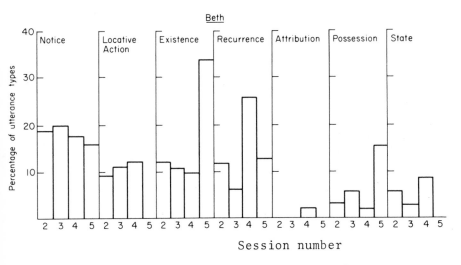

Total number of utterances per session:
    Session 2 = 33;   Session 3 = 34
    Session 4 = 64;   Session 5 =230.

Fig. 1.   Semantic-syntactic utterance types for spontaneous multiple-word utterances in sessions 2-5.

180

TABLE 2.   Mothers' responses to the children's
            utterances.

	Kate's mother	Beth's mother
Percentage of Comprehensible utterances to which mother did not respond*	19%	54%
Types of non-response:**		
>2 seconds silence	35%	28%
mother in conversation	25%	34%
child speaks again in <2 secs.	40%	38%
Questions in response to child's utterance***	36%	23%

*   Percentages are of total number of comprehensible
        child utterances for sessions 1-5.

**   Percentages are of total number of comprehensible
        child utterances not responded to by either the
        mother or the investigator for sessions 1-5.

***   Percentages are of total number of mother's
        responses to the child's utterances for
        sessions 1-5.

1, 2 and 3 was 7.25 for Kate's mother and 5.61 for Beth's
mother. It was considerably more difficult to measure
the MLU of the mothers' speech to the investigator, mainly
because of the problem of determining the end of an utterance. However, average values of about 14.0 morphemes for
Kate's mother and 20.0 morphemes for Beth's mother were
obtained after somewhat ad hoc decisions on this point had
been taken. The mothers used less subordinate clauses and
considerably more imperatives and interrogatives to the
children. However there were also some differences between
these mothers in their speech to their children and this is
clearly reflected in an analysis of their responses to the
children's utterances. None of the measures in the analysis presented here showed any developmental trend over
the five sessions and they have therefore been collapsed
into an average percentage for the purposes of this paper.
Measures were made of the frequency with which the mother
responded to an utterance of the child within two seconds
(chosen by inspection as the interval within which virtually
all responses fall); and of the outcome in cases where the
mother did not appear to respond. This was analyzed into
occasions after a child's utterance when there was at least
two seconds silence; those during and/or after which the
mother was talking to the investigator; and those after
which the child spoke again within two seconds. The
figures are given in Table 2. It will be seen that, on
average, Kate's mother failed to respond to only 19% of
Kate's utterances, while Beth's mother, on average failed
to respond to 54% of Beth's. When we look at what happened
when the mother did not respond, we can see that Beth's
mother was particularly likely to simply continue her conversation with the investigator. Kate's mother in contrast, tended to interrupt herself in conversation with
the investigator in order to answer Kate.

It is also the case that when the two mothers
did respond, Kate's mother was more likely to respond with
a question to Kate (see bottom of Table 2). This would
presumably have had the effect of extending the conversation. One could, I think, fairly deduce from these observations that there is less turn-taking in conversations
between Beth and her mother than there is between Kate
and her mother. Beth's mother made less effort to keep
the conversation going and showed less interest in what
Beth was saying. This is also demonstrated when we look
at the types of responses made by the mothers when they
did answer the child within two seconds. In both the
case of Beth and Kate, the main category of adult response
not included in Table 3 is a residual category of responses
which were judged to be conversationally appropriate to
the child's utterance but not to fall into any of the other
categories. About 20% of both the mothers' responses fell
into this category. A further 13% in Kate's case and 11%
in Beth's is accounted for by word-for-word repeats by the
mother either of what the child had just said or of what
she herself had said just previous to the child's utterance.

TABLE 3.   Types of maternal responses to the children's
            utterances

Types of response	Kate's mother	Beth's mother
Extension	33%	9%
Expansion	15%	10%
Query	2%	5%
Ignore	9%	14%
Correct	2%	11%
Ready-mades	4%	21%

Percentages are of total number of
mother's responses to the child's
utterances for sessions 1-5. They do
not sum to 100 due to utterances in
residual categories.

Categories of response type are defined as
follows (and included here are only those categories on
which the two mothers showed some differences).

Expansion.   An utterance in which the adult expands
the child's utterance to a syntactically correct equivalen
without adding any more new semantic information than is
required to render the child's utterance syntactically.

Extension.   An utterance in which the adult, in
addition to expanding the child's utterance, adds new
semantic information in excess of that required to render
the child's utterance syntactically.

Query.   An utterance in which the adult explicitly
asks the child what he/she has just said.

Ignore.   An utterance in which the adult seems to
ignore the content of the child's previous utterance,
where this utterance itself was not related to any prior
utterance of the adult's.

Correct.   An utterance in which the adult explicitl
corrects the syntactic, semantic or phonological content
of the child's previous utterance.

Ready-Made. An utterance which does not fall into any grammatical class and which is defined by Lyons (1968) as 'expressions learnt as unanalysable wholes and employed on particular occasions by native speakers'. Examples are: 'yes', 'no', 'please', 'thank you', 'oh dear', 'jolly good'.

From Table 3, it can be seen that Kate's mother responds to Kate with a high proportion of extensions and expansions relative to Beth's mother. The latter has a higher probability of either responding to Beth with a ready-made word or phrase, or of correcting the child or ignoring her previous utterance in her reply. Where Beth is responded to, therefore, she is less likely to hear an utterance that relates specifically to what she has just said or provides her with new information, but she is also more likely to be explicitly corrected about her actual utterance.

To summarize then, these two children's mothers talked to them very differently. Kate's mother seems highly responsive to what Kate says and her utterances seem to be closely related to it. Beth's mother seems considerably less 'tuned-in' to Beth's speech and less accepting of it. There are also differences in the children's own speech which indicate that the children have learnt to converse in different ways about different things.

THE IMPLICATIONS OF INDIVIDUAL DIFFERENCES

Clearly one cannot make any causal statement on the basis of two children. Indeed it is doubtful that causal statements would be at all appropriate however many children were under consideration. Rather than labouring the implication that the speech styles of the two mothers are somehow 'responsible' for the differences in their children's speech, it may be useful briefly to look at the problem from two, perhaps less common, perspectives.

Firstly there will certainly be more or less important effects of the child upon various aspects of the adult's speech to him/her from a very early age and, in particular, the effects of styles of speech may be two-way, even between a two-year old child and an adult. For instance an analysis of the investigator's (my) speech to the children indicates that the differences in their speech may have influenced the way that the investigator spoke to them. This is shown in Table 4.

TABLE 4. Types of response by the investigator to the children's utterances

Types of response	to Kate*** (Session 5)	to Beth** *** (Sessions 1-5)
Extension	27%	16%
Expansion	27%	18%
Query	3%	0
Ignore	0	8%
Correct	0	2%
Ready-made	0	10%

* Percentages are of total number of responses by the investigator to child's utterances in Session 5.

** Percentages are of total number of responses by the investigator to child's utterances in Sessions 1-5.

*** Percentages do not sum to 100 due to utterances in residual categories. About 26% of the investigator's responses to both Kate and Beth fell into the residual category of utterances judged to be conversationally appropriate but not to fall into any of the other categories. A further 16% in both cases were accounted for by word-for-word repeats of either what the child had just said or of what the investigator herself had said just prior to the child's utterance.

Only in one session with Kate, Session 5, were there enough responses by the investigator to Kate's utterances, to justify an analysis. This was due to two factors. Firstly Beth spoke directly to the investigator considerably more often than Kate did. Secondly, Kate's mother was very highly responsive to Kate's utterances and gave the investigator little opportunity to enter into conversation with Kate even had she wished to. The reverse was true in the sessions with Beth when the investigator often felt constrained to enter into some sort of dialogue with the child. These differences are in themselves very interesting and, apart from their implications for the development of language skills in the

children, they very likely reflect important features of
the developing social relationships of these children
which would bear considerably more analysis.

It will be seen from Table 4 that the way in
which the investigator responds to the two children is
somewhat different and that furthermore it is, in each
case, more similar to that of the mother to whose child
she is responding at the time than to the mother of the
other child. However, the investigator did not extend
Kate's utterances as much as Kate's mother did and she
both expanded and extended Beth's utterances more frequently than Beth's mother while ignoring and correcting
her less. She also used less ready-made utterances to
Beth than Beth's mother did. It would be possible to
argue that this was an effect of the mother on the investigator, i.e. that the investigator was imitating each
mother's speech style with her child. However, I, as the
investigator, found it much easier to carry on a conversation with Kate than I did with Beth. It is difficult to
respond informatively, for instance to expand or extend
utterances which are extremely repetitive and seem not to
relate clearly to anything in the immediate context; in
fact it is often very difficult to say anything other
than 'yes', 'no' or 'really?'. My impression is that
these figures reflect a possible influence of the child's
speech on the adult. If this is the case, then however
it was that Beth and Kate came to speak the way that they
did, it is possible that they would evoke in others who
were conversing with them, a speech style similar to that
of their mothers. That is to say, a child, by virtue of
the way that she/he talks, may be influencing the way in
which other people speak to her/him.

Secondly, if it turns out to be the case (1)
that many of the features of adult speech that have been
noted in the literature as potentially helpful to the
language-learning child are dependent for their efficacy
on the already acquired conversational skills of the child,
and (2) that individual differences in language learning
are related to individual differences in conversational
interaction between the child and others, then perhaps we
shall have to look more closely at the development of pragmatic skills in young children. Amongst other things,
this would involve investigating individual differences in
the development of turn-taking in infancy and possible
manifestations of these during the period of language
learning.

One final point is the importance of defining in
each case under discussion what the end-point of language
learning is considered to be. In superficial terms, Beth
and Kate, who are by now at school, are judged to be fluent
speakers of English. It may be, however, that there are
differences in their conversation styles and, perhaps,
skills, that may have more far-reaching implications for

their general development than a test of, say, their
syntactic or semantic abilities would show. At 25 months,
Beth was violating Grice's (1975) conversational maxims
of manner and relevance; she was neither brief, relevant
nor orderly. Kate, although the same age and not particularly advanced in other aspects of her language development, managed those skills well. On the other hand, within the context of their families, both children succeeded
in making their wishes known and both seemed happy, intelligent children with no obvious problems. We really have
no idea as yet what, if any, significance the presence of
such marked individual differences in the children's
speech might have or at what aspects of later behaviour
we should be looking for their effects.

Notes.

1.   There is a confusion in the analysis here which re-
      quires further elaboration. It appears that those
      utterances of Beth which were placed in this category
      all had the pragmatic force of demanding the mother's
      (or investigator's) attention and this was reflected
      semantically in the fact that they did not, in fact,
      call attention to the existence of an object linguis-
      tically specified in the utterance by the child. The
      utterances of Kate which were placed in this category
      did turn out, however, on reinspection, to belong to
      a genuinely semantic category as defined.

2.   Categories not included here which occurred in the
      children's speech are action-on-affected object;
      state-location of object; rejection-denial;
      non-existence   (cf. Bloom et al., 1974). A number
      of multiple-word utterances appeared to be rote-
      learnt and are also not included in the analysis.
      Examples are please mummy and thank you (mainly by
      Kate) and what's that (by Beth).

REFERENCES

Bates, E. (1975)   The Development of Conversational Skills
          in 2, 3 and 4 year olds. Pragmatics Microfiche
          1.5.

Bloom, L., Hood, L. and Lightbown, P. (1974)   Imitation
          in Language Development: If, When and Why.
          Cognitive Psychology 6. 380-420.

Brown, R. and Bellugi, U. (1964)   Three Processes in the
Child's Acquisition of Syntax.   In E. Lenneberg
(ed.) New Directions in the Study of Language.
M.I.T. Press, Cambridge, Mass.

Brown, R., Cazden, C. and Bellugi, U. (1969)   The Child's
Grammar from 1 to 111.   In J. Hill (ed.)
Minnesota Symposia on Child Psychology 2.
University of Minnesota Press, Minneapolis.

Grice, H.P. (1975)   Logic and Conversation.   In P. Cole,
and J. Morgan (eds.) Syntax and Semantics 111:
Speech Acts.   Academic Press, New York.

Keenan, E.O. and Klein, E. (1974)   Coherency in Children's
Discourse.   Paper presented at the summer meeting
of the Linguistic Society of America.   Amherst,
Massachusetts, July.

Lyons, J. (1968)   Introduction to Theoretical Linguistics.
Cambridge University Press, Cambridge.

Remick, H. (1976)   Maternal Speech to Children during
Language Acquisition.   In W. von Raffler-Engel
and Y. Lebrun (eds.) Baby Talk and Infant
Speech.   Swets and Zeitlinger, Amsterdam.

Ryan, J. (1974)   Early Language Development: Towards
a Communicational Analysis.   In M.P.M. Richards
(ed.) The Integration of a Child into a Social
World.   Cambridge University Press, Cambridge.

Sachs, J., Brown, R. and Salerno, R. (1976)   Adults'
Speech to Children.   In W. von Raffler-
Engel and Y. Lebrun (eds.)   Baby Talk and
Infant Speech.   Swets and Zeitlinger,
Amsterdam.

Sacks, H., Schegloff, E. and Jefferson, G. (1974)
A Simplest Systematics for the Organisation
of Turn-Taking in Conversation. Language 50.
696-735.

Snow, C.E. (1977)   Mothers' Speech Research: from
Input to Interaction.   In C.E. Snow and C.A.
Ferguson (eds.) Talking to Children: Language
Input and Acquisition.   Cambridge University
Press, Cambridge.

Snow, C.E. (1975)   The Development of Conversation
Between Mothers and Babies.   Pragmatics Microfiche. 1.6 A2.

Differential Socialization of Girls and Boys: Implications for Sex Differences in Language Development

L. Cherry and M. Lewis

Differential socialization of female and male children is one explanation for sex differences in behaviour. We can examine caregiver-child interaction for sex differences to ascertain if differences exist, and then consider what the implications of these differences are for the language development of children. In this paper, we will review studies of the relationship between adult-child interactional style and the language development

*An earlier version of this paper was presented at the Annual Meeting of the American Sociological Association, San Francisco, August 1975. This research was supported by a USPHS Postdoctoral Fellowship (MH-08260). The authors express their appreciation to Walter Emmerich, Roy Freedle, and Marilyn Shatz for their helpful comments on an earlier version of this paper, and to Jane Leifer for her help in the data analysis. A full description of the methods of data collection is available in Cherry and Lewis, in press.

of children, as well as studies of sex differences in these styles. We will then summarize the findings from a study of interaction between mothers and two-year-olds and discuss the implications of the study for the question we have raised.

There is a widespread belief that girls are 'better' at verbal skills than boys, learning them earlier and more quickly than boys (Bardwick, 1971; Maccoby and Jacklin, 1974; Sherman, 1971),even in the absence of any conclusive evidence that such differences exist (Cherry, 1975b). One approach to this question is to explore the possible origins of these differences, including the verbal interactions in which the child and caregiver participate.

One hypothesis about the relationship between adult-child interactional style and the language development of children is that adults adjust their speech in terms of syntactic complexity to match the level of the child's linguistic ability. The assumption underlying the 'syntactic fine tuning' hypothesis is that this simplified language input to the child is functional for learning language, since it provides a very good data base from which the child can construct the grammar of the language (Broen, 1972; Phillips, 1973; Snow, 1972). Neither the origins nor the effects of this behaviour pattern of adults has been established. Another consideration with regard to this hypothesis is that the child's direct interactions with adults, those in which he participates as speaker and hearer, are only one source of language input to the child. Indirect interactions are another, e.g. those in which the child observes. Indirect interactions may be another critical source of language knowledge for the child, since language is such an important and frequent action among people.

Few studies have addressed the question of the origins and consequences of adult-child interactional style and the child's language development. Newport, Gleitman and Gleitman's (1975) study provides disconfirming evidence for the 'syntactic fine tuning' hypothesis. The results of this longitudinal study of 15 mother-daughter pairs showed that few measures of the syntactic complexity or well-formedness of mothers' speech predicted syntactic language growth during a six-month period during the children's second and third years. A study by Cross (this volume) also provides evidence that syntactic aspects of speech are not the primary source of variation in adults' speech to the child. Her study of mother-child pairs suggests that there are major differences at the discourse or conversational level of speech between mothers of fast and slow language learners. Mothers of fast learners

used more utterances that were semantically related to
the child's preceding utterance, fewer incidences of
disrupted speech, and fewer utterances per turn at speaking, as well as a finer degree of grammatical tailoring
to the child's level of linguistic development. Adults
do speak in a style roughly appropriate to the child's
linguistic abilities, even though these studies dis-
confirm the specific 'syntactic fine tuning' hypothesis.

An alternative hypothesis about the relationship between adult-child interactional style and the
language development of children is that language development is part of the socialization process that
characterizes the child's transactions with others
(Cherry, 1976; Lewis and Cherry, 1976). Potentially
relevant characteristics of the participants in the
socialization process include sex, sibling status, and
level of cognitive and language development. Questions
such as whether the particular modifications that adults
direct to children are functional for the child's development can be addressed.

There have been few studies of sex differences
in adult-child interaction during this important period
of rapid language growth. Overall, these studies have
reported no significant sex differences, but they have
limited their analysis to adult speech variables such
as quantity of speech, lexical variation, and syntactic
complexity and have not included any conversational
measures such as question asking and answering (Fraser
and Roberts, 1975; Halverson and Waldrop, 1970; Phillips,
1973). There are, however, a number of studies which
report sex differences in mother-infant verbal/vocal
interaction (Goldberg and Lewis, 1969; Lewis and
Freedle, 1973; Moss, 1967). These studies report
greater verbal/vocal quantity and responsivity for
mother-daughter interaction than for mother-son interaction although this tendency is by no means universal-
ly reported (Maccoby and Jacklin, 1974).

In order to address the question of the differential socialization of male and female children in
verbal interaction with caregivers, and to determine if
this early pattern of greater verbal/vocal quantity and
responsivity for mother-female pairs continued into the
years of rapid language growth, we conducted a study of
interaction between mothers and two-year-olds in a play
situation. Six middle class males and six middle class
females matched for birth order were observed for 15
minutes in a free play laboratory situation. Both
mother and child were free to interact in any way they
wanted to. There were a number of toys available for
the child. The spontaneous behaviour of the mothers and
the children were recorded on audiotape; and the last
five minutes were also recorded on videotape.

The audiotape recordings were transcribed including everything that was said by the mother and the child during the play period. The transcripts were typed and coded 'blind' with respect to the sex of the child, and then these transcripts were coded according to the following quantitative and qualitative measures. Quantitative measures included: 1) total number of utterances, 2) total number of turns, 3) total number of morphemes, 4) total number of words. The qualitative measures which reflected verbal responsivity included: 1) speakers' repeating each others' utterances (other repetition), 2) mothers' use of directives (requests for action), 3) questions (requests for information), 4) acknowledgments, and 5) children's answering their mothers' questions. The reliabilities for these codes were all greater than .76.

The means for mother-female and mother-male pairs on these measures were calculated and tested for statistical significance using the Mann-Whitney U test. In terms of the number of utterances, the analysis showed that mothers of females talked more than mothers of males (149.3 versus 119.8 units respectively; p ≤ .05). Mothers of females asked more questions than mothers of males (33% versus 25% of all utterances respectively; p ≤ .05). Mothers of females repeated the utterances of their children more often than did mothers of males (65% versus 46% of all utterances respectively; p ≤ .05). The mean length of utterance (calculated according to Brown, 1973) of mothers of females was 4.40 while it was 3.68 for mothers of males (p ≤ .01). None of the other measures of either mother or child speech showed significant differences, although there was a strong trend for mothers of males to use more requests for action, directives, than mothers of females (19% versus 15% of all utterances respectively p ≤ .07).

These data support the position that there is a relationship between differential socialization and language use in mother-child interaction. It was expected that mother-female interaction would be characterized by greater quantity and responsivity of verbal behaviour. Question-asking is an initiation that usually requires a verbal response. Question-asking and answering as well as acknowledging an answer and repeating another speaker's utterance are 'conversation-maintaining' devices in that they are used to initiate and maintain verbal interaction.

The following two sequences are examples of the question-answer acknowledgment sequence. In the first, the mother asks the child about a toy piano that she is playing with. The child answers, and the mother acknowledges this by repeating the child's answer. In

the second example, the mother asks her child about a
toy horse that he is playing with. The child answers
but articulates the answer poorly. The mother gives an
acceptable articulation of the name of the toy in her
acknowledgement.

(1)   Mother: <u>Is it good?</u>

          Child: <u>Good.</u>

(2)   Mother: <u>What is that?</u>

          Child: <u>Morse.</u>

          Mother: <u>Horsey.</u> (both laugh)

In example (3) the conversation is maintained by
the mother's use of successive questions which also
function as acknowledgments of the preceding answers.
Other repetition is used also by the mother to request
confirmation of what the child said.

(3)   Mother: <u>Whatcha doin'?</u>

          Child: <u>Coloring this.</u>

          Mother: <u>Coloring this?</u>

          Child: <u>Aw done.</u>

          Mother: <u>All done?</u>

          Child: <u>Aw gon.</u>

          Mother: <u>Hmmm?</u>

          Child: <u>Aw gan.</u>

In example (4) the child is playing with a toy
truck and labels it as a 'race car'. The mother uses
her child's comment as an opening for a conversation
about the toy truck and an eraser. The child uses self-
repetition, which may function for emphasis of the
statements, while the mother uses other-repetition which
may function for confirmation of her child's statements.

          Child: <u>Have a race car.</u>

                    <u>Have a race car.</u>

          Mother: <u>Race?</u>

                    <u>What are you talkin' about?</u>

          Child: <u>Race car.</u>

                    <u>Race car.</u>

<pre>
Mother: There isn't a car.

          This isn't a race car.

Child: A truck.

Mother: That's a truck, umhmm.

          But this is an eraser.

          That's all it is.

Child: It's a truck.

Mother: It's a truck.

          Umhmm.
</pre>

Our data do not support the hypothesis that mothers are 'syntactically fine tuning' their utterances to the specific level of their children's linguistic abilities. Although the mean length of utterance of mothers' speech in our study is significantly greater for females than for males, there was not a significant difference in the mean length of utterance of the children's speech. The difference in the mothers' speech may be an incidental result of the different functions that mothers perform with their speech to male and female children. For example, questions are longer on the average than are directives expressed as imperatives, which are the most frequent type of directive in these data. The greater mean length of utterance in the speech of mothers of females may be an indirect result of mothers' greater use of questions to females than to males.

One finding to emerge from these data is that all of the significant sex differences are to be found in the mothers' speech and not in the children's. Wells (Symposium discussion) has found no significant differences between $3\frac{1}{2}$-year-old boys and girls in the purposes for which or in the contexts in which they initiate conversations with parents. However, there are significant differences in the contexts in which parents initiate conversations with boys as compared with girls. Boys were spoken to more frequently than girls when the boys were playing with toys or were engaged in similar activities, whereas girls were spoken to more often when they were engaged in 'helping' or just talking. These results provide additional support for the position that it is caregivers who are behaving differentially to their children of different sexes, and not the children of different sexes who behave differently.

Maternal language behaviour appears to be mediated by a general sex role expectation that female children.should be more verbally responsive. A compon-

ent of mothers' sex role beliefs with respect to the
speech of their children may be the expectation that
female children are or should be verbally expressive,
responsive, and talkative, while for male children this
expectation may not exist in this strong form. Girls may
be learning that this kind of behaviour is appropriate
for them. The origins of this expectation have not yet
been clearly established. Although this pattern of
greater vocal/verbal quantity and responsivity has precursors in infancy, the specific relationship between
this similar pattern in early childhood is not yet
established.

We concur with Garnica's (Symposium discussion)
observation that until we examine other aspects of
socialization processes such as teacher-child, father-
child, and sibling-child interaction, we will not have
a complete understanding of the origins of sex differences in behaviour. For example, the first author
examined sex-differentiated verbal aspects of preschool
teacher-child interaction and found that teachers verbally interacted more and used more requests for attention and action from boys, while they requested girls
to provide information (Cherry, 1975a). Further research must specify the conditions under which patterns
of sex differentiated speech behaviour exist before we
can fully understand what effect these socialization
processes have upon the language development of children.

REFERENCES

Bardwick, J. (1971)   Psychology of Women. Harper and
Row, New York.

Broen, P. (1972)   The Verbal Environment of the Language-learning Child. American Speech and
Hearing Association Monograph No. 17.

Brown, R. (1973)   A First Language: The Early Stages.
Harvard University Press, Cambridge, Mass.

Cherry, L. (1975a)   The Preschool Teacher-child Dyad:
Sex Differences in Verbal Interaction. Child
Development 46. 532-536.

Cherry, L. (1975b)   Sex Differences in Child Speech:
McCarthy Revisited. (ETS RB-75-3). Educa-
tional Testing Service, Princeton, New
Jersey.

196

Cherry, L. (1976)   Interactive Strategies in Language
    Development: A Socio-cognitive Model. Paper
    presented at Conference on Language, Child-
    ren, and Society, Ohio State University,
    April.

Cherry, L. and Lewis, M. (In press)   Mothers and Two-
    year-olds: A Study of Sex Differentiated
    Aspects of Verbal Interaction. Developmental
    Psychology.

Fraser, C. and Roberts, A. (1975)   Mothers' Speech to
    Children of Different Ages. Journal of Psycho-
    linguistic Research 4. 9-16.

Goldberg, S. and Lewis, M. (1969)   Play Behavior in
    the Year-old Infant: Early Sex Differences.
    Child Development 40. 21-31.

Halverson, C. and Waldrop, M. (1970)   Maternal Behavior
    toward Own and Other Preschool Children: The
    Problem of 'Ownness'. Child Development 41.
    839-845.

Lewis, M. and Cherry, L. (1976)   Social Behavior and
    Language Acquisition. In M. Lewis and L. Rosen-
    blum (eds.) Language and Communication: The
    Origins of Behavior. Vol. V. Wiley, New York.

Lewis, M. and Freedle, R. (1973)   Mother-infant Dyad:
    The Cradle of Meaning. In P. Pliner, L.
    Krames and T. Alloway (eds.) Communication and
    Affect, Language and Thought. Academic Press,
    New York.

Maccoby, E. and Jacklin, C. (1974)   The Psychology of
    Sex Differences. Stanford University Press,
    Stanford.

Moss, H. (1967)   Sex, Age, and State as Determinants
    of Mother-infant Interaction. Merrill-Palmer
    Quarterly 13. 19-36.

Newport, E., Gleitman, L. and Gleitman, H. (1975)
    Environmental Sensitivities of, and Constraints
    on, the Language Acquisition Process. Paper
    presented at the Seventh Annual Child Language
    Research Forum, Stanford University, April.

Phillips, J. (1973)   Syntax and Vocabulary of Mothers'
    Speech to Young Children: Age and Sex Compa-
    risons. Child Development 44. 182-185.

Sherman, J. (1971)   On the Psychology of Women: A
        Survey of Empirical Studies. Charles C.
        Thomas, Springfield, Illinois.

Snow, C. (1972)   Mothers' Speech to Children Learn-
        ing Language. Child Development 43.   549-565.

Mothers' Speech and its Association with Rate of Linguistic Development in Young Children

T.G. Cross

The inclusion of a section on interaction as a factor in language acquisition in this volume reflects an increasing interest in the aspects of language acquisition that may only be explained with reference to the social milieu in which learning takes place. Wells (1975) has argued that in concentrating on the autonomous, internal development of the child, most recent accounts of language acquisition have seriously neglected to consider the way development is influenced by the interpersonal settings in which it is embedded. Several recent lines of research have served to highlight the role of external factors in the process of language learning. Studies of the dyadic interactions between mothers and their pre-linguistic infants (Trevarthen, 1974; Bateson, 1975;

*This research was supported in part by a grant from the Advisory Committee on Child Care Research, Australian Department of Education. An earlier version of this paper has been published in Pragmatics Micro-fiche: Special Issue on Child Language, 1975. I wish to thank Katherine Kirby, Patricia Wiltshire, and John Fisher for their assistance in the preparation of the speech transcripts. I am especially grateful to Virginia Holmes for her constructive comments on earlier variations of this paper.

Stern, Jaffe, Beebe, and Bennett,1975; Snow, 1975)
have emphasized the contribution of the child's early
inter-subjective experiences with the mother in establishing conversation-like patterns of communication
which are the precursors of later conversational development and will therefore structure his early linguistic experience. Bruner (1975) has found that even the
child's entry into grammar may be traced back in development to the structure of his mother's interactions
with him in playful exchanges and to the way she interprets his prelinguistic communicative behaviour.
Nelson's work (1973, 1975) has suggested that mothers'
interaction styles may also be responsible for individual
differences in the learning strategies with which children
approach the linguistic acquisition task. Thus language
acquisition is the result of a complex interaction process beginning in the first weeks of life, in which the
mother's contribution may be very important to the
child's later development.

The aspect of language acquisition that is
probably most susceptible to external influence is the
rate of acquisition. Students of child language have
long recognized that there is considerable variation
across children in the speed with which they acquire
the formal means to express their communicative intentions. Yet very little is understood about the factors
which facilitate or inhibit their progress. While few
would doubt that the child's linguistic environment
must play some role, the importance of its contribution,
the nature of its interaction with the child's capacities and learning strategies, and the effects of variation in children's linguistic inputs are problems we
have yet to resolve.

In recent years, some progress towards a resolution of these problems has been made by an increasing number of studies which show that mothers, the
primary source of linguistic input to many children,
modify their speech in ways that may assist them in the
acquisition task. Their speech has been characterized
as much simpler in syntax and semantics, clearer, better
formed, more salient and more repetitive than had previously been supposed. Snow (1972), Broen (1972) and
others have suggested that by gradually and systematically exposing the developing child to the complexities of linguistic structure without the confusion
usually present in adult speech, mothers may be reducing
the size and difficulty of the language-learning task
and thereby facilitating acquisition.

However, very few studies have attempted to
test this hypothesis directly, and most have concentrated only on a few of the large number of input
variables that have been proposed as aiding acquisition.

Even so, the results have been largely ambiguous and have not succeeded in clarifying the role of even these few variables. For instance, Cazden (1965), Brown, Cazden and Bellugi (1969), and Feldman (1971) found that manipulating the concentration of expansions in the child's input had little effect on acquisition, while Nelson, Carskaddon, and Bonvillian (1973) have reported that in some circumstances expansions can promote growth. Brown et al. (1969) also were unable to relate the frequency of surface forms in parent speech to the order of acquisition in their children, and yet Newport, Gleitman and Gleitman (1975) have reported preliminary findings which indicate that the frequency of some surface constructions are significantly correlated with specific aspects of children's linguistic growth. Both Cazden and Brown et al. have concluded that simple, well-formed maternal speech assists the child in syntactic acquisition, but Newport et al. have reported that neither the simplicity nor the well-formedness of maternal speech predicts anything at all about language acquisition.

This paper suggests that this confusion in outcomes may result from the considerable methodological differences between studies as well as from failure to distinguish the several possible ways in which different features of parental speech may affect child acquisition. As Newport (1976) has pointed out, some features may have incremental effects on language growth (i.e. higher frequencies in the input may produce proportionately more rapid acquisition than lower frequencies), while others may affect acquisition in a threshold way, needing only to reach a minimal frequency to have maximum effects. Cross (1975) has argued that some features may have effects related specifically to the child's stage of development, while others may affect acquisition continuously throughout development. A further distinction should be made between global and specific effects on acquisition: that is, between features that may speed up the entire process and those that may only promote the acquisition of specific linguistic forms (Newport et al., 1975). This amounts to a distinction between effects on rate and on content of acquisition. Failure to make one, or several, of these distinctions may have led to the conflicting results of the studies just discussed. Further, some of the ambiguity in outcome may have been produced artificially by the use of groups of children who either spanned wide ranges of linguistic abilities or represented noncomparable levels of average ability. Cross (1975, 1977) has shown that many mothers' speech features are highly correlated with small increments in their children's linguistic ability, and that several are directly influenced by the child's communicative strategies. This being so, it is important firstly to restrict the range

of abilities of the children sampled, secondly to control precisely for their individual lingustic levels
at the outset of the study, and thirdly to collect
data in a naturalistic rather than an experimental
setting so as to leave undisturbed the child's influence on the mother's speech adjustments.

The present study was exploratory in aim and
scope. It investigated the incidence of a very large
number of maternal speech variables and manipulated
only one global child language variable, overall rate
of linguistic acquisition. Thus it was concerned only
with features that may affect the rate, not the course,
of acquisition and only with the possible incremental
effects of such features. The range of linguistic
abilities represented by the children in the sample
was restricted in an effort to control for the possibility of stage - related effects on acquisition, and a
matched-pair design was used to control precisely for
their individual linguistic levels while allowing age
and hence rate of acquisition to vary within pairs.
This design was chosen specifically to control for the
effect of the children's linguistic level on their
mothers' speech adjustments which, in most naturalistic
studies, are confounded with the effects of maternal
speech features on rate of acquisition. The aim of
the study was to narrow down the very large number of
features that have been proposed as assisting acquisition in order to establish a priority list of input
variables that could be subjected to more intensive
investigation.

METHOD

The subjects were 16 Australian-born middle
class mothers aged between 27 and 32 years. All had
been educated at tertiary level and most had Bachelor
degrees. Their husbands were all pursuing professional
occupations. Each mother had at least two children,
one between the ages of 4 and 6 and the subject-child
who was in the age range of 19 to 33 months. The
subject-children were six males and ten females with
mean length of utterance (MLU) values between 1.5 and
3.5 morphemes. These children were matched in pairs
which were equated for sex, family size, MLU, upper-
bound (the mean of their 50 longest utterances), and
their scores on a test of comprehension measuring their
ability to make appropriate responses to 100 syntactically different sentences (see Cross, 1975, for a
description of this test). The age variation of the
children in each pair was between 5 and 10 months. The
younger child was considered accelerated in comparison
with the older child, having attained the same linguistic level at an earlier age than the older child,
and was therefore assigned to an accelerated group
(AC). The older child in each pair was assigned to a

normal group (NC). The mean age difference between the
groups was 7.1 months.

The spontaneous conversations of each mother-
child pair were recorded on audio cassette and videotape at least twice within a week, yielding one hour of
tape for each dyad. The recordings were made while the
mother and child were playing with a standard set of
toys in the child's usual playroom at home. Several
precautions were taken to minimize observer contamination effects (see Cross, 1977, for details). Detailed contextual notes were taken on the spot by the
investigator and a children's speech therapist, both
of whom later transcribed the tapes. A second speech
therapist also independently transcribed the tapes
using the video records, audio tapes and contextual
notes. Discrepancies were resolved whenever possible
by comparing the transcripts and by recourse to the
original tapes. The final transcripts contained both
faithful and interpreted versions of both mother's and
child's utterances together with pause and intonation
information.

Samples of 300 sequential utterances for
each mother were then coded for more than 60 features.
Each feature was selected on the grounds that it may
have influenced the rate at which the child was
acquiring language structure. The code organized the
features under four broad headings:

1. Mothers' Syntax: This included measures of the
length, complexity and well-formedness of maternal
utterances, as well as the distribution of sentence
types.

2. Mothers' Discourse Adjustments: Here were included measures of each mother's frequency of imitations, expansions, semantic extensions and semantically new utterances. Several types of maternal
self-repetitions and any combinations of measures in
this category were also included.

3. Mothers' Speech Styles: This heading subsumed
measures of maternal volubility, conversational structure, and the analyzability of utterances.

4. Mothers' References. The mothers' utterances were
also coded for their referential relationship to the
child's or mother's ongoing activity, to persons or
objects in the recording situation, or to events that
were removed from the ongoing situation. (Further details of the code are given in the appendix to Cross,
1977.)

RESULTS

  The mean proportion of each feature in each
mother's speech sample was calculated and averaged for
each group. The mean difference between the paired
groups was tested for significance using the paired
t-test. Table 1 shows the means of each group for each
feature and the significance of the mean difference between the groups.

  Of the 60 features thus tested only 17 were
found to differ significantly between the groups. The
comparison showed that mothers of accelerated children
used significantly greater proportions of utterances
that were repetitions of all or part of the child's
preceding utterances, particularly in the form of
complete or transformed expansions, and generally in
the form of utterances that were semantically related
to preceding child utterances (i.e. the combined categories of imitations, expansions and semantic extensions)
They also produced significantly more partial repetitions
of their own preceding utterances and, almost significantly, a larger number of self-repetitions in general. Furthermore, they produced much greater proportions of 'synergistic sequences', utterance sequences
which contained either expansions or extensions and maternal self-repetitions of the same semantic material.
The AC mothers also produced significantly fewer utterances that could be argued to be difficult for the child
to analyze, in particular utterances marked in the transcripts as wholly or partially unintelligible. They
also used fewer utterances per conversation and a lower
level of preverb complexity (i.e., fewer morphemes before the main verb in their clauses). With the exception of preverb complexity, no syntactic or referential
measure significantly discriminated between the groups.

  It could be objected that some of the mothers'
adjustments may have been more correlated with the
child's age than with linguistic level, and that some,
at least, of the significant between-group differences
may have reflected the average difference in the ages
of the groups. In order to assess this possibility,
first order partial correlations, which controlled for
the children's linguistic levels, were calculated
between each of the significant features in Table 1 and
the children's ages. While no correlation with age
differed significantly from zero (most were extremely
low), the correlations for preverb complexity, unintelligibility and disfluency were strong enough (.45-
.48) to warrant caution in interpretation. Some at
least of the between-group differences observed in these
features may have been attributable to the mothers'
differential adjustments to the age differences in the
groups.

TABLE 1. The Mean Percentages of Mothers' Speech
Features for the Accelerated (AC) and
Normal (NC) Groups and Significance
Levels using the Paired t-Test.

Mother's Speech Features	AC	NC
SYNTAX		
Complexity		
Mean length utterance	4.75	4.92
Preverbal complexity	1.52	1.74*
Propositions/utterance	1.02	1.03
Single word utterances	6.00%	5.16%
Diff. child-mother MLU	2.48	2.70
Well-formedness		
Sentence fragments	6.00%	5.82%
Complete sentences	60.50%	61.03%
Minor abbreviations	18.50%	17.60%
Sentence types		
Question forms (total)	23.75%	20.83%
Wh questions	11.20%	9.21%
Yes/no questions (total)	12.54%	11.58%
Aux-fronted questions	4.54%	5.58%
Tag questions	3.33%	3.25%
Rising intonation questions	2.57%	2.26%
Occasional questions	.38%	.29%
Isolated tags	.96%	.54%
Imperatives (total)	7.08%	7.62%
Imps. (subj. deleted)	5.83%	6.00%
Imps. (subj. included)	1.27%	1.29%
Declaratives	32.02%	37.50%
Deictic statements	18.62%	19.25%
REFERENTIALITY		
Immediate references (total)	34.71%	32.00%
Refs. child activities	25.13%	22.13%
Refs. mother activities	9.08%	10.29%
Objects, persons present	6.29%	6.83%
Non-immediate events	3.42%	5.33%
SPEECH STYLE		
Unanalyzable utterances (total)	7.00%	10.50%**
Unintelligible utterances	2.00%	3.33%**
Disfluent utterances	3.08%	4.42%

Mother's Speech Features	AC	NC
Run-on sentences	1.95%	2.75%
Proportion utts/turn	1.17	1.47*
Proportion mother/child utterances	1.51	1.53

DISCOURSE

Repetitions child utterances

	AC	NC
Repetitions child utterances	22.96%	15.71%*
Exact repetitions	3.12%	2.38%
Expansions (total)	14.38%	10.87%*
Complete expansions	7.63%	4.88%*
Partial expansions	6.33%	5.08%
Elaborated expansions	2.12%	1.96%
Transformed expansions	3.67%	1.79%**

Semantic extensions

	AC	NC
Semantic extensions (total)	37.46%	31.96%
Topic extensions (noun phrase)	12.37%	11.67%
Topic extensions (pronoun)	24.25%	19.42%
Predicate extensions	.75%	.75%

Semantic related utterances

	AC	NC
Expansions + extensions (total)	60.67%	48.71%**
Expansions and N.P. extensions	35.29%	27.37%

Semantically new utterances

	AC	NC
Semantically new utterances (total)	11.83%	20.04%**
Novel, repeated utterances	9.00%	15.21%*
Novel, isolated utterances	3.42%	6.42%*

Mothers' self-repetitions

	AC	NC
Self-repetitions (total)	30.15%	24.67%
Sequential repetitions	19.50%	16.21%
Exact sequential repetitions	1.58%	1.49%
Partial sequential repetitions	8.42%	6.00%*
Transformed repetitions	7.79%	6.29%
Paraphrased repetitions	3.12%	4.08%
Nonsequential repetitions	10.52%	8.38%
Stock phrases	2.05%	2.60%

Mothers' Speech Features	AC	NC

Synergistic sequences

Synergistic sequences (total)	18.25%	10.21%**
Expansions/sequential repetitions	8.50%	4.37%**
Extensions/sequential repetitions	9.95%	5.93%**

*   p < .05, 2-tailed

** p < .01, 2-tailed

DISCUSSION

Mothers' Syntax. The most surprising result of this comparison was the failure to find significant differences in the syntactic quality of the inputs to groups of children acquiring syntax at different rates. Most recent studies of mothers' speech have concentrated on its formal differences from adult speech, assuming that by reducing the complexities and confusions normally present in adult speech it should facilitate acquisition. This view implies that children who are making rapid progress should be receiving inputs that are syntactically simpler and better formed than children developing more slowly. But this does not seem to be the case. With the exception of preverb complexity (which may reflect to some extent the mothers' adjustments to the age differences between groups), no parameter designed to assess the complexity or the grammaticality of maternal speech was significantly associated with the higher rate of acquisition.

However, this finding is not entirely an isolated one. As previously mentioned, Brown (1973) has reported that the frequency of syntactic constructions in parent speech was not related to the order of

acquisition in their children. Newport et al. (1975)
have found that neither complexity nor well-formedness
were correlated with any aspect of children's later
development, and Snow et al. (1976) have noted that
there is very little variation across socio-economic
classes in the grammatical structure of mothers' speech.
This was a study which, the authors claimed, compared
the 'mothers of potential good language learners with
the mothers of potential poor language learners'. All
these results seem to indicate a relatively minor role
in acquisition for the syntactic adjustments that
mothers make when addressing young children.

In the present study, where stage of development was restricted and the children's individual
linguistic levels equated within pairs, there also
appeared to be too little variation between mothers to
account for the considerable variation in their children's rates. Their MLUs only ranged between 4.1 and
5.4 morphemes. Even for the measures of the degree to
which their syntactic complexity matched the child's
complexity (the difference between the child's and
mother's MLUs), the differences only ranged between
1.8 and 3.3 morphemes. This lack of variation suggests that the mothers' speech register, at the syntactic level, may be quite rigid and not, as has often
been suggested, sensitive to small variations in the
listener's maturity. Cross (1975, 1977) has shown
that although many non-syntactic features of mothers'
speech are closely correlated with small increments in
their children's linguistic sophistication, most purely
syntactic features are not. Newport (1976) reports a
similar finding. Mothers seem to be unable to (or are
simply not concerned to) monitor their own or the
child's syntactic level.

The present findings, considered in conjunction with the consistent failure of recent studies to
demonstrate global effects of maternal syntactic modifications, or even to find consistent differences
across mothers in this respect, suggest that mothers'
syntax may be best characterized as a relatively uni-
form register that is used (and is possibly even acquired initially by children) as a kind of 'package'.
For this reason it may be only grossly sensitive to
differences in the linguistic abilities of the addressee, and may not vary significantly across mothers.
If this is so (and more evidence is certainly needed),
Newport's (1976) suggestion that it may have a thresh-
hold rather than a graded effect on acquisition may be
correct. It may aid acquisition simply by bringing the
structural complexity of the input well within reach of
the child's processing capacities, further simplification then being unnecessary and redundant, and perhaps
even impeding communication.

However, there is also the possibility that
syntactic modifications have their effect not in isolation but in interaction with more dynamic adjustments
that mothers make at other levels of description,
particularly at the discourse level. Cross (1977)
has argued that discourse-repair sequences, containing partial repetitions in which preverb complexity
has been reduced, should assist the child to process
utterances that were in their original form too complex
for him to comprehend. This point will be taken up
later, in the discussion of partial repetitions. It
seems that even the role of a purely syntactic feature
like preverbal simplicity may be tied to the relations
between maternal utterances rather than being effective
in isolation. The finding that the AC group received
a lower degree of preverb complexity (if it is valid
in this case) may reflect their mothers' sensitivity
within discourse sequences to the child's failure to
cope with the complexity of a particular utterance. It
may not reflect the mothers' overall sensitivity to the
child's linguistic ability. This kind of interaction
between syntactic and discourse adjustments may also
apply to the potential role of expansions. It is unlikely that expansions of child utterances could facilitate acquisition unless they were simple enough for
the child to recognize them as expressions of his own
semantic intention. Snow (1977) has argued along
similar lines. She claims that it is simplicity at
the semantic level of mothers' speech that both determines its syntactic simplicity and is critical for
the acquisition of syntax. This reasoning suggests
that, if maternal speech facilitates acquisition, then
one should find that the non-syntactic adjustments
differentiate the input of accelerated children from
those developing more slowly.

The results of this study support this hypothesis. While there was only one significant difference at the syntactic level, thirteen were found at
the level of discourse structure, and three more under
the heading of maternal speech styles. We will discuss the latter first.

The Analyzability of Mothers' Speech. The most
significant of the speech-style measures was the
number of partly or wholly unintelligible utterances
recorded in the transcripts. The AC group produced
far fewer unintelligible utterances than the NC group.
Furthermore, two other measures included under this
heading, maternal disfluency and run-on sentences,
were less frequent in the inputs of the AC group, but
just failed to reach significance. These results,
like those for preverbal complexity, should perhaps be
interpreted cautiously, as the partial correlations
between these features and the children's ages, although nonsignificant, were in the order of .46-.48.

However, the significance of the difference in the
rates of unintelligibility was sufficiently high
(p < .005) to warrant further consideration of this
factor as an inhibitor of linguistic acquisition.
This is supported by the finding of Newport et al.
(1975) that maternal unintelligibility negatively
predicted the child's linguistic growth, particularly the acquisition of noun inflections. The present findings agree with hers, but in addition they
suggest that children may be confused not only by
mothers who mumble some utterances, but also by
mothers who run sentences together without marking
their beginnings or ends, or, as in the case of the
disfluency measure, who produce a misleading pause-
structure by hesitating, word searching, or revising
their utterances.

The whole group of significant results for
the proportions of unanalyzable utterances in the
mothers' speech, if they can be verified in studies
which control simultaneously for the effects of both
linguistic level and age on maternal adjustments,
would seem to support Brown's (1973) contention that
the perceptual salience of linguistic information in
the input is a determinant of rate of acquisition.
This contention is further supported by the finding
that the proportion of utterances per conversational
turn was also significantly lower for the AC group.
One might suppose that the salience of any utterance
to the child would be interfered with by the immediate
sequential presentation of other utterances to process within a short time span, i.e. within a conversational turn. This suggests that volubility in the
mother may at times overload the child's attentional
and processing capacities, thus reducing and possibly
confusing his linguistic data base. Cn several counts,
therefore, it may be worthwhile investigating more
closely the role of maternal articulation and rate of
speech in affecting the salience and analyzability of
the child's input and hence his ease of acquisition.

The Discourse Features. As mentioned previously,
the category of discourse features contained the greatest
number of between-group differences. However, unlike the
last group of results, which were lower in the AC group,
most of the discourse features were significantly more
frequent. Thus it may be hypothesized that expansions,
semantic extensions, and partial repetitions may, at
this stage of development, assist the child to acquire
linguistic structure.

Expansions have been reported by Brown et al.
(1969) to have been more frequent in the input to Eve,

the most accelerated of his small sample, than to Adam
and Sarah. The present findings for expansions are
also compatible with the finding of Snow et al. (1976)
that the two middle class mother groups produced more
than twice as many expansions as the working class
group. On the other hand, they appear to contradict
those of Cazden (1965), Brown et al. (1969), and Feldman (1971), who were unable to demonstrate that expansions had significant effects on linguistic growth.
However, there were several methodological differences
in the present study which may account for the difference in results. The present definition of expansions was considerably broader, and included complete,
partial, elaborated, and transformed adult versions
of the child's utterance. Also, an expansion was
scored if it occurred within two conversational turns
of the child's utterance and was not required to follow the utterance immediately. But perhaps more
important were the controls instituted for the children's linguistic levels and the restrictions applied
to the range of these in the sample. Earlier work on
maternal expansions (Cross, 1970, 1975) has suggested
that in spontaneous mother-child conversations the
frequency of expansions is closely related to child
speech within a relatively restricted period of linguistic development. The relationship does not appear
to be linear, but reaches a peak frequency during
Brown's Stage II. In producing expansions, the mother
appears to be strongly influenced by the linguistic
maturity of the preceding child utterance. More telegraphic utterances received significantly more expansions than less telegraphic utterances (Cross, 1975).
However, as Nelson (1973) has pointed out, it is probably necessary for the child to be attempting to express something like a rudimentary sentence before his
mother will attempt to expand it, and several studies
using children primarily in Stages I and II have reported positive relations between linguistic level and
parental expansions (Nelson, 1973; Newport, 1976;
Blount, (1977). However, as the child's speech becomes rapidly less telegraphic and interpretation of
his intention less difficult for his parents, expansions can then be shown to be negatively related to
linguistic sophistication (Cross, 1970, 1975). The
present study sampled predominantly children in Stages
II and III and may thus have selected the appropriate
stages to observe the peak occurrence of expansions
and expansion-like adult responses, and to therefore
observe their facilitative effects.

Semantic extensions, like expansions, are
closely related to the semantic intention of the
child's preceding utterance. They differ from them in
degree: whereas expansions include all or most of the
child's words, extensions incorporate only the child's

topic (and sometimes his verb), adding new terms to
the predicate. In the present study, most of them (72%)
were referentially immediate (i.e. commented on the
child's or mother's ongoing activities), and thus presumably in the play situation encoded the child's concurrent cognitions. For this reason, it can be argued
that they should be facilitative in much the same way
as expansions, that is, by providing an adult expression
which encodes precisely the semantic relations that the
child may be considering at the time. However, although
they accounted for as many as 36% of the mothers' utterances, they did not show significant between-group differences. But when all semantic extensions were added
to the expansion category as in the semantically related category (Table 1), quite high levels of significance in favour of the AC group were reached. If
this result is considered together with the finding
that the incidence of semantically unrelated or novel
utterances was significantly lower for the AC group
(Table 1), it would appear that the semantic relationship between mother and child speech may be a very relevant factor in linguistic acquisition. In a similar
vein, Snow (1977) has shown that the great majority
of maternal utterances encode the same few semantic relations that Brown (1973) has found to underlie children's two- and three-word utterances. The present
study found that 61% of mothers' utterances for the AC
group and 49% for the NC group incorporated all or some
of the child's own semantic intention, thus explaining
how it is that mothers are able to match their children's semantic levels so closely. It seems that their
speech at this stage in their children's development is
largely a reflection of what the children are disposed
to talk about. The observations that mothers of rapidly developing children were more responsive in this
regard than mothers of slower developers seems strongly
to support Snow's contention (1977) that an input
matched to the child's semantic ability will facilitate
syntactic acquisition. By encoding only the kinds of
meanings that the child can produce himself, it should
enable him to attend to, and learn from, the form of
his mother's expressions. The present study, however,
indicates that maternal speech may be even more facilitative if it goes a step further and predominantly
encodes only those semantic relations that the child
has just produced himself, or at least are closely related to his ongoing focus of attention. It may be
primarily within these semantic and attentional constraints that the syntactic simplicity of her expressions may facilitate his acquisition process.

　　　　Partial repetitions, which also occurred
significantly more frequently in the AC group, may
assist the child in a similar way. Cross (1975) has
shown that maternal self-repetitions are almost always a response to the child's failure to make an

appropriate response to the original maternal utterance. Partial repetitions are, by definition, a reduced version of the original utterance and seem to be attempts by the mother to by-pass the complexity that prevented the child from processing the original. When the mother is successful in this endeavour (and the repetition sequence will often be prolonged until she is), the child has been permitted to grasp the meaning relatively independently of his syntactic limitations. The result of this interaction with the child's capacities is the sequential presentation of utterances conveying essentially the same meaning but varying in the level of linguistic complexity. Cross (1977) has argued that in a successful repair sequence, at least one of these utterances will have matched the child's processing capacity and permitted him to entertain his mother's communicative intention. Hearing the more complex versions at the same time may provide him with the sort of learning opportunities that expansions and extensions have been argued to do: that is, it will allow him to relate the meaning he is entertaining to a well-timed but more complex expression of it in his mother's speech. This would explain why there was a significant association between the incidence of partial repetitions in mothers' speech and accelerated development in their children.

Even more powerful than expansions, extensions, and repetitions in isolation should be combinations of these adjustments within discourse sequences. Under the heading 'Synergistic Sequences' in Table 1 are the proportions of expansions and extensions that were also repeated or paraphrased within two conversational turns of the original. In combining the semantic relevance and timing of the former with the effect of redundancy, these sequences should cumulatively (synergistically) assist acquisition. As the AC group produced a far greater proportion of these sequences than the NC group, this may be the case. By driving home the relevant linguistic information contained in semantically related utterances, such sequences may play an important role in acquisition.

CONCLUSIONS

This study set out to determine the relevance of sixty features of mothers' speech to their children's rates of linguistic acquisition, and thus by a process of elimination to construct a short list of the features that may play a major role in facilitating the acquisition process. As it was exploratory in purpose, its findings are not conclusive. The design has simply isolated a small set of features which differentiate the primary inputs to children learning language rapidly from those to children who are slower by an average of seven months, so that those features may be investigated more intensively. Not all of the features isolated need be essential to rapid acquisition. It is more likely that the set presents a 'syndrome' of the sensitive mother who is in many ways effectively encouraging her child's communicative development. Only some of the features in this 'syndrome' may in fact have relevance to linguistic acquisition. It is also very likely that the pattern of facilitative features will change throughout development in response to the child's changing linguistic requirements. Thus the set of features isolated here may have relevance only for the stage of development represented by the majority of children in the sample - too small a number on which to base confident conclusions.

However, the study has done what it was designed to do. It has suggested several plausible hypotheses about the determinants of rate of linguistic acquisition, each of which can be tested in a more intensive prospective investigation. Such an investigation is now under way, using follow-up data for the present sample. Essentially, the principal findings of the present investigation suggest that acceleration in linguistic acquisition is associated with an input that is substantially matched to the child's own communicative intentions. Mothers of accelerated children provided an input that contained greater proportions of expansions, expansion-like utterances, and semantic extensions than did mothers of children developing more slowly. They also used more partial repetitions and sequences which combine repetitions with expansions and extensions of the child's preceding utterances. They produced far fewer utterances that were new to the discourse. Their speech appeared to be perceptually more salient and analyzable; it contained fewer unintelligible and disfluent utterances and fewer run-on sentences, a lower level of preverbal complexity, and fewer utterances per conversational turn. With the exception of preverb complexity, no significant differences were found for any of the syntactic measures. It was hypothesized that it is the extent to which the mother's discourse adjustments permit the child to accurately guess her meaning that is important in acquisition. By matching the child's semantic intentions and ongoing cognitions, her speech may free the child to concentrate on the formal aspects of her expressions and thus acquire syntax efficiently. On this view the degree of syntactic simplicity in maternal speech may be of only secondary importance. Whether the features on which these groups differed are causally implicated in ease of acquisition remains to be determined. However, the results reported by Snow et al. (1976) and Newport (1976) agree substantially (where the features overlap) with those of the present study. It appears that a short list of potentially facilitative features is beginning to be replicated for quite different groups of mothers and children.

REFERENCES

Bateson, M.C. (1975)   Mother-infant Exchanges: The
    Epigenesis of Conversational Interaction.
    Annals of the New York Academy of Sciences
    263.

Blount, B.G. (1977)   Prosodic and Interactional
    Features in Parent-child Speech: English and
    Spanish. In C.E. Snow and C.A. Ferguson
    (eds.) Talking to Children: Language Input
    and Acquisition. Cambridge University Press,
    Cambridge.

Broen, P.A. (1972)   The Verbal Environment of the Lan-
    guage Learning Child. American Speech and
    Hearing Monograph No.17.

Brown, R. (1973)   A First Language: The Early Stages.
    Harvard University Press, Cambridge, Mass.

Brown, R., Cazden, C., and Bellugi, U. (1969)   The
    Child's Grammar from I to III. In J.P. Hills
    (ed.) Minnesota Symposia on Child Psychology
    2. University of Minnesota Press, Minneapolis.

Bruner, J.S. (1975)   The Ontogenesis of Speech Acts.
    Journal of Child Language 2. 1-19.

Cazden, C.B. (1965)   Environmental Assistance to the
    Child's Acquisition of Grammar. Unpublished
    doctoral dissertation, Harvard University.

Cross, T.G. (1970)   Some Investigations into the
    Nature of Linguistic Environments of Twelve
    Two-year-old Children. Unpublished manu-
    script, University of Melbourne.

Cross, T.G. (1975)   Some Relationships Between
    'Motherese' and Linguistic Level in Accelerated
    Children. Papers and Reports on Child Language
    Development 10. Stanford University. 117-135.

Cross, T.G.   (1977)   Mothers' Speech Adjustments:
    The Contributions of Selected Child Listener
    Variables. In C.E. Snow and C.A. Ferguson
    (eds.) Talking to Children: Language Input
    and Acquisition. Cambridge University Press,
    Cambridge.

Feldman, C.F. (1971)   The Effects of Various Types of
    Adult Response in the Syntactic Acquisition
    of Two to Three-year-olds. Unpublished
    manuscript, University of Chicago.

Nelson, K. (1973)   Structure and Strategy in Learning to
Talk. Monograph of the Society for Research in
Child Development 38. 1-2 (No.149).

Nelson, K. (1975)   Individual Difference in Early Semantic
and Syntactic Development. Annals of New York
Academy of Sciences 263.

Nelson, K.E. Carskaddon, G. and Bonvillian J.D. (1973)
Syntax Acquisition: Impact of Environmental
Assistance in Adult Verbal Interaction with
the Child. Child Development 44. 497-504.

Newport, E.L. (1976)   Motherese: The Speech of Mothers to
Young Children. In N.J. Castellan, D.B. Pisoni,
and G.R. Potts (eds.) Cognitive Theory 2.
Lawrence Earlbaum Associates, Hillsdale N.J.

Newport, E.L., Gleitman, L.R., and Gleitman, H. (1975)
A Study of Mothers' Speech and Child Language
Acquisition. Papers and Reports on Child Lang-
uage Development 10.   Stanford University.111-11

Snow, C.E. (1972)   Mothers' Speech to Children Learning
Language. Child Development 43. 549-505.

Snow, C.E. (1975)   The Development of Conversation between
Mothers and Babies. Pragmatics Microfiche. 1.6.

Snow, C.E. (1977)   Mothers' Speech Research: From Input to
Interaction. In C.E. Snow and C.A. Ferguson
(eds.) Talking to Children: Language Input and
Acquisition. Cambridge University Press,
Cambridge.

Snow, C.E., Arlman-Rupp, A., Hassing, Y., Jobse, J.,
Joosten, J. and Vorster, J. (1976)   Mothers'
Speech in Three Social Classes. Journal of
Psycholinguistic Research 5. 1-19.

Stern, D.N., Jaffe, J., Beebe, B. and Bennett,S.L. (1975)
Vocalizing in Unison and in Alternation: Two
Modes of Communication within the Mother-infant
Dyad. Annals of the New York Academy of Sciences
263.

Trevarthen, C. (1974)   Conversations with a Two-month-old.
New Scientist May.

Wells, G. (1975)   Interpersonal Communication and the
Development of Language. Paper presented to the
Third International Child Language Symposium,
London.

Strategies Children Use to Answer Questions Posed by Adults (Serbocroation-speaking Children from 1 to 3)

S. Savić

In this study spontaneous conversations between adults and children were analyzed. Individual
children and twins were compared to see if there is
anything specific about the way twins answer questions
posed by adults. The present paper is related to
earlier work on the acquisition of questions (Brown,
1968; Ervin Tripp, 1970; Ingram, 1972; Wode, 1974,
1975), to on-going projects in America and Europe,
and to the results of two previous papers (Savić,
1975a; 1975b) about questions in Serbocroatian.
Savić (1975a) dealt with (1) the order in which a pair
of fraternal twins produced various types of questions
and, (2) the order in which adults asked them various
types of questions. Table 1 shows these results.

Some of the main conclusions drawn by Savić
(1975a) were: (1) Questions are the most frequent
type of utterance in adult speech directed to the
child; (2) there is a marked tendency for the number
of adult declaratives to increase, and the number of
questions to decrease, around the time when children
begin to ask questions by themselves; (3) the order
in which adults ask children different types of questions does not correspond to the order in which those

TABLE 1. Adult and Twin Interrogative Systems Compared: Order and Stages

Age of child in months	Adults Order	Stages	Twins Jasmina Age in months	Jasmina Order	Danko Age in months	Danko Order
14	Šta 'What' Gde 'Where'	I	14	Šta 'What'	14	Šta 'What'
15-16	Da/ne 'Yes/no' Kako 'How'	II			17	Da/ne 'Yes/no'
	Ko 'Who'		19	Gde 'Where'		
				Da/ne 'Yes/no'	20	Gde 'Where'
17-19	Čiji 'Whose' Koji 'Which'	III	21	Kakav 'What kind of'		
	Kakav 'What kind of' Zašto 'Why'		24	Ko 'Who' Kako 'How' Čiji 'Whose'	23	Ko 'Who'
					24	Kako 'How'
20	Kuda 'Where to'	IV	25	Zašto 'Why'	25	Zašto 'Why'
23	Koliko 'How much'			Koji 'Which'	26	Kuda 'Where to'
30	Kada 'When'		31	Koliko 'How much'	27	Kakav 'What kind of'
31	Odakle 'Where from'		32	Kuda 'Where to'		Koji 'Which'
					29	Kada 'When'
			36	Kada 'When'		Čiji 'Whose'
					30	Odakle 'Where from'

question types appear in the speech of children;
(4) the order in which different types of questions
are produced differs with each child in the twin
pair.

In the second paper, four functions of
questions adults direct to children were identified,
and the way these functions change during the period
from 1 to 3 years was studied. It was concluded that
the function of questions posed by adults changes as
the child grows older. Those types of questions which
are a form of adapted adult speech addressed to children gradually disappear from the speech of adults.
These types include questions which test the child's
cognitive level (Gde živi žirafa? 'Where does a giraffe
live?'), or the child's ability to carry on a dialogue
in front of another (unfamiliar) adult (Kaži ti tetka
Miri ko tebe tuče? 'Tell aunty Mira who spanks you?'),
and those questions by which the adult expresses an emotional tie with the child (Di je mamino sunce? 'Where
is mother's sunshine?'). The child deciphers the function of such types of questions from the situations in
which the questions are realized. It can therefore be
concluded that while the child learns to take part in
various types of dialogues with adults, he also learns
that there are various contexts in which such dialogues
are realized.

The question to be dealt with in this paper
is how the child proceeds when he has to answer a
question he does not yet fully understand. Similar
studies have been done in other languages: here data
will be presented for Serbocroatian-speaking children,
comparing twins and only children.

Susan Ervin-Tripp (1970: 80) has pointed out
that 'The hearer must have an information-search method
for locating an answer'. Special attention will be devoted to four types of questions asked by adults in order to show how this information-searching method for
locating an answer works. These are questions beginning
with: (1) čiji 'whose', (2) kakav 'what kind of',
(3) zašto 'why', and (4) kada 'when'.

In judging the child's understanding of questions asked by adults, it was noted whether the child
understood (1) the question-word or (2) a significant
word (thus in 'Whose are the shoes?' the question-word
is 'whose' and the significant word is 'shoes'. The
children studied used three basic strategies to answer
questions posed by adults.

Strategy 1.   When the child does not understand
a new question-word, he answers on the basis of his experience of previously acquired types of questions. For
example, when the subjects first began to answer ques-

tions with čiji 'whose', they answered them in the same
way as they answered questions with šta 'what', which
they had already acquired. Thus (the child's age is
given before his utterance in each example; adults who
asked questions include the experimenter, E; mother, M;
and grandmother, G):

E: Čije je ovo?   Ch (1;7): Ovo

'Whose is this?'   'This'

(The experimenter takes Daddy's
aftershave lotion off a shelf.)

E: Ali čije je ovo?   Ch: Maže

'But whose is this?'   'Rub' (For rub-
                                          bing, to rub)

In Serbocroatian the question-word kakav 'what kind of'
asks for a qualification of a person or thing. It is
used (1) for an adjective in the predicate position:
Kakve su breskve? Lepe su. 'What kind are the peaches?
The pretty kind.' and (2) for an adjective modifying a
noun directly: Kakvu breskvu imaš? Lepu breskvu. 'What
kind of peach have you got? A pretty one.'. When
children first encountered questions with kakav 'what
kind of', they treated them like questions with čiji
'whose' which had been previously acquired.
For instance:

E: Kakva je lopta?   Ch (1;8): Jasminina

'What kind of ball is this?'   'Jasmina's'

(The experimenter picks a ball up
from off the floor.)

E: Jasmina, kakve su ovo   Ch (1;9): Dankove
    cipele?

'Jasmina, what kind of   'Danko's'
shoes are these?'

        This strategy is used by children for a short
period, at the very beginning of acquisition of new
types of questions. The period is longer if two types
of semantically similar questions are being learned
within a short period of time, such as, for example,
questions with čiji 'whose' and kakav 'what kind of',
which both call for a modifier of a noun ('whose' for
a possessor only, and 'what kind of' for quality).
This strategy was used throughout the second year for
'what kind of' questions by twins, significantly longer
than by the only children observed. (This strategy

appears in situations where a twin is 'caught short' by
a question of an adult or wants to answer in a hurry.)
This leads to the conclusion that the semantic feature
of possession, especially possession of objects by one
or another twin, is a very important category in the
twin situation (defined as a situation in which an
adult person and a pair of twins are involved). The
first identification that a twin child gives to an object is to which twin the object belongs. The basic
relation of possession is then extended to other persons
close to the children. For example:

E: <u>Kakve su ove naočare?</u>   Ch (2;4): <u>Bakine</u>

'What kind of glasses are   'Grandmother's'
these?'

(The experimenter is holding up a
pair of sunglasses.)

    Such data should not lead to the conclusion
that twins are slow in the acquisition of grammar. It
should be interpreted in the context of growing up in
a twin situation. When twin children (particularly in
the case of identical twins) have the same toys, clothes
or shoes, there is a need to identify these objects according to possessor. Adults are the ones who find
this kind of identification necessary, and so they frequently ask the children to which one of them a toy or
garment belongs. The frequent questions about possession which adults ask direct the attention of the twin
child to that semantic feature. The observations were
begun at the level when the children were acquiring
strategies in order to answer questions with 'whose'.
At that level, the process of input by adults was already being reflected in the output of the children.
When they acquire the procedure that an object should
be determined by possession, twins proceed to do so, as
the above example shows, even with objects that do not
belong to them personally, but to the other members of
the family.

    <u>Strategy 2.</u> <u>When the child understands the
question-word, but has not learned as yet that one and
the same question-word can be answered in various ways</u>,
he resorts to set 'stereotypes'. For instance, the
children began by answering <u>kakav</u> 'what kind of' questions with the word <u>žut</u> 'yellow' at first, Sara with
the word <u>lep</u> 'pretty', while the twins Danko and Jasmina
answered with <u>prljav</u> 'dirty', and Sanja and Maja with
<u>isti</u> 'the same'. Questions with <u>kada</u> 'when' were first
answered by stereotype expressions of time: Sara used
<u>sutra</u> 'tomorrow', Nataša used <u>posle podne</u> 'in the
afternoon', Sanja and Maja <u>u pola osam</u> 'at half past
seven', Sveta and Mileta <u>u subotu</u> 'on Saturday'. The

same phenomenon occurred in the case of za**š**to 'why' questions. Nata**š**a answered all 'why' questions with tako 'that way', Sara with zato 'because', while Sveta and Mileta used an entire phrase zato sto nemam vremena 'because I haven't got time'. For example:

M: Za**š**to si pokvario to,   Ch (1;11): Zato **š**to nemam
    za**š**to si to pokvario?   vremena.

    'Why you've spoiled it,   'Because I haven't
    why did you spoil it?'   got time.'

(Trying to mend a toy.)

and:

G: Za**š**to si se upi**š**kio?   Ch (1;11): Zato **š**to nemam
                                                vremena.

    'Why have you wet   'Because I haven't
    yourself?'   got time.'

(The grandmother is changing
 the baby and grumbling.)

Such stereotypes may mislead a listener into thinking that the child has mastered a type of question productively. Yet, the child only recognizes a given question-word, and that question-word corresponds to a particular kind of answer. He does not know how to answer such questions productively.

        Twins exhibit a variant of this second strategy. For a longer period of time than only children, they answer every **č**iji 'whose' question with the stereotype moj 'mine' regardless of whether or not the object really belonged to them or was in their temporary possession. However, a twin child hardly ever gave such an answer when the object belonged to the other child in the pair. For instance:

E: **Č**ije su ovo rukavice?   Ch (1;9): Moje.

    'Whose gloves are these?'   'Mine'

(Danko is playing with one
 pair of the experimenter's
 gloves. He tries them on.)

E: Jasmina, **č**iji je to **š**al?   Ch (1;9): Dankov.

    'Jasmina, whose scarf   'Danko's'
    is that?'

(Jasmina has put Danko's
 scarf around her neck.)

E: Jasmina, čije su to rukavice? Ch (1;9) Moje.

'Jasmina, whose gloves are   'Mine.'
those?'

(Jasmina is trying on the experimenter's other pair of gloves.)

Here too, the longer retention of the strategy is connected with the life of twins in a pair. In such a
situation, the distinction 'mine' - 'yours' (referring
to 'brother's'/sister's) is very important. Twins
master this distinction earlier than the distinction
'mine' - 'yours' (referring to other persons in the family). Hence, the distinction of possession within the
pair comes earlier than the distinction of possession
outside the pair.

  Strategy 3.   When the child recognizes the type
of question, but does not understand a word or phrase of
it, it answers by repeating a part of the question of
the adult, either (1) the part it knows, or (2) the part
it does not know.   For example:

E: Šta si dobila za Novu godinu? Ch (1;7) Dobila.

'What did you get for the   'Get.'
New Year?'

E: Šta?

'What?'

G: Šta ti je Deda Mraz doneo?

'What did Santa Claus bring
you?'

(The grandmother realizes that the
child does not know how to answer
the question formulated in such a
manner, and so makes it suit the
child.)

The significant word here is not merely 'year', but the
entire phrase 'New Year'. Although Jasmina did not know
at 1;7 what the word 'year' meant, she could answer the
question Koliko imaš godina? 'How many years old are
you?' with the stereotype dve 'two'.

E: Kakve su boje rukavice?   Ch (1;11) Boje.

'What colour are the gloves?'   'Colour.'

(The experimenter asks while the
child is playing with her gloves.)

Some children repeated part of the question in an interrogative tone. Thus:

M: Čiji je tata čika Milan?   Ch (1;11) Milan?

   'Whose father is Uncle Milan?'   'Milan?'

(A neighbour has come in, whom the
child does not recognize at first.
The mother wants to show the new-
comer how much the child knows.)

     In developing the ability to understand ques-
tions adults ask, the child has to acquire three constituent elements of the Serbocroatian language, and in
the following order: (1) how to distinguish a question
from a statement or command, (2) how to distinguish
various types of questions by their question-words, and
(3) in addition to the question-word, how to understand
what is asked in the question (the significant word).

     While the child is still developing his ability
to understand questions, he uses a series of strategies
in order to answer them. From an analysis of the
child's answers in terms of these strategies, it can be
seen which of the three constituent elements of the
language have been mastered.

     Before mastering the second and third elements,
the child can still carry on verbal interactions with
adults by simply repeating parts of their questions (he
has grasped that a question calls for an answer). When
he begins to acquire the second element, he tries to
answer a new type of question on the basis of experience
already gained, resorting to stereotypes (answering the
question-word, but not the significant word). When he
has mastered all three elements, he can answer any question in a specific situation, and it can then be said
that the child has acquired the ability to answer
questions.

     The subjects used the various strategies for
a varying length of time, yet all the strategies were
found in all the children. Some types of questions
were more difficult for all the children, so the strategies were very clearly manifested in their speech
(in the case of 'whose', 'what kind of', 'why' and
'when' questions), while with other types of questions
(in the case of 'what', 'where' and 'who' questions),
the strategies were observed less frequently.

     Twins retained certain strategies for a
longer period of time. This can be explained not by
slowness of speech development, but by the peculiari-
ties of the twin situation. The longer retention of
some of the strategies in the grammatical development

of twins does not depend only on the cognitive maturity or capacity of the children, but also on the conditions in which the children grow up. In the twin situation, the speech of adults directed to the twin
pair is more specific, adapted to the needs of communicating in such a situation. Hence the strategies for
the acquisition of grammar, in this case for answering
questions posed by adults, should be related to the
strategies adults use when communicating with a pair of
twins at an early age. One should also bear in mind
that as the twin children grow older these strategies
change or disappear from the speech of adults.

REFERENCES

Brown, Roger (1968)   The Development of WH Questions
        in Child Language. The Journal of Verbal
        Learning and Verbal Behavior   VII.

Ervin-Tripp, S. (1970)   Discourse Agreement: How
        Children answer Questions. In J.R. Hayes
        (ed.) Cognition and the Development of
        Language. Wiley, New York.

Ingram, D. (1972)   The Acquisition of Questions and
        its Relation to Cognitive Development in
        Normal and Linguistically Deviant Children:
        A Pilot Study. Papers and Reports on Child
        Language Development 4. Stanford University.
        13-18.

Savić, S. (1975a)   Aspects of Adult-child Communica-
        tion: The Problem of Question Acquisition.
        Journal of Child Language 2. Cambridge Uni-
        versity Press, Cambridge. 251-260.

Savić, S. (1975b)   Quelque Fonctions des Questions
        posées par les Adultes aus Jeunes Enfants.
        Association de Psychologie Scientifique de
        Langue Francaise, XVI-mes Journées d'Etudes.
        Barcelona. 22-24. September.

Wode, Henning (1974)   Some Stages in the Acquisition
        of Questions by Monolingual Children, Part I.
        II. Arbeitspapire zur Spracherwerk,
        Englisches Seminar der Universität, Kiel.

Wode, Henning (1975)   Der Erwerb von Fragenstrukturen
        in der Kindersprache. In G. Drachman (ed.)
        Salzburger Beiträge zur Linguistik II.
        Günter Narr, Tübingen.

Text Analysis as an Approach to the Study of Early Linguistic Operations

G.W.Shugar

Text analyses which will be reported in this paper deal with text produced by child and adult together at the stage of linguistic development when the child can produce one or two words at. a time. The paper will deal with the process by which texts may be said to be constructed conjointly, and with the linguistic operations ascribed to the child which account for his contributions to this process.

TEXT ANALYSIS AS AN APPROACH

First, some arguments will be presented adopting text analysis as a general approach to language

*This research was supported by Grant P57 from the Committee for Psychological Sciences, Polish Academy of Sciences. The author wishes to thank the editors of this volume for helpful comments on the earlier version of this paper, and also Dr. Ida Kurcz and Boguslaw Jankowski for their remarks.and also Krystyna Więcko who collected the data on the child Kasia. Thanks are also due to the mothers who cooperated in these observations.

acquisition processes. The first question that arises
is: What does text analysis mean with respect to the
child's earliest utterances? I shall rely upon Halliday's (1970) definition of text as the fundamental
function of language, through which any other language
function is realized. It is language in operation,
occurring in a given situational context; text is always systematically related to the context, which determines both content and its organization. If we
wish to examine how the child puts together the components of language and extracts the various kinds of
rules governing their combinations and uses (the 'how'
of first language acquisition), we are obliged to take
into account the multi-process context determined
socially, culturally and linguistically. At the same
time, if we envisage the child as an active agent who
utilizes his growing linguistic ability to act upon,
as well as reflect upon, his environment, then we must
relate both the demands the child makes upon language
and the demands made upon the child's language by the
environment. We require an approach which relates adult
speech to the child and child speech to the adult within
the contexts of interdependent activity (as opposed to
dealing with input to the child and child output as separate categories of phenomena in the language acquisition process). It is unquestionable that the child
acquires and uses language simultaneously. As Halliday
expresses it, it is the systematic relation to context
that makes language learnable (Halliday, 1975). The
analysis of text, by definition, allows us to examine
this relation.

But does the notion of text apply at all at
these early stages of language acquisition? Basic to
text analysis is the notion of mutually shared information. The structure proper to text is an informational
one, implying the constitutive roles of receiver and
sender (Mayenowa, 1974; Halliday and Hasan, 1973).
According to Halliday (1975) the informative function
emerges when the child starts to say something which
the interlocutor does not know; he describes it as the
one function inherent in language. However, there appears to be an earlier, more primitive informative
function served by the child's utterance once he starts
to speak. Uttering some content is a means of acting
upon the outside world, in this case transferring to a
listener some information expressed linguistically,
with effects upon the content of the next speaker's
utterance. In speaking, the child acts as if he knows
that what he utters will be taken into account by the
interlocutor who will deal with that informational
content - by adding to it, changing it, negating it,
and so on. The child acts as if he knows that he can
serve as a <u>source</u> of information which is instrumental
in producing new utterances containing novel information (new effects) as well as confirming old informa-·

tion (known effects). This type of linguistic activity
on the part of the child seems highly analogous to his
other forms of manipulative and explorative activities.
To the extent that the child deliberately pursues such
linguistic interchanges, we may impute an intentional
involvement by the child.

In complementary fashion, the adult in these
same encounters acts as if he also knows that the content of his utterance will be taken into account by the
child. As a source of linguistically expressed information, the adult adapts his utterance content to the
child's possible response. He asks questions he knows
the child can answer, and he also explicitly evaluates
the child's information (its success, appropriateness,
effectiveness). The entire enterprise of the early dialogue rests on reaching commonality of information, a
given semantic 'edifice', to use Halliday's term, mo-
mentarily erected within a given situational context.
Therefore one can say that, before the child acquires
the status of independent producer of information unknown to his interlocutor, he will produce information,
in an utterance dependency relation, that can be mutually shared with the adult.

Text analysis can only be undertaken when
there is 'text', that is to say, when there is a text
which coheres within itself as well as with the context which gives rise to it. If we admit the notion
that text can be constructed by two partners, adult and
child together, in connected utterances, then we can
begin analysis of conjointly produced text. A large
portion of the child's utterances are excluded from text
analysis. They may be considered as 'non-text', which
function as accompaniments to or instrumentals for other
activities the child is engaged in. But a considerable
portion enters a dialogue framework. These are utterances directed to an addressee who responds to the informational content of the utterance. The child engages in these enterprises early in the game, at the
one-word stage and, if we examine the process, we find
that he places his utterance in systematic and meaningful relations to the adult's utterances (this will be
referred to again in the discussion). With regard to
the textual function of language, on the basis of present data and the facts of normal child language development, the following developmental progression may be
hypothesized:

From NON-TEXT to CONTRIBUTION TO TEXT to TEXT AS OWN
PRODUCTION.

What does text analysis require as a conceptual framework? The central concepts are text, situation
and information-sharing processes. Let us consider further the concept of 'situation' in this framework.

According to Halliday, text is a situation-semantic
organization of information, whose structure is dependent upon the situation within which the text undergoes
organization. However a situation giving rise to text
is not necessarily the same situation which is referred
to in the text. There may be some degree or quality of
displacement one from the other. It seems necessary
therefore to make a distinction between two types of
situation in terms of functional relation to the text-
building process. One type is the situational context
in which receiver and sender are present and active,
that is, the situation within which text arises and to
which it contributes informationally. The other type
is the situation about which information is formulated
linguistically, to which reference is made. Both types
of situation are of necessity involved. The former provides the activity (or pragmatic context) which determines the demands made upon language, while the latter
provides the sources of information for the text-
constructing process. By adhering to this distinction
one is enabled to identify each situation type and relate them to each other. The above distinction has been
utilized in the text analyses to be reported in this
paper.

In the analyses to be presented here consideration will be given to the following range of problems
which appear to be basic to the organization of text by
child and adult in the early dialogue stage:

- the pattern of the dialogue unit (episode).
- the contribution made by the adult.
- the contribution made by the child.
- the linguistic operations ascribed to the
  child enabling him to make his contribution to the text-constructing process.

NATURE OF THE DATA

If we record the natural flow of activity of
the child at the age in question, which occurs in settings with participation of, or access to, an adult, we
find segments of activity which comprise intermittent
dialogue-type engagements of child and adult. Behaviour
stream analyses of two children over one year of early
language development (between 18 and 36 months) have
shown that text-constructing enterprises occur from
moment to moment embedded in the stream of ongoing
activity. These 'verbal episodes' occur with regularity and are of brief duration; they include about one
half of the child's total sum of utterances in observations lasting 1-1½ hours at a stretch. These episodes
may be 'lifted out' of the stream for closer inspection,
while retaining the context of prior, concurrent, and
succeeding activity and their situations. Their unitary
status is determined by criteria of sameness of partici-

pants, topic, and situation of reference. If one of
these components changes while verbal activity continues, a new unit commences. These units may be regarded as chaining together. A verbal episode chain
terminates when activity turns from essentially linguistic to other forms of activity.

The analyses reported here are based on the
following corpora from three children: 52 episodes from
a one-hour observation with Małgosia, aged 1;7, MLU in
words 1.2; 62 episodes from a one-hour observation with
Mikołaj, aged 2;0, MLU 2.0; 62 episodes from a 20-minute
observation with Kasia, aged 2;0, MLU 1.7. (The observation on Kasia has been included to extend the comparative data base; however its short duration and mass-
ing of verbal episodes render her data less varied and
representative than those of the other children, with
effects upon the results. Most of Kasia's time was
spent with picture books.) All three children were
acquiring Polish. The observations were conducted at
home with the mother in the case of Małgosia and Kasia,
and in the outdoor sandplay area with Mikołaj with
mother and another caretaker present. The observer
played a passive participant role. Observations were
transcribed from tape.

Findings of analyses of the data obtained from
one of these children (Małgosia), reported elsewhere
(Shugar, in press), have been corroborated and expanded
in the present report.

THE PATTERN OF THE DIALOGUE UNIT (EPISODE)

In the verbal episode, one of the partners,
usually the adult, starts off by referring to some situation, and focussing on some element of it as topic.
In his first connecting utterance the child usually
refers to the same situation. The adult continues to
deal with the same reference situation, but we soon
notice that the child tends to shift to a different
reference situation. This results in a corresponding
shift of the adult's reference situation so that it
matches the child's. What happens then is that the
adult and child engage in matching reference situations.
This results in a corresponding shift of the adult's
reference situation so that it matches the child's. What
happens then is that the adult and child engage in matching reference situations. The burden of the game falls
heavily upon the adult, who must identify and explicitly recognize what the child is talking about, in order
to establish commonality of reference situation. It
seems highly analogous to a hide-and-seek game. These
early text constructions seem to be purely 'reporta-
tive' in nature, with a strong playful ingredient.
Few of them seem to have an instrumental character.

Using text constructions for purposes other than the
game in itself appears to be a further complication
of the process.

The enterprise proceeds in instalments. Each
instalment may suffice and terminate the venture, but
the game usually proceeds to two, three or more instalments. If it turns out that the first instalment is a
successful one (the child's utterance is accepted as
effective), then the child readily carries on into the
second and third instalment. It is in these successive
instalments that the child begins to introduce what we
have called variations and innovations in text-construction through manipulation of topic and reference situation.

In more formal terms, the pattern may be described as follows. Utterances are organized into unitary sequences within a larger verbal episode. A
verbal episode is a single action sequence within the
behaviour stream. (The overlapping or interpenetration
of units and sub-units of sequential verbal behaviour
is a consequence of procedures applied in the analysis
of the whole behaviour stream. That is, the criteria
applied for inter- and intra-verbal episode analysis
are consistent with those elaborated for all behaviour
stream analysis. For further details see Shugar,
1976.) Three utterances are involved in each sub-unit
of a verbal episode. The first, second and third
utterances form the first sub-unit; if the third
utterance is taken up and carried further, a second
sub-unit emerges, comprised of the third, fourth and
fifth utterances; and so on. Accordingly, any utterance will occupy one of three positions in the chaining sub-units: initial, mid and final. There are two
variants which may be diagrammed thus:

Variant I	Variant II
Adult	Child
Child	Adult
Adult	Child
Child	Adult
Adult	Child
etc.	etc.

Any episode may start in one or the other variant. Which
of the two variants emerges depends upon the initiating
partner, adult or child. The variant used in an episode
has considerable consequences for the text-constructing
enterprise, since position of the utterance determines

its role in the process. The utterances in initial and final positions play a more important and responsible role than the utterance in mid position as carrier of essential information, both textual and pragmatic. Speaking in mid position, the utterer benefits both from the information contained in the initial utterance and from the back-feeding information in the final utterance. In Variant I, the adult assumes the heavier role, providing a favourable position for the child's utterance; in mid position the child utilizes information from the first utterance and benefits from that contained in the following one. In Variant II, the child is scarcely able to provide the kind of information serving such functions. However he often strives to get into the more responsible information-imparting position, particularly the initial position, by shifting the reference situation (which opens a new episode). But his inability to satisfy the demands of the role results in a return to Variant I.

To illustrate how the two variants work, here are two fragments from the data:

Variant I.

Mother: A kto kupił Małgosi buciki?   Child is sitting on
'And who bought shoes for   mother's lap.
Małgosia?'   Mother is putting on her shoes.

Child: Dziadziuś

'Grandpa'

Mother: Dziadziuś, tak ... Dziadziuś kupił...

'Grandpa, yes ... Grandpa bought ...'

Child: Mamusia

'Mummy'

Mother: Mamusia kupi, tak?

'Mummy's going to buy, yes?'

The first variant, as we see, works well. Mother supplies the text as well as the tasks and positive assessments. The child satisfies the task in the first subunit and in the second operates innovatively upon the text. Mother complies and supplies new text appropriate

234

to the child's utterance. Thus the child manipulates old text and evokes new text from the partner.

Variant II.

Child:	Kuba .. koba	Child is putting
		wooden disks into a
	(?)	small tin pail.
Mother:	Co?	
	'What?'	
Child:	Kuba .. koba .. kuba .. kuba	
Mother:	Kubeł! To wiaderko	Often used synony-
		mously; 'kubeł'
	'Bucket! That's a	usually refers to
	pail'	'garbage-pail',
		'wiaderko' refers
		to 'small pail'.
Child:	Moka ma .. makao ma	
	(Maka, makao = Małgosia? ma = have)	
Mother:	Co Małgosia ma?	
	'What has Małgosia?'	
Child:	De le ko .. wadeko .. o .. o	
	(attempt to repeat	Child shows the
	'wiaderko'? Confused	pail.
	syllables? See	
	stressed syllable	
	in model)	
Mother:	Co to jest, Małgosiu?	
	'What is that, Małgosiu?'	
E:	Co daleko?	
	'What's far away?'	
	(interprets first segment	
	of child's utterance)	
Child:	(Silence)	

The second variant does not work so well. The child's first attempt to supply text, once mother understands, is rejected and a new word substituted. The child tries to supply more text, which mother turns into text containing a new task (to repeat the new word). The child's attempt to comply is phonologically confused and she resorts to pointing out the object referred to. Variant II works poorly at this stage since the child has little text to supply.

The remainder of this paper will deal with Variant I, the more successful variant. But first let us look further at Variant II from the viewpoint of its informational value for the child.

A further example of Variant II occurred three minutes later in the observation following the second of the above fragments. The child has resumed her activity with the pail and disks and produces an utterance in the nature of an accompaniment. There is no evidence that it is intended to engage the adult's attention. But the Mother picks up the utterance, and a verbal exchange ensues.

Child: Wy da le da le ko (murmured)   Child is dropping wooden
(wiaderko?)   disks into the tin pail.

Mother: Co daleko?

'What's far away?'

Child: Da le .. e (murmured)

(echoes?)

Mother: Co daleko, Gosiu? (pause)

'What's far away, Gosiu?

Co daleko?

'What's far away?'

Child: (Silence)   Child continues to drop disks into pail.

Mother: No .. co to jest?   Mother's voice sounds en-
'Well .. what is it?'   couraging but vague.

Child: (Silence)   Child gets up from the floor, hands E some disks, goes to a plate of cherries, takes one.

It seems that the child is engaged in re-
hearsing the phonological versions heard a few minutes
previously in the same activity situation. Her mother's
concern is to check the correctness of the interpretation 'daleko = far away' of the earlier episode, and
she provides no new text. The example does not satisfy
the demands of a text-building episode: there is no
shared information. But from the child's point of view
useful information may be forthcoming from a 'failed'
enterprise. In this case, the child may have discovered
there is another and more approved word wiaderko to replace an old one kubeł, and also that there is such a
word as daleko, whose meaning is to be discovered. Con-
ceivably the child will use such information in the
future. However, there is no data in the observation
that provides direct evidence that this occurred.

Returning now to Variant I, the prevailing
variant in the data, it will be shown that this variant
offers many possibilities for the child to make successful contributions to text-constructing.

The contribution of each partner according to
Variant I will now be discussed.

ADULT'S CONTRIBUTION TO TEXT-CONSTRUCTION

The pattern of utterance organization is such
that two kinds of information are constantly being ex-
changed between partners. One type relates to propositional content, referring to objects, states and events
in the world, specifically selected from some reference
situation. The other type of information is pragmatic:
tasks, outcomes, and assessments of these outcomes.
Both kinds of information are built into the text-constructing process. The adult's initial utterance is
usually in the form of a question (setting the task)
and her final utterance takes the form of an assessment
often accompanied by new text. She may either confirm
or fail to accept, or simply 'tolerate' the outcome
(how the child handles the task). Confirmation is expressed explicitly or implicitly in a number of ways:
by repetition, acquiescing with 'yes', expansion, or a
new question, or any combination of these. If we judge
from what the adult disconfirms, there seem to be three
criterial conditions the child's utterance must satisfy. It should be an acceptable (recognizable) phonological version of the linguistic form the child is
using (that is, it must be understood). It should, at
least in some cases, be the conventionally used lexical
form (replacing 'baby talk' forms in prior usage; this
was important for one mother). But most stringently
checked was the effectiveness of the utterance as a
valid coding of a given reference situation. What the
adult confirmed was always the congruence between the
linguistic form and the referent coded, as the necessary

condition for sharing information. The adult made use
of two ways to correct the match between child's text
and reference situation. One way was to substitute
the appropriate form: she would say, 'Not a butterfly
- it's a flower'. Or she would locate an appropriate
reference situation to match the child's form: she
would produce the situation, e.g., show a picture of a
butterfly, and say, 'This is a butterfly'.

In the data analyzed a strong prevalence of
confirmations of the child's utterances was found.
This was particularly the case in the first sub-unit.
In fact, this appeared to be an important condition for
the child to engage further in active text constructing.

CHILD'S CONTRIBUTION TO TEXT-CONSTRUCTING

In terms of length, a typical verbal episode
for all three children contained three or four successive sub-units, as described above. If we examine the
contribution of the child's mid-position utterance in
the basic variant, we find an interesting picture which
suggests a particular process.

In the first sub-unit, the child supplies
direct answers to the question task set in the initial
utterance. In the vast majority of cases, this answer
is accepted (confirmed), as stated above. Starting
with the second sub-unit, and reaching a frequency
peak in the third, the child starts to manipulate the
text by introducing what have been called variations
and innovations, by means of various linguistic operations (see below). This is achieved by shifting what
is talked about: the child shifts to a new reference
situation, or, if remaining with the same reference
situation, shifts the topical focus to another situational element. The former is a major shift, requiring location of a new source of information. (This
initiates a new episode where the child gets into initiating position, as in Variant II). In the later sub-
units, however, if the original episode is sufficiently
prolonged, the child tends to revert to the simpler
direct answer. In one case (Małgosia) the child employed 'empty' vocalizations in final sub-units of an
episode. The 'empty' utterance seems for this child
to mark a withdrawal from the text-building activity
while at the same time continuing to supply an utterance in the expected position. It serves to inform
the partner of this fact, and she acts accordingly,
as the following example shows. This fragment com-
prises the sixth and seventh sub-units of a verbal
episode.

Mother:	<u>No kurka! A tutaj, co jest?</u> 'A hen! And here, what's this?'	Mother is showing a picture-book and the child looks at it from time to time.
Child:	<u>ga ge ga</u> (gę = goose sound in nursery talk)	Child is pushing her doll's pram back and forth.
Mother:	<u>A ty wiesz, że to jest gęś, tak?</u> 'And you know that's a goose, yes?'	
Child:	<u>ba ba ba ba bab ... eeee</u> (No interpretation possible)(Intonation resembles mother's previous utterance)	Child pushes the pram handle up and down.
Mother:		Mother now offers child a mouthful of food. Child opens mouth.

Analysis of the children's mid-position utterances in successive sub-units of the episode from our three sets of data provides a comparable picture, presented in Figures 1a, b and c. Percentages are based on the total number of child utterances occurring in mid-position in each successive sub-unit. (Since verbal episodes vary in length, the total number of sub-units progressively diminishes.) We note here individual differences in episode length: the two girls, Małgosia and Kasia, engaged in long episodes (up to 7 sub-units), while the boy Mikołaj regularly has short ones (4 sub-units). But there is an overall similarity in the curves for each child. Direct answering shows a falling-rising curve, while innovations and variations show a rising-falling one. There is an added curve for Małgosia (dotted line), the only child who used empty vocalizations; these utterances, devoid of meaning, dominate when the episode is overly prolonged.

As these figures show, there is a common tendency to comply with the task set at the start, then to innovate, then to fall back on direct answering in longer episodes.

<u>Reference Situation Shift.</u> Let us now examine more closely the matter of reference situation manipula-

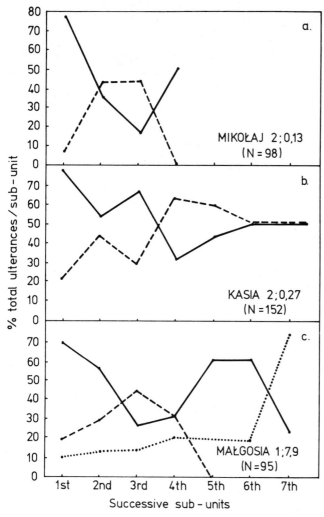

Fig. 1 (a,b,c).

Child utterance types in successive
sub-units across verbal episodes in
the variant: Mother-Child-Mother.
Percentages based on total mid-
position utterances for each sub-
unit.

Types: —————————, Direct answers;
- - - - - -, Variations and innovations; . . . . . , Vocalizations.

TABLE 1.   Sources of Reference Situations (RS) based
           Malgosia 1;7.9, Kasia 2;0.27, and Mikolaj
           Total number of episodes for each child

Utterer's role relation to Reference Situation	RS perceptually given			Spatio- RS dis
	Mal	Kas	Mik	Mal
In situ (child is active participant in RS				
a) immediate action or state (co-occurrence of activity and reference situation)	37.8	17.7	41.9	0.0
b) immediately succeeding action or state	0.0	0.0	6.5	18.9
c) immediately preceding action or state	0.0	0.0	1.6	5.6
Total	37.8	17.7	50.0	24.5
Ex situ (child is exterior to RS)				
a) recalled event	0.0	0.0	0.0	3.8
b) simulated real-life experience	0.0	1.7	0.0	7.5
c) pictured scene or event	20.8	40.3	18.4	0.0
d) non-visible but retrievable by search	0.0	1.6	1.6	5.6
Total	20.8	43.6	21.0	16.9
Sum Total	58.6	61.3	71.0	41.4

* A few episodes where RS was absent (Verbal games,

on analysis of Verbal Episodes of 3 children:
2;0.13 from one observational study each.
respectively; 53, 62 and 62.

temporal relation of Reference Situation to Utterance

| placed in time/place | | Total | | |
Kas	Mik	Mal	Kas	Mik
12.9	9.7	37.8	30.6	51.7
12.9	4.8	18.9	12.9	11.3
1.6	8.1	5.6	1.6	9.4
27.4	22.6	62.3	45.1	72.6
1.6	0.0	3.8	1.6	0.0
3.2	0.0	7.5	4.9	0.0
0.0	0.0	20.8	40.3	19.3
0.0	4.8	5.6	1.6	6.3
4.8	4.8	37.7	48.4	25.6
32.2	27.4	100.0	93.5*	98.2*

reciting).

tion. The point has been stressed that the children showed a certain versatility and ease in executing shifts from one reference situation to another as a means of locating new sources of information. The question arises as to the range within which the child executes such shifts. To establish the range of reference situation accessibility, those features were selected which serve to differentiate reference situations from the immediate activity situation, considered as the primary reference situation.

One possibility is for reference situation and activity situation to coincide or overlap, that is, the child refers to what he is doing at the time; he is then a participant in the reference situation. Another possibility concerns the degree of spatio-temporal displacement from the activity situation: the child refers to a previous activity situation or to a subsequent one, in which he has been, or will be, a participant. On the other hand, the reference situation may be otherwise displaced; it may be a situation external to the child, an event observed or presented in a picture, or a situation recreated from past experience (such as putting dolls through the supper, bath, and putting-to-bed routine). In all these cases the child is not a participant within the situation but plays an active observer role. These three relations between activity and reference situations all occur in the data.

An analysis of the data was performed to establish the range and frequency of reference situation types. The procedure was to identify reference situations for all verbal episodes and to categorize them according to two features: (1) child's role relation: participant or external observer, and (2) spatio-temporal relation to the actual activity situation. Findings are presented in Table 1.

First, if we look at the spatio-temporal relation, ignoring the role relation, we find that the perceptually present reference situation dominates over the displaced reference situation, as would be expected. The child builds text mainly on the basis of what occurs within the visual field. But at the same time there are considerable percentages of episodes having displaced reference situations. Of the latter, the largest part concern the anticipated activity situation.

Secondly, with respect to role relation in the case of two children (Mikołaj and Małgosia) there is a predominance of reference situation types involving active participation. The most frequent reference situation types where the child is an observer are perceptually given (usually in a picture).

Thirdly, considering jointly the spatio-temporal and role relations we find the lowest frequency of occurrence for maximally displaced reference situations (not perceptually given, external role). The child seldom referred to a remote situation in which he was not an active participant. Such types of reference situations may lie beyond his cognitive resources at this age.

No direct evidence is provided by this analysis as to the shifts across reference situations, but some conclusions may be drawn from the frequency with which reference situations occur. The child shifts most frequently to reference situations easily accessible as sources of new information. These are the perceptually given in both activity context and picture context, and also the forward-displaced, or anticipated, activity situation.

The shift tactic is, however, successful to the extent that the adult partner cooperates with the child. It rests upon the major text-constructor to identify the child's selected reference situation and establish it as a common starting point for the next venture in text-constructing by providing the appropriate textual material upon which the child can exercise his linguistic operations.

LINGUISTIC OPERATIONS PERFORMED BY THE CHILD

At the age in question the child is only beginning to acquire substantive linguistic material (stabilized sound patterns, appropriate lexical items) which he may independently produce; he is however apparently using certain operations upon the substantive material provided him in adult utterances.

What operations may be ascribed to the child as the means by which he is enabled to contribute to text-constructing? The children produce very little of the text on their own. Mikołaj is exceptional in this respect; he produces the most from his inner store. The girls mainly utilize the material already produced in previous utterances. The systematic relations between the child's utterance and foregoing utterance(s) may be described in terms of formal operations upon already produced text. Previous text may be both the partner's and the child's own. These comprise the means by which the child establishes meaningful structured relations. (More will be said about this in the conclusions.)

Three basic kinds of operations account for all the children's contributions to text-constructing: selective reproduction, substitution, and conjunction. The following illustrates the variations of these three kinds of operations.

I. <u>Selective reproduction of word of topical focus</u>
(one-word utterance).

  a. Without modification

1. Mother: <u>Mamusia przyjechała autem</u>
          <u>dlatego ciocia</u>...

          'Mummy came by car be-
          cause auntie...'

Mother and Auntie
(E) have just
arrived.

  Małgosia (interrupting): <u>Autem</u>

      'By car'

2. Mother: <u>Właściwie to są szczury,</u>
          <u>a nie myszy</u>

          'Actually those are
          rats not mice'

Mother and child
are looking at a
picture together.

  Kasia: <u>Szczury</u>

      'Rats'

  b. With modification: order change within a meaning
unit

3. Auntie: <u>Widzisz jak się kręci</u>
          <u>kółeczko</u>

          'See how the ring turns'
          (itself + turns = turns)

Watching the
tape turning in
the recorder.

  Kasia: <u>Kręci się</u>

      'turns'
      (turns + itself = turns)

  c. Selection between two alternatives

4. Mother: <u>Lisek grzeczny czy</u>
          <u>niegrzeczny?</u>

          '(Is) the little fox bad
          or good?'

Looking at a
picture to-
gether.

  Kasia: <u>Grzeczny</u>

      'Bad'

II. <u>Substitution</u> (one-two word utterances mainly).

  a. Replacement of QU-word by answer-word from
appropriate lexical set. (Arrow signifies replacement.) Examples:

KTO   →   Mamusia, Kasia, Niuniu, ciocia, etc.
(who)   (Mummy, Kasia, teddybear, auntie,
                etc.)

KOMU   →   Mamuni, cioci, Paniuni
(Who to/for)   (to/for Mummy, auntie, Paniunia)

CO-ROBI → alulu, miju miju, pije
(What-do)   (sleep - child's word, wash - child's
               word, drink)

GDZIE   →   tu, tam, na drzewie
(Where$_{locus}$)   (here, there, on the tree)

NA CZYM → tu, koniku
(on What$_{locus}$) (here, (on) rocking-horse)

b. Replacement of one member of QU-word set by an
    alternative member. Examples:

From CO set: krowa → kaczka → niuniu
    (What)   (cow)   (duck)   (teddybear)

From CZYJ set: Kasi → mój
    (Whose)   (Kasia's) (my)

From CO-ROBI set: usiądź →   biega
    (What-do)   (sit down)   (run)

From Z KIM set: ciocią →   tatą
    (With whom)   (with auntie) (with daddy)

c. Use of a 'general replacer'. Examples:

TEŻ (too) replaces any member of the CO-ROBI set
                                (What-do)

5. Mother: <u>Usiądź, Małgosieńko</u>   Child is standing
                             and grinding her heel
       'Sit down, Peggy'   against an object;
                             Mother is also stand-
                             ing.

Małgosia: <u>Mamusia też.</u>
           <u>'Mummy too'</u>

d. Replacement by a negative of an affirmative form.
    Examples:

NIE MA   replaces   JEST   and   TAM
(is not (there),   (is (there))   (there)
  allgone)

6. Mikołaj: <u>Ciocia, tam</u>   Child stops in front
of a strange lady in
'Auntie, there'   the yard and shows a
twig.

   Mikołaj: <u>Nie ma ciocia patyka</u>   Child put the twig
behind his back and
'Not there Auntie   uses a pathetic tone
stick' ('ciocia'   of voice.
used as vocative)

7. Mother: <u>Bo to lokomotywa,</u>   Looking at a picture
<u>jest tak?</u>   together.

'Because that's an
engine, (that) is
right?'

   Mikołaj: <u>Nie ma ... po po po ..</u>(repeating syllable
'po' until Mother
'Is not (there)...   completes word)
po-'

   Mother: <u>Pociąg</u>

'Train'

  e. Substituting one intonational pattern for another,
equivalent to substituting one sentence type for
another. Examples:

Replacing affirmative by interrogative

8. Kasia: <u>Szczury</u>   Looking closely at
picture with Mother.
'Rats'

   Kasia: <u>Tam szczury?</u> (rising intonation on final
syllable)
'There rats?'

Replacing interrogative by negative

9. Małgosia: <u>Kuku nie?</u> (rising Child knocks small
intonation) battery hard against
'Hurt not?'   her elbow.
(kuku-child's word
for a hurt)

   Małgosia: <u>kuku nie</u> (falling intonation)

'Hurt not.'

f. Dismembering a unitary form into two parts with different meanings (morphemic part-whole combining). Examples:

MA (verb of possession and/or existence) + CZYJ or KTO set words

10. Małgosia: <u>Ma Gosi</u>   Child eyes Auntie, who has sat down on
            = has + Gosia   her stool, with a
            (possessive/dative fixed unsmiling stare.
            form)

    Małgosia: <u>Ma cioci</u>   Continues to stare until Auntie gets off
            = has + Auntie   her stool.
            (possessive/dative form)

11. Mikołaj: <u>Ma munia</u>   Child places pebbles in Mother's hand.
            'Take, Mummy'
            = has + Mummy

    Mikołaj: <u>Ma Paniunia</u>   and then gives pebbles into P's
            'Take, Paniunia' hand.
            = has + Paniunia
            (pet name for 'Pani', female address form)

g. Conjoining negator with member of CO-ROBI set.

12. Kasia: <u>Nie</u> (in protesting tone)   Mother is pulling her away from the
        'no'   tape recorder.

    Mother: <u>Co nie?</u>   Mother releases child.
        'What no?'

    Kasia: <u>Nie kręci</u>   Gazing into the tape recorder
        'Not turn' window.

III. <u>Conjoining</u> (one-two word utterances mainly).

a. Adding final syllable(s) to complete a word (one-word utterance).

13. Mother: <u>Tutaj jest kartofelek, ce...</u> Mother and child are playing at cooking
        'Here is a potato, o ...' with toy pots.

    Kasia: <u>bula</u>
        'cebula' = onion

b. Adding a word to complete or expand prior
    utterance (one-word utterance).

14. Auntie: <u>Mam wszystkie w</u>   Child is transferring
            <u>ręku, wszystkie.</u>   pebbles into Auntie's
                                     hand.
            'I have (them) all
            in my hand, all'

    Mikołaj: <u>Kamienie</u>

            'Pebbles'

15. Mother: <u>Pani śpi</u>   Mother and child are
                                     looking at a picture
            'The lady is   together.
            sleeping'

    Małgosia: <u>Kocykem</u>

             '(Under) the blanket'
             = pod kocykem

c. Juxtaposing two consecutive utterances in mean-
    ingful relation (one-word utterance).

16. Małgosia: <u>Główka</u>   Child and mother are
                                     examining a picture
             'Head'   of a sleeping boy
                                     with a cap on his
    Małgosia: <u>Czapka</u>   head.

             'Cap'

d. Conjoining two 'general replacers' (two-word
    utterance).

    TEŻ (too) replacing CO-ROBI set, and DRUGI/DRUGA
    (other, next) replacing CO set

17. Mother: <u>Włożymy buty</u>   Mother is putting on
                                     child's shoe.
            'We'll put on shoes'

    Małgosia: <u>Drugi też</u>

             'Other too'

IV. <u>Combinations of above operations</u> (two-three word
     utterances).

a. Substitution + Selective reproduction.

18. Auntie: Kto jedzie?   Auntie and child are
                                     looking at a picture
              'Who is riding?'   together.

    Mikołaj: Niuniu jedzie

              'Teddybear is riding'

b. Selective reproduction + Completion of prior
   utterance (IIIb).

   Adding words from CO-ROBI set and GDZIE set

19. Mother: Słonik też   Looking at a picture.

              'Elephant too'

    Kasia: Tu też jedzie

              'Here too rides'
              = (He) is riding here too.

c. Negating embedded assertion + Selection between
   alternatives

20. Auntie: To jest małpa czy   Auntie (E) and child
              piesek?   are looking at a
                                     picture.
              'It's a monkey or a
              doggie?'

    Kasia: Nie .. piesek

              'No .. doggie'
              (=(It is) not (a monkey) + (It is)
              a doggie)

        Further examples of the above and other combi-
natory patterns are contained in IIc, d, e, g.

        The formal operations described above can be
reduced to two: substitution and conjunction. These
correspond to the interdependent axes along which any
linguistic unit is constructed, i.e. paradigmatic and
syntagmatic. Firstly, the child uses already formed and
functioning paradigmatic sets differentiated by semantic
function. These sets contain alternatives among which
the child selects with some ease. Secondly, the choice
the child will make depends apparently on at least two
variables: (a) the extent of his comprehension of the
syntagmatic context provided in the partner's text,
and (b) his intention to either stay within this context
or make a shift by changing focal referent or entire
reference situation. In respect to the latter, the child
manoeuvres intentionally and with facility inside the
available range of accessible reference situations.

DISCUSSION: RELEVANCE OF THIS STUDY TO THE ACQUISITION
OF MEANINGFUL STRUCTURES

The notion of text as operational language has
been employed as a unifying notion for dealing with
early language data emanating both from child and interlocutor. From findings derived by the methodological
procedures developed here, some conclusions may be
drawn pertaining to the child's linguistic use of meaningful relations which would reflect his current state
of cognitive knowledge about his world.

Before the child is able to put together two
or more words spontaneously, he is already connecting
his utterances to those of other speakers in a structurally meaningful way. This may be an early strategy by
which to express his knowledge of what can be meant
through language. An examination of the relations in
question shows that they comprise the same semantic relations he will predictably be producing in his first
word combinations, as numerous studies have shown
(Brown, 1973). Categories such as agent, action, object of action, location, destination, and possession
are set into relation by the above strategy. This
suggests that the corresponding cognitive structures
are already formed and operative at an earlier period
than hitherto established from empirical data.

However, restrictions upon the possible
realizations of these relations are defined by the
limitations on the range of reference situations
accessible to the child. Within this range the child
manifests on the linguistic plane a freedom and versatility characteristic of his stage of intellectual
development.

A final point refers to the adult's function
in the development described. If in fact the child is
producing in joint text construction the same meaningful relations he will in due course be producing independently, then the adult as major partner in text construction can be said to influence the learning of these
and not other meanings. An adult-prescribed selection
is involved in the process of meaning formation during
text-construction.

The reported study is an exploratory one,
since no similarly oriented work has been located in
the literature. The above statements can serve only
as hypotheses calling for further verification. A
possible approach to early operational language has
been proposed, which lends itself to examining both
basic and selective language-formative processes.
These processes are basic in the sense that language
acquisition is embedded in language in use. Text, the

only source of language input to the child, is the
carrier of information about the linguistic system
from which the child must create his own system,
given his cognitive preparation. These processes have
a selective character in terms of the informational
content transmitted from adult to child, influencing
the latter's socialization and acculturation. Both
aspects seem inextricably intertwined in the acquisition of language.

REFERENCES

Brown, R. (1973)   A First Language: The Early Stages.
Harvard University Press, Cambridge, Mass.

Halliday, M.A.K. (1970)   Language Structure and
Language Function. In J. Lyons (ed.) New
Horizons in Linguistics. Penguin, Harmonds-
worth, Middx., England.

Halliday, M.A.K. (1975)   Learning How to Mean: Explorations in the Development of Language.
Edward Arnold, London.

Halliday, M.A.K. and Hassan, R. (1973)   Cohesion in
Spoken and Written English. Unpublished
manuscript, Summer School of Linguistics,
Ann Arbor, Michigan.

Mayenowa, M.R. (1974)   Teoria Tekstu a Tradycyjne
Zagadnienie Poetyki. In M.R. Mayenowa (ed.)
Tekst i Jezyk. Problemy Semantyczne.
Ossolineum, Wrocław.

Shugar, G.W. (1976)   Behavior Stream Organization
during Early Language Acquisition. Polish
Psychological Bulletin 7. 27-36.

Shugar, G.W. (In press)   Text Construction with an
Adult. A Form of Child Activity during Early
Language Acquisition. In G. Drachman (ed.)
Proceedings of First International Child
Language Colloquium, Salzburg, December
1974. Günter Narr, Tübingen.

4
Phonology, Semantics and Syntax

Only one paper on phonetics/phonology is given in this section. Others, whose main focus appeared to belong elsewhere, are placed under what were felt to be more appropriate headings but some reference is made to them here. The overlap of semantics and syntax papers is treated in the same way.

In his experimental study, Barton demonstrates that younger children discriminate certain phonological contrasts less well than older children, thus showing that the acquisition of auditory discrimination is a gradual process. This is in agreement with the conclusions from Fourcin's experimental work (section 1) and Waterson's naturalistic study (section 5). Barton emphasizes the importance of familiarity for discrimination: features that are regularly discriminated in familiar words are less easily discriminated in the unfamiliar. Other papers dealing with phonetics and phonology are those of Delack and Fowlow, and Tuaycharoen, who deal with pre-verbal vocalizations (section 2).

The relevance of the child's participation in communication and of the pragmatic function of his early attempts at speech is evident in the semantic and syntactic studies of Bowerman, Ferrier, Griffiths and Atkinson, Smoczyńska, and Woll.

Conflicting theoretical approaches to the development of meaning are discussed by Bowerman, who draws attention to the necessity for recognizing that a child classifies experiences on the basis of many different kinds of similarities. She proposes a theory which can account for this and which includes subjective experience as an essential factor.

Smoczyńska discusses the ways semantic information is used to establish different syntactic structures. She illustrates the value of taking interpersonal function of language into account, demonstrating that the child's utterances have additional meanings resulting from their interpersonal function.

The longitudinal studies of word usage in relation to context of Ferrier, and Griffiths and Atkinson, show how the child's meanings at first differ quite considerably from the adult's. The repetitive nature of the language used to the child is shown to influence which words are acquired first and the meaning they will have, thus accounting for the idiosyncratic nature of a child's word meanings.

Woll takes the Hallidayan view that structure and function in early speech are indissoluble and shows how the relationship between them gradually changes until they become independent of each other.

Ways in which a child's early language can be seen to be based on the adult language and yet be an independent system are shown by Ingham and by Kaper. Using Persian data, Ingham compares a child's simple verbal system with the complex system of adults. Kaper explains the apparently deviant usage of adverbs of some Dutch children as being patterned on the little known colloquial usage of adults. His examples of the use of 'stored fragments' in the acquisition of syntax of Dutch children links up with Clark's paper (section 5).

Papers by Clark, Miller (section 5) and Shugar (section 3) may also be read in conjunction with this section.

The Discrimination of Minimally-Different Pairs of Real Words by Children aged 2;3 to 2;11

D. Barton

This paper offers some empirical data to the
general debate on the role of perception in the acquisition of phonology. The experiment described here is
addressed to the question of whether most phonologically relevant discriminations can be made by a child at
an early stage of his or her phonological development
or whether they are acquired as pronunciation develops.
The resolution of this question of course affects
whether various proposed phonological descriptions can
have any psychological reality.

Work by Garnica (1971, 1973) and by Edwards
(1974) has begun to investigate the claims of Shvachkin (1948) that children can make most phonological
discriminations when they begin to speak and that there
is a consistent order of acquisition of discriminations.
The present study continues this investigation. Several
methodological changes are made, to give a well-con-
trolled experiment with a task that is as simple as
possible, but where the judgement nevertheless requires
reference to some internal representation. On the assumption that children around two and a half years of

*The study reported here was supported by a
Science Research Council Research Studentship, and by
the helpful comments of Neil Smith.

age can in fact make many of the discriminations, this
experiment aimed to investigate those discriminations
that were least likely to be known.

SUBJECT AND MATERIAL

The subjects were 20 children aged between
2;3 and 2;11 who were attending various playgroups in
the area of the University.

The pairs of words to be discriminated were
chosen so that the two words were monosyllables that
differed from each other in only one phonological
feature of one segment. The words were names of objects that children were likely to know and which could
be easily illustrated.

Each pair of words was illustrated on a separate 'language-master' card. These cards are approximately 10 x 25 cm. and two channels of sound track can
be recorded on them. Instructions were recorded on
each card: for example, one card had illustrations of
the pair 'goat' and 'coat'; 'point to the goat' was recorded on one track and 'point to the coat' on the other
track. The recordings were by an adult female speaking
in a normal voice.

PROCEDURE

The children were tested individually in
sessions testing several pairs. All sessions for any
child were completed within 10 days. While being
tested the child sat on one side of the machine, a modified 'language-master', where he could see the illustrations, and the experimenter sat on the other side
where he could operate the controls. By using the recorded stimuli in this situation the possible influence
of non-linguistic cues was greatly reduced. In carrying out the task the children soon learned to feed the
cards into the machine and it was this they attended to
rather than the experimenter.

There were two stages in the experiment:

(a) Identification of the words. All the cards to
be used in the session were presented randomly one at a
time with no soundtrack. The child was asked to identify each picture in turn. If he was unable to, he was
prompted until all the pictures could be consistently
identified. If the child named a picture before the experimenter named it only once (usually by saying 'can
you see a ... anywhere?') and the child could later
identify it, then it was recorded as prompted; lastly,
if the experimenter had to name it more than once (with
perhaps some explanation of its use, etc.), then it was
recorded as taught.

This part of the session was not finished until all the words could be identified by the child. To check on taught words, it was accepted that a child could identify a particular word if he could consistently discriminate it when it was contrasted with monosyllables that differed from it in all segments. For example, one could check 'log' by contrasting it with 'cat', 'head' and 'mat'. Identification was checked in this 'non-minimal' situation and it was not necessary for the child to produce every word.

(b) Discrimination of the pairs. In this second stage the cards were presented with the sound track on. They were presented one at a time and the child responded by picking out one of the pair. When all the cards had been presented once, the procedure was repeated. Continuing like this, there were five presentations of each pair; which track was heard was random with the proviso that by the end there were at least two instances of each track for each card. If the child failed to respond at any point, the same card was repeated until the child responded. The children were not told whether or not their responses were correct. For any pair which they got right on all five trials it was accepted that they would make the discrimination (p approx. 3%). There were no further trials on these pairs, but all other pairs were continued to give a total of 20 trials per pair. A criterion of 15 correct trials in 20 trials was interpreted as meaning that these pairs could be discriminated (p approx. 2%).

RESULTS

This short paper will deal with seven pairs of words that tested a contrast in the phonological feature of voicing, a class of oppositions that is usually regarded as one of the last to be acquired (for example, by Garnica, 1971, and by Shvachkin, 1948).

It was found that whereas some errors were made with named words, more were made with prompted words and even more with taught words. Most of the failures to discriminate occurred when at least one of the pair was a taught word. (This was despite the fact that these taught words could be identified correctly in the non-minimal situation.) In these cases it was not possible to know whether the difficulty was with the discrimination or whether it lay in not knowing these taught words adequately. To avoid the interfering effects of taught words, the results are first considered excluding them. These results are given in Table 1.

The results have been scored into four categories. The first category includes cases of correct discrimination of all the first five presentations. The second category was scored when at least 15 out of

TABLE 1. Number of subjects scoring in different categories, excluding any taught words.

	log lock	back bag	frock frog	coat goat	curl girl	bear pear	guard card	To- tal
Total number of subjects tested	13	16	15	16	16	19	15	
ditto excluding any pair where either word had to be taught	3	15	0	13	12	17	10	
First 5 correct	1	14		9	10	16	9	59
15/20 correct	2	1		2	1		1	7
random				1	1	1		3
consistent bias				1				1

TABLE 2. Comparison of results for pairs containing taught words with those not containing taught words.

	pairs containing taught words	pairs not containing taught words
First 5 correct	15 (37.5%)	59 (84.3%)
15/20 correct	10 (25.0%)	7 (10.0%)
random	6 (15.0%)	3 (4.3%)
consistent bias	9 (22.5%)	1 (1.4%)
Total	40	70

20 trials were correct, i.e. when the children made the discrimination but not perfectly. These two categories, where an ability to discriminate was demonstrated, account for nearly all the results. In the remaining instances there appeared to be two distinct patterns of response: there was random responding, where the child chose randomly between the pair of pictures, and there was biased responding, where he or she consistently chose one of the pictures and ignored the other. For pairs falling in these two categories it has not been demonstrated that the children could under no circumstances discriminate them, but only that they failed to in this situation.

DISCUSSION

These figures show greater abilities than is sometimes claimed (for example, in Garnica, 1971) and there are very few cases where children did not discriminate the pairs. Furthermore, there was a high level of unequivocal responding where children got discriminations consistently right. While individual children differed a great deal in their overall results, it was not the case that some children could do all the voicing discriminations while others could do none; rather, all of the children made some of the voicing discriminations. It should be recalled that in setting up the experiment, pairs were chosen that were thought to be most likely to give difficulties.

In interpreting these results, one wants to know if this ability to discriminate is limited to pairs of words known by the children. With pairs where one or both of the words had to be taught, the subjects did less well at the discrimination task; nevertheless, most of these pairs were discriminated. The results for 40 such instances are shown in Table 2 where they are compared with known pairs.

Thus, children who had all demonstrated some ability to make some voicing discriminations found more difficulty when they did not previously know the words. With the biased results it tended to be the case that one word was taught and the other named, and that the bias was towards the named word. These taught words were scattered throughout the pairs and the results do not seem to suggest that the children were somehow avoiding sounds that were difficult to discriminate.

The use of real words is, of course, a constraint (in that not all the possible minimal pairs of English can be tested), but the difference between taught words and known words found here highlights a problem that comes with dealing with invented words. This is the problem that errors may come from not knowing the words well enough, rather than from an inability to discriminate. This may affect results obtained with the 'Shvachkin-Garnica' technique, where all the stimuli are taught: it may explain the results obtained using the technique that suggest that older children cannot make these discriminations.

Similar results to those for voicing were obtained with pairs testing other phonological contrasts, such as coronality and nasality. The voicing pairs were not significantly easier or more difficult than these other pairs; a high level of accuracy was found for all the pairs tested. We can conclude that these discriminations have been acquired at a lower age than that tested.

It is not being suggested that the features represent perceptual dimensions. Acoustically-defined perceptual variables do not bear any one-to-one relationship to phonological classificatory dimensions, and it is the latter that we are studying here. When children can make these discriminations, it is being claimed that they are using the dimensions as classificatory dimensions. The children classify differently stimuli that differ phonologically only on the dimension of voicing, and so we conclude that they use the dimension of voicing.

However, we cannot conclude from these results that all voicing discriminations can be made. It had been intended that individual pairs, such as g/k, should represent the whole class of oppositions; this possibility is implicit in much speech discrimination work. (The bias towards the pair g/k was caused by the constraint that the pairs of words be ones that the children were likely to know.) However, this is unwarranted. Perceptually, not all pairs that differ only in voicing are equally easy, and while the order of acquisition and the order of difficulty are not necessarily the same, it is possible that difficulties of discrimination limit the acquisition of some voicing pairs. That different voicing pairs differ in their discriminability can be seen, for example, in Graham and House's widely-quoted study (1971). They claim an error rate of 'more than 30%' for voicing; on closer examination it will be seen that this high error rate comes only from one of the two pairs tested, s/z (with an error rate of 52%), while the other pair, t/d, had an error rate (13%) not significantly different from the mean. It follows that we cannot refer to certain classes of oppositions as being difficult to discriminate on the basis of just some members of the class.

The abilities of younger children, between 1;8 and 2;0, have also been investigated. The results

suggest that although they have more difficulty than
the older children, they too can generally make use of
the phonological feature of voicing in discrimination.

REFERENCES

Edwards, M.L. (1974)   Perception and Production in
    Child Phonology: the Testing of Four Hypo-
    theses. Journal of Child Language 1.
    205-219.

Garnica, O.K. (1971)   The Development of the Percep-
    tion of Phonemic Differences in Initial
    Consonants by English-speaking Children:
    a Pilot Study. Papers and Reports on Child
    Language Development 3. Stanford University.
    1-29.

Garnica, O.K. (1973)   The Development of Phonemic
    Speech Perception. In T.E. Moore (ed.)
    Cognitive Development and the Acquisition
    of Language. Academic Press, New York and
    London.

Graham, L.W. and House, A.S. (1971)   Phonological
    Oppositions in Children: a Perceptual
    Study. Journal of the Acoustical Society of
    America 49. 559-566.

Shvachkin, N.Kh. (1948)   The Development of Phonemic
    Speech Perception in Early Childhood. Re-
    printed in C.A. Ferguson and D.I. Slobin
    (eds.) (1973) Studies of Child Language De-
    velopment. Holt, Rinehart and Winston, New
    York.

The Acquisition of Word Meaning: An Investigation into some Current Conflicts

M. Bowerman

The last few years have seen a rising interest in the question of how children acquire the meanings of words. In recent literature on the subject, several areas of conflicting opinion have begun to come into focus. In this study, three such conflicts are investigated through the analysis of spontaneous speech data from two children.

Briefly, the issues to be discussed are as follows: 1) What kinds of cues do children use as a basis for extending words to novel referents early in development? 2) Do all the referents for which a child uses a particular word share one or more features or are words typically used 'complexively', such that no one feature is common to all referents? 3) How do children organize and store word meanings? Controversy has centred on whether word meaning is described most accurately as a set of semantic features or in terms of prototypical referents or 'best exemplars'.

The data referred to in the following analyses come from my two daughters, Christy and Eva. Christy is the older child by 2-1/2 years. I kept detailed records on both children by taking extensive daily notes and by tape recording periodically from the start of the one-word stage. Fairly complete records are available on the way in which almost every word was used from its first appearance in the child's speech to about 24 months. Data on word use continue beyond that point but are more selective.

BASES FOR EXTENDING WORDS TO NOVEL REFERENTS

Word for Objects. In her 'Semantic Feature' theory of the acquisition of word meaning, Clark (1973, 1974b) has argued that children's extensions of words to novel objects are initially based primarily on perceptual similarity. That is, objects that are referred to by the same word are perceptually similar in some way, particularly with regard to shape, and, to a lesser extent, size, texture, movement, and sound.

Nelson (1974) has recently argued strongly against this view. Citing Piagetian theory in support, she contends that children initially lack the ability to analyze objects into perceptual components like 'round' or 'four-legged' and to use these components in isolation as a basis for classification. Nelson argues instead that children at first experience objects as unanalyzed wholes and classify them in terms of the actions associated with them and the relationships into which they enter. They regard objects as similar if they are functionally similar, e.g., if they are acted upon or act spontaneously in a similar way.

Unlike Clark, Nelson views the perceptual characteristics of objects as playing a secondary rather than a primary role in the way children form concepts. Perception is secondary because it is used not as the basis for classification but simply to identify an object as a probable instance of a concept even when the object is experienced apart from the relationships and actions that are concept-defining.

The theories of Clark and Nelson make divergent predictions about how children initially use words for objects. Clark's theory predicts that a given word will be used for objects that are perceptually similar, regardless of function, while Nelson's predicts that the word will be used to refer to objects that either function in the same way, regardless of perceptual properties, or that the child predicts would function in the same way on the basis of similar perceptual properties. Both the perceptual and the functional accounts

of categorization agree on the salience of spontaneous motion as a basis for classifying animate crea-
tures, vehicles, etc. Thus, the conflict is primarily over the relative importance of static perceptual
features like shape.

Nelson (1973a) has presented some experimental
material in support of her claim that shared function
rather than similar perceptual properties is the primary
basis for children's early object concepts, but the data
are limited (only one concept, 'ball', was investigated).
Previously-reported naturalistic data on children's
spontaneous use of words for novel objects offer little
support for Nelson's theory. For example, some of the
overextensions reported in the diary studies that Clark
(1973) drew from in formulating her perception-based
theory are clearly incompatible with a theory that
stresses the prepotence of shared function (cf. Clark,
1975). ('Overextension' refers to the child's application of a word to a referent that an adult regards as
lying outside the semantic category labelled by that
word, e.g., 'doggie' for a horse.)

The spontaneous speech data from the two subjects of the present study provide further strong evidence against the theory that functional similarity
predominates over perceptual similarity in the child's
classification of the objects to which his early words
refer. In all the data from both children, there is
only a handful of examples of overextensions of words
to new objects purely on the basis of similar function
in the absence of shared perceptual features, and these
occurred relatively late, after many object words were
already known. In contrast, there are scores of examples of overextensions based on perceptual similarity,
especially shape, in the absence of functional similarity, and many of these occurred during the early period
of word acquisition.

These data would not be incompatible with
Nelson's theory if the instances of overextension based
on perceptual cues could be interpreted in accordance
with Nelson's proposal that perceptual cues are used
primarily to predict the function of an object so that
the object can be identified as a member of a known
function-based category. However, this interpretation
is not possible in many instances. Rather, the children often disregarded functional differences, i.e.
gross disparities in the way objects act or can be
acted upon, that were well known to them in the interests of classifying purely on the basis of perceptual similarities. Some examples illustrating this
phenomenon are presented in Table 1. Eva, for
example, used the word 'moon' for a ball of spinach
she was about to eat, for hangnails she was pulling off,
for a magnetic capital letter D she was about to put on

TABLE 1. Overextensions based on perceptual
similarities, counter to known
functional differences.

Age given in years, months, days.

All examples in all tables are spontaneous; there was
no prior modelling of the word in the immediate context.

All utterances were single words unless otherwise marked.

M = Mummy;   D = Daddy

1. Eva, 'moon' (selected exx.) 1;3.26 (first use):
    looking at the moon, 1;4.2;looking at peel-side of
    half-grapefruit obliquely from below, 1;4.19:play-
    ing with half-moon shaped lemon slice, 1;4.23:
    touching circular chrome dial on dishwasher, 1;4.24:
    playing with shiny rounded green leaf she'd just
    picked; touching ball of spinach M offers her,
    1;5.2: holding crescent-shaped bit of paper she'd
    torn off yellow pad, 1;6.16: looking up at inside
    of shade of lit floor lamp,1;6.21: looking up at
    pictures of yellow and green vegetables (squash,
    peas) on wall in grocery store, 1;6.29: looking up
    at wall hanging with pink and purple circles, 1;7.7:
    pointing at orange crescent-shaped blinker light on
    a car, 1;8.4: looking up at curved steer horns
    mounted on wall, 1;8.11: putting green magnetic
    capital letter D on refrigerator, 1;8.11: picking
    up half a cheerio, then eats it, 1;8.13: looking
    at black, irregular kidney-shaped piece of paper on
    a wall, 1;11.20: 'my moon is off' after pulling off
    a hangnail (a routine usage).

2. Christy, 'snow' 1;4.10 (first use): as handles and
    eats snow outdoors, 1;4.16: looking at white tail of
    her spring-horse; touching white part of a red,
    white, blue toy boat;   looking at a white flannel
    bed pad, 1;4.17:after drops bottle and it breaks,
    spreading white puddle of milk on floor.

3. Christy, 'money' 1;3.30 (first use): holding a hand-
    ful of pennies, a button, and a bead taken from a
    bowl; she has often played with these; 1;4.11:
    scratching at wax circles on a coffee table, 1;6.7:
    putting finger through round, penny-sized hole in
    bottom of new plastic toy box,1;7.14: feeling cir-
    cular flattened copper clapper inside her toy bell.

the refrigerator, and so on. These objects all
have shape in common with the various phases of the
real moon, but the child's actions upon them were
completely dissimilar. The other examples illustrate a similar disregard for known functional differences among the objects in question. Such examples
of classification on the basis of perceptual cues
counter to known functional differences weigh heavily
against Nelson's proposal that perceptual cues play
a secondary, purely predictive role in the child's
classificatory operations.

A second factor that counts against the function-based theory of how children form object concepts
and attach words to them can be mentioned only briefly.
Nelson proposes, as a logical corollary of her theory,
that 'when instances of the child's first concepts come
to be named, it would be expected that they would be
named only in the context of one of the definitionally
specified actions and relationships' (1974:280). In
other words, 'the name of an object will not be used independently of these concept-defining relations at this
point; early object word use would be expected to be
restricted to a definable set of relations for each concept' (1974:280). According to Nelson, this hypothesis
'describes accurately what is usually termed the holophrastic stage...' (1974:280).

The early object-naming behaviour of Christy
and Eva does not accord with this prediction. Most of
their first object words (e.g., 'ball', 'bottle', 'dog',
'dolly', 'cookie') were initially uttered not when the
children (or others) were acting upon the objects in
question (or, for animate objects, watching them act)
but when the objects were static, seen from a distance
ranging from a few feet to across a room (see, for example, nos. 1, 2 in Table 3, p. 272). This suggests that
the role of function ('actions' and 'relationships') in
the child's early formulation and naming of concepts is
less crucial than Nelson proposes.

It is possible that the age at which particular words for objects are first uttered is a critical
factor with regard to this issue. That is, the earlier
an object name is acquired, the more likely it is that
it will be uttered in connection with concept-defining
actions, etc. However, Christy's and Eva's first object words were learned at 14 and 13 months, respectively, which is toward the lower end of the typical 'holophrastic' stage to which Nelson suggests her hypothesis
applies. This indicates that even if Nelson's function-
based theory accurately describes the acquisition of
object words that are learned unusually early, the theory specifies constraints on the child's methods of

formulating concepts and/or identifying new instances
of existing concepts that no longer necessarily operate
during most or, depending on the child's age at the
start of word production, all of the holophrastic period
during which the early lexicon is established.

   Words for Non-Object Concepts.   Words that do
not refer to objects often figure importantly in children's earliest lexicons (e.g., Bloom, 1973; Nelson,
1973b).   How are these words acquired and extended
to novel referents? Something other than perceptual
similarity is clearly involved in the acquisition of
words like 'more', 'allgone', 'up', etc., since the
objects or activities involved in the contexts in
which children say these words are extremely varied.
For many such words, the governing concept or cross-
situational invariance involves a certain kind of
relationship between two objects or events or between
two states of the same object or event across time.
Despite Nelson's (1974) emphasis on the importance
of relational, functional concepts, her theory does
not explain how words for actions and relationships
are acquired.   This is because in her theory,
actions and relationships are the givens by which
objects are classified; there is no account of how
these concepts themselves are formed, nor is it
explicitly recognized that they, no less than object
concepts, in fact are categories summing across non-
identical situations.   (See Bowerman, 1976b:124
for further discussion.)

   Words that reflect the child's recognition of
constancies across his own subjective experiences or reactions to diverse events are particularly resistant to
interpretation in terms of similarities among perceptual
attributes or functional relationships. Nelson (1973b)
has observed that many children acquire words of this
type (a subgroup of 'personal-social' words, in her
study) relatively early. Some examples from the Christy
and Eva data of words that were extended to new situations on the basis of similarities in subjective experience are given in Table 2. The recurrent element in
the use of 'there!' seems to have been a sense of having
completed a project, for 'aha!' it was an experience of
surprise at some unexpected object or event, for 'too
tight' it was a feeling of being physically restrained
or harassed, for 'heavy' it was a sense of physical
effort expended on an object.

   To conclude, the implications of the various
arguments presented above on the nature of children's
early bases for classifying are that an adequate theory
of the acquisition of word meaning has to be flexible
enough to account for the child's ability, even from a
very early age, to classify experiences on the basis of
many different kinds of similarities. Theories built

TABLE 2.   Words extended to novel situations on the
            basis of subjective experiences.

1.   Eva, 'there!' At 12-1/2 months in connection with
      the experience of completion of a project: as M
      finishes dressing her;   as she gets last peg into
      hole of pounding board;   after she carefully climbs
      off a high bed, etc.   Drops out until 17th month,
      then 1;4.24:   after getting a difficult box open
      (D has just shown her how), 1;4.25:   after sticking
      each of several vinyl fish on side of bathtub,
      1;4.26: after getting a rubber band onto handle of
      kiddicar, etc.

2.   Christy, 'aha!'.   From 1;6.10 in many different
      situations involving her experience of discovery
      and surprise,   e.g., 1;6.10: as opens book and
      sees new picture;   after gets up during the night
      and finds bowl of peanuts on table;   it was not
      there earlier, 1;6.13:   when M comes home with
      paper bag, 1;6.14:   when sees D taking out a cake,
      1;6.15:   after sticks hand in cannister and finds
      rice in bottom;   as finds piece of candy on M's
      dressing table, 1;6.16:   discovering and looking
      into box, 1;6.17: coming upon M who is furtively
      eating a cookie;   finding unexpected pile of tiles
      in a corner of house.

3.   Eva, 'too tight'.   From 23rd month, protest in
      situations involving physical restriction or inter-
      ference, e.g., as M holds her chin to give her medi-
      cine;   pulls down her sleeves; bends her legs up to
      change diapers as she lies on back; washes her ears,
      pulls on her hands to wash them over a sink.

4.   Christy, Eva, 'heavy'.   In situations involving
      experience of physical exertion (often unsuccess-
      ful) with an object, whether or not it is actually
      'heavy', e.g., Christy, from 1;9.12:   carrying
      books, etc., 1;9.16:   trying to lift a packet of
      oatmeal out of a box above her shoulder level;   it
      is stuck;   pushing on and squeezing a small plas-
      tic cup (which does not bend), 1;9.21:   trying to
      lift soap bubble bottle as D holds it down.   Eva,
      1;11.30:   'too heavy', trying unsuccessfully to
      unhook gas pump line on toy gas station.

---

around only one basic class of similarities, whether
perceptual or functional, are too restricted to account
for the rich diversity of ways in which children can recognize constancies from one situation to the next.

THE STRUCTURE OF CHILDREN'S EARLY WORD-CONCEPTS

Recent theorizing about the acquisition of word meaning has been predicated in part on the assumption that children identify words with one or more stable elements of meaning. In other words, it is assumed that all the referents to which a child extends a particular word share attribute(s), whether these attributes are perceptual or functional, and that the meaning of the word can be described in terms of these attributes or features. For example, all referents for a child's word 'dog' might share the perceptual feature 'four-legged' (Clark, 1973), all referents for the word 'ball' might share the functional features 'can be rolled/bounced' (Nelson, 1974).

This recent emphasis on words for which all referents are characterized by one or more common features contrasts with earlier accounts of the acquisition of word meaning. Theorists like Werner (1948), Vygotsky (1962), and Brown (1965) emphasized that children do not consistently associate a word with a single contextual feature, or set of features; rather, they use words 'complexively', shifting from one feature to another in successive uses of the word. Bloom (1973) has suggested that both kinds of word usage may occur in early development, but not typically at the same time. She argues that the association of words (at least words for objects) with consistent feature(s) requires a firm grasp of the concept of object permanence. Complexive usage reflects lack of that concept, according to Bloom, and occurs early in the one-word stage, while consistent usage does not occur until the concept is fully established during the second half of the second year.

The data from Christy and Eva do not support Vygotsky's sweeping claim that 'complex formations make up the entire first chapter of the developmental history of children's words' (1962:70), nor are they consonant with Bloom's more qualified stage hypothesis. Both children used some words for both object and non-object referents in a consistent, noncomplexive way virtually from the start of the one-word stage. In addition, they used other words complexively, but this kind of usage was not confined to the earliest period. Rather, it tended to flower a few months after the production of single-word utterances had begun and continued on well into the third year and, for certain words, even beyond. Moreover, the children's complexive use of words was somewhat more common for words referring to actions than for those referring to objects, which does not accord well with Bloom's view that complexive usage results from lack of firm mental representations of objects. In short, the complexive and the noncomplexive uses of words were not temporally ordered stages; rather, the two types of word use were contemporaneous.

Noncomplexive Words. Some examples of words used consistently for referents sharing one or more features from
early in the one-word stage are given in Table 3. Examples
1 and 2 are words for objects (cf. also examples 2 and 3 in
Table 1), while examples 3 and 4 are words for actions. The
latter two examples are particularly interesting because
they demonstrate how two children can differ dramatically
in the concepts they attach to the some word, despite what
is probably fairly similar input (see Bowerman, 1976b:135,
for discussion). Notice that Christy's word [ɑ:] ('on'
and 'off'; it was not clear if these were two words or one,
as she did not pronounce final consonants at this time) was
overextended to refer to virtually any act involving the
separation or coming together of two objects or parts of an
object. Adults would refer to many of these acts by the
words 'open', 'take apart/out','unfold', or 'close', 'join',
'put together/in', 'fold'. Eva's word 'off', unlike
Christy's, was initially used in a restricted range of contexts from the adult point of view. It referred only to the
removal of clothes and other objects from the body and did
not generalize beyond this domain for several months. During
this time Eva simply did not have a way of referring to
other kinds of separation, although she engaged in activities involving separation and joining just as much as
Christy had.

Complexes. Several different types of complexive
thinking have been described in the literature on concept formation (e.g., Vygotsky, 1962; Olver and Hornsby,
1966). Discussions of children's early complexive use
of words most frequently refer to the type Vygotsky
(1962) called 'chain complexes'. In forming a chain
complex, whether in a block sorting task or by the use
of a word, a child proceeds from one item to the next
on the basis of attributes shared by two or more consecutive items but not by all the items. In other
words, there is no stable attribute nor set of recurrent
attributes associated with the concept. For example,
item B shares something with item A (e.g., shape), item
C shares something with B (e.g., colour) but perhaps
not with A, and so on. Despite the frequency with
which children have been described as typically forming
chain complexes in their early use of words, few
examples of the phenomenon have actually been presented
in the literature.

Chain complex formation was negligible in
Christy's and Eva's linguistic development. In all the
data from both children there is only one rather limited
example. Almost all their complexive uses of words were
'associative', a pattern that Vygotsky (1962) describes

TABLE 3.   Words used noncomplexively for referents
with shared attributes.

1.   Eva, 'ball'. From 1;1.5 for rounded objects of a
size suitable for handling and throwing, e.g.,
1;1.5 (first use); as spies a large round ball in
adjoining room; then goes to pick it up, 1;1.7:
as picks up rounded cork pincushion; then throws
it, 1;1.9: as looks at a round red balloon; later,
also as handles it, 1;2.4: whenever sees or plays
with balls or balloons, 1;2.7: as holds an Easter
egg; then throws it, 1;2.8. after picking up a
small round stone, then throws it, 1;2.10: as sees
plastic egg-shaped toy, 1;2.18: as holds a round-
cannister lid, then throws it; etc.

2.   Eva, 'ice'. From 1;1.9 for frozen substances,
e.g., 1;1.9 (first use): watching M open a package
of frozen peas; she likes to eat them, 1;2.29:
reaching towards ice in a glass, 1;3.2:   rushing
towards M as M takes frozen spinach from package,
1;3.2:   after M gives her her first taste of
frozen orange juice concentrate; etc.

3.   Christy, [α:] 'on-off' (not clear if two words or
one). From 1;3.12: in connection with situations
involving separation or rejoining of parts, e.g.,
between 1;3.12 and 1;4.17 in connection with getting socks on or off, getting on or off spring-
horse, pulling pop-beads apart and putting them
together, separating stacked dixie cups, unfolding a newspaper, pushing hair out of M's face,
opening boxes (with separate or hinged lids as
well as sliding drawers), putting lids on jars,
cap on chapstick, phone on hook, doll into high-
chair, pieces back into puzzle, while M takes her
diaper off, trying to join foil-wrapped torn-
apart towelettes, etc.

4.   Eva, 'off'. From 1;2.18, in connection with separation of things from the body only (as request
or comment),   e.g., between 1;2.18 and 1;4.22, for
sleepshades, shoes, car safety harness, glasses,
pinned-on pacifier, diaper, bib. Starting at
about 1;3.23: 'open' begins to be used in other
'separation' situations, e.g., between 1;3.23 and
1;5, for opening doors, boxes, cans, toothpaste
tubes; pulling pop-beads apart; taking books out
of case, tip off door stop, wrapper off soap;
cracking peanuts; peeling paper off book cover,
etc. 'Off' still used for taking things off the
body.

in connection with children's block sorting behaviour.
In an associative complex, successive instances of the
concept do not necessarily share anything with each
other but all share at least one feature with a central
or 'nuclear' instance, e.g., the sample block given to
the child. Thus, the elements of the associative complex
are '...interconnected through one element - the nucleus
of the concept'. In contrast, in the formation of a
chain complex 'the original sample has no central significance'. In other words, 'there is no consistency in
the type of the bonds or in the manner in which a link
of the chain is joined with the one that precedes and
the one that follows it' (1962:64).

In Christy's and Eva's complexive use of words,
the central referent for a word (which will be called
here the 'prototype' to link it with a literature to be
discussed in the following section) was, with a few
exceptions, the first referent for which the word was
used. In addition, it was the referent in connection
with which the word had been exclusively or most frequently modelled. (Sometimes there were several 'prototypical' referents for a word; these all shared the
entire set of attributes that appear to have been associated with the word, as judged by the child's subsequent overextensions, and they all figured importantly
in both the adult's modelling and the child's earliest
uses of the word.) Other referents appear to have been
regarded as similar to the prototype by virtue of
having any one or some combination of the attributes
that, in the child's eyes, characterized it.

Some examples of complexive word usage that
can be characterized in terms of variations around a
prototype are given in Table 4. Consider example 1,
Eva's use of 'kick'. Some of the referents for this
word seem to share nothing with each other, e.g., a
moth fluttering vs. bumping a ball with the wheel of
a kiddicar. But all share something with the hypothesized prototypical 'kick' situation, in which a
ball is struck by a foot and propelled forward. For
instance, the moth is characterized by 'a waving
limb', while the kiddicar referent is characterized by
'sudden sharp contact' plus 'an object (ball) propelled'.
(In this example, prototypical 'kick' was not first
referent for the word, as in most of the other examples.
However, it seems to be implicit in the second referent
(a cat with a ball near its paw) and it was almost
certainly the most frequently modelled referent for
'kick'.)

Example 2 in Table 4 illustrates that for
Christy, 'night night' was associated with three primary
features that were present one-at-a-time in many of the
situations in which she used the word: beds or cribs,
blankets, and the 'nonnormative' horizontal position of

TABLE 4.   Complexively used words with prototypical
referents.

1. Eva, 'kick'.

Prototype: kicking a ball with the foot so that it
propelled forward.

Features: a) a waving limb, b) sudden sharp contact
(especially between body part and another object),
c) an object propelled.

Selected examples: 1;5.14: as kicks a floor fan
with her foot (Features a, b), 1;5.21: looking at
picture of kitten with ball near its paw (all
features, in anticipated event?), 1;5.25: watching
moth fluttering on a table (a), 1;5.22: watching
row of cartoon turtles on TV doing can-can (a), 1;6.3
and 1;6.13: just before throwing something (a, c),
1;6.20: 'kick bottle', after pushing bottle with
her feet, making it roll (all features), 1;8.6:
as makes ball roll by bumping it with front wheel
of kiddicar (b, c), 1;8.7: pushing teddy bear's
stomach against Christy's chest (b), 1;8.19: pushing her stomach against a mirror (b), 1;8.20: pushing her chest against a sink (b).

2. Christy, 'night night'.

Prototype: person (or doll) lying down in bed or
crib.

Features: a) crib, bed, b) blanket, c) non-norma-
tive horizontal position of object (animate or
inanimate).

Selected examples: 1;3.28 (first use): pushing a
doll over in her crib; from this time on, frequent
for putting dolls to bed, covering, and kissing them
(features a, b, c); 1;4.5: laying her bottle on its
side (c), 1;5.18: watching Christmas tree being
pulled away on its side (c), 1;5.26: after puts
piano stool legs in box, one lying horizontally (c),
1;5.27: after putting piece of cucumber flat in
her dish and pushing it into a corner (c), 1;6.3:
as M flattens out cartons, laying them in pile on
floor (c), from 1;6.3: while looking at pictures
of empty beds or cribs or wanting a toy bed given
to her (a, sometimes b), 1;6.31: laying kiddicar
on its side (c), 1;7.11: 'awant night night',
request for M to hand her blanket; she then drapes
it over shoulders as rides on toy horse (b).

TABLE 4 continued

3. Eva, 'close'.

Prototype: closing drawers, doors, boxes, jars, etc.

Features: a) bringing together two objects or parts
of the same object until they are in close contact,
b) causing something to become concealed or in-
accessible.

Selected examples: starting from 1;3.23 for closing
gates, doors, drawers (features a, b). From 1;5:
for closing boxes and other containers (features
a, b), 1;6.16: 'open, close', taking peg people out
of their holes in bus built for them and putting
them back in (a), from 21st month: while pushing
handles of scissors, tongs, tweezers together and
for getting people to put arms or legs together,
e.g., 'close knees' (a), 1;8.18: 'close it', as
tries to push pieces of cut peach slice together
(a); trying to fold up a towlette (a, (b?)), 1;8.25:
'open, close', as unfolds and folds a dollar bill
(a, (b?)), 1;9.16: 'open, close', after M has spread
a doll's arms out then folded them back over chest
(a), 1;11.8: 'Mummy, close me', 2;1.9: 'I will close
you, o.k.?' both in connection with pushing chair
into table (a),1;11.14: 'that one close', trying to
fit piece into jigsaw puzzle (a, (b?)), 1;11.30: 'I
close it', as turns knob on TV set until picture
completely darkens (b), etc.

4. Christy, Eva, 'open'.

Prototype: opening drawers, doors, boxes, jars, etc.

Features: a) separation of parts which were in contact, b) causing something to be revealed or become
accessible.

Selected examples:

Christy: From middle of 17th month, 'open' starts
to take over the function of 'off' (see example 3,
Table 3) for 'separation' situations, both with and
without 'revealing'. 1;4.12 (first use): for cup-
board door opening (a, b), 1;4.19: pointing to
spout in salt container that M had just opened (a,
b), 1;4.28: trying to separate two frisbees (a),
1;5.1-7: for opening boxes, doors, tube of ointment,
jars (a, b), 1;5.26: trying to push legs of hand-
operated can opener wider apart than they can go;
spreading legs of nail scissors apart (both a),
1;6.1: several times in connection with pictures

TABLE 4 continued

in magazine; wants M to somehow get at the pictured
objects for her (b), 1;6.29: request for M to un-
screw plastic stake from a block (a), 1;6.31: request for M to take out metal brad that holds 3 flat
pieces of plastic together (a), 1;7.10: request for
M to take stem off apple (a), 1;7.17: 'awant mummy
...open', request for M to pry pen out of piece of
styrofoam (a), 1;7.20: request for M to take pegs
out of pounding bench (a), 1;7.20: 'awant open
hand', request for M to take leg off plastic doll
(a), 1;7.23: request for M to turn on electric
typewriter (b), 1;7.25: trying to pull pop beads
apart (a), 1;8: request for M to turn on water
faucet (b), 1;8.5: request for M to take pieces
out of jigsaw puzzle, (a, (b?)), 1;8.6: trying to
get grandma's shoe off her foot (a), 1;8.17: 'open
light', after M has turned light off; request to
have it turned on again (b), 1;9.6: 'awant that
open', trying to pull handle off of riding toy (a),
etc.

Eva: (cf Table 3, example 4 for initial uses).
Later, 1;5.20: request for M to take apart a broken
toothbrush (a), for M to pull apart two popbeads
(a), 1;5.28: request for M to take pieces out of
jigsaw puzzle (a, (b?)), 1;6: pulling bathrobe off
M's knee to inspect knee (a, b), 1;6.9: request for
M to turn TV on (b), 1;6.18: 'open tape', request
for M to pull strip off masking tape (a), 1;7.10:
'open tangle', bringing M pile of tangled yarns to
separate (a), 1;7.14: taking stubby candle out of
shallow glass cup (a), 1;8: 'open mommy', trying
to unbend a small flexible 'mommy' doll (a), 1;8.11:
unfolding a towlette (a, b); 1;9.16: 'open slide',
request for M to set slide in yard upright (a,
(b?)), 1;8.19: request for M to put legs apart (a)
1;10.20: 'I'm open it', after rips apart two tiny
toy shoes that were stuck together (a), 2;0.3: 'my
knee open', as unbends her knee (a); 2;2.1: 'I will
open it for you', before taking napkin out of its
ring for M, does not unfold it, then says 'I open
it' as report on completed action (a), 2;7.29: 'I'm
gonna leave this chair open like this, I'm not
gonnal shut it', as leaves table with chair pulled
out (a), etc.

5. Eva, [gi] (from 'giddiup')

Prototype: bouncing on a spring horse

Features: a) horse (later, other large animals and
riding toys which one sits astraddle). b) bouncing
motion, c) sitting on toy (especially astraddle).

TABLE 4 continued

Selected examples: From 1;2.9: while bouncing on spring-horse or as request to be lifted onto it (a, b, c), 1;2.13: as picks up tiny plastic horse, then tries to straddle it (a, c), 1;2.14: getting on toy tractor (c), 1;2.15: looking at horses on T.V. (a), 1;2.17: getting on trike (c), 1;2.17: seeing picture of horse (a), 1;2.20: bouncing on heels while crouching in tub (b), 1;2.23: climbing into tiny plastic blow-up chair (c), 1;2.24: looking at hobby horse (a), 1;2.30: bouncing astraddle on M's legs (b, c). Later, continues to be used for pointing out horses, generalizes to other large animals like cows, and while pointing out or riding on trikes, tractors, kiddicars.

6. Eva, 'moon'

Prototype: the real moon

Features: a) shape: circular, crescent, half-moon. These shapes were distinct, i.e., a stretch of curved surface not enough to elicit 'moon'. b) yellow colour, c) shiny surface, d) viewing position: seen at an angle from below, e) flatness, f) broad expanse as background.

Selected examples: (see Table 1, example 1 for details and dates): real moon (all features); half-grapefruit seen at an angle from below (a, b, d); lemon slice (a, b, e); dial on dishwasher (a, c, d, e, f); shiny leaf (a, c, e); ball of spinach (a), spheres were usually called 'ball'. (There was perhaps a limited chaining effect here to the leaf, e.g. earlier in the day, through shared greenness); crescent-shaped paper (a, b, e); inside of lamp shade (a, b, d); pictures of vegetables on wall (a, b, d, e, f); circles on wall hanging (a, d, e, f); crescent-shaped orange blinker light (a, (b?), c, e); steer horns on wall (a, d, f); letter D on refrigerator (a, d, e, f); half-cheerio (a, (b?)); kidney-shaped paper on wall (a, d, e, f); hangnails (a, e).

---

an object that is usually oriented vertically. These three features are all present in prototypical 'night night' situations in which a normally vertical person is lying down in bed covered with a blanket.

For both children, 'open' was associated with a feature involving the physical separation of two objects or parts of the same object and a feature to do with something being revealed, while 'close' was associated with the opposite features of bringing together and concealment (see examples 3 and 4 in Table 4). Both members of each pair of features co-occur in prototypical 'open' and 'close' situations involving doors, boxes, drawers, jars, etc. They are found separately in such referents as turning on or off a TV, water faucet, or light (revealing and concealing without separation and joining) and taking things off or apart and putting them on or together, such as taking the stem off an apple and buckling a wrist strap (separation and joining without revealing and concealing). Examples 5 and 6 of Table 4 present similar examples of complexive word usage revolving around prototypical referents.[1,2]

Instances of complexive word usage similar to those discussed here have been remarked on by a few other investigators. For example, Labov and Labov (1974) observed that their daughter apparently identified the word 'cat', one of her first two words, with a set of features all of which characterize ordinary cats. She overextended the word to other animals that possess one or some of these features, but seemed more confident in using the word when many of the features were present. Clark (1975) notes that there are similar exemplars in the diary data from which she has drawn. She has modified her original (1973) theory of children's overextensions to account for this kind of usage by postulating that some overextensions are 'partial' rather than 'full', i.e., they are based on only a subset of the features that the child associates with the word (Clark, 1975).

To summarize, the data presented above indicate a) that children are capable of using words non-complexively from the start of word acquisition and b) that many children's 'complexive' word usages, rather than conforming to the traditional notion of an unstructured 'chain' of constantly shifting meanings, in fact reflect an internal structure describable in terms of a set of variations around a central instance (or instances) that may be termed a 'prototype'.

These findings suggest that there is less discontinuity between child and adult methods of classification than has often been supposed. First, the data from Christy and Eva provide evidence for an early ability to classify according to superordinate features (i.e., features characterizing all concept instances), a type of concept formation often thought to be beyond the capability even of children considerably older than they were at this time (e.g., Vygotsky, 1962). Second, the particular type of conceptual structure exhibited.

in their complexive use of words, a set of variations
around one or more prototypical exemplars, does not reflect a 'primitive' mode of thought that later fades
out. Rather, as recent research has demonstrated, a
large number of adult semantic categories are characterized by this kind of structure (e.g., Rosch and Mervis,
1975). The correspondence between Christy's and Eva's
complexive word usages and the internal structure attributed to adult semantic categories by Rosch and
others will be examined more closely in the following
section.

THE ORGANIZATION AND STORAGE OF WORD MEANING

A number of investigators studying concept
formation, the structure and/or acquisition of word
meaning, or semantic memory have recently focused attention on the role played by 'prototypes' or 'best exemplars' in the internal structure of natural categories
(e.g., Rosch, 1973a, b; Rosch and Mervis, 1975; Fillmore, n.d.; Anglin, in press; Smith, Shoben, and Rips,
1974). Rosch (1973b), for example found that adult subjects were able to rate exemplars of particular semantic
categories such as 'fruit' according to how well they
exemplified the category, and agreed with one another in
their ratings.

Some theorists have suggested that the representation of semantic categories (word meanings) in
terms of prototypical exemplars should be regarded as an
alternative to the more common practice of representing
word meanings as sets of semantic features. For example,
Fillmore (n.d.) argues that it may often be psychologi-
cally inaccurate to describe word meanings in terms of
sets of features specifying conditions that must be
satisfied before the word can be appropriately used. He
proposes instead that 'the understanding of meaning requires, at least for a great many cases, an appeal to
an exemplar or prototype -- this prototype being...poss-
ibly something which, instead of being analyzed, needs
to be presented or demonstrated or manipulated'. Anglin
(in press), writing with specific reference to very
young children, also suggests that word meanings are
often stored in the form of prototypes or visual schemas
that are not analyzed into components. In making
this proposal he draws upon Posner (1973), who has argued that being able to analyze a concept into a set of
attributes or features is a relatively advanced skill,
whereas the formation of prototypes is a more primitive
process that does not require featural analysis.

The data presented in the last section indicate that accounting for referential prototypes does
not have to be done at the expense of a featural analysis. Instead, both models can and should be combined,

as Rosch and Mervis (1975) have also argued. The data indicate in addition that, contrary to Anglin's argument, even very young children are capable of performing a featural analysis upon a prototypical referent and extending a word to novel referents on the basis of this analysis.

According to the model proposed by Rosch and Mervis (1975), explaining the existence of prototypical referents requires reference to the way in which features or attributes of possible referents are distributed within the category. Their model draws on Wittgenstein's (1953) notion of 'family resemblances'. According to Wittgenstein, possession of common elements is not the sole principle by which the referents for words may be linked together under a single concept; rather, for many words each possible referent has at least one and often several elements in common with one or more other referents, but no, or few, elements are shared by all referents. Rosch and Mervis hypothesized that the degree to which items are viewed as 'prototypical' members of the category labelled by a particular word is a function of the number of attributes they have in common with other referents for the word. As a corollary of this, they hypothesized also that the most prototypical referents for a given category would tend to share many attributes with each other. These hypotheses are supported by findings from a wealth of experimental studies that Rosch and Mervis conducted with adults.

The data from Christy and Eva fit the 'family resemblances' model proposed by Rosch and Mervis very well. It will be recalled that for virtually all of Christy's and Eva's complexively used words, there was one referent (or, occasionally, a small group of referents) that had one or more features in common with every other referent. In other words, in one (or a few) referent(s), the various attributes associated with the word, as judged by the way in which the child extended the word to novel items, co-occurred or clustered to the maximum degree possible.

How do categories structured around prototypical or 'best' exemplars arise? Rosch (1973b, 1974) has argued that the prototypes for certain categories, particularly physiologically determined ones, are salient prior to the categories and determine the nature of the categories. However, she doubts that all categories evolve in this manner. Some alternative sequences would be a) prototypes are formed through principles of information processing subsequent to experience with a number of particular instances of their categories (Rosch, in press) and b) frequency of exposure to given instances 'may make some items salient in a not-yet-organized-domain and may influence how that domain comes to be divided' (1973:143).

The complexive categories represented in the data from Christy and Eva appear to reflect the first-and/or last-mentioned sequence. That is, the proto-typical referent was present from the beginning and constituted the core around which the subsequent category grew, rather than being an induction made later on the basis of diverse exemplars of the category. It is difficult to assess the relative importance of language-independent cognitive activity vs. linguistic input (e.g., frequency of exposure) in drawing a child's attention to particular objects or events such that they become the growing point or prototype for a category. For some of the examples in Table 4, it seems most plausible that a particular referent for a word became more salient than other referents primarily because of the relatively greater frequency with which the word was paired with that referent in the input to the child (e.g., kicking a ball for Eva's 'kick'). For other examples, a referent may have been so salient for non-linguistic reasons that the input did no more than supply the child with a word for an item that already had special status on nonlinguistic grounds and was 'ready', in a sense, to serve as a prototype (e.g., the moon, for Eva's 'moon').

Regardless of whether prototypical referents are salient for the child independently of, or because of, linguistic input, the sequence in which complexive categories structured around a prototype appear to develop is as follows: The child hears a word modelled most frequently (often exclusively) in connection with one referent or a small group of highly similar referents: e.g., 'night night' as the child or a doll is put to bed, 'giddiup' as the child bounces on her horse, 'close' as someone closes doors, boxes, jars, 'moon' as the child looks at the real moon or at pictures of the moon. The child's first use of the word also occurs in connection with one of these referents. After a variable period of time (ranging from a few days to more than a month), the child begins to extend the word to referents that are similar to the original referent(s) in specifiable and consistent ways.

What has happened? A plausible inference is that the child has imposed a featural analysis on the original referent such that she is now capable of re-cognizing two or more of its attributes independently, i.e., in situations in which they do not co-occur blended into a single package but rather are recom-bined with entirely different contextual features. For example, the 'bringing together' of parts and the con-cealment of something, which are intimately connected in prototypical 'close' situations, can now be re-cognized independently of each other, each one being associated with the word 'close'.

The attributes that the child comes to recognize as components of a given prototypical referent
may be quite varied in nature. Some that are represented in the Christy and Eva data as presented in
Table 4 include perceptual properties or configurations
(e.g., flatness, yellowness for 'moon'; horse, or horse-
like animal for [gi]); associated actions (e.g.,
bouncing for [gi]); spatial relationships (e.g., horizontal positioning of normally vertical object for
'night night'; separation for 'open'); purpose or end
state (e.g. concealment for 'close'); the child's
viewing position (e.g., obliquely from below for 'moon'),
and so on.

The account presented above of the development
of categories revolving around prototypical exemplars is
at odds with proposals made by Anglin (in press) and
Fillmore (n.d.) in that it credits the very young child
with the capacity to perform a featural analysis on a
referent.[3] As noted earlier, Anglin (in press) suggests
that prototypes may be stored unanalyzed as visual
images. But if the prototype is unanalyzed, how can we
account for the child's ability to recognize attributes
of an original referent when they are separated from
each other and recombined in entirely new configurations?
In particular, an appeal to a global notion of 'visual
similarity' is inadequate to explain the child's extension of words to referents that are visually
dissimilar to the prototype, such as 'open' for turning
on a faucet, light, or electric typewriter as well as
for opening boxes and doors.

Another aspect of early word use that appears
to require reference to the individual features of a
prototype is the fact that some aspects of a prototypical exemplar may be more central or concept-defining for
the child than others. The evidence for this is that
the attributes of a prototype may turn up in new referents for the word with differing probabilities. Some
may always be present and hence appear to be criterial,
while others are simply characteristic but not essential.
For example, consider Eva's use of 'moon' as it is presented in Table 4. Shape was obviously the most important determinant of whether or not a given item would be
called 'moon': every referent for the word was either
round, half-moon, or crescent shaped. But in addition
to shape, almost every referent for 'moon' shared with
the prototypical real moon one or a combination of several other less critical features: flatness, yellowness, shininess, having a broad expanse as a background,
and being seen at an angle from below.

Variation in the centrality or importance of
various attributes of a prototype cannot be accounted
for when word meanings are represented as unanalyzed

wholes. In contrast, it can easily be handled by
models that represent word meanings in terms of semantic features. For example, Smith et al. (1974) propose
a model of word meaning that is similar to that suggested by Rosch and Mervis (1975) with the additional
specification that semantic features should be differentially weighted according to their degree of 'de-
finingness' for a category. Such a provision appears
essential if we are to account for phenomena like Eva's
use of 'moon'.

CONCLUSIONS

Three main arguments about the nature and development of children's early word meanings have been
advanced in this paper. A common element linking all
three has been an appeal for breadth and for the integration of theories that by themselves account for
only a portion of the data. An adequate theory of the
acquisition of word meaning must be sufficiently broad
and flexible to handle many disparate phenomena with
equal ease within a common framework. In particular,
it must come to terms with the following findings:
1) Children need not adhere to a single classification-
al principle in the early stages of word acquisition
(e.g., using only perceptual or only functional cues).
Rather, they are capable of recognizing invariances of
many different kinds, and consequently have a variety
of methods of classification at their disposal.
2) The concepts governing children's early use of words
are not necessarily either exclusively complexive, as
earlier theorists maintained, or exclusively superordinate (i.e., with features held in common by all
members of the category), as recent theorists have
implicitly assumed. Nor do superordinate categories
necessarily replace complexive ones over time. Rather,
concepts of both types can exist contemporaneously,
neither one being more 'primitive' than the other.
Finally, 3) the representation of children's word meanings in terms of feature sets or lists of conditions
that must be satisfied is not incompatible with .rep-
resentation in terms of prototypes or 'best exemplars'.
Rather, both can and should be incorporated within a
single model, just as Rosch and Mervis (1975) have
advocated in connection with adult semantic categories.

Notes.

1. The characterization presented in this paper of the
'semantic features' associated with various words
is intended as schematic rather than definitive,
for two primary reasons. First, the extent to which
certain features should be broken down is not clear.
E.g., should 'sitting' and 'astraddle' be listed

separately in the meaning of [gi]? Should 'horse' be given as a unitary feature of [gi] or should it receive some finer analysis? Second, it is obvious that an adequate representation of the meanings of these words must involve more than a listing of features; some sort of relationship holding between the features must be specified. For example, the temporal co-occurrence of a waving limb and sudden contact would not be sufficient to elicit 'kick': the two must be connected. No attempt at dealing with these problems will be attempted here, however (but see the treatment of relationships holding between semantic components in Haviland and Clark, 1974; McCawley, 1971, and other linguists).

2. A number of Christy's and Eva's overextensions of verbs reflect their awareness of cross-situational similarities or invariances that are not explicitly recognized in the way English words are used but that are formally noted in the way other languages group referents under lexical items. For example, one 'opens' the water in Spanish and one 'opens' the TV or radio in Finnish. An interesting research question is whether there is a correlation between the frequency with which children make certain overextensions in one language (e.g., 'open' for the water faucet in English) and the frequency with which the corresponding classification is formalized in other languages. A high correlation would indicate a close relationship between the cognitive factors governing the way in which children classify, i.e., what similarities among objects or events are salient to them, and the way in which the semantic categories of natural languages develop. See Clark (1974a) for some related evidence supporting the hypothesis that there is a relationship between children's overextensions and the semantic categories of natural languages.

3. There may appear to be a discrepancy between the claim made here that the child can analyze referents for words like 'open' into sets of attributes at an early age and the claim made in an earlier paper (Bowerman, 1974) to the effect that causative verbs (including 'open') are initially 'unanalyzed' by the child. In fact, however, the two arguments are not incompatible because the objects of analysis in the two cases are different: the referent event in the case of 'semantic features' of the sort discussed in this paper and the word itself, in terms of its semantic relationships to other words, in the case of the discussion of causative verbs. See Bowerman (1976a) for further discussion of this distinction, which corresponds to the distinction linguists have

often made between two aspects of meaning, reference (the relationship of a word to the (class of) item(s) which it symbolizes) and sense (the relationship the word contracts with other words in the lexicon) (e.g., Lyons, 1968).

REFERENCES

Anglin, J. (In press)   The Child's First Terms of Reference.   In S. Erlich and E. Tulving (eds.) Bulletin de Psychologie.   (Special issue on semantic memory).

Bloom, L. (1973)   One Word at a Time: The Use of Single-word Utterances before Syntax.   Mouton, The Hague.

Bowerman, M. (1974)   Learning the Structure of Causative Verbs: A Study in the Relationship of Cognitive, Semantic and Syntactic Development.   In Papers and Reports on Child Language Development 8. Stanford University. 142-178.

Bowerman, M. (1976a)   Systematizing Semantic Knowledge. Paper presented to the Midwestern Cognitive Group, Chicago, March.

Bowerman, M. (1976b)   Factors in the Acquisition of Rules for Word Use and Sentence Construction. In D. Morehead and A. Morehead (eds.) Directions in Normal and Deficient Child Language.   University Park Press, Baltimore.

Brown, R. (1965)   Social Psychology.   The Free Press, New York.

Clark, E. (1973)   What's in a Word? On the Child's Acquisition of Semantics in his First Language. In T.E. Moore (ed.) Cognitive Development and the Acquisition of Language. Academic Press, New York.

Clark, E. (1974a)   Classifiers and Semantic Acquisition: Universal Categories? Paper presented at the 73rd Annual Meeting of the American Anthropological Association, Mexico City, November.

Clark, E. (1974b)   Some Aspects of the Conceptual Basis for First Language Acquisition.   In R.L. Schiefelbusch and L.L. Lloyd (eds.) Language Perspectives: Acquisition, Retardation, and Intervention.   University Park Press, Baltimore.

Clark, E. (1975)   Knowledge, Context, and Stategy
in the Acquisition of Meaning. In D. Dato
(ed.) Developmental Psycholinguistics:
Theory and Applications. (26th Annual
Georgetown University Roundtable). Georgetown University Press, Washington, D.C.

Fillmore, C. (n.d.)   An Alternative to Checklist
Theories of Meaning. Unpublished manuscript.

Haviland, S.E. and Clark, E.V. (1974)   'This Man's
Father is my Father's Son': A Study of
the Acquisition of English Kin Terms.
Journal of Child Language 1. 23-47.

Labov, W. and Labov, T. (1974)   The Grammar of Cat
and Mama. Paper presented at the 49th
Annual Meeting of the Linguistic Society
of America, New York, New York.

Lyons, J. (1968)   Introduction to Theoretical Linguistics. Cambridge University Press,
Cambridge.

McCawley, J.D. (1971)   Prelexical Syntax. In R.J.
O'Brien (ed.) Monograph Series on Languages
and Linguistics. (22nd Annual Georgetown
University Roundtable). Georgetown University Press, Washington, D.C.

Nelson, K. (1973a) Some Evidence for the Cognitive
Primacy of Categorization and its Functional
Basis. Merrill-Palmer Quarterly of Behavior
and Development   19. 21-39.

Nelson, K. (1973b)   Structure and Strategy in Learning
to Talk. Monographs of the Society for Research in Child Development 149. 38(1-2).

Nelson, K. (1974)   Concept, Word, and Sentence: Interrelations in Acquisition and Development.
Psychological Review 81. 267-285.

Olver, R. and Hornsby, R. (1966)   On Equivalence. In
J.S. Bruner, R.R. Olver and P.M. Greenfield et
al. (eds.) Studies in Cognitive Growth. Wiley,
New York.

Posner, M.I. (1973)   Cognition: An Introduction. Scott,
Foresman & Co., Glenview, Ill.

Rosch, E. (1973a)   Natural Categories. Cognitive
Psychology 4. 328-350.

Rosch, E. (1973b)   On the Internal Structure of Per-
ceptual and Semantic Categories. In T.E.
Moore (ed.) Cognitive Development and the
Acquisition of Language. Academic Press,
New York.

Rosch, E. (1974)   Linguistic Relativity. In A. Sil-
verstein (ed.) Human Communication: Theoretical Perspectives. Halstead Press, New York.

Rosch, E. (In press)   Classifications of Real-world
Objects: Origins and Representions in
Cognition. In S. Erlich and E. Tulving (eds.)
Bulletin de Psychologie (Special issue on
semantic memory).

Rosch, E. and Mervis, C.B. (1975)   Family Resemblances:
Studies in the Internal Structure of Categories. Cognitive Psychology 7. 573-605.

Smith, E.E., Shoben, E.J. and Rips, L.J. (1974)   Structure and Process in Semantic Memory: A
Feature Model for Semantic Decisions. Psychological Review 81. 214-241.

Vygotsky, L.S. (1962)   Thought and Language. (1st ed.,
1934)   M.I.T. Press, Cambridge, Mass. and
Wiley, New York.

Werner, H. (1948)   Comparative Psychology of Mental
Development. Science Editions, Inc., New
York.

Wittgenstein, L. (1953)   Philosophical Investigations.
MacMillan, New York.

Semantic Intention and Interpersonal Function: Semantic Analysis of Noun + Noun Constructions

M. Smoczyńska

This paper is concerned with syntactic analysis of early child utterances and some related methodological problems. The central problem is: What
semantic information is essential to establish the
syntactic structure of an utterance?

Lois Bloom (1970) was the first to point out
that in order to examine the syntactic structure of
child utterances we must take into account their meaning, i.e. determine the semantic intention of the child.
This methodological claim was a breakthrough in the
study of syntactic development. Nevertheless, the methods
which are now being applied in semantically oriented
studies of child syntax are still imperfect. In this
paper some of these deficiencies will be pointed out and
some resolutions of the problem proposed.

Semantic intention is usually understood as a
set of semantic relations present in an utterance. However, in the early stages of his syntactic development
the child does not yet make them explicit by conventional linguistic means. The earliest syntactic fact is
simply the juxtaposition of two words whose referents are
related one to another in external reality. Thus, we can
ascribe meanings to child utterances only if we assume

that semantic relations correspond to objective relations holding between the elements of reality, i.e. by
applying the rich interpretation principle. This principle is used in many present studies of child syntax
(e.g. Brown, 1973). But the notion of semantic intention is limited to the propositional meaning, i.e. the
meaning which results from the ideational function of
language, if we apply Halliday's (1970) classification
of language functions into ideational, interpersonal
and textual. Semantic intention is treated as if it contained only objective relations.

However, the child is not only an objective
commentator on the events he perceives, but also a participant in the communicative process in which the interpersonal function of language is involved. Thus, child
utterances may have additional meanings which result from
their interpersonal functions. These meanings are not
usually taken into account in syntactic analysis. What
are these interpersonal meanings? Within the interpersonal function of language, the basic roles are Speaker
(I) and Addressee (YOU). In declarative utterances the
words denoting these two roles can function simply as
Agent, Possessor, Receiver or Object, as in the simulated
child utterances 1-5 given as examples in Table 1. These
roles are purely ideational.

Sometimes the Addressee's name can be used in
its interpersonal function only; e.g., in utterance 6
the word Mummy is a Vocative which serves to call the
Addressee's attention to the next declarative utterance
Baby sleeps. Such a Vocative, which will be denoted by
the symbol 'YOU$_{listen}$', is not syntactically related to
the utterance which it accompanies.

In imperative utterances the meanings of the
same words are more complex since these words play two
different roles. In utterance 7 the word Mummy is not
only an Agent (or Subject), but also, and mainly, it
expresses pressure put upon the Addressee to carry out
a request. This kind of Vocative will be denoted by
'YOU$_{do}$'. Similarly the child's name Mary, whose ideational meaning in utterance 7 is Receiver, from the
point of view of the interpersonal function expresses
Speaker's wishes, and as such it will be denoted by
'I$_{want}$'. Utterance 8 is formally declarative, but semantically it is equivalent to the imperative 7, if addressed to Mummy. Children express wishes in order to
make the Addressee realize them, not only to inform him
about their intention, as adults frequently do.

In ostensive utterances another use of Vocative
appears. In utterance 9 the Vocative serves to call the

TABLE 1. Ideational and interpersonal meaning of the words denoting speaker (Mary) and Addressee (Mummy). (Examples are the simulated utterances of a fictitious child.)

Example	Modality	Ideational meaning	Interpersonal meaning
1. MUMMY sleeps.	declarative	SUBJECT	-
2. MARY drinks.	"	SUBJECT	-
3. MUMMY'S chair.	"	POSSESSOR	-
4. MUMMY gives	"	SUBJECT	-
MARY a book.		RECEIVER	-
5. MARY kisses	"	SUBJECT	-
MUMMY.		OBJECT	-
6. MUMMY, baby	"	-	YOU_{listen}
sleeps.			
7. MUMMY, give	imperative	SUBJECT	YOU_{do}
MARY a book.		RECEIVER	I_{want}
8. MARY wants a	"	SUBJECT	I_{want}
book.			
9. MUMMY, look at	ostensive	SUBJECT	YOU_{look}
the tree.			

Addressee's attention not only to what the child says
but also to what he is speaking about (the referent).
This use of the Vocative will be denoted by 'YOU$_{look}$'.
In the two latter kinds of Vocative: YOU$_{do}$ and YOU$_{look}$,
the function of YOU$_{listen}$ Vocative is included.

The above distinctions will be shown to be
basic to a syntactic analysis, taking as an example
Noun+Noun constructions. Bloom (1970) has found that
Noun+Noun constructions can express five different meanings: Attribution, Possession, Subject+Object relation,
Location and Conjunction. It seemed puzzling that
Bloom's data contained so many Subject+Object constructions. As demonstrated by Brown (1973) this construction is not universal and therefore cannot be treated as
a basic semantic relation. On the other hand Campbell
(1976) has pointed out that the majority of Bloom's
Subject+Object constructions contain the word Mommy
which, he suggests, is a request marker rather than a
Subject. This suggestion seemed to warrant examining
this problem more closely in data from Polish-speaking
children.

The data reported here were collected from five
Polish children. Daily recordings were made of the
children in the six month period after the emergence of
the first two-word utterances. The corpora of multiword
utterances were divided for purposes of analysis into
smaller parts corresponding to successive months of syntactic development. Data available for discussion here
include: 1055 multiword utterances collected from Inka
(months I to VI; age 1;4 to 1;10; MLU in words 1.10 to
2.40), 1029 multiword utterances from Kasia (months I to
VI; age 1;3½ to 1;9½; MLU 1.25 to 2.31), 849 utterances
from Jaś (months II to VI; age 1;7 to 2;0; MLU 1.48 to
2.53), 804 utterances from Basia (months II to VI; age
1;5½ to 1;10½; MLU 1.45 to 2.29) and 819 utterances
from Tenia (months III to IV; age 1;5½ to 1;7½; MLU
1.74 to 1.82). Inka and Tenia were sisters; the other
children were unrelated.

All the Noun+Noun constructions from the corpora were analyzed. The frequency of occurrence of these
constructions was different in particular children (see
Table 2). The first part of the analysis consisted in
establishing the ideational meaning of each utterance,
which corresponds to Bloom's meaning analysis. The results are given in Table 2. In the Polish data four out
of Bloom's five categories were found; there were no
instances of Conjunction. A few other categories were
also found but they were infrequent.

Further analysis consisted in establishing the
interpersonal meanings of non-declarative utterances.

TABLE 2. Classification of Noun+Noun constructions recorded in the five children in terms of ideational meaning.

Category	Inka	Kasia	Jaś	Basia	Tenia
Attribution and Classification	4	-	-	-	3
Possession	15	15	14	4	11
Subject+Object	91	9	18	7	28
Location	36	-	14	11	10
Other	3	2	2	2	7
Unclassified	6	2	5	-	2
Total	155	28	53	24	61
Percentage of the corpus	14.7	2.7	6.2	3.0	7.4

Two categories, Attribution and Possession, were represented by declarative utterances only; therefore these had no additional interpersonal meanings which would be relevant to a syntactic analysis. The two remaining categories, Subject+Object and Location, fell into several subcategories with regard to their interpersonal meanings. The results of the analysis of these two categories are presented in detail below.

SUBJECT + OBJECT CATEGORY

Within this category only nine occurrences of declarative Subject+Object utterances were found in all the children studied. Some examples are given below. Roman numerals following the child's name indicate the month in which the utterance occurred. In the translations of the examples the nouns are sometimes provided with the subscripts Acc, Voc, Dat, Loc, Dir, which indicate the presence of case markers, respectively: Accusative, Vocative, Dative, Locative and Directional Locative.

(1) Inka IV is drinking 'coffee'. She announces:

<u>Inka kawa</u>   'Inka coffee'
(= Inka is drinking coffee)

(2) Inka VI was told that Daddy would buy her a book. On his return she asks him:

<u>tatuś książkę?</u>   'Daddy book$_{Acc}$?

(= Has Daddy bought a book?)

(3) Kasia III is watching her brother Michał eating an egg. She says:

<u>jajko Michał</u>   'egg Michał'

(= Michal is eating an egg)

(4) Basia VI wants to read. Mummy asks her <u>Co Basia będzie czytać?</u> (= What is Basia going to read?). Basia points at a newspaper:

<u>nie gazetę</u>   'not newspaper$_{Acc}$'

<u>tata gazetę</u>   'Daddy newspaper$_{Acc}$'

(= Daddy reads the newspaper)

The overwhelming majority of Subject+Object utterances were non-declarative. In these utterances the Noun described as Subject referred most frequently to the Addressee.

In imperative utterances a frequent pattern was SUBJECT/YOU$_{do}$+OBJECT, e.g.,

(5) Inka IV has knocked down the house which Daddy had built with blocks. She asks Daddy to build it again:

<u>tatuś domek</u>   'Daddy house'
(= Daddy has to build a house)

(6) Inka VI wants her book. She asks Mummy:

<u>mamusia książkę</u>   'Mummy book$_{Acc}$'

(= Mummy, give me the book)

(7) Jaś VI wants Daddy to give him a chocolate. He asks:

<u>tatusiu czekoladkę</u>   'Daddy$_{Voc}$ chocolate$_{Acc}$'

<u>czekoladkę tatusiu</u>   'chocolate$_{Acc}$ Daddy$_{Voc}$'

(= Daddy, give me a chocolate).

Among ostensive utterances a frequent pattern was SUBJECT/YOU$_{look}$+OBJECT, e.g.,

(8) Inka II takes Auntie into the room and shows her
     a lamp:

    <u>ciocia lampa</u>   'Auntie lamp'
                            (= Auntie, look at the lamp)

(9) Inka IV shows Daddy a picture of an elephant:

    <u>tatuś słoń</u>   'Daddy elephant'

    słoń tu jest   'elephant here is'
                            (= Daddy look: there is an
                            elephant).

       The name of the Speaker appears in Subject po-
sition less frequently than the Vocative reference to the
Addressee occurs, but some instances of the SUBJECT/I_{want}
+ OBJECT category were recorded, e.g.,

(10) Inka IV wants to take a pencil from Daddy. She
     says:

    <u>Inka ołówek</u>   'Inka pencil'
                            (= Inka wants a pencil)

(11) Jaś IV watches Granny drinking tea. He also wants
     some tea and asks her:

    <u>ja herbatkę</u>   'I tea$_{Acc}$'

                            (= I want some tea).

       It is worth noting that the same relation as
above can be expressed by means of a different syntactic
pattern which does not belong to the Subject+Object category, namely, the INDIRECT OBJECT/I_{want}+ OBJECT. Such
utterances have the Dative case marker on the Speaker's
name, e.g.,

(12) Kasia II wants some sugar. She asks Mummy:

    <u>Kasi cukru</u>   'Kasia$_{Dat}$ sugar$_{Acc}$'
                            (= give Kasia some sugar)

(13) Tenia III asks Mummy to give her a spoon:

    <u>łyżkę Teni</u>   'spoon$_{Acc}$ Tenia$_{Dat}$'
                            (= give Tenia a spoon)

       The proportions of utterances which represent
different subcategories within the Subject+Object group
are given in Table 3. Establishing the interpersonal

TABLE 3. Subclassification of the Subject+Object
utterances recorded in the five children.

Category	Inka	Kasia	Jaś	Basia	Tenia
SUBJECT+OBJECT proper	3	3	2	1	-
SUBJECT/YOU$_{do}$ + OBJECT	44	3	8	1	10
SUBJECT/YOU$_{look}$ + OBJECT	39	3	6	4	16
SUBJECT/I$_{want}$ + OBJECT	5	-	2	1	2
Total	91	9	18	7	28

meaning of utterances made it possible to find that the
Subject+Object category proper (declarative) was marginal
in all the five children. The Noun described as Subject
on the basis of its ideational meaning most frequently
functioned as a Vocative.

LOCATION CATEGORY

The Noun+Noun constructions which express locative relation were divided according to modality into
declarative and imperative utterances. Among the declaratives which form the category of 'Location proper' the
following three types of location were found:

I. Static location, e.g.,

(14) Inka IV is asked Gdzie jest teraz Hanka? (= Where
      is Hanka now?). She answers:

       Hanka w szkole   'Hanka at school$_{Loc}$'

                               (= Hanka is at school)

II. Dynamic location (The Subject moves to the place denoted by the Directional Locative), e.g.,

(15) Inka III takes the handbag, waves to her mother and
      says:

<u>pa, pa</u>   'byebye'

<u>Inka miasta</u>   'Inka town$_{Dir}$'

                           (= Inka is going to town)

III. Translocation of an object (The Subject causes the movement of an object to the place denoted by the Directional Locative), e.g.,

(16) Inka V puts a sweet into her mouth. She comments:

      <u>Inka do buzi</u>   'Inka into mouth$_{Dir}$'

                                   (= Inka puts a sweet into her mouth)

       In imperative utterances with the Addressee's name in Subject position the same three types of location appear:

I. Static location, e.g.,

(17) Inka II wants Grandpa to stay at home with her. She says:

      <u>dziadek domu</u>   'Grandpa home$_{Loc}$'

                                   (= Grandpa is to stay at home)

II. Dynamic location, e.g.

(18) Inka II wants Hanka to come home with her. She says:

      <u>Hanka domu</u>   'Hanka home$_{Dir}$'

                                   (= Hanka is to come home)

III. Translocation of an object, e.g.,

(19) Inka IV wants to take the dolly Bimbo out of the bed but she cannot reach it. She calls Daddy:

      <u>tatuś łóżka</u>   'Daddy bed$_{Dir}$'

                                     (= Daddy is to take it out of the bed)

Daddy does not understand the request. She explains:

      <u>Bimbo łóżka</u>   'Bimbo bed$_{Dir}$'

                                     (= take bimbo out of the bed)

In some imperative utterances the name of the Speaker appears. Such utterances have the structure SUBJECT/I$_{want}$ + DIRECTIONAL LOCATIVE, and express the child's wish to move in a given direction, e.g.,

(20) Inka VI wants to bring Daddy his shoes. She says:

<u>tatuś otwórz drzwi</u>   'Daddy open door'

<u>Inka pokoju</u>   'Inka room$_{Dir}$'

<u>butki</u>   'shoes'
            (= Inka wants to go into
            the room to get shoes)

(21) Tenia IV is tired. She says:

<u>domu Tenia</u>   'home$_{Dir}$ Tenia'

            (= Tenia wants to go home)

TABLE 4.   Subclassification of the Locative Noun+Noun constructions recorded in the five children.

Category	Inka	Kasia	Jaś	Basia	Tenia
LOCATION proper	9	-	9	8	7
SUBJECT/YOU$_{do}$ + {$\begin{matrix} LOC. \\ DIR. \end{matrix}$}	16	-	5	1	2
SUBJECT/I$_{want}$ + DIR.	11	-	-	2	1
Total	36	-	14	11	10

In the case of Inka, who produced many locative Noun+Noun constructions, imperative utterances were more numerous than declaratives. The I$_{want}$ pattern was more productive in the case of locatives than in the case of Subject+Object relation (cf. Table 3). In the other three children, declarative locatives were more frequent than imperative locatives.

CONCLUSIONS

The above analyses demonstrate that the overwhelming majority of Noun+Noun constructions formally
described as Subject+Object and Location are in fact combinations of Addressee's or Speaker's name with another
noun whose referent (object or place) is requested by the
child (as in imperatives) or pointed to (as in ostensives).
In two children, Inka and Tenia, there is a high frequency
of occurrence of the Vocative (YOU_{do} and YOU_{look}): 99 out
of 155 of Inka's Noun+Noun constructions contain a Vocative; in Tenia's data this proportion is 28/61. Since
these two children are in fact sisters, brought up in the
same family, it is probable that the high frequency of the
Vocative reflects the individual style of conversation pec-
uliar to their environment. In the writer's opinion, if
semantically declarative utterances are analyzed separately from imperatives and ostensives, striking similarities
across children, and perhaps even across languages will be
found. The importance of this methodological claim is also
supported by results concerning the development of the
transitive sentence pattern (Smoczyńska, 1976). The imperative and ostensive utterances are more likely to reflect
particular styles and individual differences in interpersonal relationship between child and adult. The interpersonal meaning of an utterance is as relevant to the syntactic analysis as the ideational meaning and it can be
established with equal ease on the grounds of the rich interpretation principle, which makes possible insights into
the real nature of numerous syntactic phenomena, especially of universals of syntactic development.

Bloom, L.M. (1970)   Language Development: Form and Fun-
     ction in Emerging Grammars. M.I.T. Press,
     Cambridge, Mass.

Brown, R. (1973)   A First Language: The Early Stages.
     Harvard University Press, Cambridge, Mass.

Campbell, R.N. (1976)   Propositions and Early Utterances.
     In G. Drachman (ed.) Akten des 1. Salzburger
     Kolloquiums uber Kindersprache.   Salzburger
     Beiträge zur Linguistik   2. Verlag Günter Narr,
     Tübingen.

Halliday, M.A.K. (1970)   Language Structure and Language
     Function.   In J. Lyons (ed.) New Horizons in
     Linguistics.   Penguin, Harmondsworth, Middx.
     England.

300

Smoczyńska, M. (1976)   Development of the Transitive
        Sentence Pattern.   In G. Drachman (ed.)
        Akten des 1. Salzburger Kolloquiums über
        Kindersprache.   Salzburger Beiträge zur
        Linguistik 2.   Verlag Günter Narr, Tübingen.

Some Observations of Error in Context

L.J.Ferrier

The present work is based on a series of observations of my one-year-old from the appearance of her
first word.   It contains four basic assumptions.

1. Mother and child are an interactional unit and it is
pointless to look at a child's production without giving
equal weight to the mother's contribution to the dialogue.

2. More interesting than the fact that the subject has
acquired a particular lexical item are the changes in
application of these items over time.

3. The child's early utterances are tied to particular
routine contextual situations and therefore the analysis
of language in the early stages must include a description
of context.

4. It is a useful research method to pay attention to the
child's 'mistakes' and a careful analysis of why the child
is making them may reveal which strategies he is relying
on in utilising maternal utterances to produce his own
novel ones.

I made weekly notes of my daughter's vocabulary
acquisitions with descriptions of the social and physical
contexts in which they were first used and utterances of
mine on which they appeared to be dependent. I noted subsequent uses of the same items and, in particular, any
misuses.

---

*This work was done as part of the Language Develop-
ment Project at the University of Bristol. Funded by
S.S.R.C. Grant No. HR 2024.

I should like to begin by bringing to the attention of those who are not parents, a few facts vital to any study of early language development. Firstly, that in the first two years of life, a baby probably averages three nappy changes per day (conservative estimate) which means that he has over 2,000 nappies changed in that period. Similarly he probably averages about 2,000 meals and 2,000 snoozes.

The second point is that, contrary to Chomsky's view that language is new and creative, mothers' language to small children is repetitious, context-tied and ritualized (Halliday, 1974). Observing my own behaviour when my daughter was about 15 months old, I discovered that whenever I took her out of her cot I said Hello my love. Where' my nice girl? Whenever I sat her in her high chair I said Upsadaisy, and whenever she sneezed I said Atchoo.

The combination of these facts means that the small baby finds himself with monotonous regularity in routine interactional contexts in which his mother produces a fairly limited and predictable set of utterances. It is both the regularity and the invariance of these routines which allows the baby to make his initial attempts at breaking the linguistic code. (My daughter's first word was Pretty which had its roots in a bed-time ritual of admiring the geraniums on a window sill halfway up the stairs.) However these interactions are idiosyncratic to particular mother-child pairs. (My daughter's earliest demand to be allowed to draw was Pussy as I constantly drew cats for her. Such demands would have been incomprehensible to anyone outside the interaction.) They also evolve slowly from day to day, week to week, under the influence of either of the two parties but particularly subject to the developing capacities of the child. For example, when my daughter was just on the point of walking she virtually refused to lie down to have her nappies changed, so involved was she with her new skill. To accommodate the nappy-changing routine to this desire, I temporarily put her nappies on while she stood on the window sill, which distraction device brought into that routine new objects, i.e. the birds on the roof-top opposite. After a week the item birds appeared in her vocabulary.

The child's early utterances are idiosyncratic for other reasons. Which items from his mother's productions a child selects for his own use will depend on the stratagems he is employing at the time. I would like to consider one stratagem hit upon by my daughter at about 16 months.

'Imitation' has had both its devotees and its detractors as a process in language development. That some children do it is well documented (Ryan, 1973); why they do it, or whether it in fact advances the productive

capacity of the child, is still in dispute. Imitation
has generally been defined as the exact repetition of
the whole or part of a preceding utterance produced by
someone other than the child and following in fairly
rapid temporal succession. This type of imitation is
fairly readily picked up by the classical research method of running a tape-recorder for set periods of time
and analyzing all utterances within that text. I would
like to suggest that there is a second type of imitation,
which I shall term 'dependency', not operating under those
temporal constraints and not so readily picked up by the
itinerant researcher, but available to the mother who can
observe her child in the repeated and routine social contexts in which they interact. Examples of this are given
below.

1. Look: At the age of 16 months one typical and repeated demand made by my subject was for drawers and
doors to be opened for her. Before this age her demands
were transmitted by gesture (pulling at the drawer or
door) accompanied by an item [ʔə̃] from her protolanguage
(Halliday, 1975). At this point I observed that my
typical reaction to such a demand was to check my interpretation of her utterance by asking Do you want to look?
She shortly afterwards produced look in exactly those
same physical contexts but as a demand form replacing
her protolanguage term.

2. Out: Shortly after the development of look, out
appeared in a similar manner. Until this time she communicated a desire to get out of her feeding chair by making
efforts to get out accompanied by her protolanguage demand.
I would once again check her message by saying Do you want
to get out? She subsequently used out as her demand form.
It was used appropriately in that specific physical context but when a week later she needed assistance to climb
into a high chair, she generalized 'out' to that situation.

3. This and That: These were used in free variation as
demands for objects out of reach and their acquisition had
a similar history. The context of their first use was the
bath, where there is a large basket of toys suspended from
the shower for use at bath time. Her gestural demand was
replaced by this and later that which were again lifted
from my check utterances Do you want this/that? This and
that were subsequently extended to any situations in which
she wanted an object out of reach and were used appropriately.

      She shortly afterwards lifted up from my check
Do you want to get up? which was then generalized to situations in which she wanted to get down. She also employed
chair from my check Do you want to get on the chair? She
then used it as a request for help to get onto tricycles,
window sills and a rocking horse.

It appeared then, that many of her early utterances were tied to repeated family routines of the sort described, in which my language was notably repetitious. But the very invariance of those routines and of my language within them allowed my daughter to hit on the pro ductive stratagem of utilizing the last word of my utterance by transforming its function to that of a demand for goods or services. The perceptual salience of sentence final position has been noted elsewhere (Slobin, 1973). (Two months after the period described she produced a beautiful example of this stratagem. I said Mummy would like one too, to which she responded Three, four, five. Note that in each case, the word lifted from the source utterance carried the tonic which presumably added to its salience.) Almost immediately the term had been acquired in those social/physical contexts in which my source utterance was embedded, she generalized it to other similar situations, sometimes appropriately and sometimes not. This process of generalization has been noted by most diarist studies and is discussed by Roger Brown (1958). It is a capacity which is obviously of enormous importance to the child's cognitive and verbal progress. I am always awed by the children's unerring ability to generalize from real ducks to Walt Disney creations which bear little relation to the real thing. It is not therefore surprisin that they sometimes stray across adult conceptual boundaries, as for example, when my daughter referred to the law mower as Daddy's vacuum cleaner.

However, a careful examination of those instance which were inappropriate suggests that the relationship between the social/physical situations and the language employed in them is not a simple one and that various categories of inappropriate usage can be analysed. To consider the ontogenesis of some other of my daughter's utterances:

4. [ϕ^h] (phew!) - an item which I systematically used for a while when I entered my daughter's bedroom each morning to be greeted by a rather offensive smell. My utterance was an exclamation and its 'application' (Lyons, 1968 : 434) was the smell. My daughter after a couple of days produced it in the same setting, i.e. her cot in the morning but when in fact the smell was absent. For her it was a form of greeting and tied initially to that particular routine. Shortly afterwards I extended its use to nappy-changing situations in which for me the utterance had the same function and application - for her the function appeared to be simply 'ostension' and its application was her nappy. She subsequently used the term outside the nappy-changing situation to refer to nappies both clean and dirty, and finally to the nappy bucket which normally contained nappies but which was, on this particular occasion, empty.

The initial use of this term as a greeting suggests that-

(a) the recurring social situation of meeting her mother in the morning was for her the dominant feature of its use and

(b) that her own noxious odour did not have the perceptual salience for her it did for me!

The fact that the term then acquired an ostensive or perhaps naming function in the nappy-changing situation indicates

(a) that which particular features of physical context an utterance is referring to is not always obvious to the language learner, and

(b) that while for me the application of my utterance was my reaction to a smell, the referent of her utterance was the object which was sometimes the cause of the smell, i.e. the nappy.

Finally, as mature speakers we tend to forget that even the humble exclamation is culture bound and has to be learned to have that particular function. (I have a notion that some of these early exclamations may in fact have an important function in delimiting the field of application later covered by specific verbs. So the accident markers 'Oh dear' and 'upsadaisy' are the precursors of such verbs as 'spill' and 'fall' which must obligatorily have attached the semantic feature 'non-purposive'.)

A further example of the confusion generated by the perceptual complexity of objects referred to, was my daughter's first acquaintance with aeroplanes. From about the time when she was one year and onwards, I frequently drew her attention to noises made by aeroplanes by use of Sh! and an accompanying raised finger. She quickly learned to respond to aeroplane noises in the same way but never in fact saw an actual aeroplane. The referent of Sh! was a disembodied noise. At about this period, she developed an interest in books. I verbally labelled a picture of an aeroplane for her and she responded with Sh! accompanied by the usual gesture but of course inappropriately in the absence of any noise. When a few days later she saw her first aeroplane, she exclaimed Bird!

Maternal utterances do not come 'labelled' as to either their function or their referents. Since children often appear to acquire these early utterances in the same repeated social/physical contexts, their initial hypotheses about both the functions and referents of their caretaker's utterances may prove to be wrong when they are later generalized beyond those first ritualized contexts.

A second area in which the child's analysis of the relationship between language and situation may initially fail is in the segmentation of maternal utterances into linguistic units. For example, in free variation with the utterance Bye-bye, my daughter produced Say bye-bye which had as its source my commands to her, in previous situations, to say goodbye to some third person. Similarly the utterance Shoes on was used ostensively, i.e. to point out shoes, and appeared to be equivalent in meaning to her utterance Shoes. Finally, she used the utterance There's Ursie (Ursie is the name of her older sister), in exactly those situations in which she used the simple utterance Ursie, i.e. as a name. It appeared that these utterances were in fact lifted wholesale from their source utterances and were for her, at this time, indivisible units. Final proof that her utterance Shoes on was in fact one unit were her productions several months later of the utterances Shoes on off and Bye-bye shoes on in which 'shoes on' was operating as one nominal. Ruth Clark (1974), in her analysis of her own children's language, has produced similar evidence of this tendency.

My data seem to suggest that, for at least some children, imitation, in the sense defined, i.e. as the use of the whole or a part of preceding maternal utterances in the same ritualized contexts, appears to be a productive strategy. It has indeed been suggested to me by Robert Hoogenraad (personal communication) that this is the method whereby all children acquire lexical items. The problem appears to be a methodological one of devising a research strategy to establish the links between the child's productions and the environmental input for those productions which may have temporally preceded them by days or weeks. The validity of the data here discussed, rests on three things (a) that I could provide instances of my own routine productions (which were constantly in use over a long period of time) (b) that my productions were virtually the only verbal input for my child (c) that I could follow all her uses of these items from their first appearance and through all their idiosyncratic contextual applications. The method employed was in fact retrospective. When my daughter acquired a new item, I checked with my current routines to see where its source might be. To acquire prospective proof would require the collection of all the mother's utterances in child-rearing contexts for perhaps months before the child's actual productions, in the hope of predicting a few of his early utterances. Hope lies in the fact that in the early days of language production, the child is rarely picking up infrequent maternal items. All his productions appear to be drawn from contexts which have a traceable history.

A further methodological point: the validity of maternal interpretations is constantly questioned by

researchers. It has been suggested by P.D. Griffiths
(Symposium discussion) that when my daughter used 'out'
as a demand to be lifted into a chair, perhaps what she
was intending to communicate was that she was 'outside'
the chair and would I please do something about it. I
think to answer this problem one has to distinguish between what her intentions were, i.e. what social act she
was attempting to accomplish, and what semantic meaning
the term 'out' had for her. Her intention was, I think,
never in any doubt (a) because her utterances were accompanied by a gesture (her leg was already half over
the side of chair at the time) which had in fact histo-
rically preceded the verbal form as a demand for help,
and (b) because she had asked for assistance to climb
into her chair several times a day in the preceding couple
of months. In a sense that particular intended meaning
had already been negotiated and agreed upon by us both.
As to what semantic meaning the term 'out' had for her, I
think that at this very early stage the utterance had no
propositional content (Dore,1975). The fact that the same
term was idiosyncratically generalized to all sorts of
contexts suggests to me that semantic boundaries for these
various locatives had not yet been established, i.e. they
were not yet semantically contrastive in the child's system. The only items which are acquired early and remain
fairly stable are nouns where the existence of a referent
compels some uniformity of usage.

Susan Ervin-Tripp (Symposium discussion) has
noted that several studies of second language learning in
children also show a sharp contrast between routine, rote-
learned units and productive structures. This difference
is even more vivid than in infants because of the length
of the routines in contrast to telegraphic new utterances.
Their source is clearly in peer interaction, e.g. let go,
get out of here, you dummy, get going, etc.

Further analysis of my daughter's idiosyncratic
usages suggests two conclusions:

1. That the social function of early utterances is
all important for the child (Dore, 1975). Language starts
as a social tool for manipulating people and objects in
his environment and only gradually approximates to adult
usage which can then accurately portray the objective
world. So, for example, the locatives 'up' and 'out'
were first and most importantly demands for assistance.
'Up' was used as a demand to be lifted, 'down' and 'out'
as a request to be lifted 'in'. 'Chair' was initially a
request to be lifted onto any flat surface and only
several months later was it used to refer to the class of
objects we call chairs. Also 'more' in its initial use
did not necessarily contain the notion of recurrence, it
was simply a general request for food. Similarly 'all
gone' was a statement that my daughter had no further
interest in her food and was not at all concerned with the

308

food's disappearance. So, in fact, the meaning covered
by the child's use of these terms may be much larger than
that served by the adult's usage and may include the
adult's antonym of that term.

2. Occasionally vocabulary items are inappropriate
because they appear to remain temporarily tied to the
action schema within which they were originally learned.
So, at 18 months, my daughter produced the utterance
Bye-bye dirty just after she had spat out a piece of half-
chewed bread. This strange utterance can only be explained by the fact that, at the stage when small children are
constantly putting inedible objects into their mouths, the
adult usually requests that the objects be spat out because they are dirty. So 'dirty' remains tied to the
initial activity of spitting objects out and only later
becomes for the child the attributive term it is for
adults. Further, when my daughter was about 16 months,
she was playing with a die on a low table. She acciden-
tally dropped it and it rolled across the floor. She immediately cried Ball; for her, at this time, the item
'ball', learned in the context of games of kicking with
mother, was defined functionally, as an object which
rolls. However, a month later it had been abstracted
from the learning context and was used to refer to pictures of balls in books and to a flat circular disc.

SUMMARY AND CONCLUSIONS

Mother and child in the first two years of life
develop an exclusive and idiosyncratic relationship in the
repeated and ritualized encounters of childcaring. Within
these encounters the mother's language is limited and context-tied, thus allowing the child to make his first attempts at breaking the linguistic code. At least some
children appear to lift items wholesale from their mother's
productions and put them to their own uses. However, the
fact that the relationship between language and the socio-
physical world is both referentially and functionally complex, leads to the child's production of inappropriate
utterances when he generalizes beyond the initial learning
context.

Finally, the social functions of the child's
early utterances appear to be developmentally dominant and
only gradually do the semantic boundaries of the items in
them approximate to those of adults.

REFERENCES

Brown, R. (1958) Words and Things. Free Press, New York.

309

Bruner, J. (1975)   The Ontogenesis of Speech Acts.
Journal of Child Language   2.   1-10.

Clark, R. (1974)   Performing without Competence.
Journal of Child Language 1. 1-10.

Dore, J. (1975)   Holophrases, Speech Acts and Language
Universals. Journal of Child Language 2. 21-40.

Halliday, M.A.K. (1974)   In Parrett H. Discussing
Language: Dialogues with W.L. Chafe, N. Chomsky,
A.J. Greimas, M.A.K. Halliday, et al.   Mouton,
The Hague.

Halliday, M.A.K. (1975)   Learning How to Mean: Explorations in the Development of Language.   Edward
Arnold, London.

Lyons, J. (1968)   Introduction to Theoretical Linguistics.
Cambridge University Press, Cambridge.

Ryan, J. (1973)   Interpretation and Imitation in Early
Language Development.   In R.A. Hinde and J.S.
Hinde (eds.) Constraints on Learning: Limitations
and Predispositions. Academic Press, London.

Slobin, D.I. (1973)   Cognitive Prerequisites for the
Development of Grammar.   In C.A. Ferguson and
D.I. Slobin (eds.) Studies of Child Language
Development.   Holt, Rinehart and Winston,
New York.

A `door´ to Verbs

P. Griffiths and M. Atkinson

During the last few years an increasing amount
of attention has been paid to young children's acquisition of word meanings and to the ways in which the meanings of particular forms change as vocabulary increases.
Most of these studies seem to have concentrated on two
areas of child vocabularies: terms which have 'concrete'
reference, and 'abstract' relational terms. A notable
gap concerns the early use of what, in an adult grammar,
would be described as verbs; forms which are applied to
actions and events rather than to individuals or abstract
relationships. This gap is somewhat surprising given the
interest which many child language researchers have recently begun to show in the ideas of the Piagetian school
of cognitive development.

Of course, the gap is not wholly unplugged. One
worthy counter-instance to our claim is Carter's (1975)
paper in which the origin of two words is traced back to
a sensorimotor morpheme. Another obvious exception (and
there are others, e.g. Ferrier's paper in this volume) is

---

* The research on which this study is based
was supported by a Social Science Research Council grant,
HR 1019, to Professor John Lyons, Department of Linguistics, University of Edinburgh. We are grateful to the
children, their parents, and the S.S.R.C.

Bowerman's (1974) study of causative verbs. She focuses on
the use by children of non-causative predicates in a causative sense.   To take an example from our own data: Jeremy,
when he was 2;1.17, requested the fastening of his shoe
by saying tight the shoe on, in other words 'cause the shoe
to be on tight'. Bowerman suggests that apparently causative verbs such as open used before this time are 'unana-
lysed' and not a complex containing a CAUSE predicate and
a stative predicate, such as BE OPEN. We are going to describe a phenomenon which is developmentally earlier than
even the use of open. We have been investigating children'
ways of verbally encoding acts of spatial separation and
assembly.

   Our study is based on weekly tape-recordings of
conversations with each of seven children, from when they
were about 15 months old until they were about 33 months
old.   The tape-recordings contain 'live' commentaries on
the non-verbal matrices of the conversations and were supplemented by weekly parental questionnaires.   See Griffiths, Atkinson and Huxley (1974) for a general description of method etc.

   Three of the children, Jeremy, Keith and
Rebecca, made a great deal of use of door as a verb - by
which we mean simply a 'doing-word'. We also recorded a
few cases of door used in the same way by a fourth child,
Gordon. (The remaining three children will enter the
picture later.) The acquisition of door was first noted
in the parental questionnaires at ages ranging between
1;7.9, for Gordon, and 2;2.19, for Keith. In all four
cases it was said to have been initially used in connection with doors. Here is an example recorded from
Keith (2;3.9):

M	Keith
	(Keith shakes a lidded beaker.)
	x, ə pennies
	(Keith takes a coin to prise off lid.)
	oh, ə stuck
	(Keith fails to get lid off - shakes beaker.)
	(Keith hands it to M, saying:)
	ə door
Open.	open (echo)
	(M struggles to remove lid.)
	stuck
	(M removes lid.)
Ooh!	Ooh!

(In this and subsequent examples: adult utterances appear on the left and child utterances on the right. Adults are identified as follows: M = Child's mother, MA = Martin Atkinson, PG = Patrick Griffiths. x stands for an untranscribable syllable.)

A reasonable hypothesis, if this had been the only situation in which it was used, might have been that Keith had noticed certain perceptual and/or functional similarities between a door and a lid of a tin and was using the form door to refer to the lid of the tin. However, in view of examples such as the following we reject this explanation. Jeremy's mother reported (1;9) that he said door to request help in extricating a pencil from his sleeve. Keith (2;5.11) said door when he wanted the lead separated from our microphone. Rebecca (1;10.3) used door to get MA to remove first a doll's shoe and then its dress. Or, again from Rebecca, this time at 1;10.17:

MA	Rebecca
Those go on there.	(MA screwing nuts on to a construction toy.)

please

(Rebecca wants the nuts off.)

door, door

Now just wait and see
a minute and I think
you'll like it.

(MA persists in screwing nuts on.)

door, door

door, door please

The predicate door seemed to have this rather wide extension virtually from its inception.

The other three children did not, as far as we know, use the form door in this way, but they could express the same meaning. Christopher and Paul achieved these effects, less sensationally, by means of out, off and open. From Jacqueline (1;4.26) we recorded, in a single session, eleven tokens of a form which we can represent as [ɔ̃gega] (its phonetic manifestation, since we cannot offer a plausible phonetically related English gloss). [ɔ̃gega] was used in only two situations:

314

several times to ask for a ping pong ball to be pushed
out of a hollow cylinder and once to request help in un-
screwing a nut. Jacqueline's family then took her away
for three weeks, on holiday, and we never heard the form
again. Nor, for several months, was there any obvious
successor fulfilling this function for her. Gordon, who
acquired door earliest (1;7.9) lost it at approximately
1;10½. At 2;1.8 his mother apparently forgetting her
earlier questionnaire entry, claimed door as a new vocabulary item signifying 'door', and one week later we a-
gain recorded it as a request for the removal of a tin's
lid. Thereafter Gordon's door disappeared once more.
During a session recorded when he was 2;4.28, he used an
unglossable bisyllabic form [dzat^ha, t^hat^ha, daʔdza] as
he tried to persuade MA to help him wrest the bottom
from a tin.(It is easier to turn them over and lift off
the lids instead.)

        Most of these uses of door etc. might seem to
be glossable by means of constructions such as CAUSE THE
DOOR TO BE OPEN or CAUSE ELEPHANT'S EAR TO BE OFF, in
which the embedded propositions, THE DOOR BE OPEN,
ELEPHANT'S EAR BE OFF, specify the end state which will
result from the performance of the desired action. Were
they causative for the children? We think not. The evidence on which to base an argument cannot be syntactic
because almost all of the 'door-utterances' we recorded
were holophrastic. One might approach the question
through pragmatics. Note that stative uses of predicates
like open, e.g. the door is open, are necessarily constative, i.e. descriptive. Now, without exception, all
the earliest uses of door in our data were requests. Requests are not constative. Therefore all we can conclude
from this line of argument is that the first doors were
not stative and, hence, might have been causative.

        What seems to seal the coffin on the causative
interpretation though is the following observation: door,
although first and predominantly used to request opening
and separation of objects, came soon to be used by three
of the children (and perhaps by Rebecca too) also in
asking for things to be put together, as in the third of
Jeremy's utterances below (1;11.8).

        M   Jeremy

                        (Jeremy looks at line of plastic
                        humanoids clasped together,
                        held by M)

                        dirty

                        xxx door, xx!

You want a door?
Like that?

(M unclasps leading humanoid.)

ə door (indignant)

Well then, there?

(M fits it to the back of the
line. This seems to be satis-
factory.)

yes

Or, from Keith (2;4.8):

PG   Keith

(Keith failing to push bung into
hole in toy telephone base, because he is putting it on upside
down.)

ə door, uh, ə there

What do you want done
Keith?   (Keith still trying.)

there

What must I do Keith?

(Keith still trying.)

uh?

What must I do?

ə door

Gordon (1;10.16) used door both for wanting a plastic man
decapitated and for wanting its head replaced. Being off
and being on are almost complementary states. It seems
therefore that door was not used to say anything about resulting states but was, rather, a semantically transitive,
but not causative, predicate meaning something like 'operate upon'. This is presumably what Bowerman (1974 :
173) has in mind when she says: 'It may be that early in
a child's development, "causative" verbs like "open" and
"break" are understood primarily in terms of the actual
or anticipated act of an agent on a patient'.

The same point can be made in connection with
Jeremy's use of off and on (a case of ontogeny recapitula-
ting ontogeny). At 1;9.1 his mother reported that he said
on not only for wanting his coat put on but also when he
wanted it taken off. At 2;2.0 she noted that he still

tended to use <u>on</u> whether he wanted items of clothing taken off or put on. And, at 2;2.7 that he used <u>off</u> for wanting his coat either on or off. If for him <u>on</u> and <u>off</u> both related to acting upon items of clothing, regardless of the end state, then naturally they would be synonymous.

In all four children we recorded <u>on/off</u> only after the arrival of <u>door</u>. Like <u>door</u>, the first uses of <u>on/off</u> were requests for action. And, again like <u>door</u>, they were next extended to dynamic constative uses, i.e. comments on ongoing actions. The last use to appear for <u>on/off</u> was stative constative, such as the final utterance in the following episode from Gordon's record (2;5.24).

MA	Gordon
	(Gordon trying to unscrew a nut.)
	<u>that off</u>
Can I do it?	
	(Gordon, still trying, says:)
	<u>no, ə mine off</u>
Who's taking it off?	
	(Gordon finally removes nut.)
	<u>see, that off</u>

We recognize that other interpretations of the last utterance are possible, e.g. past tense dynamic constative.

Keith (2;3.16) once said <u>door</u> after succeeding in undoing a nut but otherwise there are no candidates for <u>door</u> as a stative predicate. What became of <u>door</u> after its development was arrested at the request and dynamic constative stage? Well, for all the children it eventually became a noun, as it is for us. Gordon, who twice lost <u>door</u> - in the function we have been discussing - both times began to use it as a demonstrative. Jeremy (1;10.13) asked his mother to <u>do it</u> after he had failed to turn the handle of a door and from then on used <u>door</u> and <u>do it</u> in apparently free variation, as in the following examples taken from a single session (1;11.1).

M	Jeremy
	(MA produces a closed tin.)
	<u>door</u>

Put the book away first.

(After the book issue
had been cleared up, MA
obliged by opening the
tin.)

     MA   (Jeremy finds a small tin.)

                         <u>ə do it</u>

Do you want it open?

                     (MA opens it.)

There. Nothing in.

                     <u>xx door</u>

Do you want it closed?

                     (MA closes it.)

In the end <u>do</u> triumphed over <u>door</u>. For Rebecca the functions of <u>door</u> were taken over by <u>do</u> and <u>don</u> and <u>doff</u>,
which latter two meant 'on' and 'off'.

      To show the relationship between <u>door</u>, [ɔ̃gega]
etc. and the later acquisitions <u>open</u> and <u>shut</u> we have
only to illustrate the similar and comparably wide extensions of these predicates when they first appeared. Consider the following example from Jacqueline (1;8.24):

     MA   Jacqueline

                   <u>want shut me</u>

            (Jacqueline passes box to MA)

                   <u>want shut me</u>

There.   (MA opens the box. Jacqueline
                      attempts to put a brick into
                      it.)

There were other similar uses of <u>shut</u> and her mother commented that she also used the form when she wanted doors
opened. Or, consider her use of <u>open</u> a week later (1;9.0):

MA   Jacqueline

Watch. There.

> (MA fits head to a plastic man
> he had earlier decapitated.)

<u>open up, up</u>

Up?...There?

> (MA decapitates man again.)

<u>yes</u>

Paul (1;10.12) was using <u>open</u> where we would
but also in other ways, for example:

Paul

> (Paul tries to take a toy horse
> out of a tin.)

<u>horse, horse, horse</u>

> (The horse becomes wedged in
> the mouth of the tin.)

<u>stuck, stuck</u>

> (Paul tries again to get it out.)

<u>ə stuck</u>

<u>open, horse</u>

> (Paul tips up the tin. Some
> animals fall out.)

And finally, one from Jeremy (2;5.5):

MA   Jeremy

> (Jeremy tries to pull arm off a
> plastic monkey.)

<u>open it</u>

> (Jeremy uses his teeth and
> succeeds.)

<u>oh x</u>

Poor monkey.

> (Jeremy puts the arm on the
> floor.)

<u>'s open it</u>

319

The final utterance here is probably stative.
But, like <u>door</u> and <u>on</u>/<u>off</u>, stative <u>open</u> was always attested later than its use as a dynamic constative or as
a request. Why? Is this a consequence of differential
utility or is there something cognitively complicated
about statives? It is in harmony with the relatively
late development of the information-giving function noted
and discussed by Atkinson (1974), Gruber (1975) and
Halliday (1975).

REFERENCES

Atkinson, R.M. (1974)   Prerequisites for Reference.
    Paper read at BAAL seminar on applications of
    linguistics to language development. (To appear
    in <u>Edinburgh Working Papers in Lingustics</u> <u>6</u>.)

Bowerman, M. (1974)   Learning the Structure of Causa-
    tive Verbs: A Study in the Relationship of
    Cognitive, Semantic and Syntactic Development.
    <u>Papers and Reports on Child Language Develop-
    ment</u> <u>8</u>. Stanford University.142-178.

Carter, A.L. (1975)   The Transformation of Sensori-
    motor Morphemes into Words: A Case Study of
    the Development of 'More' and 'Mine'.
    <u>Journal of Child Language</u> <u>2</u>. 233-250.

Griffiths, P.D., Atkinson, M. and Huxley, R. (1974)
    Project Report. <u>Journal of Child Language</u> <u>1</u>.
    157-158.

Gruber, J.S. (1975)   Performative-constative Transi-
    tion in Child Language. <u>Foundations of
    Language</u> <u>12</u>. 513-527.

Halliday, M.A.K. (1975)   <u>Learning how to Mean: Explo-
    rations in the Development of Language</u>.
    Edward Arnold, London.

Structure and Function in
Language Acquisition

B. Woll

When interest was first focused within the
Chomskyan paradigm on the importance of the study of
language development in children, most research was
devoted to an analysis of the acquisition by the child
of the various syntactic rules of the adult speaker.
Analysis was made of early child utterances as being a
sort of reduced syntax. The development by the child of
the adult language was seen as arising from an innately
determined ability to know the major categories of
language. During the last few years, however, there has
been a reawakening of interest in functional descriptions,
both in linguistic and in behavioural terms. Roger Brown,
for instance (1973) has emphasized the importance of conversational exchange in language use and learning. The
theory of speech acts has been applied to children's conversations (Bruner, 1975; Dore, 1975). Bloom (1970)
expressed concern with a pivot-open classification in
pointing out that adults use situational information to
interpret and allocate functions to the words a child
uses. Schlesinger (1971) has challenged the basis of the
linguistic argument for innate competence and argued
strongly for an account of acquisition in terms of learning how to represent the semantic categories and relations of intended communication. Halliday (1975a and b)
has developed a functional analysis for the speech of a
child, viewing the structure of the child's utterances
as being in the first instance indissoluble from the
purposes to which he puts them. Ferrier (this vol.) has

examined in detail pre-conversational settings and
functions which give rise to language. Francis (1975)
has discussed and developed Schlesinger's valuation
rules.

This paper will concern itself with the
changing nature of the relationship between structure
and function as the child develops language. Data will
be taken from the large scale longitudinal study of child
language development now being conducted at Bristol
University under the direction of C.G. Wells. The children are recorded at timed intervals with the use of a
radio-microphone; there is no observer present in the
home at the time of the recording. Recordings take place
at three-monthly intervals of the children between the
ages of 15 months and 5½ years. The recordings are coded
in such a way as to take into account both the structural
and functional aspects of utterances in conversation. All
recorded samples of speech are first divided into conversational sequences. Sequences are defined for the
purpose of the analysis as consisting of stretches of
conversation with a shared topic and purpose between two
or more speakers. Inevitably this cannot be an absolute
criterion as topic and purpose do not always change
simultaneously. Nevertheless, most sequences terminate
either through achievement of the purpose that prompted
the initiator to start them or through abandonment of
this aim by the initiator. Sequences are characterized
as belonging to one of five types:

Control: the control of the present or future behaviour
of one or more of the participants. This may concern a
particular act or a general disposition to behave in a
particular way.

Experience: The expression of feelings and attitudes
as an affective response to a situation; with spontaneous reaction rather than considered opinion.

Representation: The exchange of information, discussion,
including considered evaluation of experience.

Social: The maintenance of social relationships.

Tutorial: A deliberately didactic intention by one of
the speakers.

Sequences are classified according to their
dominant purpose. The sequence must be considered as
a whole, as individual utterances may have a prepara-
tory or parenthetical function within the whole. Within
a sequence there may occur smaller units of conversation
which realize subsidiary purposes within the overall
purpose of the sequence as a whole. These are termed
sub-sequences. So within a sequence, of which the dominant purpose (control) is to get the child to shut the

door on coming into the house, there may be an utterance making the request (control sub-sequence); the child may interject an account of where he has been (representation sub-sequence) followed by his mother's exclamation of surprise and horror (expressive subsequence) before she reverts to the original request and the child complies (control).

Another category of sub-sequence is recognised in addition to the five which serve both as sequences and subsequences.

Procedural: concerned with the channel of communication rather than content. Such subsequences can occur to initiate or end a sequence, or occur within a sequence to rectify a communication problem due to mishearing or misunderstanding. Table 1 below illustrates how a sequence would be analyzed:

TABLE 1. Control sequence

	Child	Mother	Subsequence
(1)		Where is your apple cake you were making?	representational
(2)	Uh?		procedural
(3)		Where's the apple cake you were making?	procedural
(4)	In there		representational
(5)		Go and get them then and then Helen can play with them	control

---

Each utterance within a sequence is also coded for length, purpose, structure, relationship with previous utterances within the sequence, etc. (Further details of the coding scheme may be found in the Coding Manual produced in connection with the project (Wells, 1975).)

This type of analysis makes it possible to test various hypotheses as to the relationship between structure and function in the child's development of

language. For instance, Bernstein (1971), adapting
Halliday's systemics to the analysis of social class
difference, postulated that the various social groups
differ in the functions for which they use language
and that these differing functions give rise to differing structures, e.g. a greater use of explanation might
give rise to a greater number of subordinate clauses.
The utterances of children aged 3 1/4 years were analyzed according to the coding scheme and comparisons
made between the development of various aspects of complex structure and the development of a wide variety of
conversational functions, using the two variables of
social class and sex. On the dimensions of structural
complexity, use of manner, aspect, time reference, complex sentences, mean length of utterance, etc., there
is a significant difference between middle and working
class children. If variety in functions used is compared, however, there is no difference among children
of different social classes but of the same sex, yet
there are significant sex differences (Woll, Ferrier,
and Wells, 1975). At 3 1/4 years, then, structural
development is unrelated to function development. But
the literature acknowledges an intimate connection between the child's use of interpersonal purpose and his
development of language. Therefore, there must be a
transition in the child's development of language from
using language purely as an extension of social interaction to the point where language can be detached from
function as an essential component.

Evidence for this hypothesis has been sought
in the one- and two-word stages of linguistic development. For this, all one- and two-word utterances are
coded in one of two ways in the analysis of linguistic
structure. Some utterances are considered to be essentially unstructured, e.g., exclamations, greeting
phrases, 'yes' and 'no', and vocatives. These utterances will remain relatively unchanged in form throughout the child's linguistic development and are coded
as such. Other utterances will change drastically as
the child matures. These are coded in the first instance
as examples of a primitive structure of operator +
nominal. Examples may consist of either operator
(comment), or nominal (topic) or both. Examples are such
utterances as 'there', 'want dolly', 'issa teddy', 'more
biscuit', 'milk', etc.

Operator	Nominal
there	
want	dolly
issa	teddy
more	biscuit
	milk

It is this group of structured utterances which will
be examined here; this will be done with reference
to the structure of the conversations in which they
occur, and in particular the concern will be with the
operators, those elements which closely resemble predicates in a case system, and function in an interpersonal purpose system. This distinction into operator
and nominal is similar to that made by Braine (1963)
and others. These are not like any one form class in
adult grammar but help the child to achieve desired situational changes. It is proposed that these operators
be regarded at first as labels used by the child to denote conversational rather than sentential purpose. The
child appears to use them to label the purpose of the
conversation in which he is engaged. Similar observations have been made of the role of gesture in children's early utterances, when gestures often accompany
and indeed seem part of the child's intentions.

At this operator and nominal stage which occurs with both one- and two-word utterances, children's conversations are characterized by a curious sort
of inflexibility. Once in a conversation they are unable to change its direction to reach more quickly and
easily the shared goal. The inability of children to
use structured utterances in different subsequences is
surprising, since they can evidently use unstructured
utterances for that purpose.

Two conversations representing the holophrastic and the two-word stage are given in Tables
2 and 3 respectively.

The similarity between the two conversations,
despite the difference in MLU, is accounted for if the
operators are regarded at this stage as serving as
identifiers of each of the social functions of speech,
as labels of global conversational purposes. In Table
2, the child is unable to respond to the mother's
procedural utterance. She is bound up in a control
subsequence determined by her use of 'look'. Only the
use of the unstructured exclamation is a direct response
to the mother's attempts to share the experience with
her. In Table 3 there is a similar rigidity in the
child's responses to the mother's question. Again, only
by the use of an exclamation is she able to move on to
a different function. The structured utterances are
equivalent to the functions they realize.

A change occurs, however, during the two-word
stage, partly connected with a change in the child's
intonation system. The child begins to use structure
independently of function, although there is no appreciable increase in MLU. The operators used previously
acquire much more flexible use.

TABLE 2.   Conversation representing the holophrastic stage

Child	Mother	Function analysis	Subsequence
(1)			
Look		operator-control of attention	control
(2)			
Look (pointing out of window)		operator-control of attention	control
(3)			
Look, look		operator-control of attention	control
(4)			
	Someone's playing some music	attempt by mother to interpret focus of child's attempt to control her attention	procedural
(5)			
Eee		exclamation - rejection of mother's interpretation	procedural
(6)			
Look		operator-control of attention	control
(7)			
Look		operator-control of attention	control
(8)	It's the fireguard, isn't it Kate? against the window	another attempt by mother to interpret focus	procedural
(9)			
Look		operator-control of attention	control
(10)			
	So you can't get out	last attempt by mother	procedural

TABLE 3. Conversation representing the two-word stage

Child	Mother	Function analysis	Subsequence
(1)	Where's all the birdies	initiation of con-versation ques-tion with known answer	representa-tional
(2) Birdie, oh		nominal - osten-tion	representa-tional
(3) There birdy		operator and no-minal-ostention	representa-tional
(4) Birdy, birdy, birdy		nominal repeated-ostention	representa-tional
(5)	Birdy	acknowledgement by mother	representa-tional
(6) Ah		exclamation of affection	expressive
(7)	Ah	acknowledgement of affection	expressive
(8)	There's one, look	mother ostends (answers ori-ginal question)	representa-tional

In Table 4 this child, with a MLU of under two, is better able to express his intentions through varying the functions used. For example, he can use 'Paul' both as an answer to a question (2) and a rejection of his mother's statement (5). He can append 'no' to 'Paul' as an operator (12) or use it as an unstructured negative. He can support his position with an appeal to the evidence ('look' (10)). He is able to use the structures available to him as a means of expressing the functions he chooses to express. His utterances are no longer bound by a rigid connection with function.

328

TABLE 4. Use of structure independently of function

Child	Mother	Function analysis	Subsequence
(1)			
	What's that?	conversation initiator	representational
(2)			
Paul, Paul, Paul		answers question appropriately - nominal	representational
(3)			
Picture Paul		answers question appropriately - nominal	representational
(4)			
	That's not Paul	mother rejects answer	representational
(5)			
Paul		child rejects - nominal	representational
(6)			
	That's not Paul it's a little girl	mother rejects again; offers explanation	representational
(7)			
No Paul (= no it's Paul)		child rejects again; unstructured 'no' plus nominal	representational
(8)			
	No it's a little girl	mother rejects again; repeats previous explanation	representational
(9)			
No Paul (= no it's Paul)		child rejects again; unstructured 'no' plus nominal	representational

Child	Mother	Function analysis	Subsequence
(10)			
Look		control of atten-tion-operator child redirects her attention to the picture	control
(11)			
	No it's not	mother rejects answer	representa-tional
(12)			
No Paul (= it's not Paul)		child acknow-ledges operator and nominal	representa-tional
(13)			
Not Paul		child repeats operator and nominal	representa-tional
(14)			
	No it's not Paul is it?	mother acknow-ledges	representa-tional
(15)			
Not Paul		child acknow-ledges mother's statement; operator and nominal	representa-tional
(16)			
	Mm	further mutual acknowledgements	representa-tional
(17)			
Not Paul		further mutual acknowledgements	representa-tional

330

Conclusions

The child comes to his first attempts at
linguistic conversation with experience in the use of
non-linguistic cues to signal general pre-linguistic
conversational purpose, e.g., pointing, grabbing,
whining, etc. The first structural utterances link
topics and purposes. But for a child to progress in
language these must become independent choices. They
become qualitatively different at this stage, per-
mitting the child to develop a wide range of vocabulary and structure to express any function arising in
conversation.

Any study of language acquisition must include both these processes of language acquisition:
how the child isolates and internalizes structures
and also which functions he realizes with them. Further investigation of the relationship of structure
and function is necessary to provide an adequate explanation of how language develops from complete context dependency to the relatively independent choices
of the adult speaker.

REFERENCES

Bernstein B. (1971)   Class, Codes and Control. Vol.1
Routledge, London.

Bloom, L.M. (1970)   Language Development: Form and
Function in Emerging Grammars. M.I.T. Press,
Cambridge, Mass.

Braine, M.D.S. (1963)   The Ontogeny of English Phrase
Structure: The First Phase. Language 39. 1-13.

Brown, R. (1973)   A First Language: The Early Stages.
Allen and Unwin, London.

Bruner, J.S. (1975)   The Ontogenesis of Speech Acts.
Journal of Child Language 2 1. 1-19.

Dore, J. (1975)   Holophrases, Speech Acts and Language Universals. Journal of Child Language
2 1. 21-40.

Francis, H. (1975)   Language in Childhood. Paul Elek,
London.

Halliday, M.A.K. (1975a)   Explorations in the Functions
of Language. Arnold, London.

Halliday, M.A.K. (1975b)   Learning How to Mean: Explorations in the Development of Language.
Arnold, London.

Schlesinger, I.M. (1971)   Production of Utterances
and Language Acquisition. In D.I. Slobin
(ed.) The Ontogenesis of Grammar. Academic
Press, New York.

Wells, C.G. (1975)   Coding Manual for the Description of Child Speech. University of Bristol
School of Education.

Woll, B., Ferrier, L., and Wells, C.G. (1975)
Children and their Parents - Who Starts the
Talking, Why, and When? Paper presented at
the Language and the Social Context Conference, Stirling.

Comparison of the Verbal System in Child and Adult Speech in Persian

B. Ingham

The theme of this paper is the disjunction between surface form and grammatical function. Comparison is made between the verbal systems of child and adult speech. Cases are investigated where forms in the two systems which can be regarded as phonologically identical may be used with different grammatical functions. The designation of grammatical function is reached by locating the system of contrasting forms in which it operates and also by reference to the context of situation. Three main areas of the child's language are investigated which illustrate a degree of independence from the adult system: 1) The function of the verbal affixes be- and -d; 2) The division of verb lexemes into two classes, Stative and non-Stative, and 3) The existence of negative forms not occurring in the adult systems.

The material was recorded from a single child between the ages of 1:10 and 2:00. The child, the writer's daughter Maryam, had Persian as her first language and was at the time living in an environment in which Persian was the main language of communication. This consisted of three adults speaking only Persian, and two adults and an older brother with both Persian and English. Data were collected in the home in the evenings and at weekends over a period of ten months and comprised some 520 different utterances with notes on idiosyncratic uses of particular lexemes.

333

The discussion is in terms of 'grammatical categories', using this term in the way exemplified by the work of F.R. Palmer (1965) and J. Carnochan (1970) especially. It indicates a system of contrasting 'terms' operating throughout a given class of elements with similar forms as exponents of these terms. Forms are classed as exponents of a particular grammatical term if they involve the same morphological structure and can be seen from the context to have the same function. Two forms will be discussed here, the first involving a suffix generalized as -d and the second lacking this -d and showing prefix be- in the affirmative. These two forms as shown in Table 1 are involved in the categories of Mood, Aspect and Tense in the adult language. The suffix -d appears in completive structures and in the past non-completive and past intentional while be- is involved in the intentional. Since the term 'category' is defined here as a set of contrasting terms represented by separate forms, it follows that if a particular verb has only one form then it cannot be said to involve any grammatical categories since there is no contrast. Even if the morphological structure involved is the same as that of a particular tense or aspect in the adult language, one cannot be sure that the child intends to indicate that tense or aspect.

This type of situation is commonly found in the lexical field and studies such as that of Griffiths and Atkinson (this volume) have shown how a child may use a lexeme with a semantic field considerably different from that of an adult. The child studied here produced the following two examples of this type of non-correspondence between child and adult lexical usage. Firstly she frequently used the noun ab-bazi 'water-game' to indicate types of play which did not involve any particular toy, e.g. playing with a velvet blanket on the floor. In this game no water was used and there was no indication that she meant the blanket to symbolize water. Secondly she used the verb kutah kardan 'to shorten', to indicate arranging an object in a particular way, for instance the blanket in the game described above. This verb was also used when trying to put a teaspoon inside an opened envelope. The claim made here is that this type of non-correspondence may also be found at the grammatical level and that particular morphemes may be used by the child with a different function, in this case the affixes be- and -d as shown on pp.341-342. The study concentrates on the development of a system of Mood differentiation which was just beginning to emerge at 1;10. Unfortunately no information is available on earlier stages of the child's speech. However, if it was along the lines of the Persian-speaking child studied by Doroudian (1975), it is likely that the forms acting as exponents of the two moods appeared at much the same time at the earlier stage but as unanalyzed forms.

Comparison of the child's system with the adult's shows
that as far as the grammatical categories are concerned,
the child begins with what is the primary category for
the adult, i.e. Mood, and does not first distinguish
Tense and Aspect, which are secondary. As can be seen
from Table 1, the adult system shows a primary category
of Mood to which all forms in the verb system are re-
ferable, being either exponents of Event or Intention
mood. All Event mood forms are then distinguished for
Aspect giving Completive and non-Completive. Comple-
tives are then further divided into Perfective and non-
Perfective while non-Completives are divided in the
affirmative into continuous and non-continuous. The
category of Tense divides both Event and Intention mood
forms into Present and Past with the exception of non-
Perfective Completive forms of the Event mood which are
regarded as outside this system. The two systems differ
in that the child uses the forms with a more generalized
function than the adult. Therefore not as many terms
are needed to describe her system, i.e. a form which is
referred in the adult system to the categories of Mood
and Aspect as Event mood, non-Perfective Completive
aspect, for the child only indicates Event mood, with
distinctions of Aspect being irrelevant. A further difference is that the child's verbal system showed a
semantico-syntactic division of verbs into two classes
which can be called Stative and non-Stative (see pp. 338-
339). These two classes showed clearly different
grammatical systems and involved different semantic
features. This classification is however quite absent
in the adult language.

The marked difference between the two systems
raises the theoretical question of whether the child's
system is purely an imperfect attempt at the adult system or whether it constitutes a separate system in its
own right. This type of discussion has of course been
conducted in relation to phonology. The studies of
Smith (1973) and Waterson (1970, 1971a, 1971b, 1976)
are representative of the first and second view respectively. However while a phonological system is an
abstract system of linguistic 'signs' none of which
bears lexical or grammatical significance, a grammatical system has a definite link with meaning and context, and one can therefore have recourse to factors
of the situation in deciding what the grammatical
function of a given form is in the child's language
and whether or not it has the same function as a
similar form in the adult language. As an example of
this, four forms of the verb xα- 'to want' are considered:

a) míxαm   'I want'   b) némixαm 'I don't want'

c) béxαm   'that I should want' d) náxαm   'that I should
                                            not want'

Of these a) and b) show a prefix mi- while c) shows a
prefix be-. The child's general output had only
bɑ́xɑm and nɑ́xɑm. However from the context of use it
was clear that these were to be taken as equivalents
to the adult mɪ́xɑm and némixɑm meaning 'I want' and
'I don't want'. Some examples of forms with mi- did
occur sporadically but only as echoes of adult forms
with mi- in the preceding discourse, as in the following conversation:

child	nɑ́tunam	'I can't'
adult	man ham némitunam	'Nor can I'
child	mɪ́tuni	'Yes you can'

The child did not produce forms with mi- otherwise. Consideration of the context of use of these verbal forms
seems to indicate that the child's verbal system was
different from that of the adult because her possibilities for expression were different and more limited.
More specifically the majority of utterances were concerned with a fairly limited time span, i.e. the immediate present, near future, and near past. Utterances
were either statements or questions about present states
or actions occurring within this limited time span or
were recommendations or requests for the near future.
Examples of typical utterances are given below. In
those marked 'non-verbal' the notion 'to be' is expressed by suffixing the subject pronoun affixes to the
complement, as in the adult language. Where the adult
form is significantly different, it is given in brackets
after the child's form.

1. Statements, non-verbal

(a) lulú-e-hɑ It is a ghost (the suffix -hɑ
is an expletive).

(b) kɑb-e mamɑ́r-e It is Maryam's bed.

(c) mese erɪ́k-e He is like Eric.

(d) unɑ sɑ́g-an bóz-an They are dogs and billy-
goats (abusive).

(e) xɑnóm-am I am a lady.

2. Statements, verbal

(a) kolɑ́ sares ka:dam I have put a hat on his
head.

(b) lulú kesedam-ɑ I have drawn a ghost
(-ɑ a form of -hɑ above).

(c) asapaín sod   It has become angry.

(d) peydá sod   It has appeared.

(e) doktó: umadé mamaro apú bedane   The Doctor has come to give Maryam an injection.

(f) o:tád   It has fallen down/is about to fall down.

(g) rih(t)   It has spilt/is about to spill.

(h) sikás(t)   It has broken/is about to break.

(i) masíneso báxam   I want his car.

(j) ino nátunam kutá konames   I cannot arrange this. (lit. This (obj.) I cannot shorten it.)

3. Questions, non-verbal

(a) mamár-e?   Is it Maryam's?

(b) kaáz-e?   Is it paper?

4. Questions, verbal

(a) rah(r)?   Has he gone?

(b) geréhri?   Have you got (it)?

(c) indá-sti?   Are you here?

(d) nádari?   Haven't you got (any)?

5. Recommendations

(a) míz besinam   Let me sit at the table.

(b) bó-ohtam (bíyoftam)   Let me fall down.

(c) béde pilíz   Give (it) please.

(d) mamár estax bére   Let Maryam go to the swimming pool.

(e) bébinimes   Let us see it.

(f) máno biyares birún   Bring me out. (lit. Me (obj.) bring it out.)

(g) beram indza peydá besam soku béta:se Let me go here and (then) appear so that Shokooh will be afraid.

(h) <u>xonak náse</u>   Let it not get cool.

6. <u>Requests</u>

   (a) <u>péparam</u>? (<u>bé</u>param)   Shall I jump? (<u>be</u>->pe-
                                       before <u>p</u>)

   (b) <u>bó-ohtam</u>? (<u>bíyoftam</u>)   Shall I fall down?

   (c) <u>pópusam</u>? (<u>bépušam</u>)   Shall I put (it) on?
                                       (<u>be</u>-> <u>po</u>- before <u>pus</u>-)

   (d) <u>mamar bóxore</u>?   Shall Maryam eat (it)?

   (e) <u>ɑs bóxoradetes</u>?   Shall she eat soup?
       (<u>bóxorateš</u>)   (lit. Soup, shall she
                                       eat it?)

   (f) <u>nárize</u>?   Shouldn't it spill?

The grammatical system shows a division into two
classes of verb which can be labelled 'Stative' and
'non-Stative'. 'Stative' verbs are not distinguished
for Mood and occur only in sentences of type 2 and 4,
i.e. Verbal Statements and Verbal Questions. These
have only one stem characterized by the absence of
modal affixes (4(c)(d)) with the exception of the verb
<u>xɑ</u>- 'to want', which shows a prefix generalized as <u>be</u>-
in the affirmative (2(i)). 'Non-Stative' verbs are <u>dis</u>-
tinguished for Mood and have two stems, one like the
verb <u>xɑ</u>- sharing a prefix generalized as be- in the
affirmative (5(a)-(g), 6(a)-(e)) and unprefixed in the
negative (5(h), 6(f)), and a second showing a suffix
generalized as -d (2(a)-(h), 4(a), (b)). In 4(a) and
(b) the suffix <u>is</u> realized as <u>r</u>, while in 2(g) and (h)
it is realized as <u>-t</u>. The variations were phonologically predictable <u>and</u> further examples are given in
the Appendix. In this class of verbs the second stem
occurs in sentences of types 2 and 4, i.e. Statements
and Questions like 'Stative' verbs, while the first
stem occurs in sentences of types 5 and 6. These may
be statements of intent (5(a), (b), (g)), requests
(5(c), (d), (f)) or recommendations (5(e), (h)). In
the interrogative they are requests for permission
(5(a)-(d)) or requests for approval (5(e), (f)). Type 5
are all glossed with 'Let -' for ease of reference.
However it may be that the 'intent' type (5(a), (b),
(g)) would be better glossed 'I think I will - ' where
the agreement of the interlocutor is expected but not
asked for (see Appendix). The morphology of the two
verb-classes is shown below with the verbs 'to want'
<u>xɑ</u>- of the 'Stative' class and 'to see' <u>di-/bin</u>- of
<u>the</u> 'non-Stative' class. The prefix <u>be</u>- <u>harmonizes</u>
with the stem <u>xɑ</u>- giving <u>bɑ</u>-. (Further examples
are given in t<u>he</u> appendix, pp. 344-345.)

1. Stative (Actual state only)

   bǎxɑm   'I want'   nǎxɑm   'I don't want'

2. Non-Stative

   Mood 1 (Actual event)

   dídam   'I saw, see'   nádidam   'I didn't, don't see'

   Mood 2 (Intended or desired event)

   bébinam   'Let me see,   nábinam   'Let me not see

             I want to see'   I don't want to see'

If we compare this with the full system of forms in the adult verbal system given in Table 1, we notice that although the adult system distinguishes Mood, Tense and Aspect the child distinguishes only Mood, and that only for one class of verbs. In particular it is interesting to note that the child's system lacks Present non-completive forms with mi- such as míre 'he goes, will go'. As mentioned earlier, these occurred sporadically in answer to adult forms with mi-. Also three examples were recorded where Mood 2 forms were used as responses to adult forms with mi-; these responses seemed to function as statements rather than recommendations. They occurred in the following conversations:

1. adult: mísuze   'It will burn (you)'

   child: násuze   'It won't burn (me)'

2. adult: míbore   'It will cut (you)'

   child: nábore   'It won't cut (me)'

3. adult: míbine   'He will see'

   child: nábine   'He won't see'

Even after the child had begun to use non-Completive forms with certain verbs of the same semantic type as Class 1, i.e. máxam 'I want', míse 'It is possible', némise 'It isn't possible', mítuni 'You can', the majority of verbal forms functioning as statements were in the Completive, i.e. oftadám 'I fell down'; and later also in the Past perfective of the Completive, oftadé budam 'I had fallen down'. The latter however did not seem to differ functionally from the Present perfective Completive.

The normal use of the mi- forms is to express general facts, i.e. mísuze 'It burns', habitual events,

TABLE 1. Tense, mood and aspect systems of Persian (Indicating forms occurring in child's language)

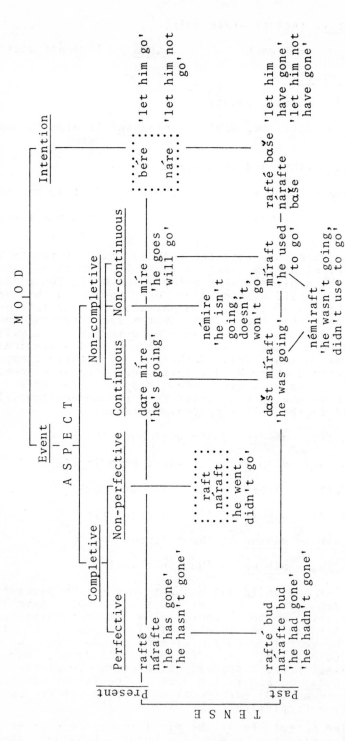

····· Forms occurring in the child's language

Examples are given in the 3rd person singular only.

i.e. ziád mixore 'He eats a lot', future events, i.e.
fardá miad 'He will come tomorrow' or continuing present
events, i.e. dare mísuze 'It is burning'. Of these the
first three were outside the child's range of experience
and observation while the fourth could also be expressed
by the -d form i.e. suxt 'It has burnt', this usage being
common in situations of urgency (for example oftád 'It
has fallen, is about to fall', rixt 'It has spilt, is
about to spill'). It seems therefore that the mi- forms
were not used because the majority of the messages which
the child wished to convey regarding actual events fitted
more easily into the frame of the -d form and this was
therefore adopted as the form expressing all actual events
in contrast to intended or desired events. Brown (1973)
gives a similar interpretation of grammatical function to
mine in his analysis of the beginnings of the tense system
in English. In the analysis of the -ing form he says 'all
present forms refer to action and events of temporary
duration, but since these do not contrast with permanent,
instantaneous and timeless action and events, it is not
clear that "temporary duration" is part of what the child
intends to express' (1973:319).This makes contrastive
ability the basis for the assignment of a particular form
to a given function. Referring to an earlier stage, where
the child had only one unmarked verb form, Brown describes
(317-318) how this one form can be understood by the
parent in one of four meanings: (a) Imperative, (b) Past,
(c) Intention or prediction and (d) Progressive of present
temporary duration. He regards this however as 'expanding'
or 'glossing' by the parent and does not say that the child
intends these to be separate. Slobin (1971:185) referring
to the same material, takes this a stage further and
suggests that the child has already understood these functions and expresses them implicitly. In this paper it is
considered that there is only one grammatical function or
meaning for one form of a verb from a given class in a
given structure, although, as shown above with the examples
of the -d form it may have different semantic references.
It may be that there is more justification for Slobin's
type of interpretation for a system with only one form.
However as Brown points out (1973:318, footnote 17) it is
difficult to obtain evidence other than that of context
and mature expression for the child's intentions.

It is possible to suggest, in line with the
'defective performance' view, that when the child uses
forms with be-, she is collapsing the adult distinction
of mi- and be- in her performance in favour of the
more frequently heard form, whereas in her competence
the two remain distinct. However on the basis of the
context of use of the examples and the type of lexemes
involved in each case, it would seem that the child
has a simpler system for Class 2 verbs which does

not include mi- forms, and in which the -d form substi-
tutes for mi- forms. For Class 1 verbs only a form to
express actual states is necessary. In the adult
language these would have mi- (with the exception of the
verbs 'to be' and 'to have' which show no prefix). Here
again she uses be-, thus minimizing her prefix system
without confusing the 'Actual' use of be- for Stative
verbs with the 'Intentional' use of be- for non-Stative
verbs. A further argument in favour of the view that the
child has her own well-constituted but simplified system
is that certain morphological structures were produced by
the child which did not occur in adult speech. These
occurred at a later stage than the one referred to in this
paper, at 2 years 6 months. The relevant structure was a
negative of the Continuous aspect as distinguished from
the non-Continuous where the adult language has only one
negative for the two, i.e.:

Adult Form		Child Form	
Continuous	Non-Continuous	Continuous	Non-Continuous
dαre míre	míre	dαre míre	míre
'he/she is going'	'he/she goes, will go'	'he/she is going'	'he/she goes, will go'
	némire	dαre némire	némire
'he/she is not going will not, does not go'		'he/she is not going'	'he/she does not, will not go'

The form dαre némire seems to be a linguistic creation
resulting from the child's analysis of the linguistic
data she hears.

REFERENCES

Brown, R. (1973)   A First Language, The Early Stages.
    Allen and Unwin, London.

Carnochan, J. (1970)   The categories of the verbal
    piece in Bachama. African Language Studies XI.
    83-112.

Doroudian, M. (1975)   The acquisition of Persian and
    English syntax. Ph.D. Thesis, University of London.

Lambton, A.K.S. (1957)   Persian Grammar. Cambridge
    University Press, Cambridge.

343

Palmer, F.R. (1965)   A Linguistic Study of the English
     Verb. Longmans, London.

Rastorgueva, V.S. (1964)   A Short Sketch of the Grammar
     of Persian. Trans. S.P. Hill. H.H. Paper (ed.)
     International Journal of American Linguistics II.

Slobin, D.I. (1973)   Cognitive Prerequisites for the
     Development of Grammar.   In C.A. Ferguson and
     D.I. Slobin (eds.) Studies of Child Language De-
     velopment. Holt, Rinehart and Winston, New York.

Smith, N.V. (1973)   The Acquisition of Phonology: a
     Case Study. Cambridge University Press, Cambridge.

Verhaar, J.W.M. (ed.) (1967-1972)   The Verb 'Be' and
     its Synonyms. Parts 1-5, Dordrecht-Holland.

Waterson, N. (1970)   Some Speech Forms of an English
     Child - a Phonological Study.   Transactions of
     the Philological Society. 1-24.

Waterson, N. (1971a)   Child Phonology: a Prosodic
     View. Journal of Linguistics 7. 179-211.

Waterson, N. (1971b)   Child Phonology, a Comparative
     Study.   Transactions of the Philological Society.
     34-50.

Waterson, N. (1976)   Perception and Production in
     the Acquisition of Phonology. In W. von Raffler-
     Engel and Y. Lebrun (eds.) Baby Talk and
     Infant Speech.   Swets and Zeitlinger,
     Amsterdam.

APPENDIX

VERBS OCCURRING IN THE CHILD'S LANGUAGE

In the following list only simple stems are listed.
Approximately thirty additional items were also recorded
which were of the compound type using one of the following stems preceded by a nominal or adjectival element
such as dúst daram 'I like'. The adult form is given in
brackets where it is significantly different from that
of the child. The elements t d r and n are realizations
of the -d suffix elided in pausal position.

Class 1

This class has only four members and these show
less structural homogeneity than Class 2. 'To be' and
'to have' are both regularly declined without the mi-

344

as in the adult language. The verb 'to have' was the only one which was declined with all persons. The others are shown in the forms in which they were attested.

báxɑm	náxɑm	'I want, don't want'
-	nátunam	'I can't'
dáram	nádɑram	'I have, haven't'
-sti	nis(t)	'You are, he/she isn't'

Class 2

The forms given are the 3rd person singular of Mood 1 and the 2nd person of Mood 2 or the form occurring if the latter was not attested. The suffix -d has the forms -d -t -r and -n.

Mood 1, 3rd person sing.		Mood 2, 2nd person sing.	
ɑó:d	(ɑvórd)	bíɑr	'to bring'
a:dɑ́h(t)	andɑ́xt	bénnɑz	'to throw'
ban(n)	(bast)	béban(n)	'to bind,close'
-		bébor	'to cut'
bo:d	(bord)	bébar	'to carry'
bud		-	'to be' (bɑ́še 'let it be')
dɑd		béde	'to give'
did		bébin	'to see'
geréh(r)	(geréft)	bégir	'to get'
gozó:s(t)	(gozó:št)	bézar	'to put'
-		bógu	'to say'
imɑ́d	(umɑ́d)	bíɑ	'to come'
kan(n)		békan	'to pluck'
ka:d	(kard)	bókon	'to do'
kesé:d	kešíd	békes (békeš)	'to pull' (to pull)
mun(n)		bémun	'to stay'

<u>mɑlíd</u>		<u>bemɑ́l</u>	'to rub'
<u>nesé:d</u>	<u>nešést</u>	-	'to sit' (<u>bé-</u> <u>sinam</u> or <u>ne-</u> <u>se:nɑ́m</u> 'Let me <u>sit</u>, I want to sit')
<u>o:tɑ́d</u>	(<u>oftɑ́d</u>)	<u>oh</u> (<u>bĭyoft</u>)	'to fall' (also <u>bó-ohtam</u> 'Let me fall, I want to fall')
<u>paríd</u>		<u>bépar</u>	'to jump'
<u>pusó:d</u>	(<u>pušíd</u>)	<u>pópus</u> (<u>bépuš</u>)	'to put on (clothes)'
<u>rah(r)</u>	(<u>raft</u>)	<u>bórou</u>	'to go'
<u>rih(r)</u>	(<u>rixt</u>)	<u>bériz</u>	'to spill'
<u>sikɑ́s(t)</u>	(<u>šekɑ́st</u>)	-	'to break' (<u>sike:nɑ́m</u> 'Let me break, I want to break')
-	-		'to burn' (<u>nɑ́-</u> <u>suze</u> 'It will not burn', see above, p. 339.
<u>sos(t)</u>	<u>šost</u>	-	'to wash' (<u>bó-</u> <u>suram</u> 'Let me wash, I want to wash')
<u>sod</u>	<u>šod</u>	-	'to become' (<u>bésam</u> 'Let me become, I want to become')
<u>taspún(d)</u>	(<u>cašpúnd</u>)	<u>bétaspun</u>	'to stick on (transitive)'
<u>ta:síd</u>	<u>tarsíd</u>	-	'to be afraid' (<u>béta:se</u> '..so that she will be afraid')
<u>xaríd</u>		<u>béxar</u>	'to buy'
<u>xɑbíd</u>		<u>béxɑb</u>	'to sleep'
<u>xo:d</u>	(<u>xord</u>)	<u>bóxor</u>	'to eat/drink'
<u>zad</u>		<u>bézan</u>	'to hit'

The verb 'to be' is exceptional in the above list in
that it appears with the stem -st- as a Class 1 verb
and in the stems bu- and bɑs- as a Class 2 verb. It is
possible that the child did not relate these phonologically quite different stems to one another since they
were used with somewhat different lexical functions. The
stem bu- referred to events in the recent past, i.e.
mán budam 'I was (the one who did it)'; kí bud 'Who was
it (at the door, on the telephone)?'. The stem -st-, on
the other hand, was used normally as a grammatical negator peydɑ nís 'It isn't visible' or as a lexeme meaning 'to be present', i.e. nístan 'They aren't here'. As
mentioned earlier, the copulative use of 'to be' is most
frequently expressed in Persian by adding the subject
pronoun affixes to the complement (see p.336). However,
whether we interpret these stems as two separate lexemes
or as the only verb to distinguish aspect in the child's
language, it illustrates the point made by the studies
edited by Verhaar that the verb 'to be' often behaves
exceptionally.

`Blacky Always has a Tail´: Some Observations on Apparently Superfluous Adverbs in Child and Adult Language

W. Kaper

Observation of the language use of Dutch children aged three years and older revealed that they occasionally inserted the adverb <u>altijd</u> 'always' into sentences where it seemed to be superfluous. Consider the examples (1) to (6):

(1)   <u>Dat groene</u> (sc. broekje) <u>is altijd van jij</u>. 'That green one (sc. knickers - in Dutch singular -) always belongs to you.' (E 3;5.24)

(2)   <u>Welke nummer is deze nummer altijd?</u> 'Which number is this number always?' (E 4;6.15)

(3)   <u>Moortje heeft altijd een staart</u>. 'Blacky (a toy-dog) always has a tail.' (H 3;1.15)

(4)   <u>Kleine wagens en grote wagens heeft altijd witte wielens.</u> 'Small cars and big cars always has white wheels.' (H 3;2.8)

(5)   <u>Pappa, vroeger was altijd de kachel uit.</u> 'Daddy, the stove always used to be out.' (H 3;7.1; what the child is trying to say is that it was not burning a few days ago).

(6)   <u>Hier begint Nienke z'n haar altijd.</u> 'Here always begins Nienke's hair' (H 5;4.22; pointing to the back of his head).

E and H are the abbreviated names of two brothers (E is about two years older than H), whose interesting and deviant utterances were regularly noted between the ages of

347

about 2 and 7 years. Ages are given in years, months and days respectively following each utterance. At first sight one is tempted to think that the use of the adverb is meaningless in these sentences. The question arises whether this is a typical phenomenon in child language which does not occur in adults' speech and whether there is any explanation for it. There are certainly utterances of the parents and of other adults which may well be compared to these sentences; see the examples (7) to (10):

(7)   Het ruíkt altijd zo heerlijk! 'It always smells so delicious!' (mother).

(8)   Dit is altijd een nare halte, hè? 'This is always an unpleasant stop, isn't it?' (mother).

(9)   Wat een raar beest is dat toch altijd. 'What a queer beast that (sc. a cat) always is.' (father).

(10) Dat vind ik altijd zulke schattige kopjes, deze. 'I always think these are such lovely cups.' (aunt).

It is reasonable to suppose that such adult sentences have given rise to the insertion of the apparently superfluous altijd in (1) to (6), the more so as the children's mother very frequently used altijd in this way. Snow has remarked (Symposium discussion) that the frequency of such adverbs in adult Dutch (also in the Dutch spoken to young children) is very high. My tape recordings of adults speaking to a little girl of about two show an average of about 18 superfluous adverbs per 100 sentences, which is not in contradiction with Snow's comment, but there may be individual differences. Moreover, I will not rule out the possibility that children aged three to five years pick up some speech habits overheard from their parents' conversation with other adults. However, I think it improbable that children would simply be trying to make their sentences 'sound adult' by using a certain number of adverbs per sentence, as Snow suggested, because this presupposes a linguistic consciousness exceeding the competence of a child. It may be more fruitful to hypothesize that altijd has some meaning, both in the adult sentences and in those spoken by the children. Why do we feel that latter to be deviant?

In (7) to (10) altijd means that every time we are in a certain situation (walking in a flower garden, waiting at a tram-stop, seeing a cat, or looking at some tea-cups), we have the same impression. In (1) to (6) the meaning is similar in that it indicates that again and again the child finds the same state of affairs. The difference is, however, that the children's utterances do not refer to subjective impressions, but to objective facts. Evidently the children did not yet appreciate this subtle difference. The phenomenon is not confined

to Dutch children: D.I. Slobin has observed that his
three-year-old son also overused <u>always</u> as a marker of
the habitual (Symposium discussion).

    In (11) to (13) the problem is slightly more
complicated:

(11)   <u>Ik ga soms altijd tot half vijf tellen.</u> 'I some-
        times always am going to count till half past
        four.' (E 5;7.15)

(12)   <u>Wanneer komt er soms altijd zo'n groene kaft van</u>
        <u>de 'Levende Talen'</u>? 'When comes sometimes al-
        ways such a green cover of the Modern Languages
        (a periodical)?' (E 6;5.5)

(13)   <u>Ja hij doet het altijd wel es.</u> 'Yes, he always
        now and then does.' (H 5;0.27)

These examples seem to present a contradiction: if something is 'always' the case, it cannot happen 'sometimes'
or 'now and then'. But consider number (12). The boy E
had a strongly marked sense of regularity and obviously
it had struck him that at long intervals a green cover of
the periodical Levende Talen was delivered at the parental home. As mentioned above, it is quite normal to express such a regular recurrence of events by the use of
the adverb <u>altijd</u>; <u>soms</u> 'sometimes' on the other hand indicates that the event did not occur very often. The
combination of these adverbs is unusual indeed, but the
child avails himself of a potential linguistic construction which is commonly neglected. Adults do this as
well; consider the striking resemblance between (13) and
(14):

(14)   <u>Daar let ik altijd wel eens op.</u> 'I always now and
        then <u>pay attention</u> to such things.' (woman-teacher).

As a matter of fact the combination of <u>altijd</u> with <u>meest</u>,
'mostly', the opposite of <u>soms</u>, is no less contradictory,
and yet the construction <u>meest altijd</u>, meaning 'mostly'
is certified by the authorized Dutch Van Dale dictionary
(1961, s.v. <u>altijd</u>).

    The suggested explanation does not hold for the
examples (15) and (16):

(15)   <u>Vanmiddag heeft ie altijd geen joghurt</u>, 'This
        afternoon he always doesn't have any yoghourt'
        (H 4;0.23)

(16)   <u>Doe 'k altijd vanmiddag!</u> 'That's what I <u>always</u> do
        this afternoon! (H 4;1.19, in reply to the ques-
        tion: 'Will you shine up your other shoe to-day?'
        In reality he wanted to do it in the morning of
        that day).

Vanmiddag 'this afternoon', indicating a fixed time of
the present day, is incompatible with altijd. Evidently
the child does not yet apprehend the exact cognitive
function of the former adverb, a frequently observed
phenomenon (Bloom, 1970:228 ff.; Kaper 1959:145 ff.).
Utterance number (5) corroborates such an uncertainty.

According to Kraak (1966:138) the structure
hij werkt altijd niet 'he always doesn't work' is ungrammatical, in contrast to the grammatical hij werkt
niet altijd 'he doesn't always work'. It is of course
usual to replace altijd niet 'always not' by nooit
'never'. Not only children, however, but also adults
may occasionally use the construction objected to, as
is evident from (17) and (18) respectively:

(17)   Ik ga altijd niet huilen, als jij de deur dicht
        doet bij mij. 'I am always not going to cry, when
        you shut the door on me.' (E 3;11.11)

(18)   Ik kan het altijd niet vinden. 'I always can't
        find it.' (father).

Is altijd niet in these sentences equivalent to nooit?
The emphasis on altijd in (18) sets one thinking. The
father does not want to say that he never can find something, but he is annoyed at the fact that it happens
again and again that he can't find it. The emphasis on
altijd underlines this 'again and again' and that may be
the reason why the fusion with the negation element does
not occur. The not yet four-year-old E is unlikely to
notice differences of this kind, but nevertheless there
is an undeniable correspondence between the structures of
(17) and (18). E wants to assert that it is always the
case that he is not going to cry when his father shuts
the door, which is formally expressed by inserting altijd
into the sentence ik ga niet huilen.

The preceding discussion aims to show that, although undeniable deviations may occur in child language,
there is no essential difference between sentence structures produced by children and by adults. An alternative
explanation was advanced by R. Clark (Symposium discussion)
that the construction 'always not' instead of 'never' may
reflect some more general characteristic of child syntax.
A child may add to a sentence an introducing sentence
fragment which grammatically ought to cause some modification in the sentence, but without making the modification,
e.g.,

(19)   Why did - he went?

This suggestion could be reformulated in the
following way: a child may combine a familiar sentence
fragment with another familiar one, which may result in

an ungrammatical sentence. In the case of (17) <u>ik ga</u>
<u>niet huilen</u> is combined with <u>altijd</u>; there is no intro-
ductory fragment in Clark's sense, but the modification
(the substitution of <u>nooit</u> for <u>altijd niet</u>) is indeed not
made.

The resulting ungrammatical sentence may represent a construction that is grammatical in another language. Clark's example, for instance, has a striking
counterpart in Swedish, where constructions like (20) are
possible:

(20)   <u>Sov gjorde han.</u> 'Slept did he.'

The fact that the child combines familiar sentence fragments, producing constructions which are possible sentences in other languages, may indicate universal processes in the creation of language. This could
be a promising line of research, and further observations
about this phenomenon are being collected. These observations support the position that child language cannot
be seen as a language <u>sui generis</u>, but that children's
constructions can always be related to adult constructions, either in the child's mother tongue or in some
other language. As a matter of fact, even seemingly contradictory constructions which might be considered as
typical of child language also occur in adults' speech.
A very convincing example is (21):

(21)   <u>Ik deed het altijd nóóit.</u> 'I always <u>never</u> did.'
        Spoken by an aunt of the children, a 76-year-old
        lady.

The contradiction in terms is apparent, not real, for
the lady merely wanted to say that she did not do something, and that this was the case every time. The phrase
construction, then, resembles that of (17) and (18), but
<u>niet</u> is replaced by <u>nooit</u>, a common means in Dutch to
express emphasis in negation.

The mere fact that in adult language the ad-
verb <u>nooit</u> can be used to deny something emphatically,
irrespective of whether the denied event is supposed to
occur once or several times, accounts for the misuse of
this word in examples like (22) and (23):

(22)   <u>Daarnet, toen ik het geef, toen lust hij het</u>
        <u>nooit meer.</u> 'Just now, when I give it, then he
        never likes it any more.' (E 4;6.18)

(23)   <u>Nou wil Pappa nooit.</u> 'Now Daddy never <u>will</u>.'
        (Meaning something like 'Now Daddy always refuses
        to do it'; H 4;0.5)

In the course of his language acquisition the child must
learn the constraints on the use of the adverb in this

meaning. The problem has previously been briefly discussed in Kaper (1959:8 ff).

Entirely meaningless is <u>meer</u> 'any more' in combination with <u>niet</u> 'not' in the sentences (24) to (26):

(24)   <u>Dat zijn niet wantjes meer.</u>   'These are not mittens any more.' (E 3;5.24)

(25)   <u>Ik is er niet; ik ben niet Erik.   Ik ben nog niet Erik meer.</u>   'I isn't here;   I am not Erik.   I am not yet Erik any more.' (E 3;5.25)

(26)   <u>Een hond hééft al geen voeten meer;   een hond heeft póten.</u>   'A dog already doesn't <u>have</u> feet any more; a dog has <u>paws</u>.' (H 5;3.14)

In (24) and (25) E protests against a usual denomination; it would have sufficed to say <u>dat zijn niet wantjes</u> 'these are not mittens' and <u>ik ben niet Erik</u> 'I am not Erik' respectively. The latter wording is realized, but it is followed by a more extensive utterance in which presumably the sentence fragments <u>nog niet</u> 'not yet' and <u>niet meer</u> 'not any more', opposites in meaning, are combined. Such a contamination of parts of different sentences overheard in parental speech has been found more than once in child language (Kaper 1959:XX). This observation is also relevant to Clark's discussion of (17). Consequently, here too, adult expressions seem to be the model on which a contradictory sentence of the child is constructed.

Very interesting in this context is (26). The information is simply that a dog does not have 'feet' but 'paws';   both <u>al</u> 'already' and <u>meer</u> 'any more' are superfluous additions. But for what reason does the child emphasize <u>heeft</u> 'has', and not <u>voeten</u> 'feet' as contrasted with <u>poten</u> 'paws'? Here not only the structure, but also the intonation of the sentence reveal the influence of the language use of the mother. She produced utterances like (27):

(27)   <u>'t Hóéft al niet eens meer.</u>   'It already doesn't <u>have to</u> any more' (meaning something like 'I'm not even interested any more').

There are more examples of the same kind, e.g. (28) compared with (29) and (30):

(28)   <u>Dáár zat ie niet in, hij staadde.</u>   '<u>There</u> (sc. in the merry-go-round) he wasn't sitting in, he standed.' (H4;8.21)

(29)   <u>Dáár gaat het niet om!</u>   '<u>That</u>'s not the point!' (both father and mother).

(30)   Dáár wacht ik niet op! 'I am not waiting for that!'
        (mother),

where the illogical emphasis on daar 'there' instead of
the contrastive stress on zat 'was sitting' in the child's
utterance (28) may be due to the stressed daar in sentences like (29) and (30) of the parents. The evidence
discussed in this paper supports the conclusion that
child language should be studied in continual comparison
with adult language, and first of all with the performance of the parents. Child language is not a language
which can be studied independently of the adult language,
because it is a continuous attempt to get into conformity
with a model.

REFERENCES

Bloom, L. (1970)   Language Development: Form and
        Function in Emerging Grammars. M.I.T. press,
        Cambridge, Mass.

Kaper, W. (1959)   Kindersprachforschung mit Hilfe des
        Kindes: Einige Erscheinungen der kindlichen
        Spracherwerbung erläutert im Lichte des vom
        Kinde gezeigten Interesses für Sprachliches.
        Wolters, Groningen.

Kraak, A. (1966)   Negatieve Zinnen: een Methodolo-
        gische en Grammatische Analyse. de Haan,
        Hilversum.

Van Dale, J.H. (1961) Groot Woordenboek der Nederlandse
        Taal. Achtste geheel opnieuw bewerkte en
        zeer vermeerderde druk, door Dr. C. Kruyskamp.
        Martinus Nijhoff, The Hague.

5
Processes of Acquisition

The closer cooperation between linguists and psychologists has resulted in a growing interest in relating Piaget's theories of cognitive development to the development of language. Sinha and Walkerdine discuss concept formation in Piaget's theory and compare it with the theory of Bruner and others, more particularly as regards the acquisition of conservation and the interrelationship between language and cognition. Ingram's paper is concerned with Piaget's sensorimotor period. He establishes three stages in language development and attempts to clarify Piaget's sensorimotor stages in order to relate them to the stages in language development. The other papers in this section deal with more specifically linguistic questions.

Clark proposes a theory of syntactic development in which 'imitation' plays a major role. Perceptual discrimination reduces what is internalized out of the whole utterance, and storage is in the form of unanalyzed 'chunks' or 'fragments'. Production is based on such

familiar chunks. Cognitive development also has a role in
the theory. The use of pre-established routines is seen
as the basis of speech production as has been shown to be
the case in adult usage.

Waterson shows how a gradual increase in complex
ity in phonological development takes place. Here, too,
familiar chunks play an important part in the production of
new and larger structures. The same kind of processes
appear to operate in the production of syllable, word, and
sentence, something that is reminiscent of Piaget's vertical décalage.

There is a great deal of common ground between
Clark's hypothesis of syntactic learning and Waterson's on
the learning of phonology. Both show evidence of the same
kind of learning based on input which is constrained by
limited perceptual discrimination. Fragments or chunks of
language material are stored and form the basis of production, and combinations of such familiar chunks are used in
the production of larger stretches of utterance. Bowerman's hypothesis on semantic learning (section 4) also has
much in common with Clark and Waterson. Further support
for this kind of learning comes from Felix in his study of
the acquisition of German as a second language, and from
Kaper (section 4) for Dutch.

The importance of studying the child's developing communicative competence for the analysis of syntactic
development is emphasized by Greenfield and Miller. These
studies, made independently, the one for English and the
other for German, both show that it is the non-redundant
information that the child expresses in dialogue. Adults
similarly eliminate redundant information in elliptical
utterances; this indicates a degree of continuity in the
way language is used in childhood and adulthood.

The paper by Felix is the only one concerned
with second language learning. He finds a reversal of
learning processes in second as opposed to first language
learning. In the second language, a large number of syntactic structures is acquired while the vocabulary is
very small whereas in the case of a first language, a
large vocabulary is acquired before syntax.

A picture of integrated language development is
beginning to emerge. There appears to be some similarity
in the way syntactic, semantic and phonological learning
takes place, and there is evidence that children process
speech along the same basic principles as adults. These
approaches to child language studies, together with the
study of the mutual influence of cognitive development
and language development suggest interesting lines of
research.

Conservation: A Problem in Language, Culture, and Thought

C. Sinha and V. Walkerdine

Traditionally, the ability to conserve, as measured by the classical Piagetian experiments (conservation of liquid and solid volume, length, weight, number etc.) has been conceived of as a universal, supra-cultural cognitive competence, the attainment of which is independent of the particular social context within which any individual develops. It is the accepted Genevan view that the effect that 'environmental factors' have upon the attainment of conservation is confined solely to the rate of development - the substance of what is eventually acquired remains unaffected. This conception of conservation as a universal derives from the priority accorded in Piagetian theory to logico-mathematical knowledge, as well as from cross-cultural experimentation (Price-Williams, 1961). In contrast to other theorists, Piaget contends that the fundamental source of the developmental process is to be found in the actions of the young child. Cognitive development, as seen by Piaget, consists of the gradual construction and

---

*The research reported in this paper was carried out as part of the Project 'Language Development in Pre-School Children', directed by Gordon Wells, and was funded by S.S.R.C. Grant No. HR2024.

reconstruction by the child of increasingly effective
schemata based upon successive stages of co-ordination
of the logic of actions. Knowledge, for Piaget, is not
derived from percepts (sensory input) alone, or from the
symbolic representation of such sensory information,
e.g., in language, as is maintained by most empiricist
psychologists, but from the internalization and symbolic
representation of the actions performed upon objects.
'Logico-mathematical concepts presuppose a set of operations that are abstracted not from the objects perceived
but from the actions performed upon these objects, which
is by no means the same' (Piaget and Inhelder, 1969:49).
Cognition, therefore, is not merely a reflection of the
real world, even a reflection mediated through symbolic
representation. On the contrary, cognition is a constructive act, and one which furthermore constructs its
own object. It follows, therefore, that for Piaget,
language, in common with other symbolic systems, is a
secondary intellectual process. The child can only express in language the conceptual schemata that he has
already internalized. 'There is a logic of co-ordination of actions. This logic is more profound than the
logic attached to language, and it appears well before
the logic of propositions, in the strict sense'.
(Piaget, 1969:122). 'A symbol (is a) signifier with a
figurative context different from and assimilated to,
operative intelligence, which is the symbol's source
and reference' (Piaget, 1966:99).

It is upon this foundation that the entire
edifice of Piagetian theory rests, including the theory
of stages, the different types of décalage, and the ir-
reversibility of cognitive development. And it is from
this position that Piaget denies to language, or any
other representational system per se, a decisive influence upon the course and outcome of cognitive development.

The theoretical stance adopted by Piaget is in
contrast with the developmental theory proposed by
Bruner, Olver and Greenfield et al. (1966), in which central importance is accorded to systems and modes of representation; for Bruner, cognitive growth is characterized by successive stages in which the universe of
the child is predominantly represented in one of three
modes, the enactive, the iconic and the symbolic; the
enactive mode being linked to the organization of motor
responses, the iconic mode to the organization of visual
perception, and the symbolic mode to the emergence and
organization of language. An implication of this theory
is that within each mode of representation, the elements
of the world-as-represented are organized as a system;
the exemplar par excellence of this is language, with
its complex structure of interrelated levels (semantic,
syntactic, phonological) from content to expression,
comprising successive hierarchies of syntagmatic and

paradigmatic relations. Very little work, however, has
been devoted to investigating possible equivalent systematic organizations in other representational modes,
though Olver and Hornsby (1966:69), following Vygotsky
(1962), note with respect to the development of the concept of equivalence that 'it is not only the "semantics"
of equivalence that changes with growth - the features
of the environment used as the basis of equivalence -
but the syntax of equivalence formation as well'.

There are a number of important implications
consequent upon Bruner's theory that differentiate it
from Piaget's theory: the most important of these relates to the influence of 'environmental factors'. If
the major determinant of cognitive development is the
manner in which the child represents her experience of
the world, then differential experience of the representational systems themselves will presumably affect not
only the rate but also the final outcome of the developmental process. This emphasis on the plasticity and
cultural specificity of development distinguishes Bruner,
along with the Soviet tradition of Vygotsky and Luria,
from Piaget, who has emphasized the universal and supra-
cultural aspects of development characterized by the
a-contextual and a-temporal forms of logico-mathematical
knowledge. Despite the differences between the two
theoretical stances, in their confrontation with the
problems posed by the conservation experiments they have
many elements in common. The conservation problem, like
many of Piaget's classical experiments, relies in essence upon the examination of the attempts, successful
or unsuccessful, on the part of the child to resolve the
apparent contradiction between appearance and reality,
between what she sees and what, at a certain level of
development, she knows.

For Piaget and the Genevan theorists, the
problem is essentially one of the development of logico-
mathematical structures of thought (reversibility, as-
sociativity, identity, closure) in which actions performed by the subject are cognitively dissociated from
the perceptual attributes of the object on which the
actions are performed. The operations of thought are
thus seen as strictly autonomous from the objects of
thought. The contradiction between the appearance
of the changing spatial extension on different dimensions of the object, and the reality of its unchanging
volume/weight, unaffected by operations performed upon
its distribution in space, serves to disequilibriate
the cognitive structure and eventually cause an advance in knowledge leading to re-equilibriation at a
higher structural level.

For Bruner, the appearance/reality contradiction is not merely the trigger to the more fundamental

dynamic of structural development, as it is for Piaget;
rather, the contradiction between appearance and reality
itself constitutes the central cognitive problem:
'appearance is defined by iconic representation, reality by symbolic' (Bruner et al., 1966:200). In discussing conservation of Liquid Volume, Bruner maintains that
Piaget has conflated the notion of identity - the enduring 'sameness' of the liquid through its transformation, a conception whose genesis and development Piaget
has himself traced in his studies of the development of
the notion of object permanence - with the notion of
equivalence of quantity. Bruner goes on to emphasize
the importance of the lexical items used in the experiment, in particular the word 'same', which does not differentiate between identity and equivalence. He suggests that the refinement, through language, of the notions of identity and of perceptual, or attributional,
similarity, is a necessary (though not sufficient) condition for the emergence of the notion of equivalence
of quantity and for conservation.

The motor of development, for Bruner, consists of the conflicts between the different modes of
representation. It is only with the development of language (in this case, the lexis of dimensional and relational terms) that the conflict between the enactive and
the iconic is resolved; until this time, the child will
remain perceptually dominated - he will take appearance
for reality.

Representational factors indeed play a part in
Piaget's theory, although it is assumed that the same
structures underlie that which is represented in any me-
dium. However, the structure of the operative system
may develop at different rates according to the mode in
which it is represented. This principle lies behind the
phenomenon of vertical décalage, in which the developing
organism may recapitulate in one representational mode,
a structure already developed in another mode (or level
of functioning). For example, the infant will construct
a certain motor representation of topological space, including elementary instances of reversibility, before
she is able to construct imaginal representations of the
same structure. The counterpart to such vertical décalage is horizontal décalage, in which a level of operative intelligence is achieved with respect to one physical range, before the same level is achieved with respect to a different range, even though structurally the
problem confronting the subject is the same in each case.
It is well known, for example, that conservation of volume precedes that of weight. The question at issue here,
for Piaget, is the relationship between 'knowledge of
objects' and logico-mathematical knowledge, and it is a
question that has never satisfactorily been resolved
within Piagetian theory. As Inhelder (1972:104) said:

'comparatively little attention has been paid to features of the object favouring the attainment of knowledge'. Nevertheless, in the conservation experiment,
it is precisely the 'features of the object' - the
liquid, plasticine etc. used in the experiment - which
mislead the pre-operational child into believing that
its volume or weight has undergone transformation along
with its shape.

Recently, attempts have been made to extend
Bruner's conception of perceptual dominance in theories
which seek to explain the observation that very young
children of two to four-and-a-half years appear, under
certain circumstances, to be able to conserve. Mehler
and Bever (1967) and Bryant and Trabasso (1971) have
advanced two different hypotheses to account for apparent conservation by very young children, both of
which relate perceptual dominance to changes in the
structure and capacity of young children's memory.
Mehler and Bever conducted experiments on children
aged 2;4 - 4;7, to investigate conservation of numerical inequality, using clay and candy pellets. Children
were first asked to make a judgement about the equality
of two rows:

O O O O O

O O O O O

The array was then transformed, and two pellets added
to the lower row:

O O O O O

O O O O O O O

In the case of the clay pellets, the children were asked
to judge which row had more. With the candy pellets,
they were asked which row they wanted to keep for eating. Successful responses with the clay pellets were
highest between the ages of 2;4 and 2;7 and lowest between the ages of 3;8 and 3;11, rising again between
4;4 and 4;7. Mehler and Bever concluded that 'rules
that allow them (children) to be successful at a younger
age can be tapped if motivation is sufficiently strong'
(Mehler and Bever, 1967:141). Similar results were obtained in experiments involving conservation of volume
inequality, which showed a dramatic decrease in con-
servation-type responses after the age of about 3;6.

Mehler and Bever's findings can be summarized
as indicating that the path of conservation ability
follows a U-shaped curve with increasing age; their explanation for this phenomenon suggests that 'perceptual
domination' is in fact a result of the application of

specific perceptual strategies in making judgements
about quantities, strategies which are themselves
rooted in changes in the structure and scope of memory
in the course of early childhood. Mehler (1972) expresses this position as a theory of impoverishment
of rich innate dispositions. He draws a comparison
between this view and Chomsky's proposal that there
exists an innate linguistic ability. Mehler maintains
that it is unreasonable to suppose that the child constructs increasingly rich strategies ex nihilo, and
counters this view with the suggestion that children
start with initial rich, global capacities, which are
gradually lost as a result of reliance on later, more
specific strategies. He further suggests that the
beliefs of two-year-olds may be based to a great extent on a phenomenal mnemonic capacity (Mehler, 1972).
He cites the experiments (Mehler and Bever, 1967) as
evidence that very young children can perform very
well in global situations involving unstructured
events, simply by virtue of their high capacity to
register these events in memory. Memory traces thus
develop from global to more analytic systems, which
enable the child to rely less on 'sheer memory' and
more on rules and regularities. This departure from
reliance on memory occurs, according to Mehler, at
around the age of three-and-a-half years, and gives
rise to a total change in performance, whereby the
child relies more on what he sees (appearance) than
what he believes (reality). The different performances on the clay and the candy pellet tasks is offered as evidence that high motivation preserves reliance on the part of the child on what he believes
rather than on what he sees. Piaget, commenting on
Mehler's innatist hypothesis, wrote: 'as the great
biologist Dobzhansky has said, though predetermina-
tion is impossible to disprove, it is on the contrary,
and I would add, precisely for that reason, completely useless' (Piaget, 1968:979).

Several other criticisms have been offered
of these experiments, by Beilin (1968) and Piaget
(1968), who both pointed out that conservation of inequality is not the same as conservation of equality.
It was in the former that Mehler and Bever's most
conclusive results were obtained. Beilin maintained
that because of this, Mehler and Bever had conflated
two different transformations, addition and relocation. When he tested these separately, the results
did not conform to those of Mehler and Bever. Beilin,
however, used a different experimental procedure, which
required that the child give verbal responses, involving
the use of the words 'same', 'different', 'more' and
'less'. He noted that children may understand 'more'
in one of two possible ways - either relationally, or as
'more of', i.e. addition. Piaget suggested Mehler and
Bever's subjects had not yet reached the stage where

they evaluate number by reference to length, and therefore used more primitive topological evaluations based
upon 'heaping' or 'crowding'. Piaget also considered
that the words used in the experiment were of considerable importance - young children were not always able
to understand 'more' and 'less' consistently, but 'a
lot', 'a little' and 'not a lot' gave rise to more consistent answers. Piaget also mentioned that young
children do not understand the words 'same' and 'different', whereas older children begin to do so, and so
are subject to more conflict: 'it is worth noting that
non-conservation indicates an effort to dissociate variables; very young children and severely mentally retarded subjects pay no attention to these variables,
whereas older normal children pass through a stage of
non-conservation as they re-organize relations which
they cannot yet grasp in full'(Piaget, 1968:978). It
remains the case, then, that Piaget considers the
child's failure to comprehend the particular linguistic input in the experimental setting to be a result of
cognitive developmental patterns, rather than a con-
tributory source of them.

Bryant and Trabasso (1971) also claim to have
observed conservation behaviour in very young children.
Bryant (1969) showed that while five-year-olds were
able to distinguish horizontal, vertical and oblique
lines in simultaneous presentations, they were not
successful on successive presentations of the same stimuli. He suggested that Piaget's demonstration (Piaget
and Inhelder, 1941) that children below the age of
eight years cannot make transitive inferences from perceptual input (e.g. given that A > B and B > C, they
cannot infer A > C) may have been influenced by the
fact that the arrays were never presented simultaneously. In other words, Bryant claimed that their failure
to make transitive inferences may have been due to memory failure. Bryant and Trabasso (1971) trained
four-, five-, and six-year-olds on a series of direct
comparisons of the lengths of simultaneously-presented
pairs of sticks, without ever allowing the children to
see the actual lengths of the sticks. There were five
sticks in all (ABCDE) all of different lengths, and the
subjects were trained to make judgements of which of
the pairs AB, BC, CD, DE were longer or shorter. The
training on the various pairs was conducted in random
order. Bryant and Trabasso then tested the children's
ability to make transitive inferences on pairs such as
AC. They pointed out that the only conclusive demonstration of transitive inferences was on the pair BD. Only
in this case has each of the rods been both longer and
shorter in the initial comparison. It is, therefore,
the only pair which cannot be solved by the subject
focusing on the absolute length of one of the rods in
the pair, and by 'parrotting' a verbal label attached
to one of the sticks during the initial training

procedure. Bryant and Trabasso observed successful performance on this task at all ages, although the BD pair
was consistently more difficult than the others. They
argued that 'lower performance in the critical BD pairs
is not due to a failure to make inferences but to a
failure of retention of the information contained in
the initial comparisons' (Bryant and Trabasso, 1971:458).
In other words, it was a mnemonic, not a logical, de-
ficiency that produced failure.

From this conclusion, Bryant (1971) went on to
challenge Piaget's assertion that young children do not
understand invariance. An adult, he claimed, solves the
conservation problem in the following way:

A = B and B = B'   therefore   A = B'

A young child may understand this, but because of limitations of short term memory may be unable to co-ordi-
nate the two judgements involved in the task, in the
absence of the simultaneous presentation of the arrays
A, B and B'. After the transformation, then, the child
generates two conflicting hypotheses about the arrays
- they are equal or they are unequal - and, because she
is unable to retrieve the initial judgement from memory,
bases the choice of hypothesis upon the immediate configuration. Non-conservation is nothing but a failure
to resolve conflict due to inadequate memory capacity.
Bryant (1971) conducted a further experiment of conservation of inequality. He presented four-year-olds
with an array of two unequal rows of counters, which
they correctly judged to be unequal, and then placed
each row of counters in identical glass beakers, so
that they appeared to occupy equal volumes. The majority of children correctly judged which beaker contained more counters, where a simple 'perceptual'
judgement would have led to an equality judgement. It
should be noted, however, that the word 'same' was not
used in the experiment, and one of the arrays was initially coded as having 'more' before the transformation took place, and it could be that the result was
due to the maintenance by the subject of the 'more'
labelling through the transformation. For this reason,
the experiment is not a conclusive demonstration that
the hypothesis-conflict theory is correct, or that it
is not logical ability that underlies conservation.
Nevertheless, it is clear from the evidence that under
certain conditions the immediate perceptual input need
not dominate children's responses in a conservation
task, which suggests that 'perceptual domination' is a
rather catch-all term which may miss the subtlety of
what is actually happening.

The experimental evidence offered by Mehler
and Bever (1967) is also compelling, and strongly suggests that some early form of equivalence judgement

does indeed precede a stage of non-conservation. The
theoretical explanations advanced by them are less convincing, however, in the light of more recent evidence.
An experiment by Gelman (1972) gave no support to any
hypothesis that qualitative changes in the bases of
children's numerosity judgements take place between
three and six years of age. Gelman's finding that the
criteria children use in making numerosity judgements
vary according to absolute number, and that very young
children can treat number as invariant provided that
the number is small enough, was confirmed by investigations by Smither, Smiley and Rees (1974), Lawson,
Baron and Siegel (1974), and Winer (1974).

Gelman (1972) noted that the classical Piagetian experimental paradigm required an adult-like performance from the child on a whole number of different
cognitive, linguistic, perceptual and social dimensions,
not all of which are related in a simple manner to the
logical abilities postulated by Piaget to underlie conservation ability. In particular, following many investigators, e.g. Green and Laxon (1970), she drew attention to the problems posed by the use of certain
words - 'same', 'different', 'more', 'less' - in the
task, and the consequent focusing of attention onto
different aspects of the experimental situation which
constitute the context for the use of the words. Gelman concluded that 'the conservation task is, at minimum, a test for logical capacity, the control of attention, correct semantics and estimation skills'
(Gelman, 1972:89).

Particularly interesting in this regard is
the experimental technique employed by Gelman (1972)
to elicit judgements of numerosity by her young subjects. Having established that numerosity judgements
of small numbers (two and three toy mice) were based
neither on length, as suggested by Mehler and Bever
(1967), nor density, as suggested by Piaget (1968),
but in fact on actual number, she altered the normal
procedure for testing number invariance. Rather than
simply transforming the appearance of the array and
asking the child if its number had changed, she surreptitiously performed one of two operations; transforming either the number of the array (subtraction) or
its appearance (displacement, or relocation), and asked
the child to make an equivalence judgement, recording
the surprise reactions by the children. Such reactions of surprise were much greater for subtraction
than for displacement operations, leading Gelman to
conclude that expectations of invariance had been
violated. There are three important things to note
about this procedure. Firstly, there was only one
question asked of the child to establish invariance,
whereas in the classical Piagetian procedure two consecutive judgements are required of the subject, be-

fore and after the transformation. Secondly, the procedure eliminated the vocabulary of equivalence - no
relational or dimensional terms occurred in the speech
of either experimenter or subject. Thirdly, neither
displacement nor subtraction operations were performed
overtly, as they are in the classic Piagetian paradigm.
Instead, Gelman employed a 'magic' paradigm in which
operations were performed surreptitiously, and the
child's expectations of invariance were deduced from
his expressions of surprise.

The first of these observations has also been
made by Rose and Blank (1974), who point out that the
experimental requirement that the subject make two consecutive judgements may be taken by the child as a cue
to confirm a change in the initial configuration and
relation, and to alter his initial judgement, since 'in
the normal (non-experimental) course of events, one
would never ask the identical question twice if a significant change had not occurred in the material that is
not being observed'(Rose and Blank, 1974:499). When,
similarly to Gelman (1972), Rose and Blank asked the
children to make only one judgement in a number conservation task, after witnessing the transformation, significantly more children succeeded in giving correct
answers than in the traditional experimental procedure.

Gelman's 'magic' paradigm is similar to an
experimental technique used by McGarrigle and Donaldson
(1975) who administered number and length conservation
tests to four- to six-year-olds under two different conditions. In the first condition, the standard procedure
was used. In the second procedure, the transformation
of the array was effected, not directly by the experimenter, but by a toy teddy bear who was 'trying to spoil
the game'. In other words the transformation of the
array was seen by the child as accidental, rather than
as the result of a deliberate, intentional act on the
part of the experimenter. Significnatly more children
conserved under this second condition than were able
to do so when the standard procedure was used. McGarrigle and Donaldson argue that the child iterprets the
intention behind the experimenter's instruction within
a framework constituted by his significant actions within the experimental context. They emphasize that their
approach to the question of language comprehension within the experimental setting differs from arguments that
linguistic input, or certain key lexical items (relational and dimensional terms), are simply not understood. Their contention, rather, is that the child, in
the experimental as well as the naturalistic setting,
is actively seeking to match utterance to ongoing activity in such a way as to reconstruct the meaning intention
of the speaker, within the extra-linguistic context. The
particular interpretation put by the child on the experimenter's utterance will be determined by non-

linguistic rules (Clark, 1973) based upon certain
critical features of the situation, including the
activity which the experimenter directs towards the
array. They emphasize that data from recent language
acquisition studies demonstrate that it is possible
to understand an utterance in one context but not in
another (Huttenlocher, 1973; Ryan, 1973); and that
it is the social interactions of the child with its
mother and other adults which enable the meaning intentions of the latter to be mapped onto the utterances that they address to the child.

In an earlier study, Donaldson and Wales
(1970) drew attention to the richness and complexity
of the possible interpretations of the word-pair
'same/different' and 'more/less'. For our purposes,
we can say that the word 'same' combines several different meanings. In the first place it can refer to
enduring identity. That is, when an identity is
translated across space or time, it retains its identity. In the second place it can refer to attributional similarity - usually, but not necessarily, similarity of perceptually observable attributes. This
may be of an absolute nature - i.e. two or more objects
may be different tokens of the same type, and are thus
similar in all respects or attributes - or of a relative nature, i.e. two or more objects are alike in some
one or more respects, but not all. In a similar
fashion, the word 'different' may refer either to identity or to attribution. The lexico-grammatical (syntactic)distributions of the two words are therefore
asymmetrical. An analysis of the word-pair 'more/less'
reveals a higher degree of symmetry, but there are
nevertheless certain important discontinuities relating
to the use of the word, as Donaldson and Wales point
out: 'in effect, "more" is ambiguous. It may be used
in a simply additive sense as well as in a strictly
comparative sense' (1970:249).

In a more recent study, Webb, Oliver and
O'Keefe (1974) have confirmed Donaldson and Wales's
(1970) report that very young children interpret
'different' to mean the same as 'same', and have argued
that the interpretation of the word 'different' progresses through four developmental stages. It is only
at the age of about three-and-a-half years that children begin to use the criteria of attribution, in the
negative sense implied by the use of 'different'.

Clearly, the above analysis is of great importance in the consideration of the classical conservation test. Indeed, the experimental procedure employed, the 'méthode clinique', gives full recognition
to the importance of the verbal elements of the problem,
by demanding that the child, in order to demonstrate
full conservation, should be able fully to justify his

solutions to the problem in a verbally explicit manner,
rather than merely offering yes/no responses which remain ambiguous in the experimental context. However,
the 'justification criterion' is no more than a negative recognition of the problem, for it rests upon the
ability of the child already to control the interleaved
systems of language and cognitive operations, and says
nothing about the process by which such control actually develops. The analysis is more relevant, however,
to Bruner's theorization of the conservation task as an
experimental concatenation of the notions of equivalence
and identity, since equivalence is directly related to a
particular instance of the attributional use of the word
'same'. The evidence of both Donaldson and Wales (1970)
and Webb, Oliver and O'Keefe (1974) supports Bruner's
(1966) contention that the primitive notion of identity
precedes that of equivalence. However, such considerations point to the conclusion that the role of language,
and in particular of relational and dimensional terms,
in the conservation task, and for that matter in cognitive development generally, is by no means a simple
one. Peisach (1973), comparing the descriptive dimensional language of conservers and non-conservers, concluded that comprehension of dimensional language was a
necessary but not sufficient condition for conservation.
Lapointe and O'Donnell (1974) attempted to relate the
development of comprehension of the words 'same' and
'more' to the use by children of perceptual features of
the array in the investigation of number conservation.
They concluded that the young child's progress towards
conservation ability depends upon a series of overlapping, or interleaved, factors. The most important
of these related to the increasing sophistication of
the child's knowledge of the language of dimensional
and logical relations, and to the transition of the
basis of equivalence judgements from perceptual features
such as length and density to that of numerical correspondence. We have already seen how the pattern of development of the lexis of dimensional and relational
terms such as 'same/different' and 'more/less' follows
a pattern that is consistent with the hypothesis that a
primitive 'identity-equivalence' notion precedes an
'attribution-equivalence' notion. Further, that the
term 'more' can be used in a sense consistent with
either a judgement of relation or a relocation action
('give me more ...'). It is clear that there must
exist an independent course of language development
which is not tied to any single cognitive problematic,
or any single interpersonal setting; yet it is equally
clear that the development of the language of numerical
and other logical relations is closely linked to the
internalized co-ordination of these relations, and of
course to the ability to express them appropriately in
a communicational setting.

The experiments reported in this paper were carried out as part of the Bristol University School of Education Language Development Project, and attempted to address themselves to the problem of the complex interaction between language and its context in determining the interpretation of task demands in conservation tasks.

EXPERIMENT 1

Subject. The subjects were drawn from two sources: (a) 19 children aged 3;6, 16 aged 4;0, and 11 aged 4;6, all participants in the project Language Development in Preschool Children. No control was introduced into the sub-sample for sex or social class, but the full LDPC sample was matched for these factors; (b) 11 children aged 5;0-5;11, 10 aged 6;0-6;11, and 10 aged 7;0-7;11, approximately evenly distributed as to sex, with no controls introduced for social class, all pupils at a local Primary School.

Procedure. The standard Conservation of Liquid Volume test, along with a test of Compensation, was administered to all subjects. The full Piagetian criteria of conservation were operated on the Conservation test. On the Compensation test, however, a behavioural criterion for success was implemented, rather than one of verbal justification. The procedure for the Compensation test was as follows: the child was given a standard beaker containing orange squash 'to drink'. He was then shown a tall, thin cylindrical beaker into which the experimenter poured orange squash. The experimenter told the child to shout 'Stop!' when 'we've both got exactly the same to drink'. In all cases, the Compensation test was administered immediately after the standard Conservation task, when the child had already had the opportunity to note the levels reached by equal volumes of liquid in the different containers.

Results. The results revealed, as was expected, that no children below the age of 5;0 were able to conserve, and that the number conserving displayed a steady increase with age thereafter (see Table 1). The data from the Compensation task, however, revealed contradictory and surprising results (see Tables 2 and 3). Of 19 children tested at age 3;6, 14 achieved our criterion of success. Thereafter, there was a sharp decline in the number of children achieving Compensation at age 4;0, only 3 children out of 16 succeeding at that age. Thereafter, there was a slowly ascending number of children achieving Compensation. At all ages below 7;0 the Compensation task was only slightly easier than the Conservation task, except at 3;6, when the majority of children succeeded in compensating while all failed to conserve.

TABLE 1. Conservation test results

| | A G E | | | | | |
	3;6	4;0	4;6	5	6	7
SUCCEED	0	0	0	5	4	7
FAIL	19	16	11	6	6	3
TOTAL	19	16	11	11	10	10
% SUCCEED	0	0	0	45.45	40	70

TABLE 2. Compensation test results

| | A G E | | | | | |
	3;6	4;0	4;6	5	6	7
SUCCEED	14	3	3	7	7	7
FAIL	5	13	8	4	3	3
TOTAL	19	16	11	11	10	10
% SUCCEED	73.68	18.75	27.27	63.63	70	70

TABLE 3. Comparison of Compensation and Conservation test results

AGE	-Comp -Cons	-Comp +Cons	+Comp -Cons	+Comp +Cons	TOTAL
3;6	5	0	14	0	19
4;0	13	0	3	0	16
4;6	8	0	3	0	11
5	4	0	2	5	11
6	3	0	3	4	10
7	3	0	0	7	10

Discussion. Our results seem to indicate that, although there was no suggestion that very young children are capable of conserving in the usual sense of the term, the progress of compensation ability follows the U-shaped curve noted in the experiments of Mehler and Bever. Indeed, the critical age involved, three-and-a-half to four years, appears identical to that in Mehler and Bever's findings. In this context it is interesting that Webb, Oliver and O'Keefe (1974) found that it was only after the age of three-and-a-half years that their subjects were able to correctly select objects that were 'different' from a target object on at least one perceptual dimension. It would appear that before this age there is no differentiation between the notions of attribution and identity, and consequently no systematic connection between the child's use of relational terms and peceptual properties of the objects to whose relations they refer. Our suggested interpretation of these results then is that the three-and-a-half year-old children have not yet begun to master the complex rules governing the relationship of the words 'same' and 'different' with the notions of identity, equivalence and perceptual (attributional) similarity. Such an interpretation is supported by observation that these children would reply 'yes' with equal conviction when asked of the two beakers in the conservation task 'are they the same?' and 'are they different?'. Until these notions are at least partially disentangled, the stage of 'non-conservation proper', with its implications of 'perceptual domination', cannot occur.

Later on, at least by four years of age, the dimension of 'perceptual similarity', attributionally coded in the word 'same' and rendered salient by the repeated questioning of the child by the experimenter, will be isolated in this particular context with respect to the perceptual feature - level of liquid. Before this level of development is attained, the child appears to be free to reproduce, from memory, a 'pseudo-compensation' response - this response is not, of course, an operational compensation proper - indeed, true compensation, accompanied by the ability to provide verbal justifications, appears to develop more slowly than conservation (Gelman and Weinberg, 1972).

By the age of four years, however, neither conservation nor pseudo-compensation can be achieved by the child, precisely as the result of the beginnings of the integration of the child's linguistic and cognitive/perceptual knowledge. Several aspects of the actual utterance addressed to the child - e.g. Have you got exactly the same amount of orange to drink as I have? - direct the child's attention towards one particular aspect of the experimental context. In the first place, the word 'same', for the young child, now codes attributional similarity as well as identity - its semantic

relation to its context has undergone an expansion,
but has not yet fully stabilized into a set of rules
which can specify the particular sense of the word
intended in the utterance. In the second place, that
word is embedded in an utterance whose function is one
of attributional questioning - and whose mood is interrogative. Which attribute of the liquid is being top-
icalized and questioned - quantity or configurational
similarity - the child can only decide, in the absence
of a consolidated system of semantic relations, by reference to the context. Within the particular interpersonal context of the experimental situation - defined as it is by repeated interrogations respecting
attributes which immediately succeed actual changes in
certain attributes - the child naturally focuses upon
the attribute of liquid level. Thus, it is these multiple processes of social, cognitive and linguistic development, combined at the micro-level of representational integration, which we would suggest are the
cause, and not the result, of 'perceptual domination'
as a cognitive phenomenon during the (structural) stage
of pre-operational thought.

The results, however, are open to an alternative explanation - that offered by Mehler and Bever
(1967). It could in fact be that the child's initially
high memory-capacity for 'absolute' judgements - in
this case the level of liquid reached by the liquid in
the cylinder during the first conservation transformation - simply becomes impoverished by the age of four
years, rather than becoming necessarily superseded by
the linguistic and perceptual strategies described
above. Experiment 2 was designed to eliminate this
hypothesis, and to provide further support for our own
interpretation.

EXPERIMENT 2

Subjects. All subjects were drawn from the sample
of the project Language Development in Preschool Children and comprised 9 children aged 3;6, 23 aged 4;0 and
11 aged 4;6. No controls were operated for sex or
social class.

Procedure. The procedure for Experiment 2, which
we named the 'lot/little' test, was as follows: a
large toy horse and a small toy dog were placed in front
of the subject, who was told by the experimenter 'here
is the big horse, he likes a lot to drink, here is the
little dog, he likes a little to drink'. A standard
beaker containing orange squash was then placed in front
of each animal, the horse's beaker containing more than
the dog's. The squash from the dog's beaker was then
poured into a tall, narrow cylinder, and the squash from
the horse's beaker was poured into another standard
beaker. After this transformation, the level of liquid

in the tall cylinder was higher than that in the standard beaker. The child was then told: 'remember, the big horse likes a lot to drink and the little dog likes a little to drink. Now give them their drinks.'

Results. The results showed that at both 3;6 and 4;0 the majority of children succeeded in correctly assigning the beakers to the respective animals, but that at age 4;6 there was a sharp decline in the numbers of children succeeding. The distribution was significantly different from that expected through chance, ($p < 0.01$,) see Table 4), and a contingency coefficient revealed no significant correlation between the scores on the compensation and 'lot/little' tests.

TABLE 4.   Lot/Little test results

	A G E		
	3;6	4;0	4;6
SUCCEED	6	20	3
FAIL	2	1	6
TOTAL	9	23	11
% SUCCEED	66.66	86.96	27.27
Transitional	1	2	12

Discussion. It should be noted that we do not claim that this task demonstrates conservation ability among very young children, for the reasons that the child is not required to conserve a relation of equality, but one of inequality, and that the criterion of success is operational, and requires no verbal justification on the part of the child. But more important is the difference between the language of the experimenter in the classical conservation task and that in the 'lot/little' test. The 'lot/little' test eliminates the relational terms 'same', 'more' and 'less', and also eliminates the procedure of repeatedly questioning the child as to equivalence - a procedure which, as Rose and Blank (1974) point out, implies some sort of change. This difference is reflected in the mood-choice of the experimenter's utterance, which is imperative rather than interrogative. These combined differences in procedure, we suggest, lead the child to attend to functional, or actional, aspects of the situation rather than to its peceptual attributes, enabling the four-year-old child to maintain a primitive 'identity-equivalence' judgement across the transformation of the array, even when on the compensation task he is by now using the perceptual attributes of the array as the basis of an incorrect judgement. Many of the four-and-a-half-year-old children, however, were observed, after the transformation had taken place, to spontaneously re-code the liquid quantities in terms of the words 'big' and 'small'. Such a re-coding appears to interact with perceptual-attributional (or 'iconic') representational knowledge to produce failure on the task.

The fact that these children succeed until 4;0 years on this task also discounts the possibility that their failure at the same age on the Compensation task was due simply to memory failure for they are clearly able to remember to which animal to assign each liquid quantity. Clearly, this sort of equivalence-memory is not adequate to achieving conservation, in that it is not systematically integrated with their perceptual-attributional judgements. Such a re-integration does not occur until conservation and compensation proper are attained at a considerably later age. The results of both Experiment 1 and Experiment 2 are represented in Figure 1.

CONCLUSION

The general conclusion that we would draw from these experiments is that language, in a broad sense, neither simply reflects cognitive structure, nor supersedes, as an organizing system, other modes of representation, and in a narrower, experimental context, that its role extends beyond simply directing subjects' attention. Rather, through its interaction with and 'meta-representation' of the iconic'and socio-cultural representational systems, it defines and transmits for the subject the specific interpretation of the context which is required, or appears to be required, of him. The conception of an underlying universal a-contextual structural 'level' becomes questionable in its interpretation, as does the separation in concrete situations of different representational modes and systems. We would suggest, in fact, that 'structure' is itself not a generalized reflective abstraction, but an actual construction which takes place more or less ad hoc as a result of micro- and macro-level interactions between modes and structures of representation within particular inter-personal and cultural contexts. In the terms suggested by Steiner (1974), structure does not exist except in and through the particular representation it acquires within any given situation.

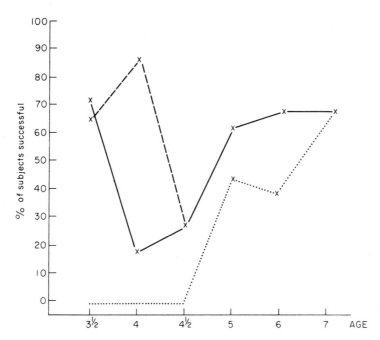

Fig. 1.   A comparison of the distributions of Conserva-
          tion, Compensation and Lot/Little test scores
          by Age.

KEY

——————————————— Compensation

· · · · · · · · · · · · · · Conservation

- - - - - - - - - - - - - - Lot/Little test

REFERENCES

Beilin, H. (1968)   Cognitive Capacities of Young Child-
          ren: A Replication. Science 162. 920-921.

Bruner, J.S., Olver, R. and Greenfield P. et al. (1966)
          Studies in Cognitive Growth. Wiley, New York.

Bryant, P.E. (1969)   Nature 224. 1331.

Bryant, P.E. (1971)   Cognitive Development. British
    Medical Bulletin   27. 3.

Bryant, P.E. and Trabasso, T. (1971)   Transitive In-
    ferences and Memory in Young Children.
    Nature 323. 456-458.

Clark, E.V. (1973)   Non-linguistic Strategies and the
    Acquisition of Word-meanings. Cognition 2.2.
    161-182.

Donaldson, M. and Wales, R. (1970)   On the Acquisition
    of some Relational Terms.   In J.R. Hayes (ed.)
    Cognition and the Development of Language.
    Wiley, New York.

Gelman, R. (1972)   Logical Capacity of Very Young Child-
    ren: Number Invariance Rules. Child Develop-
    ment   43. 75-90.

Gelman, R. and Weinberg, D. (1972)   The Relation be-
    tween Liquid Conservation and Compensation.
    Child Development   43. 371-383.

Green, R.T. and Laxon, V.J. (1970)   The Conservation
    of Number, Mother, Water, and a Fried Egg
    Chez l'Enfant. Acta Psychologica 32. 1-20.

Huttenlocher, J. (1973)   The Origins of Language Com-
    prehension.   In R.L. Solso (ed.) Theories in
    Cognitive Psychology, Lawrence Earlbaum,
    Hillsdale, New Jersey.

Inhelder, B. (1972)   Information-Processing Tendencies
    in Recent Experiments in Cognitive Learning
    - Empirical Studies.   In S. Farnham-Diggory
    (ed.) Information Processing in Children.
    Academic Press, New York.

Lawson G., Baron J. and Siegel, L. (1974)   The Role of
    Number and Length Cues in Children's Quanti-
    tative Judgements. Child Development   45.
    731-736.

Lapointe, K. and O'Donnell, J.P. (1974)   Number Con-
    servation in Children Below Age Six: Rela-
    tionship to Age, Perceptual Dimension and
    Language Comprehension. Developmental
    Psychology   10.3. 422-428.

McGarrigle J. and Donaldson, M. (1975)   Conservation
    Accidents. Cognition 3/4. 341-350.

Mehler, J. (1972)   Knowing by Unlearning. Paper presented at the International Seminar of the Centre International d'Etudes de Bio-Anthropologie et d'Anthropologie Fondamentale.

Mehler, J. and Bever, T.G. (1967)   Cognitive Capacities of Young Children. Science   158. 141-142.

Olver, R. and Hornsby, J. (1966)   On Equivalence. In J.S. Bruner, R. Olver, and P.M. Greenfield, et al., Studies in Cognitive Growth. Wiley, New York.

Peisach, E. (1973)   The Relationship between the Knowledge and Use of Dimensional Language and Achievement of Conservation. Developmental Psychology   9.2.   189-197.

Piaget, J. (1968)   Quantification, Conservation and Nativism. Science   162.   976-979.

Piaget, J. (1969)   Language and Intellectual Operations. In H. Furth   Piaget and Knowledge. Prentice Hall, New York.   Trans.   from (1963) Le Langage et les Opérations Intellectuelles. In Problèmes de Psycholinguistique: Symposium de l'Association de Psychologie Scientifique de Langue Française. Presses Universitaires de France, Paris.

Piaget, J. and Inhelder, B. (1941)   La Développement de Quantités Physiques chez l'Enfant. Delachaux et Niestlé, Paris.

Piaget, J. and Inhelder B. (1969)   The Psychology of the Child.   Routledge and Kegan Paul, London.

Price Williams, D.R. (1961)   A Study concerning Concepts of Conservation of Quantities among Primitive Children. Acta Psychologica   18. 297-305.

Rose, S.A. and Blank, M. (1974)   The Potency of Context in Children's Cognition: an Illustration through Conservation. Child Development   45.   499-502.

Ryan, J. (1973)   Interpretation and Imitation in Early Language Development.   In R. Hinde and J.S. Hinde (eds.) Constraints on Learning. Academic Press, London.

Smither, S.J., Smiley, S.S. and Rees, R. (1974)   The Use of Perceptual Cues for Number Judgement by Young Children. Child Development   45. 693-699.

Steiner, G. (1974)   On the Psychological Reality of
     Cognitive Structures: A Tentative Synthesis
     of Piaget's and Bruner's Theories. Child
     Development   45. 891-899.

Vygotsky, L.S. (1962)   Thought and Language. M.I.T.
     Press, Cambridge, Mass.

Webb, R.A., Oliver, M.E. and O'Keefe, L. (1974)   In-
     vestigations of the Meanings of 'Different'
     in the Language of Young Children. Child
     Development   45. 984-991.

Winer, G.A. (1974)   Conservation of Different Quanti-
     ties by Pre-School Children. Child Develop-
     ment   45. 839-842.

Language Development during the Sensorimotor Period

D. Ingram

As the study of the relation between language and cognition progresses, it is becoming clear that one of the significant issues is the relation between linguistic milestones of development and Piaget's stages of cognitive development. Currently much interest is being generated by the notion of cognitive prerequisites to language (cf. Slobin, 1973). That is, what cognitive developments must occur in order for language to advance. Piaget's theory is quite clear in this regard.

'Articulate language makes its appearance...at the end of the sensori-motor period, with what have been called "one-word sentences".' (Piaget and Inhelder, 1969:85)

Or,

'Once he is in possession of the semi-signs described in obs. 101 and 102 (stage 6 behaviours:DI), the child will quickly learn to speak, his progress following the lines with which Stern's investigations have made us familiar, word-sentences, sentences of two words, and complete sentences which soon come to be linked one with another. This

brings us to the second phase of development of
representation, corresponding to Stages I and II
(these are part of the preoperational period and
beyond sensorimotor development: DI).'(Piaget,
1962:221)

Piaget argues, therefore, that true language development awaits the end of the sensorimotor period.

Despite this, Piaget mentions the fact that
linguistic communication does occur during the sensorimotor period.

He states:

'It was, as a matter of fact, during this fifth
stage (of imitation: DI) that J., L. and T. began
to make their first clumsy efforts to reproduce
the words of adults.' (Piaget, 1962:53)

He goes on to say:

'Before the sixth stage, during which the child
becomes capable of deferred reproductions, which
are correct at first attempt, imitation naturally
takes place through controlled trial and error.'
(Piaget, 1962:54)

For example, Jacqueline at stage 5, age 1;3.8, would say
the French word parti 'left' when people left the room
or when things came to an end. The productions of this
word were phonetically variable. At stage 6, deferred
imitations appeared.

'J began to reproduce certain words, not at the time
they were uttered, but in similar situations, and
without having previously imitated them.

Thus at 1;4.8 J. said in step as she was walking, although she had never uttered these words
and they had not been said in her presence immediately
before.' (Piaget, 1962:63)

The nature of language during this period is quite restricted. First, 'The first use of language is mainly
in the form of orders and expressions of desire'
(Piaget, 1962:222). It is tied to the child's current
actions, and not used to recount past events. Also,
these words are not yet signs. Rather than being fixed
in meaning, they are highly variable- 'they still have
the disconcerting mobility of the symbol, as distinct
from the fixity of the sign.' (220) For example, J.
used bow-wow in a few days' time for dogs, cars, and
men. Language in the sensorimotor period for Piaget
then, is the use of single word utterances in the last

two stages, where these utterances are highly pragmatic
in function, i.e. to give orders, desires, etc. They
are highly variable in reference and have yet to become
social signs.

These observations of Piaget constitute strong
claims about the relation of cognition and language.
Since Piaget did not focus on language, however, the
specifics of linguistic milestones in relation to cognitive ones are lacking. For example, if adult words are
attempted at stage 5, does the child use its own spontaneous vocalizations meaningfully before that? Also,
since examples are given from only three children, and
mostly from one of these, Jacqueline, it may be that
other children show greater variation between linguistic and cognitive development than Piaget suggests. Because of these factors, Piaget's claims about language
and cognition constitute empirical hypotheses that
need to be subjected to closer investigation.

This paper reports on research undertaken to
examine more closely the relation between linguistic
and cognitive development in the first two years of
life. Since the topic is so broad, the work is clearly heuristic in nature. There have to be some substantive preliminary findings before comparative work can
begin. To date, there have been detailed observations
of linguistic and cognitive stages, but usually in
isolation from each other. For example, Bloom (1973)
makes very specific observations of the linguistic development of her daughter Allison, then goes on to speculate about the relation to cognitive development,
since cognitive milestones were not recorded. This
approach can be justified, however, in that we need to
have a clear idea of what the linguistic stages are
before they can be compared to the cognitive ones. This
is also true for the cognitive stages of Piaget. For
example, stage 6 of sensorimotor development is very
vaguely delineated in Piaget's theory, and its exact
nature needs to be established before comparisons can
be made. Once stages are established, research could
then begin to compare the development in the two areas.
Even here, however, one will need to be careful in
selecting those behaviours which will be actually observed. These require some preliminary work on determining those areas of cognition that appear to be especially important for linguistic development. The
rest of this paper briefly outlines the way the author
has attempted to answer some of these questions over
the last three years.

STEP 1: THE LINGUISTIC STAGES

Before any comparison between language and
cognition can be made, the first requirement is to find

the significant linguistic advances that take place in
the early development of language.   In the last few
years, there have been several studies on the nature
of the first utterances used by children, e.g. Ingram
(1971), Bloom (1973), Halliday (1975), Greenfield and
Smith (1976).   In Ingram (1974), these various studies
are reviewed and it is concluded that the actual facts
from one to another are quite similar, although the
theoretical interpretations vary.   The major finding
was that there are three distinct periods or stages of
linguistic development between the appearance of the
first word and the frequent use of multimorphemic utterances.   These are summarized in Table 1.

        The first period is one which lasts for se-
veral months and is marked by the use of single-word
vocalizations.   These words are used in a variety of
different functions, e.g. to request, command, etc.,
and do not appear to be propositionally complex.   That
is, they do not reflect semantic roles such as Agent,
Act, etc.   During the second period around 1;6 several
new developments occur.   At this point, one-word utterances do become interpretable as semantic relations.
The evidence for this comes from the contexts in which
they are used and the sequences in which they occur. At
the same time, dialogue emerges, and the vocabulary
undergoes rapid growth.   A month or two later, when the
vocabulary reaches around 50 words, two-word combinations appear.   The following months are marked by an increasing ability to combine words.   The functions of
language use also increase in this period, with the addition of what Halliday (1975) calls the imaginative
and mathetic functions.   In the imaginative function,
language is used in play or pretence.   The mathetic function is one where language is used by the child to talk
about the world in order to better understand it.   Several months later at the end of this period and the beginning of the third, two further advances take place.
There is the onset of references to past events and the
first appearance of the informative function.   The latter marks the fact that the child is now aware of
language as a means of communicating information between
people.   It is at this point that the child's first
sincere information questions appear.   During the third
period language becomes a means for the child to convey
his ideas, discuss past and future events, and request
new information.

        These periods are essentially the same as the
three phases described by Halliday (1975).   I have altered them in a few ways, however, and consequently
have avoided the use of the term 'phase'.   These linguistic milestones clarify some of the relevant behaviours that appear over time and can be used in comparison to cognitive stages.

TABLE 1. Characteristics of the three stages of linguistic development between the first word and multi-morphemic utterances.

Period	Age	Characteristics
1	0;10-1;5	One word at a time. Words used in a variety of functions, e.g. as wish, request, etc. Small vocabulary.
2	1;6-2;0 or later	(Beginning)
		One word at a time at onset. Use of single words in semantic roles such as Agent, Object. Use of sequences of one-word utterances. Onset of dialogue. Rapid growth of vocabulary.
		(One or two months later)
		Vocabulary up to 50 words, onset of multi-word sentences.
		(Several months later)
		Onset of information function, onset of reference to absent situations.
3	2;0-3;0	One word utterances no longer used, onset of ideational, interpersonal, and textual functions (cf. Halliday, 1975).

STEP 2:   THE COGNITIVE STAGES

If the three periods described in Ingram
(1974) are to be compared to Piaget's stages of sensorimotor development, it is first necessary to develop ways
to determine a child's particular cognitive stage of
development. This issue is discussed in Ingram (in
press). In many ways, it may be several years before
research produces enough findings for this to be done
with any certainty. There are two major reasons for
this. First, it is necessary to establish the notion
of stage in Paiget's theory. In the three books Piaget
wrote on the sensorimotor period (1952, 1954, 1962),
he focused on stages of individual behaviours, e.g.
stages of causality, imitation, etc. He spent relatively little time on the question of how to determine
overall, i.e. across all abilities, when a child is at
any particular stage. Piaget's focus is reflected in
research done in recent years on the sensorimotor period. Décarie (1965), for example, looked primarily
at stages of object permanence. The most ambitious
study to date, Uzgiris and Hunt (1975), also is primarily concerned with determining stages on the basis of
individual behaviours rather than general stages. This
is important because Piaget notes that the behaviours
for one stage may begin during the previous one. Thus,
success on a task for stage 5 does not necessarily mean
that the child is at stage 5. Before comparisons with
language can begin, we need some reliable way to satisfactorily establish a child's development through each
of the sensorimotor stages. A summary of Piaget's
six stages is given in Table 2.

The second problem is that the stage that is
most important in comparison to linguistic development,
i.e. stage 6, is very unclearly defined relative to the
other stages. This stage is crucial because it marks
the transition from sensorimotor to symbolic intelligence. The second Piagetian period, symbolic intelligence, is usually referred to as a time when 'representation' appears, i.e. the ability to internalize the
world. (This is obviously an oversimplification, cf.
Furth 1969.) Ways to distinguish stage 6 of the sensorimotor period from representation, however, are lacking.
For example, in Piaget (1954), stage 6 in every case is
representation, i.e. the same period. In fact, the only
place that Piaget discusses a difference between stage 6
and representation as distinct periods of development is
in Piaget (1962). There he mentions two differences. In
stage 6, the onset of symbolic play is seen in 'symbolic
schemas', i.e. symbolic play restricted to activities
related to the child, such as pretending to sleep. Also,
stage 6 has verbal schemas rather than preconcepts,
verbal schemas being highly variable as discussed earlier.
The general lack of differences between stage 6 and

TABLE 2.   A summary of Piaget's six stages of
            sensorimotor development.

Stage 1   (birth to 0;1)   The Use of Reflexes

           Child shows reflexes that are foundation of
           future development, e.g. sucking reflex,
           vocalization.

Stage 2   (0;1 to 0;4)   Primary Circular Reactions

           Child develops abilities focused on its own
           body, such as thumb sucking. Will vocalize
           when adult does, and will turn head towards
           sounds it hears.

Stage 3   (0;5 to 0;8)   Secondary Circular Reactions

           Child's activities on external objects
           create reactions which hold its interest.
           The activities are repeated to make the
           event occur again, e.g. swinging arms to
           make rattle move.

Stage 4   (0;9 to 0;11) Co-ordination of Secondary
                         Schemes

           Child uses activities of previous stage as
           means to achieve ends, e.g. hitting or
           moving parent's hand to move it away from
           an object the child desires. Child begins
           to attempt imitation of novel sounds.

Stage 5   (1;0 to 1;4)   Tertiary Circular Reactions

           Interest develops in nature of objects.
           Through exploration with new events and
           objects, child attempts to determine their
           novelty. Also, child develops new means to
           achieve goals, such as using a stick or
           string to obtain an object. When confronted
           with a problem, will actively experiment to
           solve it.

Stage 6   (1;4 to 1;6   Invention of New Means through
           or 2;0)   Mental Combinations

           Child can solve problems through reflection
           and anticipation of events. Object permanence
           is obtained - child is aware of independent
           existence of objects. First instances of
           symbolic play appear , e.g. child will pretend
           to sleep, eat, etc. In general child develops
           a mental representation of reality.

representation makes it difficult to establish whether a child is at one stage or the other. Therefore, one needs to define stage 6 more clearly in order to make a comparison with general linguistic developments.

Ingram (in press) is essentially an attempt to solve these two problems. The first step was to establish more clearly in Piaget's own data the nature of the sensorimotor stages. To do this, the observations in Piaget's three books were re-arranged in chronological order for each child. This made it possible to see the general stages for each child and how various cognitive milestones appeared in relation to one another. The data show that success on individual tasks does not always indicate that the child is at a particular sensorimotor stage. Also, the data present a clearer picture of the language development of Piaget's three children in comparison to the cognitive stages. Jacqueline began to use her first words during stage 5 of sensorimotor intelligence, and many of Piaget's examples of verbal schemas, e.g. the use of 'bow-wow' actually occurred in stage 5, before symbolic play and other stage 6 behaviours.

To further examine general stages in both language and cognition, chronological data were taken from three older diary studies (Shinn, 1900, Hogan, 1890, and Preyer, 1895), and three recent ones (in Church, 1966), and compared to the data from Piaget's three children. While these diaries obviously did not do the kinds of experiments that Piaget did, it was still possible to determine general cognitive stages from the observations. For example, Preyer mentions that his son Axel at age 1;1 took off and put on the cover of a can 79 times. This is clearly a stage 5 behaviour. The comparison of the nine children on language and cognition revealed the following very general findings: that Period 1 in language development (see Table 1) covered sensorimotor stages 4 and 5; that Period 2 coincided with stage 6; and finally, that Period 3 marks the onset of representation. These findings are presented with a great deal of caution since they are based on ad hoc observations. It is quite interesting, however, to speculate on the possibility that Halliday's use of the mathetic function versus the informative one may be a valuable way of distinguishing stage 6 of sensorimotor development from later representation.

STEP 3: A LONGITUDINAL STUDY

With some notion of what to expect linguistically and cognitively from young children, a longitudinal pilot study of four children (three girls, one boy) between the ages of 0;7 to 1;7 was undertaken. It was expected that the children would be on the verge of

stage 4 at the start of the study and in stage 6 when
it ended. Each child was visited in the home at two
week intervals, with two observers always present.
During the visits, observations of the child's cognitive stage, and audiorecordings of the child's language were made. While Piagetian tasks were given,
the focus was on general stages rather than specific
ones for individual behaviours. Thus, success at a
stage 5 behaviour did not automatically mean that
stage 5 was achieved. The three researchers on the
project met weekly and discussed the visits. These
meetings were used to reach a consensus on the child's
current general stage of development. Each child's
use of language was also discussed as well as the reports from each mother of her child's recent developments. All tape recordings were transcribed and included a fine phonetic transcription of the child's
utterances, all adult utterances directed to the child,
and a description of the context of the utterances.

The findings will be reported in Ingram, Ingram and Neufeld (in preparation). The analysis is not
complete at the time of writing but some general observations can be made. Three of the children appear
to be developing along the lines found in the diary
studies. That is, Period 1 coincides with stage 5, and
more rapid language development has taken place with
the onset of stage 6 cognition. The fourth child, however, is quite different in language. While her cognitive abilities have been the same (or slightly slower)
than the other three children, her language is quite
advanced. Her first words appeared in stage 4, and
stage 5 marked the onset of multi-word utterances. By
stage 6 many of her utterances were of more than one
word. In her case, it appeared that stage 5 was sufficient to allow syntactic development. When looking
for a reason for this difference between her and the
others, one striking factor stood out, namely, the
fact that this child was very advanced in her imitative abilities. While imitation stages for the other
children were usually one stage behind the general
cognitive stages, the stages for this child were
either advanced or on a par. We have examples on tape
of her attempting to imitate phrases during stage 5
far beyond her understanding. When unsuccessful at
finding an object hidden with one invisible displacement, she would say where'd it go? This tendency
could be better understood by looking at the mother-
child interaction. She was a first born and the mother
was very concerned about her language development. As
a result, she spent a great deal of time each day with
the child training her to imitate. This intense daily
interaction led to the child's learning a large vocabulary and advanced syntax. Also, interestingly, the
child is very clear in her pronunciation, and rarely

babbled on the tapes. We are currently comparing the child's language during stage 5 to that used later by the other children, when matched on MLU. We hope this will shed some light on whether or not syntactic development during the sensorimotor period differs from that which occurs when representation appears. Overall, our impressions are that the attainment of stage 5 in general, and in imitation in particular, are important for the development of syntax. In terms of the results of the diary comparisons, the longitudinal data suggests that while Period 2 usually coincides with stage 6 of sensorimotor development, it may begin in stage 5.

REFERENCES

Bloom, L. (1973)   One Word at a Time.   Mouton, The Hague.

Church, J. (ed.) (1966)   Three Babies: Biographies on Cognitive Development. Vintage Books, New York.

Decarie, T.G. (1965)   Intelligence and Affectivity in Early Childhood.   International University Press, New York.

Furth, H. (1969)   Piaget and Knowledge. Prentice-Hall, Englewood Cliffs, New Jersey.

Greenfield, P. and Smith, J. (1976)   The Structure of Communication in Early Language Development.   Academic Press, New York.

Halliday, M.A.K. (1975)   Learning How to Mean: Explorations in the Development of Language. Arnold, London.

Hogan, L. (1898)   A Study of a Child.   Harper, New York and London.

Ingram,   D. (1971)   Transitivity in Child Language. Language 47.   888-910.

Ingram,   D. (1974)   Stages in the Development of One-word Utterances.   Paper presented to the Child Language Research Forum, Stanford University.

Ingram,   D. (In press)   Sensorimotor Intelligence and Language Development. In A. Lock (ed.) Action, Gesture, and Symbol: The Emergence of Language.   Academic Press, New York.

Ingram, D., Ingram, J. and Neufeld, W. (In preparation)
A Longitudinal Study of Language Development
during the Sensorimotor Period.

Piaget, J. (1952)   The Origins of Intelligence in
Children. Trans. by M. Cook. International
Universities Press, New York.

Piaget, J. (1954)   The Construction of Reality in
the Child. Trans. by M. Cook. Basic Books,
New York.

Piaget, J. (1962)   Play, Dreams, and Imitation.
Trans. by C. Gattegno and F.M. Hodgson.
Norton, New York.

Piaget, J. and Inhelder, B. (1969)   The Psychology of
the Child. Trans. by H. Weaver. Basic Books,
New York.

Preyer, W. (1895)   The Mind of the Child. Appleton,
New York.

Shinn, M. (1900)   The Biography of a Baby. Houghton
Mifflin, Boston.

Slobin, D. (1973) Cognitive Prerequisites for the
Development of Grammar. In C.A. Ferguson and
D.I. Slobin (eds.) Studies of Child Language
Development. Holt, Rinehart and Winston, New
York.

Uzgiris, I. and Hunt, J. McV. (1975)   Assessment in
Infancy. University of Illinois Press,
Champaign.

Some Even Simpler Ways to Learn to Talk

R. Clark

This paper aims at outlining a model for
speech production in the early stages of language
development. The model is fragmentary, but ways in
which it will need to be supplemented will be indicated.

According to traditional models of language
development, children absorb information about linguistic structure through interpreting and analyzing the
speech that they hear. By this means they construct linguistic rules that form their competence,
but this competence cannot find full expression in
production because of performance constraints on short-
term processing.

The model presented in this paper differs
from the above in two main ways. In the first place,
it does not represent syntactic competence as central

---

*Apologies to Fodor 'How to learn to talk:
some simple ways' in Smith and Miller (eds.) 1966.

I wish to acknowledge the helpful comments
made by Paul Meara and Sandra Foubister on drafts of
this paper.

392

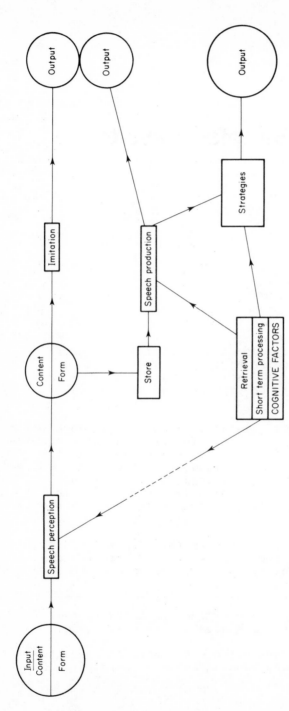

Fig. 1. First steps towards a model of language development.

This diagram illustrates those aspects of the model which have been mentioned so far. The perception of utterances is influenced by short term processing, among other factors. The utterance as perceived by a child is reduced from the adult utterance both in content and in form. Imitation may be either immediate or deferred. In either case, the output reflects closely the way the child perceived and interpreted the input. But speech production may also involve the use of simple strategies for modifying stored items, and these may result in outputs which are longer and apparently more complex than straightforward imitations. Deferred imitation is influenced by retrieval of stored items from long term memory.

to speech production or reception. On the contrary, imitation figures prominently in the model. Discussions of imitation have usually adopted one or other of two conflicting points of view. Either the child is copying mechanically the forms of adult utterances, without interpreting them fully, or he is forming an adequate interpretation of what the adult says, which he then expresses according to his own system of syntactic rules. This model will try to take account of both mechanical and semantic factors in imitation.

The second major difference between this model and other approaches to language acquisition concerns the role attributed to performance factors. Performance factors have most often been conceived of as short term processing constraints operating during production to prevent syntactic competence being fully realized in speech. As already mentioned, syntactic competence does not figure prominently in this model of language development. Short term processing constraints are considered here to have more influence on speech reception than speech production, so that what is stored by the child is subject to distortions at the input stage, but it is realized fairly directly in output.

According to the present model, performance constraints on production have more to do with the re-trieval of stored imitations from long term memory, than with short term processing, though I shall also be considering simple strategies of speech production, to which short term processing constraints may be relevant insofar as the function of these strategies seems to be to bypass any need for the planning of utterances in speech production, and enable it to occur in the absence of elaborate competence (see Figure 1).

Before presenting further details of the model it will be necessary to review very briefly discussions in the literature of comprehension, of the role of parental speech in the development of syntax, of imitation, and of speech production.

COMPREHENSION

Many people consider that children's knowledge of the structure of their language far exceeds what they can make manifest in their speech. If this is so, then they must acquire this knowledge through processing the speech that they hear, and identifying those aspects of situations to which specific properties of utterances relate. In order to identify which linguistic forms signal a particular meaning, children must be capable of interpreting the meanings of utterances in the first in-stance independently of the linguistic code. They must also be capable of noting the formal characteristics of utterances which constitute elements of the code.

But a wealth of research on semantic development in recent years has demonstrated that a child's
interpretation of an adult's utterance often captures
only a part of the adult's intention, and may distort
it. To pick but a few examples of the many pertinent
studies: Ervin-Tripp found that two- and three-year-
old children often fail to respond appropriately to the
particular wh word in a question (Ervin-Tripp, 1970)
(see also Savić, this volume, eds.). For example, they
respond to 'who' questions as if they were 'where',
'what' or 'what do' questions; Donaldson and McGarrigle
have shown that interpretations by three-to-five-
year-old children of structures including quantifiers
are heavily influenced by what should be irrelevant
aspects of the situation the utterances describe (1974).
Eve Clark has shown that interpretations of prepositional phrases by children aged between one-and-a-half and
two-and-a-half are determined by what they consider to
be the natural spatial relationships between the objects
described, and not by the particular preposition used
(Clark, 1973). Huttenlocher and Strauss, studying
children of five years of age and upwards, found that
cases of comprehension of instructions depended on how
the object the child was holding in his hand was referred to in the sentence. Thus children's interpretations of the input are influenced by conceptual factors which give rise to situational expectations. These
will need to be added to the diagram in Figure 1, feeding into the speech perception box (see Figure 3, p.406).

Clearly, children in the early stages of language acquisition are not capable of constructing anything like full interpretations of the utterances they
hear. But how much of the form of adult utterances are
they capable of registering? Here again, research
studies are revealing limitations on children's ability
to register formal aspects of the speech they hear.

Firstly, children do not apparently attend to
the whole of an input. Shipley, Smith and Gleitman
(1969) have suggested that children fail to attend to
adult utterances if they begin with unfamiliar material.
Bever has proposed that children use simple strategies
in speech perception, rather than attempting a complete
analysis of the input (Bever, 1970). Two-year-olds, he
suggests, scan the input for adjacent noun-verb sequences which can be interpreted as agent-action constructions, whereas four-year-olds treat the first noun in
the sentence as the subject of the verb. Among the 'operating principles' which Slobin proposes is 'pay attention to the ends of words'. He shows how, as a result
of this principle, the age at which children learn to
express particular concepts is influenced by the devices
their native languages use to express them (Slobin,
1973a).

Secondly, although another of Slobin's 'operating principles' is 'pay attention to the order of words and morphemes', it seems that children do not always do so. Other research suggests that even though children's spontaneous speech may reflect the word order of their native tongue, their interpretations of adult speech are not always sensitive to the order of constituents. So whilst they may be noticing the word order, they are not interpreting its function. For example, De Villiers and De Villiers (1974) found that under M.L.U. 1.5 word order played no part in the interpretations by children of instructions to make objects perform actions on each other. Chapman and Miller (1975) found that children aged between 1;8 and 2;8 used the correct word order in the production of subject-verb-object sentences significantly more often than they decoded such sentences correctly in a comprehension task. Chapman and Miller suggest that children are able to put syntactic rules to use in production before they can use them in interpreting sentences. But perhaps their use of standard word order in production does not depend on competence at all, but can be traced to the origin of the sentences in imitation.

With regard to the form of utterances, then, no less than the content, the evidence suggests that constraints exist on children's capacity to note all its aspects and identify their functions. It will be necessary to add a box representing these constraints, or 'operating principles', to the diagram in Figure 1. The nature of the operating principles will be dictated by short term processing restrictions, and in their turn the constraints will influence speech perception (see Figure 3, p.406).

If the present claim is correct, why has it always been widely assumed that children put syntactic knowledge to use more fully in comprehension than in production? A number of research studies have supported this claim, but they are open to criticism. For example, Fraser, Bellugi and Brown (1963) found that children performed better on a comprehension task than a production task. However, their methods of measuring comprehension and production have been questioned by Baird (1972) and Fernald (1972) respectively. Shipley, et al. (1969) claimed that among their sample of children aged between 1;6 and 2;6 whose speech was telegraphic, those that were linguistically more mature responded better to well-formed than to telegraphic speech. Their suggestion was that these children were capable of registering aspects of other people's speech which they were unable to formulate in their own speech. However, in their description of how the subjects were divided into linguistically mature and less linguistically mature groups, Shipley, Smith and Gleitman point out that this was done on the basis of median utterance length, which, they further point out, correlated with use of function words and inflections. In fact, then, the linguistically mature children were not producing speech which was entirely telegraphic, so if they responded better to well-formed than to telegraphic speech, this need not mean that they were comprehending more than they were producing. Smith made a similar claim with regard to the superiority of comprehension over production in connection with three- and four-year-old children (1970). However, she took a child's ability to imitate a structure as evidence that he could comprehend it, and I shall argue below that this is not justified.

Starr (1974) found that children, producing only single word utterances themselves, could discriminate between grammatical subject-verb-object and ungrammatical subject-object-verb constructions. Their ability to discriminate was shown by their preference for listening to the grammatical sentences. However, it may take very little knowledge for the children to be able to make this discrimination. Let us suppose, for example, that they attend mainly to the ends of sentences. The nouns in object position in the grammatical sentences would then be more familiar to them than the verbs at the end of the ungrammatical sentences, and this might account for their preference. Their preference certainly does not prove that they are fully aware of the function of the word order, as Starr seemed to be implying. As for Starr's finding that children producing longer utterances showed an equal preference for grammatical and ungrammatical sentences, the implications of this are hard to determine.

Klima and Bellugi (1966) made a more moderate claim regarding the relationship between comprehension and production. They claimed from their study of developing negative and interrogative structures in the speech of Adam, Eve and Sarah that when the children were currently producing particular structures they could also comprehend these structures in the speech of others. They cite the following examples as evidence for the comprehension of interrogatives:

Mother: Who are you peeking at?

Child: Peeking at Ursula.

Mother: Who are you playing with?

Child: Robin.

The authors infer comprehension of 'who', but these responses may reflect a very simple syntagmatic strategy, for the child is supplying a word to complete the sentence fragment at the end of the adult utterance. ·

Such a strategy may be relevant to the well-known finding that children progress from syntagmatic to paradigmatic responses in word association tasks (Ervin, 1961).

Some recent discussions have viewed more sceptically children's ability to decode grammatical cues in comprehension, (e.g. Bloom, 1974). In one discussion, my colleagues and I concluded that my son at age 2;9 was depending almost entirely on cues outside the verbal message in his interpretations of adult utterances (Clark, Hutcheson and Van Buren, 1974).

For the above reasons the model of language development presented in this paper depicts imitation as central rather than competence derived from interpretation and analysis of the input, though the stored imitations, which I shall maintain constitute a child's linguistic repertoire, do not fully reflect the form, or fully encapsulate the meaning, expressed in their models (see Figure 1). It is no longer possible to expound models which propose that processing constraints on speech reception are moderate, and allow the development of a competence whose expression is prevented by severe processing constraints on production. After all, it is speech reception that is paced by the speed of other people's utterances, and hence is more likely to suffer because of limited channel capacity. Speech production can take its own time.

Before turning to a discussion of imitation and strategies in speech production, I shall consider briefly the role of parental speech in the development of syntax.

THE ROLE OF PARENTAL SPEECH

The study of the special characteristics of mothers' speech to children is thriving, as this volume shows. Some effects of the way parents talk to children have been identified. For example Blount (1972) has proposed that adults define social roles for their children through the way they interact with them in conversation, and that the effects of this training are shown in variations from culture to culture in the frequency with which children use sentences of different functional types. However, research has been far less successful in establishing correlations between structural properties of adult and child speech. For example, Brown, Cazden and Bellugi (1968) found no relationship between the incidence of structures in parental speech and their order of emergence in the speech of Adam, Eve and Sarah. As Cross (this volume) has pointed out, it is not enough to show that both children's speech and mothers' speech to children become increasingly complex as the children grow older, since the increase in complexity of mothers' speech may be a reaction to developments in the children's own syntax, rather than the cause of their development.

Some psycholinguists have a theoretical bias against attributing the course of language development to external factors, such as the characteristics of mothers' speech, since they adopt a child-centred approach and suppose the course of language development to be determined by characteristics of the child himself. However, if we accept that what children attend to in adult speech is a function of their processing mechanisms and their conceptual understanding, and that these develop as the child grows, we may look for interactions between the structure of adult utterances and the mechanisms by means of which children process them. And we can do this without losing sight of either the child's perspective or the objective characteristics of the mother's speech.

To give a simple example, if children of a particular age are only attending to the ends of sentences, then what we should be looking at is a relationship between the structures the child produces and the way that adults typically end their sentences. This approach is more likely to bring positive results than a global comparison of child speech with the relative frequencies of whole sentences of various types. In fact it is very likely that length of sentence and position in sentence and other such factors influence the likelihood of a structure being acquired. Consider for example the fact that early negatives typically begin with the word 'no'. This is a word that often occurs on its own as a complete utterance, and so may very readily be imitated even by a child with limited imitative capacity. Furthermore, 'don't' usually emerges before 'can't' or 'won't'. This too can occur on its own as a complete utterance whereas the others cannot. Elliptical utterances in parental speech may contribute to the development of the yes/no question form. In fact they definitely did in the case of my own elder son. His first spontaneous negative yes/no questions emerged after a period of a few days during which he would copy adult elliptical tag questions, and later after copying them prefix them immediately to a further utterance (Clark, 1975).

Adam: It's cold.

Mother: Isn't it.

Adam: Isn't it.   Isn't it dark too.

Wh questions are another area of syntax whose development may be the product of an interaction between properties of adult syntax and children's processing

strategies. The form of children's interim questions
resembles that of adult dependent questions, which occur typically in subordinate clauses at the end of sentences, where they are, perhaps, most likely to be attended to (Clark, 1974a).

It may be, then, that the rate of syntactic
development in children could be related to the frequency of usage by the mother of elliptical structures
and other such syntactic devices that are adapted to
the formal constraints of children's processing mechanisms for input.   These mechanisms will be represented in the 'operating principles' box to be added
to the diagram in Figure 1 (see Figure 3).

On the other hand, some proposals regarding
parental training procedures attribute to children the
ability to relate and compare successive sentences, and
it seems to me unlikely that children could profit from
such learning opportunities. For example, Brown, Cazden and Bellugi (1968) draw attention to the technique
of rephrasing a question which a child does not understand, in the form of an occasional question, e.g.
'What do you want?' would be rephrased as 'You want
what?' They suggest that this informs the child that
the question in its latter form, which he can more
readily understand, is equivalent to the question in the
form first presented. However, it is not obvious that a
child can retain and compare the formal aspects of both
versions of the question at the same time as concentrating on interpreting the adult's intention. Similarly,
Ervin-Tripp, describing Kobashigawa's finding that adults
often repeat sentences with minor variations, argues
that 'the semantic equivalence of formal alternatives,
given maintenance of the external situation across the
sentences, would be apparent'. It would only be apparent if the child were capable of giving the alternatives
his attention, and retaining the relevant formal features for long enough. It may be that the function of
such repetitions is limited to maximizing the probability that the child will understand what the adult is saying in one formulation or another (see Ervin-Tripp,
1973).

IMITATION

The view that children comprehend a great deal
which they may not be able to express has not failed to
influence studies of imitation. One major approach to
imitation is to believe that children form fairly complete interpretations of the adult models, whose meaning they formulate according to their own syntactic rule
systems. If the child's rendering of the adult utterance is inadequate, blame is attached in such models to
the mechanisms interfering with output. Where findings
suggest that imitations are equivalent in length and

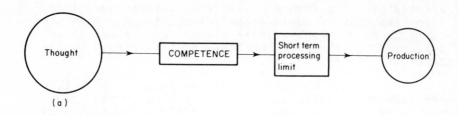

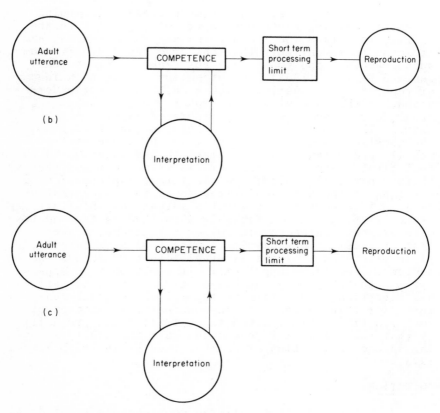

Fig. 2. Traditional performance models.

(a) Production.

(b) Imitation with performance constraints conceived as equal to constraints on production.

(c) Imitation with performance constraints conceived as less stringent than in production.

complexity to spontaneous utterances, it is postulated
that performance constraints affect both processes
equally. Where findings suggest that imitations are
longer or structurally more complex, that is accounted
for in terms of less stringent performance restrictions
on imitation than on production (e.g. Smith, 1970;
Slobin, 1973b). These two approaches are represented
in Figure 2 a, b and c.

But according to other explanations of imitation children do not necessarily interpret the model
fully before attempting to repeat it. For example,
Brown and Fraser (1963) proposed that when two- and
three-year-old children imitate they are storing up a
corpus of utterances from which they can later gradually extract information about the structure of their language. Apparently, then, when they first copy the utterances they are not fully aware of the meaning potential carried in their structure. Fraser, Bellugi and
Brown (1963) have also proposed that three- and four-
year-old children may copy structural features of utterances mechanically, without full understanding. This
would account for the superiority of their performance
in imitation tasks over comprehension tasks. In the
case of the younger children, the imitations are not
superior to spontaneous utterances. Rather they resemble them in length and structure. The reason for
this, according to Brown and Fraser, is that spontaneous
utterances are nothing but imitations that have been
stored for later reproduction.

Though differing from the above models in the
matter of whether children interpret what they imitate,
Brown and Fraser's model resembles them in postulating
performance constraints. Both the spontaneous utterances and the imitations of the children are viewed as
reduced forms of adult utterances. Brown and Fraser
seem to be proposing two processes to account for the
reduction. Factors such as stress and word order apparently influence the perception of the models in imitation. But Brown and Fraser also postulate a length
constraint on production which affects both imitations
and spontaneous utterances. It is not clear why this
mechanism is necessary to the model, given that reduction has already taken place on input. Their model
seems more consistent without this production constraint.

As is clear from this brief summary, discussions of imitation in the literature are riddled with
paradox. The main controversial question seems to have
been 'Is imitation mechanical or does it involve interpretation according to rules of competence?'.

But this opposition seems to oversimplify the
process. It is clear from the discussion of comprehen-

sion above that children may only extract a certain amount of the meaning intended by an adult speaker. Furthermore, they may only register a part of the form of an adult utterance. Perceptual constraints will determine what portion of the formal material they will register for reproduction, and conceptual constraints will determine what meaning they will attach to that portion of form. An imitation will be a representation of the model utterance which is reduced in both form and meaning, its character being determined by conceptual factors and by formal constraints. And not only will form and content be reduced, but elements of form may be distorted, not merely reduced. A child may infer some aspect of meaning which was not part of the adult's original intention at all. And he may assimilate the utterance that he hears to a similar sequence of words more familiar to him and reproduce it in an altered form. A further consideration is that form and content may be competing for his limited attentional capacities. All these processes can take place without any syntactic rules being employed in sentence interpretation or imitation at all.

One form of evidence often used to support the view that children structure material according to their own rules when they are imitating is that they often alter the word order of the original. However, although Slobin and Welsh (1968) hold to this view, some of their own examples of changes in word order in imitations by Echo provide strong evidence that mechanical processes are involved in imitation, e.g.

Model: The candy is marple, the shoe is marple.

Imitation: Shoe marple an' a candy marple.

Although no syntactic rule would dictate the order of conjoined sentences, very many of Echo's imitations of such sentences reverse the order in the original. This is just what one would expect if imitation was affected by short term memory constraints. Whilst it is true that Echo has structured the material linguistically to some extent by treating the sentences as units, rather than transposing parts of sentences, this does not alter the fact that mechanical elements are involved in the process. After all, some prior structuring of the material is involved in any mechanical repetition procedure. One's digit span in a foreign language would not be as long as in one's native language. Further examples of mechanical influences in imitation, in which shorter units are transposed, are discussed in Clark and Van Buren (1973) and in Clark, forthcoming.

Is imitation mechanical then or does it involve interpretation and reconstruction according to the rules in a child's competence? The answer must be that there are mechanical aspects to imitation, that imitation does not always involve a complete and accurate interpretation, nor is it always reconstruction according to the rules of competence. Similarities between spontaneous utterances and imitations need not be due to their both being formed according to the same syntactic rules, but may be due to the spontaneous utterances having originated as imitations.

On the basis of this analysis of comprehension and of imitation, it is denied that children build up syntactic competence as a result of interpreting adult utterances and relating aspects of their form to aspects of their meaning. It is proposed instead that children imitate utterances overtly, or merely record them for delayed imitation; that their imitations are subject to the formal and conceptual influences discussed above; that structures children imitate are not fully comprehended by them and that their imitations constitute a repertoire of linguistic structures from which they only gradually extract information about the structure of their language which enables them to generalize the structures to new lexical items. (Because this analysis is gradual, the 'stored fragments' box in the amended diagram, Figure 3, is linked only by a dotted line to 'analysis', and thence to 'competence'.) In the meantime they employ a variety of very simple strategies for making their linguistic repertoire go further in speech. Some of these strategies will be mentioned in the next section.

The above proposal is an extension of Brown and Fraser's suggestion (1963) that a child's repertoire of stored reduced imitations is the corpus from which he gradually induces grammatical rules. Subsequently Brown and Bellugi (1964/1970) were led to postulate the 'induction of latent structure' as a process in language development. They found that many of Adam's, Eve's and Sarah's utterances could not have originated as reduced imitations since they were not merely adult-like structures with bits left out. Rather, Brown and Bellugi commented 'they are mistakes which externalize the child's search for the regularities of English syntax' (1970:90). It will be the contention of the next section that more of these child-like utterances than Brown and Bellugi allowed can be explained in terms of imitation, plus certain other simple strategies.

PRODUCTION

As we have seen, various people have suggested that speech perception depends on simple processing strategies, rather than on a full semantic and syntactic analysis of the input. However, even those who acknowledge that speech perception depends on such strategies may believe that speech production depends on rules, and

that the structure of a sentence is planned, at least
in part, before it is uttered (e.g. Cohen, 1966; Fodor,
Bever and Garrett, 1974). A favoured way of explaining
syntactic errors in children's speech is to attribute
them to the effect of length constraints, or other short
term processing restrictions, rather than to lack of
competence (e.g. Bloom, 1970; Bellugi, 1971).

However, Braine has attacked the idea that a
length constraint is responsible for the idiosyncratic
nature of children's early actor-action constructions.
'It seems to me that what is probably happening in these
utterances is that the child, lacking complete command
of the English rules for making action phrases, is constructing such phrases simply by seizing on some salient
feature of the action for which he has a word readily
available. Sometimes the word chosen happens to be a
verb, sometimes the English object noun, sometimes the
location, if that is an important part of the action for
him, and sometimes something salient that is none of
these. His choice is pragmatic and not determined by
syntactic or semantic structure. The process at work, I
suggest, is essentially similar to that by which the one-
word so-called holophrases are produced.' (Braine, 1974:
455.)

It seems to me that even with utterances longer
than two words a similar 'holophrastic process' is taking
place. Sequences of such words adopted in imitation may
function as single units and enter into longer sentences
in the way that Braine has suggested single word holophrases do. All fall down water, said of a tree lying in
a stream, is a particularly clear example, since there
seems little doubt that 'all fall down' was acquired as
an integral verbal unit from use in the child's game
'Ring-a-ring o'roses'. But I have cited further evidence
for the widespread influence on syntax of the coupling of
stored sequences of words to another word, or another
such sequence, without internal modification of the established string (Clark, 1974a). Such a device may explain
so called 'topic/comment' constructions (Gruber, 1967)
which are frequent in child speech. Phrasal verbs, such
as get it are learnt as units, then simply coupled to
nouns, without the pronoun being dropped, to produce sequences like Get it ladder.

The idiosyncratic nature of children's output
is often cited as evidence for rule-governed creativity,
but the 'holophrastic process' is but one of the simple
strategies that can account for such deviations from
adult structure. Other strategies are evident from the
speech of my own children. For example, two different
ways of expressing the same idea, each perhaps origina-
ting as an imitation, may simply be amalgamated in a
composite utterance such as 'That's not the right thing
I wanted to do' - apparently an amalgam of 'That's not

the right thing to do' and 'That's not the thing I
wanted to do' (see Clark, forthcoming). These strategies of speech production have been added to the
diagram in Figure 3, p.406. Like the operating principles which affect speech perception, they are adapted
to short term memory constraints.

If, as I am suggesting, speech production, at
least in the early stages, depends largely on repro-
ducing stored sequences, or combining or fusing them in
simple ways, do performance constraints have no influence whatever on speech production? I would suggest
that there are performance constraints but that they are
not constraints on short term processing capacity. To
suppose that there is a limit to processing capacity in
sentence production is to assume that the structure and
content of sentences needs to be planned in advance. But
it has been argued in the case of adult speech that pre-
established routines lie at the basis of speech production (Olson, 1973). It seems plausible to me that this
is so of children too. It is characteristic of English
syntax that optional constituents which were not fully
intended at the outset of an utterance may readily be
added as an additional aspect of the situation claims
the speaker's attention. Adults can add constituents in
this way without the rhythmical flow of their speech
being interrupted. Perhaps successive one word utterances (Bloom, 1973) and replacement sequences, or build
ups, (Braine, 1971; Weir, 1962) in children's speech
are due to their lack of facility for finding the words
and phrases that they need sufficiently rapidly. But
this is a matter of rapid retrieval from long term memory rather than of short term processing - a performance limit due to insecure competence. (I am referring
to lexical competence, though Braine has attributed replacement sequences to insecure syntactic competence
(1974). Both explanations may be correct but relevant
to different stages of development.)

The recognition of the role of retrieval in
sentence production allows for a plausible explanation
for the fact that imitations may be longer and more
complex than spontaneous utterances. It is precisely
the retrieval of lexical items from long term memory
which is facilitated when a model is available for imitation.

LANGUAGE DEVELOPMENT IN OUTLINE

The way I see language development is as follows. Children imitate linguistic messages in recurrent contexts, and their version of the message may get
retained as a 'stored fragment', to use Cazden's phrase
(1968). The form of these stored fragments and the
meaning the child attributes to them only partially represent the form and the meaning of the model.

406

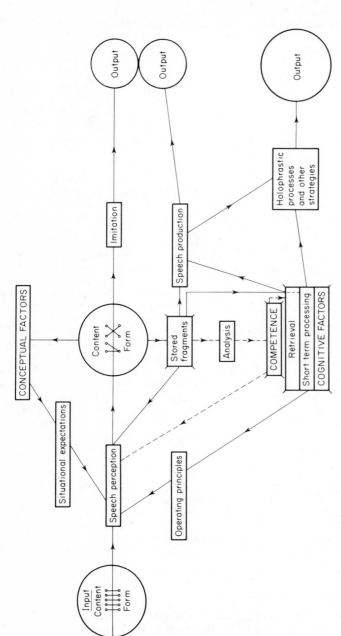

Fig. 3. The model.

This diagram has several limitations. For example, it attempts to represent in one picture short-term processes affecting the perception and production of utterances, together with the long term changes arising out of these processes. Furthermore, the meaning of the arrows joining different boxes is not the same: some represent the transfer of material, some represent the order of events in a process, some represent short term influences on processes and some long term influences on systems (named in capital letters). Also, there are many hierarchical relationships between the processes represented which I have been unable to depict graphically. I hope that despite these deficiencies, the diagram will help to clarify the arguments in the paper rather than obscuring them.

The input has elements of content associated with specific elements of form. The perception of the content is influenced by situational expectations, which are in turn affected by conceptual factors. The perception of the form of an utterance is influenced by operating principles, which are themselves influenced by cognitive factors, such as short term processing constraints. The version of the utterance as received by the child may be reduced in content, reduced in form, and form and meaning may be mismatched and distorted in the ways described in the section on imitation above. I have tried to represent some of these modifications in Figure 3 by using circles to represent elements of content and elements of form, and lines to represent links in the child's mind between these.

Once registered by the child, the piece of language may be reproduced immediately as an imitation, or it may be stored for future reproduction. Furthermore, what the child has learnt about the world from interpreting the utterance will influence his conceptual framework.

When the stored fragments are reproduced at a later date, they are subject to restrictions on speech production affected by cognitive factors, such as limitations on retrieval. Having been retrieved, they may be reproduced as they originally stood, or they may be processed by simple production strategies, such as the holophrastic process, 'coupling' and 'amalgamation' as described above in the section on speech production. If they have been so processed, they may emerge as longer and more complex sequences than the immediate or deferred imitations, though with the grammatical errors characteristically produced by such strategies (Clark, forthcoming). Children's speech is often called 'creative'. This means that they construct novel sequences which they may never have heard before. This creativity is usually attributed to the operation of syntactic rules in speech production, either alone (Fodor, 1966), or modified by performance constraints (Bellugi, 1971). But I am treating many of the novel utterances produced by children as very simple modifications of imitations.

As the repertoire of stored fragments builds up, it comes to influence speech perception, and thus the acquisition of further stored fragments, in that children assimilate sequences they hear to familiar sequences. This process of assimilation gets in the way of their noting new aspects of syntactic and morphological structure, and is an additional factor in accounting for discrepancies between adult models and the child's rendering of them, e.g. They won't tooken down copies from They weren't taken down. 'Weren't' is assimilated to 'won't' which is a word already familiar to the child. ('Tooken' may also be the product of assimilation - the 'take' in 'take -en' being assimilated to 'took'. On the other hand, it may be an example of grammatical creativity, which probably affects morphology earlier than it affects syntax.) The stored fragments also influence cognitive factors, such as short-term processing, since the amount of material that can be processed is a function of the familiarity of the material (Olson, 1973).

In the course of time, I believe, through regular use of a sequence children come gradually to be able to generalize from it by substituting new lexical items. This is the beginning of creativity based on rudimentary syntactic rules. But I believe children can only do this with highly familiar sequences (see Clark, 1974a), and that in the first instance they may only be able to modify one constituent at a time. Where generali ations are evident in the structure of children's speech at an earlier stage, they may be based on semantic, rather than syntactic knowledge. For example, De Villiers and De Villiers (1974) found that 87% of the 'agent-action', 'action-object' and 'agent-action-object' sequences of eight children with MLU between 1.00 and 1.5 had an animate noun as agent and an inanimate noun as object (see also Bowerman, 1973). As time goes on, the repertoire of stored fragments may be gradually analyzed for more elaborate information about syntactic structure, which will be accumulated in the child's competence. As the child's competence develops, it will eventually begin to influence the way speech is interpreted, though all the evidence, touched on briefly in the section on comprehension above, suggests that this is a slow process. The growing competence will also gradually begin to influence short term processing restrictions, in the way stored fragments do, since structured materials are more readily remembered, once the child is aware of the structure. I have tried to reflect in Figure 3 my view that competence is slow to develop by representing all the connections associated with it by dotted lines.

It is conceivable that children could be learning something about syntactic structure through listening to adult speech, even though this knowledge is not put to use for the time being. Even without being manifest in either production or comprehension, competence could be developing through attention to adult speech and analysis of it, rather than, as I have suggested, through the gradual unpacking of the content and structure of sequences already in the child's repertoire.

Starr (1974) has made such a proposal. She has postulated performance restrictions preventing the use of competence in comprehension similar to those usually invoked to explain defective syntax in speech production. Starr proposed that children aged between one and two could express their competence in judgements of the grammaticality of sentences, if in no other way. However, De Villiers and De Villiers (1974) found that the ability to judge the grammaticality of sentences on the basis of word order emerged much later than the ability to use word order cues in comprehension. So there is as yet not enough evidence that grammatical knowledge is present before it can be used in comprehension or production.

As the child develops, the repertoires of stored experience, and the systems that develop through their aid, are growing and altering. A child's repertoire of stored fragments will increase and there will be more stored material to which inputs can be assimilated. Also, the semantic constraints on speech perception will alter according to conceptual growth. The formal constraints will alter as children's memory capacities increase, enhanced by their greater familiarity with linguistic forms. I have marked the corners of some of the boxes in Figure 3 to represent this dimension of growth. However, many that have not been so marked will also be changing with age. For example, as the child builds up grammatical competence through examining stored fragments, his powers of analysis will be developing, partly as a result of their being used in this way. Also, the processing strategies for speech production will increase and become more elaborate as development proceeds.

Perhaps changes of perceptual strategy with age can be accounted for in terms of developmental changes in other psychological systems. Many treatments of perceptual strategies work on the assumption that the sentence is being processed sequentially, from beginning to end (Kimball, 1973; Fodor, Bever and Garrett, 1974). However, until children have enough knowledge of the language to be able to recognize words rapidly as they are presented and retain them while the rest of the utterance is produced, their recall of utterances will be subject to a recency effect. Cook found that the ability to identify the object of a verb in a relative clause is enhanced if the verb object sequence is at the end of a sentence (Cook, 1975; see also Clark, 1974b). Perhaps the transition of Bever's experimental subjects from a 'noun-verb' strategy to a 'first word in sentence' strategy (see section on comprehension above) is a function of their growing ability to recognize and retain the first word in the sentence.

The reader may feel that the diagram presented in this section and my discussion of it take us

rather far from the 'simpler ways to learn to talk'
suggested in the title of this paper. But, though
language development is presented here as a process
involving complex and changing relationships between
a number of cognitive systems, the child is all the
time credited with only simple strategies for perceiving and producing utterances.

CONCLUSION

My general conclusion is that the role of
performance factors in linguistic development is not
restricted to preventing competence from being fully
expressed. Performance limitations prescribe the way
in which competence develops, through influencing perceptual strategies, and hence determining what information is acquired. They also dictate the kind of strategies that will be used to keep communication going
whilst competence is developing.

REFERENCES

Baird, R. (1972)   On the Role of Chance in Imitation,
Comprehension and Production Test Results.
Journal of Verbal Learning and Verbal Be-
havior 11. 474-477

Bellugi, U. (1971)   Simplification in Children's Lang-
uage. In R. Huxley and E. Ingram (eds.)
Methods and Models in Language Acquisition.
Academic Press, New York.

Bever, T.G. (1970)   The Cognitive Basis for Linguistic
Structures. In J.R. Hayes (ed.) Cognition
and the Development of Language. Wiley, New
York.

Bloom, L. (1973)   One Word at a Time. Mouton, The
Hague.

Bloom, L. (1974)   Talking, Understanding and Thinking.
In R.L. Schiefelbusch and L.L. Lloyd (eds.)
Language Perspectives:Acquisition, Retarda-
tion and Intervention. Macmillan, London.

Blount, B. (1972)   Parental Speech and Language
Acquisition. Some Luo and Samoan examples.
Anthropological Linguistics 14. 119-130.

Bowerman, M.R. (1973)   Early Syntactic Development: a
Cross-Linguistic Study with Special Reference
to Finnish. Cambridge University Press,
Cambridge.

Braine, M.D.S. (1971) The Acquisition fo Language in Infant and Child. In C.L. Reed (ed.) The Learning of Language. Appleton-Century-Crofts, New York.

Braine, M.D.S. (1974) Length Constraints, Reduction Rules and Holophrastic Processes in Children's Word Combinations. Journal of Verbal Learning and Verbal Behavior 13. 448-457.

Brown, R. and Bellugi, U. (1964) Three Processes in the Child's Acquisition of Syntax. In Harvard Educational Review 34.2. 133-151. Reprinted in Brown, R. (1970) Psycholinguistics. The Free Press, New York.

Brown, R., Cazden, C. and Bellugi, U. (1968) The Child's Grammar from I to III. Reprinted in C.A. Ferguson and D.I. Slobin (eds.) (1973) Studies of Child Language Development. Holt, Rinehart and Winston, New York. From J.P. Hill (ed.) (1968) Minnesota Symposia on Child Psychology 2. University of Minnesota Press, Minneapolis.

Brown, R. and Fraser, C. (1963) The Acquisition of Syntax. In C.N. Cofer and B. Musgrave (eds.) Verbal Behaviour and Learning. McGraw-Hill, New York.

Cazden, C. (1968) The Acquisition of Noun and Verb Inflecctions. Child Development 39. 433-438. Reprinted in C.A. Ferguson and D.I. Slobin (eds.) (1973) Studies of Child Language Development. Holt, Rinehart and Winston, New York.

Chapman, R.S. and Miller, J.F. (1975) Word Order in Early Two and Three Word Utterances: Does Production precede Comprehension? Journal of Speech and Hearing Research 18. 355-372.

Clark, E.V. (1973) Non-linguistic Strategies and the Acquisition of Word Meaning. Cognition 2. 161-182.

Clark, R. (1974a) Performing without Competence. Journal of Child Language 1. 1-10.

Clark, R. (1974b) Aspects of Psycholinguistics. Symposium on Linguistics and Mathematical Education. U.N.E.S.C.O. ED-74/CONF. 808/8, Nairobi, September 1st-11th.

Clark, R. (1975) Adult Theories, Child Strategies and their Implications for the Language Teacher. In J.P.B. Allen and S.P. Corder (eds.) Edinburgh Course in Applied Linguistics 2. Oxford University Press, London.

Clark, R. (Forthcoming, 1977) What's the Use of Imitation? Journal of Child Language.

412

Clark, R., Hutcheson, S. and Van Buren, P. (1974)
Comprehension and Production in Language
Acquisition. Journal of Linguistics 10.
39-54.

Clark, R. and Van Buren, P. (1973) How a Two Year
Old Orders Words About. Edinburgh Working
Papers in Linguistics 2. 76-89.

Cohen, L.J. (1966) Comments on 'Competence and Per-
formance' by J. Fodor and M. Garrett. In
J. Lyons and R. Wales (eds.) Psycholinguistics
Papers. Edinburgh University Press, Edinburgh.

Cook, V.J. (1975) Strategies in the Comprehension of
Relative Clauses. Language and Speech 18.
204-212.

De Villiers, J.G. and De Villiers, P.A. (1974) Com-
petence and Performance in Child Language:
Are Children Really Competent to Judge?
Journal of Child Language 1. 11-22.

Donaldson, M. and McGarrigle, J. (1974) Some Clues
to the Nature of Semantic Development.
Journal of Child Language 1. 185-194.

Ervin, S. (1961) Changes with Age in the Verbal Determinants of Word Association. American Journal
of Psychology 361-372.

Ervin-Tripp, S. (1970) Discourse Agreement: How
Children Answer Questions. In J.R. Hayes (ed.)
Cognition and the Development of Language.
Wiley, New York.

Ervin-Tripp, S. (1973) Some Strategies for the First
Two Years. In T.E. Moore (ed.) Cognitive
Development and the Acquisition of Language.
Academic Press, New York.

Fernald, C. (1972) Control of Grammar in Imitation,
Comprehension and Production: Problems of
Replication. Journal of Verbal Learning and
Verbal Behavior 11. 606-613.

Fodor, J.A. (1966) How to Learn to Talk: Some Simple
Ways. In F. Smith and G.A. Miller (eds.)
The Genesis of Language: a Psycholinguistic
Approach. M.I.T. Press, Cambridge, Mass.

Fodor, J.A., Bever, T.G. and Garrett, M.F. (1974)
The Psychology of Language. McGraw Hill,
New York.

413

Fraser, C., Bellugi, U. and Brown, R. (1963) Control of Grammar in Imitation, Comprehension and Production. Journal of Verbal Learning and Verbal Behavior 2. 121-135.

Gruber, J.S. (1967) Topicalization in Child Language. Foundations of Language 3. 37-65.

Huttenlocher, J. and Strauss, S. (1968) Comprehension and a Statement's Relation to the Situation it Describes. Journal of Verbal Learning and Verbal Behavior 7. 300-304.

Kimball, J. (1973) Seven Principles of Surface Structure Parsing in Natural Language. Cognition 2. 1-47.

Klima, E.S. and Bellugi, U. (1966) Syntactic Regularities in the Speech of Children. In J. Lyons and R.J. Wales (eds.) Psycholinguistics Papers. Edinburgh University Press, Edinburgh.

Olson, G.M. (1973) Developmental Changes in Memory and the Acquisition of Language. In T.E. Moore (ed.) Cognitive Development and the Acquisition of Language. Academic Press, New York.

Shipley, E.F., Smith, C.S. and Gleitman, L.R. (1969) A Study of the Acquisition of Language: Free Responses to Commands. Language 45. 322-342.

Slobin, D.I. (1973a) Cognitive Prerequisites for the Development of Grammar. In C.A. Ferguson and D.I. Slobin (eds.) Studies of Child Language Development. Holt, Rinehart and Winston, New York.

Slobin, D.I. (1973b) Introduction to: Studies of Imitation and Comprehension. In C.A. Ferguson and D.I. Slobin (eds.) Studies of Child Language Development. Holt, Rinehart and Winston, New York.

Slobin, D.I. and Welsh, C.A. (1968) Elicited Imitation as a Research Tool in Developmental Psycholinguistics. Working Paper No.10. Language Behaviour Research Laboratory, University of California, Berkeley. Reprinted in C.A. Lavatelli (ed.) Language Training in Early Childhood Education. University of Illinois Press, Illinois. Also in C.A. Ferguson and D.I. Slobin (eds.) Studies of Child Language Development. Holt, Rinehart and Winston, New York.

Smith, C.S. (1970)   An Experimental Approach to
        Children's Linguistic Competence.   In J.R.
        Hayes (ed.) Cognition and the Development of
        Language. Wiley, New York.

Starr, S. (1974)   Discrimination of Syntactical Errors
        in Children under Two and one half Years.
        Developmental Psychology   10.   381-387.

Weir, R.H. (1962)   Language in the Crib.   Mouton,
        The Hague.

Growth of Complexity in Phonological Development

N. Waterson

A widely recognized principle is exemplified in this paper: that of progress from a simple beginning to greater complexity. The findings presented should therefore have a wider application than to the one case study on which most of the evidence is based, more particularly because the language development of the child in question showed the typical features of other children's acquisition of language (cf. Ingram, this vol.).

A longitudinal study of the child's phonetic and phonological development, made in the context of his language development in general, has convinced the writer that to get a fuller understanding of the processes involved, growth of complexity should be studied at the several levels of language: semantic, phonetic, phonological, lexical, and syntactic, taking into account their interrelations together with the increase in amount of language used. However, the data available are not adequate for this and as work on child language has not yet reached the point when such complete studies are being made, reports covering only some of the aspects will continue to make a contribution and here only limited interrelations are considered.

It has often been said that children learn the coarse, gross contrasts of language first and in this paper an attempt is made to illustrate this at the phonetic and phonological levels, showing at the same time how such development is related to increases in vocabulary size, syntactic complexity, and amount of language use. In a short paper of this nature it is not possible to give a full longitudinal description of the phonetics and phonology, so a restricted aspect has been selected for consideration. What will be demonstrated is increase in syntagmatic differentiation and length of utterance. Only a brief outline will be given - a more detailed description will be available elsewhere (Waterson, forthcoming).

Increase in syntagmatic differentiation is illustrated in relation to syllable, word, and sentence. Particular reference will be made to syllable structure, consonantal contrasts within syllables and words, contrasts of syllables within words, and word contrasts within sentences. A differentiated vowel system was acquired very early, as is often the case, so vowels are not included in the discussion. That syntactic patterns are learnt in a similar way to the phonological is implicit but a great deal more is involved in the learning of syntax (cf. for instance Clark, Miller, this volume; Bruner, 1975, Dore; 1975).

It will be shown that increase in length, in degree of differentiation, and in amount of use at the levels of syllable, word, and sentence was achieved in a manner that was similar in many respects. Progress was from short, simple utterances in which there were few articulatory contrasts and only simple syllable patterns, to quite long ones containing a large number of contrasts. The phonetic and phonological development of the child who is the subject of this study proved to be remarkably systematic and this suggests that something of the same strategies and hence possibly the same neural processes were involved in the creation of the phonological structures of syllable, word, and sentence.

The evidence put forward in this paper shows that there are interrelations between the different levels of language dealt with, that is, the phonetic, phonological, lexical, and syntactic, and with amount of language use, and that in the early stages increase in complexity did not take place at the same time and at the same rate in them all. The picture that emerged is rather that if there was progress at one level, there was often little or no progress at another. This suggests that the child's overall organization for language was such that it was not possible for him to cope with growth at all the levels at the same time. Then at around 1;6 to 1;7 there was progress at a faster rate and at several levels at once; it was as if he had developed an organization which enabled him to process language material in a more efficient way and this speeded up his learning and use of language.

The main concern of this paper will be with the child's production. The important role played by perception and auditory salience in the acquisition of the phonological system has been described in detail elsewhere (Waterson, 1970, 1971a, 1971b, 1971c, 1976). Briefly, at the start the child was found to produce his forms of words mainly on the basis of those parts of the adult models which had the greatest auditory salience and were at the same time semantically salient for him. Auditory salience, to put it oversimply, involves mostly stretches of relatively low frequency (F1 and F1 transitions), relatively high intensity, and relatively long duration (see Waterson, 1976). The child was paying a great deal of attention to F1 and F1 transitions when beginning to speak and these have been found to be important in the auditory perception of babies in the prespeech period (Fourcin, this volume). He thus scanned the speech signal but made use of only a small part of it. To begin with, he operated with a very limited set of articulations, producing a limited number of sounds which he used in restricted contexts in short utterances of one or two syllables. These sounds were then used in a wider range of contexts so that the number of syntagmatic contrasts within his utterances increased, as also did his word patterns. As time went on and as he gained more experience, his perceptual discrimination, and the amount of attention he was able to give to the speech signal, appeared to improve because he began to take less salient features of the models into account and gradually produced more and more new sounds. These again first appeared in restricted contexts and later in a wider range. The syntagmatic differentian in his utterances and hence also in his phonological system thus increased. Increase in length of utterance was first achieved by the use of what was familiar - either by repetition of an item or by the combination of familiar items, as shown by Clark for syntax (Clark, 1974, and this volume).

The aspect of language development dealt with in this paper is a small part of a longitudinal study of the phonetic and phonological development of the writer's eldest child. The period covered by the study starts at the beginning of the one-word utterance stage, at ten and a half months, and ends at around two years when the child was using relatively complex two-part multi-word utterances. Data of the child's linguistic and general development were collected daily and some notes were made of the context of use. When the data were analyzed, it was found that the type and number of articulatory contrasts within a syllable, contrasts of syllables within a word, and contrasts of words within a multi-word utterance were important factors in relation to what the child was able to produce at different stages of language learning. This indicates that syntagmatic differentiation (that is, contrast within the sequence of an utterance) is very important for child language studies and indeed for studies of speech processing in general. It seems probable that increasing differentiation in a child's phonetic and phonological systems reflects his growing ability to perceive and recognize more in the speech signal, as well as his increasing ability for planning, production, storage and retrieval. There is some discussion of this point in Waterson, 1976.

Examples of syntagmatic differentiation in a one-word utterance and a two-word utterance are given below to clarify what is meant by the term. The degree of differentiation within the four-syllable one-word utterance [helikɔptə] 'helicopter', first used at 2;2, is compared with that of the four-syllable two-word utterance [mama, popo] 'mama, potty', first used at 1;4. The same type of phonetic feature description is used here as in the writer's other studies of child phonology (see Waterson references).

In [helikɔptə] the syllable structure is CVCVCVCCV, three open, CV, syllables and one closed, CVC. Each syllable is different: [he - li - kɔp - tə]. In the CVC syllable a difference in place of articulation has to be made (velar [k] to bilabial [p]) which must involve greater difficulty in production than a CV syllable where no such contrast needs to be made.[1] The word begins with a breathy onset [h] and there is a contrast of manner of articulation within the sequence: lateral [l] and plosive [k, p, t]. There are four changes in place of articulation: alveolar [l] to velar [k], to bilabial [p], to alveolar [t]; there are changes in lip position: from spread in [heli], to rounded in [kɔp], to neutral in [tə],and there are also changes in tongue position in the dimension of height and also in relation to front, back, and central positions in the mouth. Tongue height changes from half-close [e], to close [i], to half-open [ɔ], to half-close [ə], and the start is with front tongue position in [heli], moving to back in [kɔp], and central in [tə]. There are also several changes involving voicing and voicelessness: the voiced stretches are [eli], [ɔ] and [ə] and the voiceless are [h], [k], and [pt].

In the two-word utterance [mama, popo], there are only open, CV, syllables, so there are no place and manner contrasts within any of the syllables, and there

is a minimum of contrasts in the whole utterance as
both words have repeated syllables,that is, (CV)[2]. Only
one place of articulation, bilabial [m, p], is involved
and there is only one manner of articulation contrast:
nasal [m] and (oral) [p]. Only one change in lip position is made: from relatively spread in [mama], to
rounded in [popo], and there is one change in tongue
position and tongue height: from relatively front and
open in [mama] to back and half-close in [popo]. There
is voicing throughout the first word [mama] and changes
from voicelessness, [p], to voice, [o], in the two syllables of the second word.

When the two utterances, [helikɔptə] and
[mama, popo] are compared in terms of the syntagmatic
contrasts involved (bearing in mind also the accents and
pitch changes which are of a different nature), it becomes clear that a one-word utterance like [helikɔptə]
in which a large number of articulatory changes is involved, needs much more skill in planning and production
that a two-word utterance with very few contrasts like
[mama, popo], and may therefore be described as having a
higher degree of complexity. Its production would seem
to be more complex even allowing for the fact that a
two-word utterance involves the selection of two appropriate items from the memory store and their organization into a sequence, whereas in the case of a one-word
utterance only one selection is made and no arrangement
in a sequence is required. The high degree of complexity of 'helicopter' may well be one of the reasons why
the child did not attempt it until 2;2 despite the fact
that helicopters were phenomena almost as frequently
commented upon in his environment as planes. 'Plane'
[plein] is much simpler and was first attempted at 1;6,
as [beim]. Structural complexity thus appears to be one
of the reasons for the late production of this word,
cf. Ferguson and Farwell (1973) who drew attention to
phonologically determined selectivity in word acquisition.

The concept of syntagmatic differentiation as
used in this paper has now been demonstrated and it is
plain that the more syntagmatic differentiation there is,
the greater is the degree of complexity. Growth of complexity in phonetics and phonology will now be illustrated and related to growth in vocabulary, syntactic development, and to amount of language used. As mentioned
earlier, only the briefest indication can be given here
because of limitations of space. In the illustration
that follows, selected examples are given which are representative of the increases in syntagmatic differentiation.

GROWTH IN COMPLEXITY

In the detailed longitudinal study, the phonetic and phonological development of the child is divided

into seven stages on the basis of linguistic changes
that took place, and the same divisions are used here.
The stages and ages are given below. It will be seen
that they vary in length, stages 1 and 7 being the
longest and stage 4 the shortest.

Stage 1	0;10.14 to 1;2.21	
Stage 2	1;2.21 to 1;4.10	
Stage 3	1;4.11 to 1;5.7	
Stage 4	1;5.8 to 1;6.0	
Stage 5	1;6.0 to 1;7.10	
Stage 6	1;7.11 to 1;8.3	
Stage 7	1;8.4 to 2;2.0	

There is, of course, some overlap from one stage to the
next. Some changes that took place in one stage had
their beginnings in the previous stage. The child was
babbling at the start of the study and was still babbling in Stage 6. He was also using a 'protolanguage'
(Halliday, 1975), communicating by a system of vocalizations accompanied by gestures and actions, up to stage
3 when communication became more fully verbal without
dependence on non-verbal actions. The earlier stages of
development are described in more detail than the later
as the latter followed along very much the same lines
and it is felt that by stage 5 the way growth in complexity took place has been made clear. The description
of the growth of complexity now follows.

Stage 1. The child's vocabulary was very small
and was acquired very slowly over a long period of time;
some of the words occurred only once. Plosives, nasals,
and vowels were the only sounds used apart from one
example of a labial glide. These are sounds that were
familiar from babbling and their perception and production
was thus well-practi ed. At this time the child used only
one-word utterances of both one and two syllables and these
had few consonantal contrasts. Syllable structures of
one-syllable words were CV, VC and CVC, the latter being
the only ones with contrasts within the syllable. Systems at C were P (plosive) and N (nasal), i.e. PV [ba:]
'Bob', NV [nou] 'no', VP [ʌp] 'up', VN [æn] 'Anne',
PVP [gʊd] 'good', and PVN [boun] 'bone' and [bæŋ] 'bang'.
Two-syllable words had open, CV, syllables only, and were
mostly of a reduplicated structure, i.e. the whole or
part of the syllable was repeated, $(CV)^2$, so that there
were no contrasts at C within the structure. The possibilities were $(PV)^2$, [dada] 'dada', [kʊku:] 'cuckoo',
and $(NV)^2$, [mama] 'mama'. There was one word of CVCV
structure, with a contrast of P and N, PVNV, [bi:nə]
'Bina'. Two-syllable words had one accent but there was

one two-syllable utterance with two accents, [go wei]
'go away', and it had the same intonation as the two-
word adult model. The child did not use 'go' nor 'away'
separately so his [go wei] was intermediate between a
one-word sentence and his first two-word sentences which
had two accents.[2]

The only words of the CVC structure, [gʊd],[boun]
and [bæŋ] had a contrast at onset and ending as in the
adult models. In [gʊd] there is no contrast of manner
of articulation, onset and ending both being plosive,
but there is a place contrast, velar [g] and alveolar
[d]. Features of voice and voicelessness are treated
prosodically as relating to the syllable and not as part
of consonantal contrasts so are not included in the discussion (see Waterson, 1971b). [boun] has a place of
articulation contrast of bilabial [b] and alveolar [n],
and there is also a manner contrast, oral [b] and nasal
[n]. [bæŋ] has the same oral-nasal contrast but a
different place contrast: bilabial [b] and velar [ŋ] .
There was one three-syllable utterance,[pɔppɔppɔp] 'pop
pop pop', (PVP)[3], with no place or manner contrasts.
This was used onomatopoeically.

At this time, when language use was infrequent
and words were acquired with long intervals between each,
the child was able to manage the place and manner contrasts in the few words used. This may be compared with
the situation later on in stage 3, when the rate of vocabulary growth was faster and new words of the CVC
structure had no place or manner contrasts, nor did two-
syllable words, the only ones being of the (CV)[2] structure. Thus at the start the child's learning seemed to
be on the basis of individual items, whereas later it
appeared to be by pattern (see stage 3).

Stage 2. The rate of growth of vocabulary and of
amount of language use increased and a number of new
vowel sounds were acquired so that the child now had
most of the vowels of English but not all the diphthongs
and triphthongs (cf. Jones, 1962). Plosives, nasals,
and the labial glide were still the only consonants.
There was one new syllable structure, V, and two new
word structures, V and VCV, in neither of which were
there any consonantal contrasts involved.

Examples:

V   [uː] 'the letter "u"', [aː] 'the letter "r"'

VCV [ɪtɪ] 'Kitty', [æpʉ̥] 'apple'.

The first increase in utterance length from one word to
two took place at this time. Two-word utterances are
analyzed as two-word sentences on account of their accentuation (that is, by virtue of having two accents as

opposed to one which was the case in one-word utterances), by intonation contour, and by their relation to the context (cf. Bloom, 1973).

The structure of these first two-word sentences was similar to that observed in other English children (e.g. Bloom, 1970; Clark, 1974) and was a) repetitive: for example, a repeated word as [gɔn, gɔn] 'gone, gone', with the structure {gɔn}^{2} (Braces, { }, represent sentence structures) b) differentiated: two different words in a sequence, i.e. a sequence of one-word utterances, as [daun, ʌp] 'down, up', {{daun} {ʌp}}; or two words expressing a semantic relation: [æpɯ gɔn] 'apple's gone', {æpɯ gɔn}. The only functions of the two-word sentences were comments (declaratives), requests, and vocatives. As would be expected from the fact that only plosives and nasals were involved (the labial glide was still used only in 'go away') there were few contrasts relating to place and manner within the two-word utterances. Such contrasts as occurred are shown below phonologically in relation to the C systems in the structure of the sentences.

Examples:

Contrasts at C (relating to manner) are P and N.
(P = plosive system, N = nasal system)

Utterance	Sentence structure	Maximum contrasts
[gɔn, gɔn]	{PVN} {PVN} = {PVN}^{2}	{P--N}^{2} i.e. P--N--P--N
[gʊd, gʊd]	{PVP} {PVP} = {PVP}^{2}	P
[nau, nau]	{NV} {NV } = {NV^2}	N^2
[ʌp, daun]	{{VP} {PVN}}	P--N
[daun, ʌp]	{{PVN} {VP}}	P--N--P
[mama, popo]	{{ (NV)^2} { (PV)^2}	N--P
[æpɯ gɔn]	{VPV PVN}	P--N

Contrasts at P and N (relating to place) are p, t, k.
(p = bilabial, t = alviolar, k = velar).

Utterance	Sentence structure	Maximum contrasts
[gɔn, gɔn]	{kVt} {kVt} = {kVT}^{2}	{k--t}^{2} i.e k--t--k--t
[gʊd, gʊd]	{kVt} {kVt} = {kVt}^{2}	{k--t}^{2} i.e k--t--k--t
[nau, nau]	{tV} {tV} = {tV}^{2}	t
[ʌp, daun]	{{Vp} {tVt}}	p--t
[daun, ʌp]	{{tVt} {Vp}}	t--p
[mama, popo]	{{(pV)^2} {(pV)^2}}	p
[æpw̥ gɔn]	{VpV kVt}	p--k--t

From the above it may be seen that the greatest number of contrasts, P--N--P--N and k--t--k--t, occurred in a repeated-word sentence, in {gɔn}^{2}. Where there was no repetition, the maximum contrast was less: P--N--P and t--p in {daʊn, ʌp} and P--N and p--k--t in {æpw̥ gɔn}. In the other cases there were fewer contrasts.

At this time there were two longer utterances in use with accentuation and intonation as in the adult models: [ə: gɔn, nou mɔ:] 'all gone, no more' and [gʊnai, nou, nɔt nau] 'goodnight, no not now'. Both were used as indivisible units and with specific functions so were intermediate between a one-word and a four-word sentence, cf. [go wei] in stage 1. Interestingly, these longer utterances are no more complex in terms of consonantal contrasts than the two word sentences; no new contrasts are involved and the maximum contrast is P--N--P--N and k--t in {{gʊnai}{nou} {nɔt nau}} as shown below.

Examples:

Contrasts at C are P and N.

Utterance	Sentence structure	Maximum contrasts
[ɔ: gɔn, nou mɔ:]	{{V PVN} {NV NV}}	P--N
[gʊnai, nou, nɔt nau]	{{PVNV} {NV} {NVP NV}}	P--N--P--N

Contrasts at P and N are p, t, k.

Utterance	Sentence structure	Maximum contrasts
[ɔ: gɔn, nou mɔ:]	{{V kVt} {tV pV}}	k--t--p
[gʊnai, nou, nɔt nau]	{{kVtV} {tV} {tVt tV}}	k--t

The child was thus using the same sort of contrasts in his planning and production of these longer utterances as in the shorter ones and this may be one of the reasons why he was able to use these sentences which were so much longer than those in his general usage.

Stage 3.   There was a big increase in vocabulary size and in amount of language use. No further instances of actions instead of words were recorded so there was obviously greater reliance on language for communication. There were no new syntactic functions and no increase in utterance length other than the appearance of the first three-syllable word. There was, however, an appreciable increase in the number of two-word sentences and more of the non-repetitive, differentiated type began to be used. The word 'gone' was very productive, being combined with 'mama', 'dada', 'car', and 'Bob'. Apart from a few new sounds in some isolated words, namely [br] in [bre:] 'bread', [f] in [fɔ:] 'four', and [l] in [deil] 'tail', plosives and nasals were still the only consonants that were used and there was little new in syllable or word structure. The biggest expansion in the vocabulary was in words of the familiar PV, (PV)^2, and PVP structures in which there were no consonantal contrasts, e.g. [gu:] 'goose', [dɔ:] 'door', [bə:] 'bird', [gaʊ]'cow'; [pæpæ] and [bæbæ] 'Patrick', [beibɪ]'baby', [bæbu:] 'birdie'; [gʌk] for 'truck', 'jug', 'cake', [dɪk] and then [gʌk] for 'stick'.

In stages 1 and 2 nearly all the adult models of the words the child attempted had only plosive and nasal consonants. Now the child was attempting words in which the models had other sounds as well but he continued to use only plosives and nasals and this resulted in his attempts being less like the models than was the case earlier. He was still responding only to what was auditorily most salient in the models. For instance, 'cheese', adult [tʃi:z] was   [di:] and 'rope', adult [roup] was [oup].   The CVC structure words acquired during this period had no contrast at the C places. Thus 'truck', adult [trʌk] and 'jug', adult [dʒʌg] were both [gʌk], PVP and kVk, and 'moon', adult [mu:n] was [mu:m] NVN and pVp. Hononyms, resulting from the child's production of words based on the same sets of salient features in the models, appeared in the child's speech at this time, e.g. [di:] for 'cheese' and for 'tea', [bɔ:] for 'ball' and for 'paw'. New two-syllable words were of a reduplicated structure, mostly (PV)^2, see the examples above. The first three-syllable word, 'banana', had open syllables only and consisted of a single syllable followed by a repeated syllable, CV(CV)^2. It had alternative forms with one syllable, [ba] PV, and two syllables, [nana] (NV)^2. The three-syllable form was a combination of these: PV(NV)^2 [banana].

The two-word sentences had the same sort of contrasts as in stage 2. Only the differentiated types are examined here as the repeated types had no contrasts, e.g. $\{mɔ\cdot\}^2$ 'moth, moth', $\{gɑ:\}^2$ 'car, car', $\{ɑ:\}^2$ 'ah, ah', $\{nou\}^2$ 'no, no'.

Examples:

Contrasts at C are P and N. Contrasts at P and N are p, t, k.

Utterance	Sentence structure		Maximum contrasts	
[dada gɔn]	$\{(PV)^2\ PVN\}$	$\{(tV)^2\ kVt\}$	P--N	t--k--t
[mama gɔn]	$\{(NV)^2\ PVN\}$	$\{(pV)^2\ kVt\}$	N--P--N	p--k--t
[ba: gɔn]	$\{PV\ PVN\}$	$\{pV\ kVT\}$	P--N	p--k--t
[gɑ: gɔn]	$\{PV\ PVN\}$	$\{kV\ kVt\}$	P--N	k--t
[mɔ: di:]	$\{NV\ PV\}$	$\{pVtV\}$	N--P	p--t
[mama ʌp]	$\{(NV)^2\ VP\}$	$\{(pV)^2\ Vp\}$	N--P	p

In these differentiated, non-repetitive two-word sentences, the maximum contrast is N--P--N and p--k--t, in {mama gɔn}; this is less than the maximum in the repetitive example in stage 2 but more than the maximum in the differentiated types.

Of the three longer utterances used, one was repetitive, with four accents, and had no contrasts: [a: ba:, a: ba:] 'ah Bob, ah Bob', and the other two were composed of combinations of familiar words: 'dirt' and 'oh' with the old-established 'go away', i.e. [də:t, gu: əwʌ:] 'dirt, go away' and [ou, gou əwei] 'oh, go away', with simple contrasts of plosives and labial glide. The two latter examples had three accents as in the adult models but were intermediate between two- and three-word sentences since 'go away' was still used only as a single indivisible unit, i.e. as a word.

The acquisition of CVC structure words in a simpler form in this stage than in stages 1 and 2, that is without a contrast at onset and ending, cannot be explained as being due to motor constraints as the child had already shown himself able to produce and use words of this structure with a contrast, for instance [gʊd] 'good', [bæŋ] 'bang' and [boun] 'bone' in stage 1, and [gɔn] 'gone', [kot] 'coat', [də:t] 'dirt' and [daʊn] 'down' in stage 2. Nor can it be said to be due to a limited memory span as he was producing utterances that were longer than a one-syllable word with several contrasts, for instance in the differentiated two-word

utterances such as [dada gɔn] 'dada's gone', P--N,
t--k--t, and [mɔ: di:] 'more cheese', N--p, p--t. The
reason for it may well be that, aside from increase in
complexity taking place at other levels of language,
there was a change in the way the child was coding language. The evidence shows that he was now responding
to adult models in a patterned way (cf. the homonyms
and the expansion of the vocabulary by the acquisition
of words of established structures, PV, (PV)[2] and PVP),
and this would suggest that he was learning by pattern
recognition and was developing a coding system by classification in addition to coding by individual item,
which appeared to be the earlier strategy. The absence
of contrast in CVC structure words would thus be explained as a processing constraint. The child had to
handle the storage, retrieval, and planning of a growing number of items with ever-increasing frequency as
the vocabulary and language use continued to expand. He
was also producing more two-word utterances. He thus
had to develop a new organization, or new coding systems in order to be able to handle the more complex language he was needing to use as his cognitive and social
development was advancing, and it seems that he had not
yet acquired a complex enough system to handle a large
number of words of anything but the simplest structure.
It seems his working capacity was stretched to the full
and he was therefore not able to cope with consonantal
contrasts in the words he was now acquiring, nor with
any increase in the number of syntagmatic contrasts in
two-word utterances, as shown above, nor indeed with an
increase in utterance length, apart from the three
simple examples already described.

Stage 4. Although there was still no increase in
utterance length (apart from the use of two four-word
utterances of very simple structure), a great change
took place during this stage, the shortest of all the
stages. Not only was there a further big increase in
amount of language use and in vocabulary growth (again
especially in words of established structure) but a new
range of sounds, continuants, came in and were used in
several words. These were sibilants and fricatives,
sounds that are less salient in the adult models than
the plosives and nasals to which the child had been responding earlier. This means that for some time before,
he must have been discriminating more in his perception
and recognizing more, and was now ready to attempt these
new sounds. He was obviously aware of the contexts in
the models in which they occurred because he was producing them appropriately in several words. The production of these less salient sounds of the models is in
line with the acquisition of plosives and nasals, that
is to say, the first to be produced were those in contexts in which they had the greatest auditory salience
in the models, the less salient being produced later, in

Stage 6, showing that the non-production in such contexts was not due to an inability to produce the particular sounds but rather because they had not been given
attention.

The continuant sounds the child was now attempting required more skill not only in perceptual discrimination but also in production. The articulators have to
be in a posture of close approximation to achieve friction, neither completely in contact as in plosives and
nasals, nor well clear of each other as in vowels. The
appearance of sibilants and fricatives in stage 4 is not
seen as resulting primarily from a production difficulty
which had been overcome but as arising from the child's
increased perceptual discrimination, the need for their
production not having arisen until the child was able to
discriminate them and recognize them as functional. As
the child's babbling was not recorded, it is not known
whether these sounds formed part of the babbling repertoire but they do not appear to have been well-practised
as their production was not always successful. However,
the inaccurate production may well have reflected inaccurate identification of the sounds as well as difficulty in production.

Another factor that points to the child's increased perceptual discrimination is that whereas before
this stage, very few words changed in form from the one
in which they were first acquired, now they began to get
more variable in form as the child changed his production
to match the models more closely (see Waterson, 1976),
and the instability of the form of words which has often
been noted in the speech of young children, appeared in
his speech. His established words began to change and
some of his homonyms diverged, e.g. 'stick' changed from
[gʌk] to [gɪk], 'cake' from [gʌk] to [gek]. However,
new ones continued to be acquired, e.g. 'duck' was acquired as [gʌk], like his 'truck' and 'jug'. Words in
simple form changed more quickly to a more differentiated
one, e.g. [beip] for 'plate' and 'grape', quickly diverged to [bleit] and [geip] respectively.

Attempts at the friction and sibilance of the
models were made with varying degrees of success. Friction was achieved at several places, i.e. bilabial,
labio-dental, dental, and velar; and sibilance was produced at the palatal, palato-alveolar, and alveolar
places. Attempts in initial position tended to be af-
fricated.

Examples:

Fricatives

	Initial	Final
bilabial	[bβæ] 'fly'	[gu:ɸ] 'goose'
	[βɔ:] 'four'	[kaʊɸ] 'cow/calf'
labio-dental	[fɔ:] 'four'	[bɪf/bəf] 'beef'
dental	-	[gu:θ] 'goose'
velar	[ɣɔn] 'gone'	-

Sibilants

	Initial	Final
palatal	[dɟu:], [ɟʰu:] 'shoe'	-
palato-alveolar	[dʒein] 'chain'	[dɪʃ] 'dish'
		[ʊ ʃ] 'vest'
		[ʊʃ/ɪʃ] 'fish'
alveolar	-	[geips] 'grapes'
		[dadaz] 'dada's'

      The new sounds were used mostly in one-syllable words and brought new consonantal contrasts into use so that a higher level of complexity was reached in monosyllables before disyllables which continued to be mostly of the reduplicated type with no consonantal contrasts, e.g. [bebe] 'biscuit', [tɪtɪ] 'Kitty', [gʰ₁agʰ₁a/ɟʰjaɟʰja] 'Geoffrey', [mɛmɔ̃] 'lemon'. The first few examples of non-reduplicated two-syllable words appeared, each having a closed syllable: [bəu:n] 'balloon' and [pebl/bʌbl] 'table'. The labial glide [w] was now used more widely, for instance [wæ] an alternative form of 'fly', [wæ] one of the forms of 'eye' (the others were [ʌ], [jæj], [æj] and lastly [aɪ]), and [wæ̃wæ] 'barrow'. The use of new contrasts resulted in new word structures. For instance, in addition to the established structures with P and N, such as PV, PVP, PVN, VP, VN, NVN, there were now PVS [dɪʃ] 'dish'; VS, [ɪʃ] 'fish', [ʊʃ] 'vest'; PVF, [bɪf/bəf] 'beef', [kaʊɸ] 'cow/calf', [gu:θ/gu:ɸ] 'goose', and PSVN, [dʒen] 'chain' (S=sibilant system, F = fricative system, PS = affricated sibilant system). The few new disyllabic structures were PVVN [bəu:n] 'balloon', PVPVL [pebl/bʌbl] 'table' (L= liquid system), and PLVSVS [prəʃəʃ] 'precious' (PL = plosive with liquid release). One new three-syllable word, [pe:toto] 'potato', came into use. It was of the same structure, namely CV(CV)^2, as the one acquired in stage 3 but the systems at C places were different, PV(PV)^2 of [pe:toto] contrasting with PV(NV)^2 of [banana]. The increase in the number of different word structures meant that the whole phonological system had increased in complexity.

The use of differentiated, non-repetitive two-word sentences became even more frequent and for the first time they greatly outnumbered the repetitive type. The consonantal contrasts in the majority of the two-word sentences were still of the familiar plosives and nasals but there were a few that contained words with the new continuant sounds, for example:

[dadaz yʃ] 'dada's wash'   {(PV)^{2}S VS}   P--S

[dʒen ba:p] 'Bob's chain'   {PSVN PVP}   PS--N--P

[prəʃəʃ beibɪ] 'precious baby' {PLVSVS (PV)^2} PL--S--P

The phonological structure of two-word sentences was thus beginning to grow more complex with new contrasts involving S, PS, and PL.

At the syntactic level several new relations were expressed in two-word sentences, for instance, the possessive relation: {mama εə}'mama's hair', {dada dau} 'dada's towel'; the use of a qualifier of quality: {puə ba:} 'poor Bob', {prəʃəʃ beibɪ} 'precious baby'; and listing: {b bl, bε } 'table, chair'.

One three-word utterance and two four-word utterances were recorded. The three-word utterance was of the listing type: [du:, dli:, fɔ:] 'two, three, four'. The four word utterances were repetitive; one had no consonantal contrasts and the other had only one, as shown below.

Utterance	Sentence structure	Maximum contrasts
[dada di:, dada di:] 'dada's tea, dada's tea'	{(PV)^2 PV}^{2} {(tV)^2 tV}^{2}	P t
[ai, ai, nou, mʌ] 'eye, eye, nose, mouth'	{{V}^{2}{NV}{NV}} {{V}^{2}{tV}{pV}}	N t--p

This is consistent with the earlier stages where the few
longer utterances contained no more contrasts than were
found in general use.

By the end of this stage there was thus an increase in vocabulary size; an increase in the number of
different sounds; and a consequent increase in the differentiation within two-word sentences. There was also an increase in the use of differentiated two-word sentences and
in the syntactic structure of such sentences, and more
language was used in general. However, there was no increas
in word length nor in sentence length. The child thus appeared to be learning to process speech at a more complex
level in short utterances before starting the regular use
of longer utterances.

Stage 5. This stage saw a sudden increase in utteranc
length. Several new three syllable-words were acquired and
the first four-syllable word appeared. Three-word utteranc
began to be used relatively freely and several utterances o
four and five words were recorded. This increase in utterance length coincided with a great deal of verbal play duri
which the child used repetitive utterances of up to twelve
words in length, although there were never more than six di
ferent words in any one such stretch, e.g. [dada ti: ɔ: gɔ
bʌbu: ti: ɔ: gɔn, mama ti: ɔ: gɔn] 'dada's tea is all gone'
Patrick's tea is all gone, mama's tea is all gone', and [pu
mama, puə dada, puə mæm, puə gɑ:, puə gaga] 'poor mama, poo
dada, poor man, poor car, poor tractor'. This verbal play
lasted throughout the five weeks of this stage. The syntact
structures involved were of the type often used by the chil
in his everyday speech, as also were most of the word combi
nations, and the majority of the stretches of verbal play h
only the well-established plosive and nasal consonants. It
seems that this kind of play, with familiar articulations,
familiar syntactic structures, and very familiar words together with some more recently acquired, facilitated the
planning and production of longer utterances by providing
practice through the use of what was familiar. The verbal
play is thus a further example of the use of the familiar i
the production of something new, in this case longer utterances, and is reminiscent of babbling during which children
spend quite a lot of time repeating familiar patterns in se
quences of relatively long stretches (cf. Tuaycharoen, 1977
The verbal play was similar to one of the pre-sleep mono-
logues described by Weir (1962) but took place during the d

In this stage the vocabulary expanded at an even
faster rate than before. There was not much in the way of
new articulations. Alveolo-palatal affricates [tɕ] and
[dʑ]began to be used: [tɕi:z] 'cheese' and [ʥæm]
'jam'. The instability in the form of words noted in
the previous stage increased. Sounds acquired earlier
were now used in a wider range of contexts, for example
the lateral began to be used in post-vocalic position:
[aḷa], then [elən] ' Helen', [pi:ḷou] 'pillow',

[kʰjaiətli] 'quietly'. The possibilities of syntagmatic contrasts within one-syllable words became greater,
for instance [pɪn] 'pin', [byʃ], then [bʊʃ/bəʃ] 'brush',
[bi:s] 'piece', [geɪt] 'gate', [dʒæm] 'jam', [bred̥]
'bread', [gl̩af] 'glove'. The contrasts are evident from
the transcriptions and phonological representation is
therefore not given. The first use of a word with complex onset and complex ending was recorded: [gl̩eps]
'grapes'.

There were more examples of two-syllable words
with a closed syllable and with a higher degree of syntagmatic differentiation, e.g. [βʌβain] 'robin',[gærɪʃ]
'garage', [tɔ:təs] 'tortoise', [bʌʔn] 'button', and for
the first time there were two-syllable words with abutt-
ing consonants, -CC-. Examples are [a:ntɪ] 'auntie',
[kʰjaiətli] 'quietly', [a:kjʊ] 'thank you'. Three-
syllable words still had repeated syllables and there
were some new structures: $(CV)^2CV$, $(CV)^2CVC$ and $C(V)^2CV$.
The earliest three-syllable words had only the familiar
plosives and nasals but now there were some with continuants: lateral continuant [1] and labio-dental fricative
[v].

Examples:

Teddybear	[tedibɛə]	$(CV)^2CV$	$(PV)^2PV$
marmalade	[mɑ:mʌeid], [mɑ:maleid],	$(CV)^2CVC$	$(NV)^2LVP$
	[me:me:lot], [mʌ:mæleit]	and	and
		$(CV)^2CV$	$(NV)^2VP$
cauliflower	[gahava]	$C(V)^2CV$	$P(V)^2FV$
butterfly	[bʌʔəvæ], [bæʔævæ]	$C(V)^2CV$	$P(V)^2FV$

The one four-syllable word was also repetitive, with
simple contrasts, as was the case with the first two-
and three-syllable words. The example is [ma:tota:to]
'tomato', N(VPV)P(VPV). This was used in free variation
with the disyllabic form [ma:to] NVPV, cf. the first
three-syllable word [banana] which had shorter alternant
forms, monosyllabic [ba] and disyllabic [nana].

As a result of the greater number of articulatory contrasts within words, and the increase in the
number of such words, there was greater syntagmatic differentiation in the two-word utterances than before.
Sometimes the form of words differed in two-word utterances from that used in isolation in a way that reduced
the number of articulatory contrasts. For example,
'dog's eye' was [dœei] with frontness of articulation
throughout instead of backness in 'dog' [dɔg] and frontness in 'eye' [aɪ] but 'dog's nose' was [dɔʔ nou] with
backness throughout; 'go on' [gou ɔn] with backness and

rounding throughout but [gɶ bæ] for 'go back' with frontness instead of backness in 'go'. 'Man' was usually
[mæn] but 'the man's gone' was [mæ̃ gɔn] or [mæ̃ gɔm], with
no place closure for the nasality at the ending of 'man'
and sometimes with bilabial place of articulation of the
final nasal of 'gone' harmonizing with the bilabial place
at the onset of 'man': similarly 'moon' was [mu:m] or
[mu:ɲ] but 'the moon's gone' was [mũ: gɔɲ] or [mu: gɔɲ]
again with no closure at the end of the first word.

This stage saw the start of the use of inflections though probably not as yet with grammatical function but rather resulting from attention being paid to
less salient features,e.g. [dadaz dauu] 'dada's
towel',cf. [dada dau] in stage 4; [dadaz ɪʃ] 'dada's
fish'; [mɶ gḷeps] 'more grapes'. Function words too
began to appear, again showing an increase in perceptual
discrimination, the child now paying attention to the
weak unstressed words in adult utterances.

Examples:

[baʔ gɔn ɪn gɑ:dn]   'Bob's gone in the garden'.

[bɪʔ æ gaga]   'bit of tractor'.

[dada ən mama]   'dada and mama'.

The structure of three-word sentences was
mostly a combination of a familiar two-word sentence and
a one-word sentence, e.g. {mama gḷa gɔn} 'mama's glove's
gone' was a combination of the previously used {mama
gḷa} and {gɔn}; {oupʊ geit dædɪ} 'let's open the gate
for daddy' was a combination of {oupʊ geit} and {dædɪ}.
Four-word sentences were similarly combinations of
shorter sentences, e.g. {mɔ: bʊbaiɲ ækjʊ mama} 'more
pudding thank you mama' was a combination of {mɔ:
bʊbaiɲ} and {ækjʊ mama}. The early use of combinations
of ready-made utterances in the formation of longer
utterances has been pointed out and illustrated by
Clark in her study of her son's acquisition of English
syntax (Clark, 1974, and this volume). The other possibility was repeating one or more items as in {{tu:
æpl} {ʌn æpl}} 'two apples, one apple'; {{bʌbu:ɪn}
{bʌbu: ɪn}} = {bʌbu: ɪn}[2] 'let Bobby in, let Bobby in'.
The five-word sentences were very repetitive and of a
stereotyped structure such as was used by the mother
when pointing out and naming objects in the environment
or in picture books: {{mæm} {ɲaɲa mæm} {tu: mæm}}
'man, another man, two men'; {{bɛə} {ɲaɲa bɛə} {tu:
bɛə}} 'bear, another bear, two bears'.

To begin with, mostly familiar sounds (plosives and nasals) and mostly familiar words were used
in the three-, four- and five-word sentences and there

were not many contrasts within them, that is to say, the degree of syntagmatic differentiation was not great.

Examples:

Three-word sentences: {gou bæ æn} 'go back Anne'; {mama tou gɔn} 'mama's toe's gone'; {n̦o, ŋo, bʌbu:} 'no, no, Patrick'.

Four-word sentences: {a:l gɔɲ, nɶ̃ mɔ:} 'all gone, no more'; {baʔ gɔn ɪn gɑ:dn} 'Bob's gone in the garden'; {pɪˑ, pɪˑ, gaʊ, gaʊ} 'pig, pig, cow, cow'.

Five-word sentences: {pɪˑ, n̦an̦a pɪˑ, tu: pɪˑ} 'pig, another pig, two pigs'; {mæm, n̦an̦a mæm, tu: mæm} 'man, another man, two men'.

But at this time a few two-word sentences had the possibility of contrasts with liquids, [l, r], and sibilants, for example: {hʌḷou tʃi:z} 'hullo cheese'; {tu: t͜si:z} 'two cheeses'; {oʊpm gærɪʃ} 'open the garage'. Once again it is seen that new, longer utterances were first produced with familiar articulations and a relatively low degree of syntagmatic differentiation compared with the level of differentiation possible in shorter utterances.

Increase in complexity of the child's phonetics and phonology in relation to growth in vocabulary, syntax and amount of language use has now been demonstrated and as development continued along much the same lines, the last two stages are considered only very briefly.

Stage 6.   The rapid increase in vocabulary and amount of language use continued. Words were acquired in more differentiated form than before and those acquired earlier in reduplicated form became more differentiated. Some words were acquired in simple form but progressed rapidly to a closer match to the models, e.g. 'saucer' started as [ohə] and [œhə] and changed to [dʒodʒə] and then to [soʔsɔ]. More of the less salient sounds of the models were produced, for instance the lateral began to be used more freely and in several contexts: [el] 'letter ʻlʼ ', [tauəl] 'towel', [l̩ʌk] then [loc] 'lock', [klɔk] 'clock', [ʌl̩ɪ] 'elephant',[ʌl̩ɪ] 'lovely'[ʔelou] 'fellow', [bu:l̩uɲ] 'balloon'. The affricate [dʒ] became more common: [dʒan] 'John', [dʒan] 'swan'. The less salient nasals, those in unaccented intervocalic position began to be produced: [e:nɪ] for 'Rooney', previously [ehẽ]; [ʌnɪ] for 'honey', previously [ahu:]; and [enɪ] 'any'.

In addition to the repetitive type of three-syllable words, such as PV(PV)[2] [baikʊkʊ] 'bicycle', NV (PV)[2] [ma:toto] 'tomato', there were now some examples in which the three syllables differed, for example:

[piḑama] 'pyjamas', [u:brelə] "u' for umbrella' = 'umbrella', [bæcberi] 'blackberry' (which, however, soon
changed to the simpler two-syllable [bætɪ]). By the end
of this stage, the use of three-syllable words was beginning to increase but they were not yet widely used.
A five-syllable word appeared in a highly repetitive
form of 'tomato': [ma:totototo] N((PV)^2)^2. There was
now a wide range of different word structures.

Sentences of two, three and four words were
used freely in differentiated form. Five-word sentences
were used in repetitive and in differentiated form, the
latter being combinations of familiar shorter sentences.

Examples:

Repetitive: {{babɪ iə} {babɪ ŋaŋa iə}}
                 'Bobby's ear, Bobby's other ear'.

Differentiated: {mama, də:tɪ ænd ɔ: wet}
                  'mama, dirty hand's all wet'.

This was made up of three units: {mama}, {də:tɪ ænd}
and {ɔ: wet} which had all been used before. Six-word
sentences were repetitive only:

Repetitive: {{ʌn bʌbu: bu:t} {tu: bʌbu: bu:t}} 'one
Patrick's boot, two Patrick's boots'; {{mama nɪk} {mama
nicɪ mama gaga}} 'mama, look at Nick; mama Nicky is
using mama's tractor (grasscutter)'.

A few more inflected forms began to be used:
'ing' forms, e.g. [bə:dɪ ʔɪŋɪŋ] 'birdie's singing';
[mama kʌmmɪŋ] 'mamma's coming'; plural 's': [tu: pɪns
gɔn] 'the two pins have gone'; possessive 's': [mama's
dɑ:lɪ] 'mama's darling'; third person singular 's':
[iə kʌms dædɪ] 'here comes daddy'.

More function words came into use showing the
child's increasing awareness of the weak unstressed
words in the adult models. Some of the function words
(those underlined in the examples) harmonized with the
context as can be seen from the transcription.

Examples:

[bɪʔ ɪ dʑæm pʊpʊ] 'a bit of jam for my pudding'.

[bɪʔ ɪ ḑæm] 'a bit of a stamp'

[bʌbu: geʔ ʔə] 'Patrick will get it'.

[iŋk ek mama pɪn] 'ink out of mama's pen'.

[mama ɔʃ ɪt] 'mama 'll wash it'.

Stage 7. There was steady progress with increasing complexity at all levels. Continuant sounds were used in a wide range of contexts and the child was now responding to the least salient and the least easily discriminable sounds in the adult models, for instance, the liquids [r] and [l], the semi-vowels [j] and [w], and the fricatives [θ] and [ð] but he was not always producing them correctly. The previous uses of [w] were mostly not in the contexts where they occured in the adult models, for example [wæwæ] for 'barrow', [wæ] for 'fly'. Now [w] was used where the model had [w] but it was sometimes omitted: [wɛəz flai?] 'where's the fly?' but [mamaz ɔʃɪŋ] 'mama's washing'. [j] was used in initial position: [wɛə ɑ: ju en?] 'where are you 'n'?', [jes] 'yes'. [r] was variously [r], [j], [w] or [z], or nothing: [ri:d] 'read', [rʌn] or [ʌn] 'run'; [j] in [kjas] 'across', and in [kʌŋgiju:] 'kangaroo'; and [w] in [wʌnɪŋ] 'running', [kwʌs] 'cross' and [dʒafwɪ] 'Geoffrey', [z] in [zeizɪns] 'raisins'. Several clusters were now used: [pleɪɪŋ] 'playing', [glasɪs] 'glasses', [blou] 'blow', [klous] 'clothes', [twɛəf] 'twelve', [flai] 'fly', [stjʌc] 'struck', [tʂi:] 'tree'. The child responded to adult [θ] and [ð] with sibilants, labio-dental fricatives and the glottal stop: [fu:] 'through', [wɪf] 'with', [zɪs] and [ʔɪs] 'this', [zɛə] 'there'.

Pronouns and the copula began to be used and the number of unstressed words per sentence increased; by the end of the stage more than one often occurred, for instance: {'ketu 'sɪŋɪŋ, is 'goɪn tə'boɪʊ} 'the kettle is singing, it's going to boil'; {'kʌp 'ti: fɔ: 'bʌbu:, 'pɔ:r it ɪn 'bʌbu:s 'kʌp} 'a cup of tea for Patrick, pour it in Patrick's cup'; {'wɔt ə jʊ 'gɔt ɪn mai 'hænd? } 'what have I got in my hand?'; {'iəs mai 'tauzəz fə 'mʌmɪ} 'here's my trousers for mummy'; {'mænz nʌt̚ 'kwʌʂ, 'es iʔ?} 'the man's not cross, is he?'; {'zis ʌns vɔ: 'mama, 'zɪs ʌns vɔ: 'bʌbu:} 'this one's for mama, this one's for Patrick'. As may be seen from the examples, utterance length increased to eight and nine words.

Some inflections with grammatical function were now used fairly regularly. For instance, the plural: [tu: βa:s] 'two flowers', [tu: waɪs] 'two flies', [ɪtɪ bai i:tɪŋ bʌbus zeizɪns] 'little boy eating Patrick's raisins'; possessive 's': [beibɪz piɭou] 'baby's pillow', [bʌbu:s tʃɛə] 'Patrick's chair', [bʌbu: af mamas peɲ] 'Patrick wants to have mama's pen'; third person singular present: [bʌbu: a:s mamaz ʔɔʃɪŋ] 'Patrick hears mama's washing', [bʌbu: ɔnts pendil] 'Patrick wants a pencil', [ɔf mama gous] 'off mama goes'. Past tense forms were also used, e.g. [bʌbu: gɪt̚ blænkɪt] (said when the child was going off to get the blanket) and [bʌbu: gɔt blænkɪt] (said when he came back with it), [mama du: ɪt] (a request for something to be done) and [mama du:d ɪt] (when it was done).

436

It was towards the end of this stage that the greatest increase in grammatical complexity took place and it is significant that it did not take place until the vocabulary was quite large, language use was quite fluent and the phonological system was well-developed, and the child was able to pay attention to and discriminate the weak, non-salient stretches of the adult models.

SUMMARY

Growth in length and in complexity of syllable, word, and sentence is now summarized below.

Growth in Complexity and Length of Syllable and Word. The first words were mostly monosyllabic and the structure thus coincided with that of syllables so a separate account of syllable structure is not given. The first monosyllabic words had the structures CV, VC, CVC; the ones of greatest length being those of the CVC and some of the CV structures. The first few CVC words had a contrast at the onset and ending, e.g. [boun] 'bone', but when the vocabulary was expanding rapidly, words of such structure had a sameness in place and manner of articulation at the onset and ending; this may be viewed as a repetition of a consonant within the syllable, i.e.

CVC　　[gʌk] $\underset{\smile}{\text{CVP}}_k$　　[beip] $\underset{\smile}{\text{CVP}}_p$　　[mu:m] $\underset{\smile}{\text{CVN}}_p$

These later became differentiated, with contrasts at onset and ending: [trʌk], [greip], [mu:n].

Two-syllable words at first had open syllables only and a repeated syllable so no consonantal contrasts were involved, e.g. [be:be:] 'biscuit'. The two syllables gradually became differentiated: [bebit],[bɪkɪʔ].

The first three-syllable words similarly had no closed syllables and had a repeated syllable. They consisted of a combination of a single syllable and a repeated one, e.g. [banana] $PV(NV)^2$, [pe:toto] $PV(PV)^2$. Gradually more complex structures came into use: $(NV)^2LVP$ [me:me:lot], $P(V)^2FV$ [gahava], and these were followed by fully differentiated ones: PLVPVPVS [plætɪpʊs] 'platypus', PVSVPV [taisɪkʊ] 'tricycle'.

The first four-syllable word was similarly repetitive: [ma:tota:to] C(VCV)C(VCV) and consisted of familiar syllables with a simple contrast of N and P: N(VPV)P(VPV).

The first five-syllable word was another form of 'tomato' and was also very repetitive: [ma:totototo] $CV((CV)^2)^2$ again with the familiar contrast of NV and PV: $NV((PV)^2)^2$.

It has been seen that one-syllable words and reduplicated syllable words were used before differentiated two-syllable words were acquired. Three-syllable words followed slowly until differentiated two-syllable words were being used freely, and it was some time before four- and five-syllable words came to be used regularly, in fact, not until after the age of two. How greater differentiation took place within words over a period of time in the same child's phonological development has been described in separate studies (Waterson, 1970, 1976), the phenomenon being essentially the same, a wider use of the familiar appearing to make possible the production of what was new, in this case the use of more familiar features and a minimum of syntagmatic differentiation when a new contrast was being attempted.

Growth in Complexity and Length of Sentence. Increase in length and complexity of sentence shows a parallel to that of syllable and word. Speech began with one-word sentences and the first two-word sentences were mostly repetitive:

[gɔn, gɔn] 'gone, gone' {gɔn}^{2} cf. the structure of

[gɑ:, gɑ:] 'car, car' {gɑ:}^{2} the first two-syllable words: (CV)^2

Differentiated, non-repetitive two-word sentences, consisting of familiar words began to be used more:

[mama gɔn] 'mama's gone' {mama gɔn}

[mɔ: di:] 'more cheese' {mɔ: di:}

and when they outnumbered the repetitive type and were used freely, three-word sentences came into use. These mainly consisted of a combination of familiar shorter sentences, that is to say, they consisted of familiar ready-made units; for instance {mama gḷa gɔn} 'mama's glove's gone' consisted of the frequently used {mama gḷa} and the very common {gɔn} and {mæ ge:k dada} 'more cake dada' was made up of {mæ ge:k}, the usual request for cake, together with the name of the person to whom the request was addressed, the familiar {dada}. These may be compared with the structure of the first three-syllable words which were a combination of familiar syllables, PV and NV: PV(NV)^2 and PV(PV)^2.

Sentences of four and more words were also first repetitive in form:

Four-word sentence:

{ɑ: ba:, ɑ: ba:} 'ah Bob, ah Bob' {ɑ: ba:}^{2}

{dada di:, dada di:} 'dada's tea, dada's tea' {dada di:}^{2}

Five-word sentence:

{bɛə, ŋaŋa bɛə, tu: bɛə} 'bear, another, bear,
                                two bears'

{{bɛə} {ŋaŋa bɛə} {tu: bɛə}}

Gradually, when more of the differentiated type began to be used, even longer sentences came into use, as seen in stage 7.

CONCLUSIONS

It has been shown that increase in length and in complexity of the syllable took place in a similar way to that of monosyllabic words. A parallel in the way one-, two-, three-, four-, and five-syllable words were acquired is evident in that increase in length first took place by the repetition of some part or by the use of what was familiar, i.e. CV syllables and P and N systems. This same kind of process was seen in the increase of sentence length and complexity which was achieved by the repetition of words or by the use of a combination of familiar short sentences. There was thus a parallel in the way increase in length and complexity (syntagmatic differentiation) took place at the levels of syllable, word, and sentence. The similarity of this to Piaget's vertical décalage was pointed out to the writer by G.P. Ivimey, University of London, Institute of Education (personal communication).[3]

Growth at the phonetic and phonological levels has been seen to be from the simple to the complex. When speech first began, the syllables, words and sentences were of very simple structure and were short in length. Increase in complexity first took place in single syllable words and sentences and when there was an increase in word and sentence length, there was no great increase in their complexity. Through the use of the familiar, sentences of greater complexity and greater length were produced than would otherwise have been possible at the particular stage of development; progress was thus closely related to the use of what was familiar. Words and sentences with repeated elements were used frequently to begin with when the particular structure involved was becoming assimilated into the phonological system. The number of repetitive elements gradually decreased and the differentiated increased.

From the account given in this paper, it has been seen that increase in utterance length involves greater complexity not only in terms of the number of syllables within a word, or of words within a sentence but also in relation to the degree of differentiation or number of contrasts within the syllable, word and sentence, whether the articulations involved are new or familiar, whether the consonants at the beginning and ending of a syllable are the same or different, new or familiar, and whether there is a high or low degree of differentiation within the words concerned. This suggests that phonetic and phonological complexity brings its own constraints on utterance length.

The fact that new, longer utterances were first produced with familiar articulations and a relatively low degree of syntagmatic differentiation compared with the level of differentiation possible in shorter utterances leads to the speculation that as far as processes of planning and production are concerned, the overall complexity of longer utterances with a low level of syntagmatic differentiation does not greatly exceed that of shorter utterances consisting of fewer items but having a higher degree of differentiation. The selection of items from the memory store and their arrangement in a particular sequence must in itself involve quite complex operations so the structure of longer utterances must be relatively simple at first. If this were not so, children would start using longer utterances much earlier than they do. Further support for this speculation comes from the fact that longer utterances are produced by repetition and by the combination of established units: either syllables, words, or short sentences; the use of repetition and of established, ready-made units must economize on planning. Further careful observations and testing are needed to assess the validity of this speculation.

This particular child's language development was especially patterned and systematic. Being highly intelligent,[4] he may have hit on a useful strategy early which enabled him to process speech efficiently. On the other hand, it is possible that this systematicity became evident because the child happened to be very vocal and was recorded daily, so that most phases of development were captured. Whatever the reason may be, the evidence suggests that similar neural processes were at work in his processing of syllables, words and sentences. It is interesting that the same kind of growth in complexity at word level has been reported in the phonological development of a Spanish-speaking child (Marlys Macken, Stanford Child Language Project; personal communication); similar use of the familiar when learning the new has been reported in the emergence of language from babbling in a study of a Thai baby (Tuaycharoen, 1977), and the use of ready-made units has already been demonstrated in the acquisition of syntax (e.g. Clark, 1974). The same sort of repetitive and differentiated use of words in early sentences has been noted in the literature both for English, for instance Bloom (1973) and in other languages, for example in Dutch, by Schaerlaekens (1973). It is thus likely that this type of development is not idiosyncratic to the child reported on here.

It has been demonstrated that at first increase in complexity does not take place at the same rate and at the same time at all the different levels of language. The semantic level and cognitive development have not been considered in this paper but it may well be that these are the levels at which progress is fastest as so much depends on the child's understanding of the world around him for his language learning (cf. Slobin, 1973). Language learning is very individual. Some children may advance faster at one level than at another and it may be that not all advance at the phonetic and phonological levels so far ahead of syntax as the subject of this paper, cf. for instance Joan Velten, whose phonetic and phonological development was relatively slow (Velten, 1943). A great deal more work needs to be done before general statements can be made.

The main conclusions that can be drawn from the observations presented in this paper may be summarized as follows. The evidence suggests that the principle of vertical décalage may apply at the level of language learning - further studies are needed to test this. The major constraints on utterance length (leaving aside the question of cognitive constraints) depend on structural complexity and non-familiarity at the various interrelated levels of language. Language experience makes familiar what has been acquired and hence enables progress to be made in the acquisition of what is new; thus experience of language is clearly an essential part of the process of language learning just as experience is necessary for the acquisition of other human skills. The child's ability to process language is very limited at first and he operates within his limits so that when there is a major advance at one level there may be little or no progress at others. The acquisition of word forms first takes place by processing each item as an individual unit, but later, learning proceeds by pattern recognition, and classification is by pattern as well as by individual item so that speech processing becomes more efficient and the rate of learning increases.

Longitudinal studies of a larger number of children and in relation to different languages, showing the interrelations of development at the various levels of language may show that what has been illustrated here is typical of language development. It may be that such studies could lead to a better understanding of how speech is processed. A practical advantage of this type of analysis is that it provides a means for assessing the relative complexity of words and sentences by taking into account the number of syntagmatic contrasts involved. Such an analysis is more complicated than MLU (mean length of utterance) as a way of arriving at some kind of comparability in the language development of children but it provides some indication of what is within his capacity at the particular time. This could be very important for the teaching of the deaf and those with language disorders.

Notes.

1. Difference of place of articulation within a syllable must involve some difficulty in production because the majority of children's early words have open syllables and do not have such contrasts.

2. The question of whether one-word utterances are sentences or not is irrelevant to this paper; they are referred to as sentences for convenience of exposition, but see Dore, 1975, for a discussion of the problem.

3. For Piaget's 'vertical décalage' see Sinha and Walkerdine, this volume.

4. The child has always been around two years ahead of his peers at school.

REFERENCES

Bloom, L. (1970) Language Development: Form and Function in Emerging Grammars. M.I.T. Press, Cambridge, Mass.

Bloom, L. (1973) One Word at a Time: The Use of Single-word Utterances before Syntax. Mouton, The Hague.

Bruner, J.S. (1975) The Ontogenesis of Speech Acts. Journal of Child Language 2. 1-19.

Clark, R. (1974) Performing without Competence. Journal of Child Language 1. 1-10.

Dore, J. (1975) Holophrases, Speech Acts and Language Universals. Journal of Child Language 2. 21-40.

Ferguson, C.A. and Farwell, C.B. (1973) Words and Sounds in Early Language Acquisition: Early Initial Consonants in the First 50 Words. Papers and Reports on Child Language Development 6. Stanford University. 1-60.

Halliday, M.A.K. (1975) Learning How to Mean - Explorations in the Development of Language. Arnold, London.

442

Jones, D. (1962)   An Outline of English Phonetics (9th edition). Heffer, Cambridge.

Schaerlaekens, A.M. (1973)   The Two-word Sentence in Child Language Development. Mouton, The Hague.

Slobin, D.I. (1973)   Cognitive Prerequisites for the Development of Grammar. In C.A. Ferguson and D.I. Slobin (eds.) Studies of Child Language Development. Holt, Rinehart and Winston, New York.

Tuaycharoen, P.   (1977)   The Babbling of a Thai Baby; from Early Communicative Interaction to Speech. Thesis for the Ph.D., University of London.

Velten, H.V. (1943)   The Growth of Phonemic and Lexical Patterns in Infant Language. Language 19. 281-292.

Waterson, N. (1970)   Some Speech Forms of an English Child: a Phonological Study. Transactions of the Philological Society 1-24.

Waterson, N. (1971a)   Child Phonology: a Prosodic View. Journal of Lingustics 7. 179-211.

Waterson, N. (1971b)   Child Phonology: a Comparative View. Transactions of the Philological Society 34-50.

Waterson, N. (1971c)   Some Views on Speech Perception. Journal of the International Phonetic Association 1. 81-96.

Waterson, N. (1976)   Perception and Production in the Acquisition of Phonology. In W. von Raffler-Engel and Y. Lebrun (eds.) Baby Talk and Infant Speech. Swets and Zeitlinger, Amsterdam.

Waterson, N. (Forthcoming)   A Prosodic Approach to Language Acquisition: the Phonological Systems of an English Child.

Weir, R.H. (1962)   Language in the Crib. Mouton, The Hague.

Informativeness, Presupposition, and Semantic Choice in Single-word Utterances

P. M. Greenfield

This study of development within the period
of single-word utterances indicates that children acquire the ability to express a variety of semantic functions during this period. They do so by combining a
single word with a variety of situational elements - gesture, object, person, etc. But given that in any particular situation the child is limited to but one verbal
element, is it possible to characterize which situational
element is selected for linguistic encoding? This is the
problem to which this paper is addressed. My hypothesis
is that the principle of informativeness can generally explain which element is selected. Informativeness is used
in the information theory sense of uncertainty. Uncertainty exists where there are possible alternatives. But uncertainty must be defined from the child-speaker's point
of view. Information in this sense, then, is relative to
the child. The question has been raised (D. Crystal, Symposium discussion) as to how, in principle, for this stage
of development, can you know that the intuitions of uncertainty and informativeness that you have can be ascribed
to the child? Linguistics as a discipline has been accustomed to taking language as a privileged type of behaviour. If we accord equal weight to behaviour in other
modes, the problem is no more serious at the one-word stage
than at later points in the language acquisition process.
In fact, we are always in the position of making inferences
about mental processes from regularities in external behaviour. In the case of uncertainty and informativeness,
these regularities can be specified by sets of rules appropriate to different types of referential situation. .

This distinction between information and certainty is the psychological basis for the distinction between assertion and presupposition in language. One type of presupposition is pragmatic presupposition, the appropriate context for uttering a sentence (Keenan, 1971). Presumably then, the pragmatic assertion would be the sentence itself. A pragmatic presupposition is assumed rather than stated. I want to show that this parallels the situation in single-word utterances: what, from the child's point of view, can be assumed is not stated; what cannot be assumed or taken for granted is given verbal expression by the single word. And it is the relatively certain element that is assumed, the relatively uncertain one that is stated. In this way, the cognitive distinction between certainty and uncertainty forms the psychological basis for the linguistic distinction between presupposition and assertion.

Logical presupposition is closely related to pragmatic presupposition, but involves a relation between sentences rather than between a sentence and its nonverbal context. One sentence presupposes another just in case the truth of the second sentence is a necessary condition for the truth or falsity of the first. The major psychological relation between the two concepts of presupposition is that a pragmatic presupposition is represented nonverbally, whereas a logical presupposition is a linguistic form. Another hypothesis of this paper is that the psychological basis for logical presupposition lies in early dialogue.

I shall illustrate these notions with one type of situation involving an inanimate object undergoing changes of state. The concept of informativeness will be used to predict when the child will encode the object verbally and when he will encode the change of state. Discourse must be drawn from a point in development where there is evidence that a child is capable of expressing both alternatives - object and state change. I shall, furthermore, analyze a discourse sample where it is known that the child has the vocabulary to encode either element because both kinds of element are in fact encoded at different times during the discourse. But which element will be expressed when? I should like to argue that there is a set of rules based on the concept of informativeness which can make such predictions; the rules are as follows:

(1)   When an object is not in the child's possession, it becomes more uncertain; in this case his first utterance will encode the object.

(2)   When the object is securely in the child's possession while it is undergoing its process or state change, the object becomes relatively certain and is not encoded first. Instead, action or state change is encoded first. (The

idea of using distance from the child as a way
of assessing informativeness in situations involving an object undergoing actions comes from
Veneziano (1973).)

(3)   Once the most uncertain or informative element in
the situation has been encoded, be it object or
action/state, it becomes more certain and less
informative. At this point, then, if the child
continues to encode the situation verbally, he
will now express the other aspect, heretofore
unstated.

The scene presented in Table 1 illustrates the
application of these rules; it involves the object word
car and three action or state changes, byebye, down and
beepbeep. The data come from a larger longitudinal study
of two children, Matthew and Nicky (Greenfield and Smith,
1976). One can look at the use of these words in the ongoing situation to see whether Matthew's choice of object
(car) rather than one of the action/state words (byebye,
down, beepbeep) reflects informational properties of the
situation.

At the beginning of the scene (Table 1), Matthew
names an absent object. Its action/state is known from
the noise; uncertainty lies in the identity of the invisible object. Hence in choosing car rather than byebye,
Matthew is encoding the most informative aspect of the
situation. (If, in this situation, he had said byebye
rather than car, his utterance would have been in viola-
tion of Rule 1, which states that the child's first utterance should encode the object if it is at a distance from
the child.) Once, however, the identity of the car is
established by his utterance and his mother's questions,
What's the car doing? Where's it going?, action/state
becomes less certain relative to object and Matthew responds byebye. Here dialogue turns pragmatic presupposition into a primitive form of logical presupposition, for
the questions actually represent linguistically two
possible presuppositions of Matthew's assertion byebye:
The car is doing; the car is going. Next, Matthew wants
his own car, but he is at a distance from it, and so his
possession is relatively uncertain. At this point he encodes the object. Next, he is pushing his car, now in
his possession and its identity established by the preceding utterance. Uncertainty now shifts to its action/
state, and he encodes it with byebye, hmm (if one wants
to consider this imitation of a motor noise to be a
word), and beepbeep. Next, however, he hears an invisible
car pass by outside and so he goes back to car rather than
byebye.

In the next scene his own car has fallen down
and so he encodes the object rather than its action/state,
for as the object, his own car is no longer a certainty

TABLE 1.   Object and Action/State Discourse at 1;6.18.

Preceding context	Speaker action	Object action
	M hears	car going by outside
		car
What's the car		
doing?		
Where's it going?	M	byebye:byebye
	M pointing to	his car
	whining	car, car
You want your car?	M about to push	his car byebye
	M pushing .	his car byebye
		hmm (car sound)
	M patting	his car beepbeep
	M hears	car going by outside
		car! car!
	M hears	car going by outside
		car
	M looking for	car has fallen down
	whining	car
Whatcha doing?	M throwing	his car down
		down, down
	M has thrown	car down
		car
	M hears	car going by outside
		car
	M looking for	his car
		car

Note: Solid horizontal lines indicate intervening child speech. Broken horizontal lines indicate no intervening child speech, but intervening adult speech.   M=Matthew. Underlining indicates speech while non-underlining describes the nonverbal aspects of the referential situation. For each speech event, the child's utterance is placed under the single element in the situation that has been given verbal expression.   The first column under speaker action identifies the speaker, the second, his action or state.   Similarly, the first column under object action identifies the object, the second its action or state.

for him. Note here that informative and 'new' are not identical for Matthew. The concept that an assertion encodes
'new' information while a presupposition contain the 'old'
(or 'given') is the basis for some adult psycholinguistic
experiments by Haviland and Clark (1974). Applying this
notion to the present situation, we would be led to the
prediction that Matthew would now encode the 'new' change
of state (down) rather than the 'old' object (car). But the
opposite is the case, as Table 1 shows. Although car is
'old' in the scene, it is uncertain because it is out of his
grasp. Thus, for nonverbal context, no simple equation of
informativeness with new information is possible even though
the perception of information functions as the psychological
basis for the given-new contrast. Other attributes defining
the child's perception of the ongoing situation must also be
taken into account.

The analysis continues with the next scene.
Matthew now has car in hand and is throwing it down; object has become relatively more certain, action/state relatively less. Mother asks Whatcha doing? and Matthew
says down as we would predict. (While Matthew's utterance is preceded by a question, this particular question
does not presuppose either the object or its action/state.)
Note that this scene is the only one that begins with the
expression of action/state rather than object and, correlatively, is the only one that begins with object in
hand. It thus confirms the importance of physical
possession as a psychological criterion of certainty from
the child's point of view. Once the car has been thrown
down and its action/state expressed, object certainty de-
creases, and Matthew now expresses the object, car. In
the next scene Matthew once again names an absent car
which he hears going by outside. Finally, Matthew names
the object he is searching for. Thus, Matthew's choice
of object or action/state word accurately reflects the
continually shifting balance between information and
certainty.

Table 2 presents another example of this type
of analysis applied to Matthew's corpus, this one involving another object and situation and occurring about
a month later. In these scenes, Matthew is having difficulty getting his skates on and off. Therefore, trying to look at the situation from Matthew's point of view,
we conclude that action/state is more in question, is less
taken for granted, under present circumstances than is
the object. Hence, we would expect more frequent expression of action/state than object, which is exactly what we
find. In fact, action/state is expressed six times, object only three. Let us compare these scenes with those
presented in Table 1. In the latter, the object was often
out of hand, and, correlatively, was expressed relatively
more often than in the former.

In the first scene presented in Table 2, object
is expressed when it is not yet in Matthew's possession,

TABLE 2.   Object and Action/State Discourse at 1;7.21

Preceding context	Modality	Event
	M goes over to and ˎ picks up	skates (s)ka(tes)
	M trying to put whining repeats	skates on on (s)ka(tes)
	M trying to put whining repeats	skates on on
	M has put down trying to put whining	skates skates on (s)ka(tes)
They go outside		
Do you want to put your skates on?		yeah
	M holding onto skates whining	on, on
a skate?	M whining	on yeah
		Mother putting on skates ashoe
	M whining	on
	M whining	ashoe, ashoe
	M tugging	skates off on

Note: Solid horizontal lines indicate intervening child
speech.   Broken horizontal lines indicate no intervening
child speech, but intervening adult speech. M=Matthew.
Underlining indicates speech while non-underlining describes the nonverbal aspects of the referential situation.
For each speech event, the child's utterance is placed
under the single element in the situation that has been
given verbal expression.   The first column under speaker
action identifies the speaker, the second, his action or
state.   Similarly, the first column under object action
identifies the object, the second its action or state.

hence, relatively uncertain from his point of view.
Next time the object, (s)ka(tes), is uttered, it is
after on; in other words, action/state has become a
known because of Matthew's previous utterance. In the
second scene, skates occurs at the one point that the
skates are not in Matthew's hands. Here, the object
has become relatively less certain, and this uncertainty
is resolved with skates. In the final scene, skates are
all too much connected with Matthew, and he restricts
himself to encoding action/state, again in accord with
the prediction from an informational analysis.

Comparing sequences of single-word utterances
to two-word utterances proper, one sees that the former
clearly lack the fixed word order of English syntax. A
sequence is defined as a succession of single-word utterances encoding different aspects of a single referential
situation. For instance, at the top of Table 2, 'Matthew
goes over to and picks up his skates' is considered one
referential event, 'Matthew trying to put skates on' a
second one. A single sequence cannot span the two events.
In the examples, for instance, object sometimes preceded
action/state, as in car. byebye, (Table 1) while the reverse order also occurred as in on. skates. (Table 2)
This analysis of scenes involving the encoding of objects and their actions or states indicates that word
order in sequences of single-word utterances reflects the
shifting pattern of uncertainty in the ongoing event, as
seen from the child's point of view. If so, then the addition of English syntax with the onset of two-word
utterances means that the child has learned that a fixed
word-order rule must override the informational structure of the situation as a determinant of word order.
The child temporarily loses the ability to use word order
to signal the difference between relatively certain and
uncertain aspects of the situation. This ability does
not return until years later when the child learns how to
use certain surface structure syntactic devices involving
variable word order to signal the topic-comment distinction, for example (Hornby, 1971).

An important point is the continuity between
psycholinguistic functioning in infancy and adulthood.
This is demonstrated by telegraphic ellipsis in adult
speech, for it requires nonverbal context in order to be
comprehended (Holzman, 1971). Holzman presents an example
in which one person says to another, pretty dress. Its
comprehension depends on following the speaker's gaze to
someone wearing a dress. The perception of someone wearing a particular dress is pragmatically presupposed by
the assertion pretty dress.

In adult speech, as in child speech, there is
also continuity between the role of verbal context and
nonverbal situational structure. Consider the following
example from Holzman's (1971) article:

Question:	Answer:
<u>When are you going?</u>	<u>Tonight</u>

Clearly the single-word utterance is perfectly natural
in adult conversation. The response presupposes the proposition <u>You are going</u> contained in the question; this
functions as 'old' information. Only the 'new' information is expressed in the answer.

Adult-child dialogue at the stage of single-
word utterances involves exactly the same process as that
described for the adult-adult example just given. Compare
this example from Nicky, the other child in the study,
spoken at 1;6.4:

Question:	Answer:
<u>What do you want?</u>	<u>Showel</u> (shovel)

Again, the answer supplies all the information the ques-
tioner was seeking (new information) and no more. What
is presupposed from the question - <u>You</u> (the child) <u>want</u>
<u>something</u> - is not expressed in the answer. Hence,
single-word answers to questions follow the same principle as spontaneous single-word utterances: express
the single most informative element; and this principle
operates for both children and adults in dialogue. Thus,
when the child's utterance is produced in relation to
verbal context, the certain element is the 'old' information, 'given' in the preceding utterance. The uncertain element expressed verbally by the child is thus always 'new' information as defined by Haviland and Clark
(1974) after Chafe (1970). The situation for dialogue
thus contrasts with single-word utterances produced in
relation to purely nonverbal context: the informative
element is always 'new' information. The perceptual/
cognitive distinction between information and certainty
on the nonverbal plane is, through further development,
thus transformed into the beginnings of the given-new
distinction on the verbal plane.

I have developed other rules which make similar predictions about semantic choice in other types of
situation. For instance, in the case of scenes involving an agent and his or her action, the child generally
takes the agent for granted and encodes the action. Agent
uncertainty seems to arise for the child in particular
kinds of situation: (1) in the case of absent agents, as
when the child names a person whom he can hear making a
noise in another room; (2) when there is conflict over
agency, a question in the child's mind as to who should
perform some action; (3) when the child desires a change
of agent. In these cases the child will encode agent
rather than action or state. An example of the first
sort occurs at 1;1.3 when Matthew says <u>daddy</u> upon hearing

his father, not yet visible, come in the outside door
and start up the steps to his apartment. An example of
the second sort is documented in the film Early Words
(Greenfield, May and Bruner, 1972) at 22 months of age.
Matthew says self, trying to discourage his mother from
buttering his bread for him so that he could carry out
the action himself. An example of the third sort occurs
at 1;7.4. Matthew has been trying unsuccessfully to cut
his meat with a knife, when he hands the knife, an in-
strument, to his mother, saying mummy. Here the Agent
case is again used to signal a desired change of actor.
Another example illustrates the same point, but both alternative Agents are verbalized. At 1;8.10 Matthew's
sister Lauren says Let me do it; Matthew answers mummy,
explicitly replacing the Agent of the verbal context, me,
with mummy. This is also an example of paradigmatic substitution: that is, mummy can fill the same semantic/
grammatical spot as me in the sentence Let me do it. The
reply mummy presupposes someone will do it. This proposition is also presupposed by the original utterance Let
me do it; it is thus 'old' information. Once again, the
child's answer expresses only 'new'information.

The principal difference between the young
child at the single-word stage and the adult is that the
adult is capable of adding words when the information
cannot be transmitted by nonverbal context, whereas the
child is not. Despite this difference, ellipsis, incomplete sentences formed by adults, shows that basically
the same process of information analysis described for
earliest child language operates in adult speech. Because children generally talk about the here and now, a
common process of information analysis means that an
adult will often analyze a given referential situation
in the same way as the child. This commonality does not
in any way imply that the child speaker is aware of the
listener's perspective, of what might be 'old' or 'new'
information for the listener. The power of a process of
information extraction common to child and adult is that
it can make verbal communication between child and adult
possible long before the child has developed any such
awareness of the listener's point of view. A cognitive
process common to mature speakers and language learners
thus enables the still egocentric child to communicate
from an impressively early point in the language learning process.

REFERENCES

Chafe, W.L. (1970)   Meaning and the Structure of Lan-
        guage. University of Chicago Press, Chicago.

452

Greenfield, P.M. and Smith, J.H. (1976)   The Structure of Communication in Early Language Development. Academic Press, New York.

Haviland, S.E. and Clark, H.H. (1974)   What's New? Acquiring New Information as a Process in Comprehension. Journal of Verbal Learning and Verbal Behavior 13.   512-521.

Holzman, M.S. (1971)   Ellipsis in Discourse: Implications for Linguistic Analysis by Computer, the Child's Acquisition of Language, and Semantic Theory. Language and Speech 14.   86-98.

Hornby, P.A. (1971)   Surface Structure and the Topic-comment Distinction: a Developmental Study. Child Development 42.   1975-88.

Keenan, E.L. (1971)   Two Kinds of Presupposition in Natural Language.   In C.J. Fillmore and D. Langendoen (eds.) Studies in Linguistic Semantics.   Holt, Rinehart and Winston,   New York.

Veneziano, E. (1973)   Analysis of Wish Sentences in the One-word Stage of Language Acquisition: a Cognitive Approach.   Unpublished master's thesis, Tufts University.

Pragmatic Constraints on the Linguistic Realization of `Semantic Intentions´ in Early Child Language

M. Miller

The aim of this paper is (a) to point out some reasons for the theoretical and empirical inadequacy of the concept of 'reduction transformations' which developmental psycholinguists following Bloom (1970) have used to describe and explain the elliptical linguistic realization of 'semantic intentions' in early child speech (one-, two-, and three-word-utterances) and (b) to present empirical evidence for the assumption that already at this developmental stage children vary the degree of the linguistic realization of 'semantic intentions' in a systematic manner and that an analysis of pragmatic regularities, which define this systematic behaviour, can answer certain open questions in the reconstruction of a logic of early syntactic development (developmental grammar).

The data on which this paper is based derive from a longitudinal study ('Kognitive und soziale Determinanten des Spracherwerbs') of the language acquisition of two middle-class children and one lower-class child (from the 17th month until the end of the 4th year). This language acquisition project, which is financially supported by the Max-Planck-Institut für Bildungsforschung (Berlin), has been running under the writer's direction since September 1971 at the Deutsches Seminar, Universität Frankfurt. The analyses, which

are briefly discussed in this paper, are considered
more extensively in Miller (1976), a report on the
first phase of that project.

THE INADEQUACY OF THE CONCEPT OF 'REDUCTION TRANS-FORMATIONS'

Bloom (1970) introduced the concept of 'reduction transformations' in order to describe and explain the now generally accepted observation that the
child usually intends to convey with his utterances
more structural meaning to his hearer than an analysis
of the surface forms of these utterances alone would
indicate. This observation can be traced back to the
method of 'rich interpretation' (cf. Brown (1973) and
Miller (1976)), which for its part has been justified
by certain discovery procedures such as 'replacement
sequences' and the distribution of explicitly expressed
semantic relations in an extensive corpus of a child's
utterances.

Bloom tries to account for the observed regularities of child ellipsis by postulating 'reduction
transformations' whose mode of operation is restricted
by certain conditions which reflect a cognitive limita-
tion of the child (in Bloom's own words: 'an inability
to carry the full structural load of the underlying representation' (1970:169)). Another explanation has
been given by Fodor, Bever, and Garrett (1974), who
suggested a 'mechanical computational constraint'.

There are many theoretical and empirical arguments (cf. Miller, 1976) which show that the concept of
'reduction transformations' and the 'cognition hypothesis' (cf. Cromer, 1974) alone represent an inadequate
solution to the description and explanation of child
ellipsis. This paper will, however, be confined to two
crucial counter-arguments to the conception of 'reduction transformations':

1. If children's 'reductions' are not random but rule-
governed (in a stronger sense than mere compliance with
a gradually rising complexity limit of surface structure
forms) the question arises: what, in Bloom's formal
treatment of 'reduction transformations', determines
which categories of the syntactic deep structure are eliminated in the resulting surface structure? Bloom suggests only that cognitive and linguistic constraints
interact in some as yet unspecified manner to influence
the transformationally derived surface structure form.
This statement has neither descriptive nor explanatory
value. Bloom's analysis essentially fails to account
for the rules underlying 'reduction' in early child
language.

2. The notion of 'reduction' as an aspect of the child's syntactic competence and the notion of 're- duction' as a mechanical computational constraint' give the appearance of irrelevance to the observation that certain surface structure forms, which are <u>pre- dicted</u> by Bloom's grammar, nevertheless do <u>not</u> occur in the very extensive corpora of children's utterances studied by the writer. This observation, however, can be given an interesting and systematic interpretation within a theoretical framework different from either Bloom's 'reduction transformations' or Fodor, Bever, and Garrett's 'mechanical computational constraint'.

In what follows it will be argued that there are pragmatic constraints which explain the system of children's 'reductions' or better, the rules of ellipsis in early child language. This, it would seem, speaks in favour of a position which holds that an adequate ana- lysis of the syntactic development of the child necessi- tates an investigation of his developing '<u>communicative competence</u>'.

CONTEXT-REFERENTIAL (DEICTIC) ACTS AND ELLIPSIS

Let us assume for a moment that a child, pro- ducing the two-word utterance <u>schuhe an</u> 'shoes on' with a certain terminal intonation contour (cf. the investi- gation of the correspondence between different terminal intonation contours and different types of illocutionary acts in early child language in Miller, 1976) conveys to his mother the meaning: 'Mother, please put my shoes on' by constraining the choice among potential nonverbal constituents of his utterance to a very narrow set of cognitive elements which are available perceptually, in- tentionally, or in immediate memory (cf. Rommetveit, 1968). This assumption, however, would normally pre- suppose fully developed role-taking on both sides of the verbal interaction, that is to say: a communicative competence a child of that age does not yet possess. But what then makes communication between children, younger than two years, and their parents function so well? There are at least two reasons:

1. There is from the outset a restricted sphere of discourse between the child and his parents.

2. There are certain context-referential acts (cf. Miller, 1976), which describe and explain the regulari- ties of the child's verbal reductions. So a child, at a given complexity limit of the surface structure of his utterances, from a communicatively egocentric per- spective (unconsciously) ensures that the full meaning of his elliptical utterances will be grasped by a hearer.

Take, for example, the following utterances of Simone (utterances of the child are on the left, utterances of adults are on the right. M = mother, Ma = Max Miller = Simone's father). The nonlinguistic context and certain paralinguistic features of utterances are represented within square brackets. Paralinguistic vocalizations are represented within parenthesis. The symbols ⁻, ´, ˋ at the end of children's utterances distinguish progredient, rising, and falling terminal intonation contours. The age of the children is stated in years, months and weeks thus: 1;9.2=1 year 9 months, 2 weeks. MLU signifies the mean length of utterance of the child. For further symbols used in the transcript please cf. Miller (1976):

Simone (age: 1;9.2/MLU: 1.09)

(a)

                [Simone and her parents are taking a walk in a park]
[Simone is sitting in a baby carriage]
[Simone's parents meet friends and talk to them]

runter⁻ [wants to get out of
'down'   the carriage]

                [Simone's parents continue to converse with their friends]

raus⁻ [complaining]
'out'

(whines)

raus⁻ [whining]
'out'

[still sitting in the carriage]

          . . . .

(b)

                [a few minutes later]
[Simone has gone to the sand box with her parents]

M: Simone! Wir backen jetzt Kuchen!

'Simone! Let's make a cake!'

karre (=Kinderwagen) rein‾
'in carre'

Kuchen-
'Cake-'

karre rein‾
'in carre'

Willste in die Karre
rein?
'Do you want to go in
the carriage?'

karre‾
'carre'

In die Karre.
'In the carriage.'

[puts Simone into the
carriage]

. . . .

        The corpus in which these utterances of Simone
occur includes 1635 utterance tokens and 267 utterance
types. Of these only two types (three tokens) were
three-word-utterances. The syntactic complexity limit
seems therefore to be confined to the combination of two
words in this developmental phase. Of the following surface forms predicted by 'reduction transformations'

   (a)   (b)

>raus   rein
'out'   'in'
karre   karre
'carre' (= carriage)   'carre'
mone (=Simone)   mone
'mone'   'mone'
mone raus   mone rein
'mone out'   'mone in'
karre raus   >karre rein
'out carre'   'in carre'
mone karre   mone karre
'mone carre'   'mone carre'

Simone actually uses in spontaneous utterances only
those marked with the symbol > (cf. the presentation
of 'Bloom's reduction transformations and the sample
strings resulting from its operation' in Brown (1973:234).

From the child's <u>communicative egocentrism</u>, which can be described as the child's inability to separate the deictic centre of communicative acts from his own person, it follows that the child expresses certain parts of his 'semantic intentions' only implicitly. These parts of his 'semantic intentions' refer to the deictic centre (which for the child is always the child himself) and its role in the communication act comprising certain constant assumptions the child maintains about the role of his interlocutors in the communication act (cf. the discussion of deictic acts in Fillmore (1972)). In other words, the child uses only those surface structure forms (predicted by Bloom's 'reduction transformations') which from his own communicative perspective express non-redundant semantic information explicitly.

In case (b) <u>karre rein</u> 'in carre' this means that the argument which stands in the semantic relation 'agentive' (AGT) (mone) to the predicate 'rein' is not expressed in surface structure because this argument refers to the child himself. In case (a) <u>raus</u> 'out' this means that furthermore, in addition to case (b), the argument which stands in the semantic relation 'locative' (LOC) (karre) to the predicate 'raus' is not expressed in surface structure because this argument refers to the place where the child himself is already situated. (As analyses in Miller (1976) show, these derivational constraints, in case of local deixis, are independent of the subcategorization of the relational semantic concept 'locative' in 'position', 'source', and 'goal'.)

<u>Formal representation</u>:

(a)

$$AGT(x, LOC(y, P_2)) \quad\longrightarrow\quad V_p \quad (\text{'raus'})$$
Cond.: x = speaker (child)
$\qquad$ y = location of speaker (child)

(b)

$$AGT(x, LOC(y, P_2)) \quad\longrightarrow\quad N_y + V_p \quad (\text{'karre rein'})$$
Cond.: x = speaker (child)
$\qquad$ y ≠ location of speaker (child)

(The formal representation of semantic structures and their mapping into surface structure forms is expressed using a system of logic which is a modified form of the advanced predicate calculus as described in Reichenbach (1947) and Carnap (1958) and other works, e.g. Brekle (1970) and King (1974). This formal representation fulfills two purposes:

1. it allows the representation of the relational
nature of semantic cases: semantic relations are represented as higher-order predicates;

2. it allows the characterization of two aspects of
early child language which are relevant in this connection:

    (a) the representation of word-order rules, and

    (b) the representation of rules of ellipsis.

Word-order rules are expressed by giving syntactic constituents of the surface structure subscripts in conformity with matching logical symbols of the semantic
representation. Rules of ellipsis are expressed by
certain pragmatic conditions that state which parts of
the semantic representation are not expressed in surface
structure.)

      Nearly 12,000 utterances which two children
(social middle-class) produced at the age of 19 to 22
months have been analysed (Miller, 1976). This period
started when these children began to produce two-word-
utterances. At the end of this three-month period they
began to produce four-word utterances (Simone: MLU 1.008-
1.46; Meike: MLU 1.009-1.75). The data contain no
counter evidence to the above mentioned rule of local
deixis which states that the child never verbalizes a locative if this refers to the place where the child himself is already situated.

PERCEPTION OF CONTEXTUAL ALTERNATIVES AND THE ACQUISITION
OF SYNTAX

      There is another subclass of context-referen-
tial acts whose mechanism is personal deixis; this sub-
class demonstrates how the content of pragmatic constraints undergoes developmental change and how this relates to the syntactic development of the above mentioned
two children within the period of two-word utterances and
the transition period from two- to three-word utterances.

      Three developmental phases can be outlined:

1. In a first developmental phase the child produces
utterances like schuhe an 'shoes on':

Simone (age: 1;9.2/MLU: 1.09)

                      [preparing to go for a
                      walk]

(grumbles)

schuhe an⁻ [complaining]
'shoes on'
          [takes a shoe]

M: Ja, zieh dir doch die Schuhe
an, Simone! Das kannst du
ganz alleine!
'Right, put your shoes on,
Simone! You can do that by
yourself!'

schuhe⁻ [complaining]
'shoes'

Ma: (yawns) Maxe setzt sich
daneben.
'Maxe will sit down beside
you.'

schuhe⁻ [complaining]
'shoes' [moves close to Ma and
holds a shoe out to him]

schuhe⁻ [whining]
'shoes'

Ja, mach's doch mal alleine,
Simone! Zieh'n dir mal
alleine an, den Schuh! Hm?
Probier's mal alleine! Hm?
'Do it yourself, Simone!
Put the shoe on by yourself!
Hm? Just try it by your-
self! Hm?'

nein [complaining]
'no'

Soll dir Maxe die Schuhe
anziehen?
'Should Maxe put them on?'

schuhe⁻ [complaining]
'shoes' [impatiently]

M: Na ja, Maxe soll dir mal'n
bisschen helfen! Nich?
'Well, Maxe should help you
some, shouldn't he?'

Ma: Ja, gut, helf ich dir. Maxe
zieht dir den Schuh an.
'O.k., I'll help you. Maxe
will put your shoe on.'

. . . .

Formal representation:

$$AGT(x,BEN(y,OBJ(z,P_3))) \longrightarrow N_z + V_p \quad (\text{'schuhe an'})$$

Cond.: x = mother/father } interaction routine
      y = child

In utterances like <u>schuhe an</u> the arguments that stand
in the semantic relation 'agentive' (AGT) (mother) and
'benefactive' (BEN) (child) to the predicate 'an(ziehen)'
have not been expressed in surface structure. As discussed above, these arguments of the semantic representation of <u>schuhe an</u> are not explicitly expressed by the
child, not even in the form of replacement sequences,
because these implicit arguments refer to the deictic
centre and its role in the communication act comprising
certain 'interaction routines' which determine the 'semantic roles' of the communication participants.

2. In a second developmental phase the child produces
utterances like <u>mama ummachen</u> meaning something like
'Mama, please turn over the (milk) can':

Meike (age: 1;10/MLU: 1.75)

                    [Meike is playing with a milk can]

<u>kipp⁻ umkippen</u>
'tip'

<u>mama ummache⁄</u> [gives M the can]
'mama turn over'

                              M: Nee. <u>Mama will nichts
                                 umkippen</u>.
                                 'No. Mama will not
                                 turn over anything.'

<u>leine (=alleine) mache⁻</u>
'do it alone'

[takes the can again, wants
to pour milk into a cup]

                    [nothing leaks out of the can]

<u>geht nich˘</u> [holds the can out to M]
'doesn't work'

                              <u>Geht nich?</u>
                              'Doesn't work?'

<u>mama suchen⁄</u> (=versuchen)
'mama try'

                              <u>Mama versucht's. Na ja!</u>
                              'Mama will try it. All
                              right.'
                    . . . .

Formal representation:

$$AGT(x, OBJ(y, P_2)) \longrightarrow N_x + V_p \quad \text{('mama suchen',} \\ \text{'mama ummache')}$$
Cond.: $x \neq$ speaker (child) (contextual alternative)

In these utterances the arguments that stand in the semantic relation AGT (and possibly BEN) to the predicate are only expressed in the surface structure, if they do <u>not</u> refer to the child himself. This can be explained by the assumption that, whenever the child at the time of his utterances perceives <u>contextual alternatives</u> to potential referents of arguments which have been expressed only implicitly up to that time (that is, whenever the child rejects certain 'interaction routines' which have been valid for him up to that time), he tends to express this argument explicitly, if it does <u>not</u> refer to himself as the deictic centre of the communication act.

       A quite cogent illustration of this regularity can, for example, be found in the two-word utterances using the modal adverb 'auch' 'too', 'also':

<u>Meike</u> (age: 1;9.2/MLU: 1.35)

(a)

              [Tea-time]
              [Meike is drinking milk]
              [M and Ma are drinking tea]

[drinks milk]

<u>mama auch</u>`
'mama too'

              [M and Ma talk to each other]

<u>maxe auch</u>`
'maxe too '

              Ma: <u>Was auch? Maxe trinkt</u>
                    <u>auch Milch.</u> Hm?
                    'What too? Maxe is
                    drinking milk too,
                    isn't he?'

(laughs)

              . . . .

(b)

              [a moment later]

<u>auch milch</u>‾
'milk too'
[goes to Ma]

              [perceives Ma turning
               to his cup]

<u>auch</u>‾
‾too'   M: [gives Meike a cup
                                            filled with milk]

. . . .

<u>Formal representation</u>:

(a)

AUCH(AGT(x,OBJ(y,P$_2$))) ➤ N$_x$ + auch ('mama auch',
                                             'maxe auch')

Cond.: x ≠ speaker (child) (contextual alternative)

(b)

AUCH(AGT(x,OBJ(y,P$_2$))) ➤ auch + N$_y$ ('auch milch')
Cond.: x = speaker (child)

       Whenever the 'grammatical subject' of two-
word utterances with 'auch' has <u>not</u> been explicitly expressed in surface structure, it <u>refers</u> to the child
himself. Whenever at this developmental phase it has
been expressed, it does <u>not</u> refer to the child himself.
This can easily be expla<u>ined</u> by the approach presented
here since 'auch' has a predicative and a deictic function. As a deictic particle 'auch' always refers to
some contextual alternative.

       The achievement of this second developmental
phase may be summarized with the statement of the following <u>developmental principle</u>:

In connection with the perception of contextual alternatives (cf. Olson, 1972) the child partly replaces his
context-referential acts by syntactic constructions in
order to improve the pragmatic adequacy of his utterances.
This, however, leads to further construction problems
for a child who only produces two-word utterances. These
construction problems define the third developmental
phase.

3. If, for example, a child now produces <u>mama ummachen</u>
instead of <u>dose ummachen</u> ('turn over can'), <u>the argument</u>
which stands <u>in the</u> semantic relation 'objective' (OBJ)
(dose) to the predicate has not been explicitly expressed, whereas it still remains explicit in utterances
like <u>dose ummachen</u> where the absent 'agent' refers to
the <u>child himself.</u> Within the scope of this paper it
may be conjectured however, that arguments that stand in
the OBJ relation to the predicate have already been explicitly expressed in an earlier developmental phase
- due to the perception of contextual alternatives; that
is, certain context referential (deictic) acts have been

replaced by syntactic constructions which develop a certain autonomy (a point to be considered in a moment). And the construction problems which now arise for the child in that in any case his two-word utterances fail to meet his own standards concerning the pragmatic adequacy of his utterances are intensified by the following fact: the pragmatic rule, that an absent 'agent' must be taken to refer to the child himself, can finally be shaken by an intended persistent misunderstanding on part of the hearer. As can be inferred from the following utterances of Simone, the child solves these construction problems by expanding his two-word utterances to three-word utterances:

Simone (age:1;10.3/MLU:1.46)

[under her bed-cover and
 pretending to sleep]

Ma: Darf Max- Maxe
auch'n biss-Maxe
will auch'n bisschen
schlafen. Ne?
'Can Max- Maxe wants
a little- Maxe also
wants to sleep a
little. Hm?'

auch lafe⁻ (=schlafen)
'sleep too'

[slips under the
bed-cover beside
Simone]

Maxe schläft schon.
'Maxe is already
sleeping.'

auch läft⁻ (=schläft)
'sleeps too'

Wer schläft auch?
'Who is sleeping
too?'

mone auch läft⁻
'mone sleeps too'

[pushes Ma away from her
bed-cover]

[sits down again on
the bed-cover]

Jetzt hat sich der
Maxe hingesetzt. Ne?
'Now Maxe has sat
down, hasn't he?'

auch heia⁻ auch⁻
'too sleep too'

Hm?

auch heia
'sleep too'

Maxe soll auch heia
machen?
'Maxe should sleep
  too?'

mm [denying]

Macht die Simone heia?
'Is Simone going to
sleep?'

(complains)

Ach Mone! Nun sei
doch nich so grausam
zu mir. Ich will doch
auch'n bisschen heia
machen. Hm?
'Oh Mone! Now don't be

mone auch heia⁻ [softly   so mean to me. I'd like
'mone sleep too' complaining] to sleep a little too.
                              Hm?'

. . . .

Formal representation:

$$\text{AUCH}(\text{AGT}(x, P_1)) \rightarrow N_x + auch + V_P \quad (\text{'mone auch läft'},$$
$$\text{'mone auch heia'})$$

Cond.: x ≠ hearer (contextual alternative)

We may summarize the achievement of this
third developmental phase with the slight modification
of our earlier developmental principle: In connection
with the cumulative perception of contextual alternatives
the child begins to replace his context-referential acts
by syntactic constructions and finally expands his syntactic constructions in order to effect the pragmatic
adequacy of his utterances.

It goes without saying that this developmental mechanism is only one aspect or one dimension of a
developmental grammar. Taking into account the results
of other language acquisition projects during the last

years as well as of our own research, there seems to
be enough empirical evidence to assume at least the
following three interdependent developmental principles
pertaining to the very early acquisition of languages:

1. The development of relational semantic concepts
like 'agentive', 'objective', etc., which presuppose
the cognitive development of the child, determines and
constrains the child's process of formulating and testing hypotheses about the syntactic surface structure
of his language.

2. The impulse behind this process of formulating and
testing hypotheses can be found in the continuously re-
appearing discrepancy between the child's elliptical
realization of 'semantic intentions' and his own developing pragmatic standards concerning the communicative adequacy of his utterances.

3. Once context-referential acts have been replaced
by syntactic constructions, syntactic rules develop a
certain autonomy; that is, they determine the child's
production and perception of speech to such an extent
that the child now expresses certain substructures of
his semantic representations largely independent from
situational contexts. The acquisition of syntax thus
leads, as Grace de Laguna (1927) stated it, to 'a progressive freeing of speech from its dependence on the
perceived conditions under which it is uttered and heard,
and from the behavior which accompanies it'.

In this way, if one takes the perspective of
the child, new syntactic forms make possible the communicatively adequate elliptical realization of successively more complex semantic structures. These in turn
determine the child's reconstruction of syntax, once
the child is pressed by his social interaction to
successively decentre his communicative perspective;
that is, to notice a discrepancy between what his
'semantic intentions' are and what can objectively be
conveyed by his utterances.

Although there is strong empirical evidence
for partly reducing the learnability of syntax to the
pragmatic development of the child, it would nonetheless be dishonest to conceal that this circularity in
the acquisition of syntax, semantics, and pragmatics
- though it might close certain gaps in the reconstruction of a developmental grammar - is at the present state of affairs rather a heuristically meaningful hypothesis than an empirically well attested research outcome.

REFERENCES

Bloom, L. (1970)   Language Development: Form and Function in Emerging Grammars. M.I.T. Press, Cambridge, Mass.

Brekle, H.E. (1970)   Generative Satzsemantik und transformationelle Syntax im System der eng- lischen Nominalkomposition. Wilhelm Fink, München.

Brown, R. (1973)   A First Language: the Early Stages. Harvard University Press, Cambridge, Mass.

Carnap, R. (1958)   Introduction to Symbolic Logic and its Application. Trans. by W.M. Meyer and J. Wilkinson. Dover, New York.

Cromer, R. (1974)   The Development of Language and Cognition: The Cognition Hypothesis. In B. Foss (ed.) New Perspectives in Child Develop- ment. Penguin, Harmondsworth, Middx., England.

Fillmore, Ch.J. (1972)   Ansätze zu einer Theorie der Deixis. In F. Kiefer (ed.) Semantik und ge- nerative Grammatik. 2 Bände. Max Niemeyer, Frankfurt.

Fodor, Bever, and Garrett (1974)   The Psychology of Language. McGraw-Hill, New York.

King, R.T. (1974)   Modern Semantic Theory: a Critical Analysis and an Application to the Study of German Prepositions. Ph.D. dissertation. Rice University, Texas.

de Laguna, G. (1927)   Speech: Its Function and De- velopment. Indiana University Press, Bloomington. 2nd edition (1963).

Miller, M. (1976 in press)   Zur Logik der frühkind- lichen Sprachentwicklung-Empirische Unter- suchungen zum Erwerb kommunikativer Fähig- keiten. Klett Verlag, Stuttgart.

Olson, D.R. (1972)   Language Use for Communicating, Instructing, and Thinking. In I. Carroll and R. Freedle (eds.) Language Comprehen- sion and the Acquisition of Knowledge. Wiley, New York.

Reichenbach, H. (1947)   Elements of Symbolic Logic. Free Press, New York.

Rommetveit, R. (1968)   Words, Meanings and Messages. Academic Press, New York.

Some Differences between First and Second Language Aquisition

S.W. Felix

In this paper three major differences between
first and second language acquisition will be outlined.
It will be shown that in the earliest stages of development the second language (L2) learner's linguistic competence is fundamentally different from the one commonly
attributed to a child acquiring his mother tongue. Many
of the syntactic structures typical of early first
language (L1) acquisition do not occur in the speech of
children who learn a second language in a natural environment, i.e. without receiving any type of formal instruction. Furthermore, the order in which certain sentence
structures emerge is essentially different in first and
second language acquisition. Consequently there is reason
to believe that in some areas L1 and L2 learners do not
pursue either the same or similar strategies to achieve
adult competence.

---

*I gratefully acknowledge invaluable advice and
criticism from various people in our research group,
notably from Henning Wode, Deitrich Lange, and Dieter
Furkmann. I also wish to thank Christa Meyer for her
help in collecting the data.

Certain properties of early L2 utterances as well as the particular order in which structures are acquired can be directly related to the fact that the L2 learner makes use of his first language experience. However, contrary to the claims of many theories of interference, e.g. Nemser (1971) and Selinker (1972), there is strong evidence to suggest that the L2 learner does not simply transfer L1 structures onto L2, but rather utilizes his prior linguistic knowledge on a much more abstract level. There is no indication in my data that interference plays more than a marginal role in second language acquisition in a natural environment (see Felix, 1976).

Traditionally, problems of second language acquisition have been primarily dealt with in the context of foreign language teaching, where typically the learning process is guided and controlled by various types of formal instruction. This kind of research has for the most part concentrated on the question of how teaching material and teaching methods should be structured in order to ensure quick and effective learning. Investigations on how children acquire a second language in a natural environment are very few in number and have been started only in the last few years. The more recent studies, e.g. Dulay and Burt (1974a, 1974b), and Boyd (1975), have been mainly concerned with the emergence of verb and noun inflections. With few exceptions (see Hakuta 1974), the order in which various inflectional endings are acquired seems to roughly parallel the one determined by Brown (1973) for first language acquisition. As for L2 syntactic development little if anything is known.

In the absence of detailed empirical data, some researchers, e.g. McNeill (1965), Corder (1967) and others, have claimed that first and second language acquisition must by and large involve the same basic psycholinguistic strategies and processes. Differences are seen above all in the influence of non-linguistic factors, such as motivation, memory span, general maturity, etc. However, the crucial question if and to what extent these factors determine the development of linguistic structures in the L2 learner, has hardly ever been discussed.

The studies by Huang (1971) and Ravem (1974), who observed the acquisition of English by a Taiwanese boy and two Norwegian children respectively, seem to lend support to an L1 = L2 hypothesis. Both authors found striking parallels between first and second language acquisition of interrogative and negative structures. Contrary to these findings, the early stages of L2 development, in particular the acquisition of sentence types, will be shown to be fundamentally different from first language acquisition. Consequently the two processes are neither totally the same nor completely different. Rather, it seems that the relationship between first and second language acquisition has to be specified in terms of different structural levels and areas.

THE DATA

For the past years a group working at Kiel University has observed some English-speaking children, aged four to seven who were acquiring German as a second language in a natural environment, i.e. without receiving any kind of formal instruction. In this paper data will be presented from Guy, seven years old, and his sister Julie, five years old.

The children were observed for a total period of eight months. Two investigators visited Guy and Julie at their home two to three times per week. Each visit lasted approximately $2\frac{1}{2}$ to 3 hrs. and was tape-recorded. The tapes were subsequently transcribed in conventional orthography with comments on the situational context.

The parents of Guy and Julie had both received a college education. Before the family moved to Germany, the children had not been exposed to German. At home they always maintained English, as the parents spoke little or no German. Guy was enrolled in a local school two months after the family arrived in Germany. At the same time Julie started going to kindergarten. The two children heard the new language primarily from their peers. Only rarely were they exposed to German conversations among adults. Apart from weekends, Guy and Julie spent roughly half of their day in a German-speaking environment. With the exception of the two investigators and some of Guy's school teachers who had a moderate command of English, the children mixed only with monolingual German speakers.

The corpus contains only spontaneous utterances. No formal experiments were carried out. In general, the two investigators joined in the children's activities whatever these happened to be. Most of the time they played in the basement with the children's toys. During the summer time they frequently played in the garden or took the children for a walk to the nearby airport or city park to provide for some situational variation. Although it was originally intended to administer some accompanying tests, both Guy and Julie proved to be not very co-operative in anything that remotely resembled an artificial communication situation.

SUCCESSIVE ACQUISITION OF SENTENCE TYPES

During the first two to three months, Guy and Julie produced only three different multi-word utterance types:

(a)   sentence imitation

(b)   noun phrases, usually of the form adj + N

(c)   copular sentences

The term sentence imitation refers to those utterances which, from their very first occurrence, were fully grammatical, both syntactically and morphologically. Compared to other utterances produced during the same developmental stage, they showed a surprisingly high degree of structural complexity. They furthermore occurred only for a relatively short period of time and then disappeared. These properties seem to indicate that the children learned and stored such structures as wholes and did not generate them by rules of grammar. Here are a few examples from Guy:

(1)   sprechen Sie Deutsch.   'do you speak German'

(2)   lass das doch sein.   'cut it out'

(3)   möchten Sie eine Tasse Kaffee.'do you want a cup of
                                       coffee'

(4)   hau ab, du Doofmann.   'get out of here, you
                                       idiot'

        The majority of non-copular two-word utterances produced during the initial stage consists of a noun preceded by an adjective or mein 'my':

(5)   grün Baum.   'green tree'

(6)   grosse Auto.   'big car'

(7)   meine Tasche.   'my bag'

(8)   viele Ball.   'many ball'

These noun phrases show grammatical word order, but deviate from adult usage in that the adjective-noun agreement is not yet fully established. Structures such as (5) - (8) occurred either as answers to a 'what is that?' type of question or as spontaneous utterances by which the children described visual impressions.

        Apart from sentence imitations and two-term noun phrases the predominant structure in Guy's and Julie's early speech was the copular sentence:

(9)   dast is ein Wind.   'that is a wind

(10) dies ein Haus.   'this is a house'

(11) das gut.   'that good'

(12) das ist grün. 'that is green'

(13) das ist for du. 'that is for you'

(14) das für die Turm. 'that for the tower'

In these early copular sentences the copula was frequently, but not regularly, missing. The subject of the sentence was always a pronoun, never a noun. In predicate function nouns emerged chronologically first, later adjectives appeared, and finally prepositional phrases (see Felix, 1976 in press). During this early period no main verb sentences occurred. The developmental priority of the copular sentence is furthermore demonstrated by the fact that both children used this structure even in situations in which the adult language requires a different sentence type. Thus Julie asked the writer to put a box on a shelf, by using the copular sentence du da ist das 'you there is that' with the apparent intention of an imperative, while simultaneously pointing to the shelf. In another situation Julie and the writer were drawing pictures on two sheets of paper. After a while Julie looked over and asked was ist du? 'what are you'. The context made it quite clear that the girl wanted to know what was being drawn. The utterance was intuitively interpreted correctly and the answer given: I'm drawing a tree.

After this initial stage other sentence types started to appear. The first non-copular sentence structures to occur all contained an auxiliary as the only verb constituent. This construction, though with certain restrictions, is also permissible in adult German:

(15) ich kann das. 'I can (do) that'

(16) du kann hier. 'You can (play) here'

(17) du musst so. 'You must (do it) this way'

(18) ich muss nicht Schule. 'I need not (go to) school'

Approximately two weeks later a growing number of main verb sentences were recorded:

(19) ich essen Banane. 'I eat banana'

(20) du bleib hier. 'You stay here'

(21) ich komme gleich. 'I come soon'

(22) ich gehe raus. 'I go outside'

These data show very clearly that the L2 learner acquires the different sentence structures in a distinct chronological order. It is particularly striking that Guy and Julie produced in the earliest period, apart from sentence imitations and isolated noun phrases, only copular sentence structures which they used even in situations in which the adult language - both English and German - requires a different sentence type. In contrast to this, L1 learners have been shown to produce a multitude of different structures as early as the initial two-word stage. Bowerman (1973) observed at least 12 different structures in the speech of her subject Kendall at an MLU (mean length of utterance) of 1.48. Sentences containing verbs are among the earliest and most frequent multi-word utterances of L1 learners, whereas Guy and Julie acquired main verb sentences distinctly later than copular structures. Similarly, Bloom (1970) found at an MLU below 2.0 five different relations underlying the frequent N + N combinations. None of these structures appeared during the early stages of Guy's and Julie's L2 development. In particular, neither child ever produced a two-term S + O utterance which seems to be typical of early L1 acquisition (but see Smoczynska this volume. Eds.)

Compared to the structural diversity in the early speech of L1 learners, Guy's and Julie's competence during the first three months of their L2 development seems to be amazingly restricted.

WORD ORDER

A typical phenomenon of early L1 acquisition is that the children use different word orders to express the same grammatical relation. Although many sentences show adult word order, there are numerous examples in which constituents are combined in a way which is not permissible in the adult language. A few examples of grammatical and ungrammatical word order from Bowerman's (1973) data are presented in Table 1. Variation in word order was also observed by Park (1974) in his study on German first language acquisition. Park found examples of all six mathematically possible two-term combinations of subject, verb, and object in the speech of a Swiss girl at age 2;0 to 2;4. Contrary to this, Guy's and Julie's declarative sentences showed only one particular word order for each grammatical relation. Both in copular and later in S + V/Aux + O sentences the word order was always in strict accordance with the corresponding structures of the adult language. Deviant word order occurred only much later in connection with the placement of adverbs and various German inversion transformations.

Typical examples of early child language are furthermore utterances which do not directly reflect structures of the adult language but seem to represent the child's own grammatical system. Some of the by now classical examples from Braine (1963), frequently ignored in recent discussions on language development, are

TABLE 1. Grammatical and ungrammatical word order in L1 production (data from Bowerman, 1973)

S = subject, V = verb, O = object.

Grammatical	Ungrammatical
S + V	V + S
(23) Kendall swim	(28) hug Mommy
(24) Mommy sleep	(29) see Kendall
V + O	O + V
(25) look Kendall	(30) doggie sew
(26) bite ... finger	(31) Kimmy kick
S + V + O	O + V + S
(27) Kimmy ride bike	(32) Mummy bite Kendall

allgone shoe, byebye man, see hot, nightnight office, etc.
None of the L2 learners we observed ever produced comparable utterances. Guy's and Julie's declarative sentences
could always be matched with corresponding structures of
the adult language. Although the two children frequently
overgeneralized adult structures (see Felix in prep.),
there is no indication that, in forming basic sentence
types, they used rules which do not exist in the target
language.

VOCABULARY

The third difference concerns the acquisition
of lexical items. Although Guy and Julie rapidly acquired
new syntactic structures, their vocabulary remained
surprisingly small during the entire period of observation. After five months of acquiring German neither child
was recorded to produce more than 40 different nouns and
20 different adjectives. Since during the early stage
only noun phrases and copular sentences were used productively, the children's knowledge of verbs developed
even more slowly. Even after Guy and Julie had acquired
most basic sentence structures, interrogatives, negatives,
and certain types of embeddings, their vocabulary was so
small that they frequently had to resort to English lexical

items. This seems to indicate that the development of syntactic structures is largely independent of the size of the vocabulary. In contrast, L1 learners appear to acquire a substantial number of words before they start to combine these to form syntactic constructions. Thus Bloom's (1970) Kathryn used at least 100 different nouns, 21 adjectives, and 23 verbs at MLU 1.32.

Apart from size, our L2 learners' early vocabulary also differs in quality from the one of L1 learners. Whereas pronouns appear to be relatively rare in early L1 utterances, they were the most frequently used words in Guy's and Julie's speech. The two children freely used das 'that' and dies 'this' to denote objects whose German name they did not know. This strategy often resulted in semantically empty or uninterpretable utterances. Thus Julie occasionally 'described' pictures with sentences such as das ist das und das ist das 'that is that and that is that'.

DISCUSSION

If the early stages of first and second language acquisition are compared, two facts appear to be particularly striking: (a) the L2 learner produces fewer different structures than the L1 learner; (b) certain utterance types, such as allgone shoe or see hot, which cannot be directly related to corresponding syntactic patterns of the adult language, are restricted to first language acquisition and do not seem to occur in the speech of L2 learners.

In the light of current theories (McNeill 1970; Roeper 1973) which claim that the knowledge of certain grammatical relations is innate and hence does not have to be acquired, the comparatively small number of different syntactic structures in early L2 speech will be difficult to explain. Why should the L2 learner who is both cognitively and intellectually more advanced than the L1 learner and who has furthermore the benefit of prior linguistic experience, express his intentions during the initial stage primarily through copular sentences and certain types of isolated noun phrases, whereas the L1 learner produces a multitude of different structures as early as the two-word stage? If the L1 learner verbalizes a large variety of grammatical relations as soon as he starts to construct multi-word utterances, why should the L2 learner not be able to do the same?

It seems that this fundamental difference between early first and second language development can only be explained if we assume that the L1 learner does not construct his earliest multi-word utterances on the basis of syntactic rules. Bloom (1973) was among the first to present evidence suggesting that the L1 learner, at the

earliest stage of development, combines words to express
relations between cognitive concepts. Only later does
the child discover the syntactic principle of language
and will then acquire the various grammatical categories
and structures of the adult language. Consequently the
earliest two-term utterances express conceptual, not
grammatical relations. Before the child starts to acquire
adult rules, he will pass through a pre-syntactic stage
of development during which utterances are constructed on
the basis of non-syntactic properties of words.

If we accept Bloom's (1973) theory, the reason
for the differences between first and second language
acquisition seems to be clear. Due to his past linguistic
knowledge the L2 learner is already familiar with the syntactic principle of natural languages. He knows that
words cannot be randomly combined, even if the underlying
conceptual or semantic relation is clear. Verbal utterances have to be constructed in accordance with certain
grammatical rules. This is what the L1 learner does not
yet know at the beginning of his language development.
He has to discover, i.e. acquire the knowledge of, the
syntactic principle. Consequently he will at first construct his utterances according to some other, i.e. non-
syntactic rules.

Because of his linguistic experience, the L2
learner does not have to go through the pre-syntactic
stage of development characteristic of early first language acquisition. Consequently we do not find in the
L2 learner's speech any of those utterances (allgone shoe,
see hot, etc.) which do not conform to syntactic patterns
of the adult language, but which are presumably constructed on the basis of conceptual relations. The L2 learner's
first task will be to discover grammatical regularities
and syntactic structures in the language he is exposed to.
It is clear that his learning capacity imposes restrictions
on the number of structures he can acquire at a time. Consequently we find during the first months of development
only very few different utterance types. As the L2 learner
advances, he acquires more and more new structures. For
reasons which cannot yet be explained, at least Guy and
Julie began with the copular sentence. However, it is
conceivable that other L2 learners might choose a different type of structure to start with. What is important
is not so much the particular order in which various
structures emerge, but rather the fact that the L2 learner
produces at first only a small number of different
utterance types.

In contrast to the L2 learner, the L1 learner
who has presumably acquired a relatively large variety
of congnitive concepts by the time his language development begins, will attempt to express verbally at
least the majority of conceptual categories and relations
with which he is familiar. Consequently his early speech

will show a correspondingly large variety of different utterance types. Some of these utterances may in fact look like mere simplifications of adult structures. However, a superficial similarity cannot be considered sufficient evidence for the assumption that the child does in fact construct his sentences according to the same or similar rules as the adult speaker.

It seems that the differences between first and second language development outlined in this paper lend very strong support to the claim that the L1 learner's early utterances express conceptual, not grammatical relations. If the opposite were assumed, the L2 learner would appear to be a retarded, rather than a cognitively, intellecutally, and linguistically more advanced child.

REFERENCES

Bloom, L. (1970)   Language Development: Form and Function in Emerging Grammars. M.I.T. Press, Cambridge, Mass.

Bloom, L. (1973)   One Word at a Time. Mouton, The Hague.

Bowerman, M. (1973)   Early Syntactic Development: a Cross-Linguistic Study with Special Reference to Finnish. Cambridge University Press, Cambridge.

Boyd, P. (1975)   The Development of Grammar Categories in Spanish by Anglo Children Learning a Second Language. TESOL Quarterly 9. 125-135.

Braine, M.D.S. (1963)   The Ontogeny of English Phrase Structure: the First Phase. Language 39. 1-13.

Brown, R. (1973)   A First Language: the Early Stages. Allen and Unwin, London.

Corder, S.P. (1967)   Significance of Learners' Errors. IRAL V/4. 162-169.

Dulay, H. and Burt, M. (1974a) Natural Sequences in Child Second Language Acquisition. Language Learning 24 37-53.

Dulay, H. and Burt, M. (1974b) A New Perspective on the Creative Construction Processes in Child Second Language Acquisition. Language Learning 24. 253-278.

Felix, S. (1976 in press)   Interference, Interlanguage, and Related Issues. In C. Molony and H. Zobl (eds.) German in Contact with Other Languages. Scriptor Verlag, Kronberg/Taunus, Germany.

Felix, S. (In prep.)   Linguistische Untersuchungen zum englisch-deutschen Zweitsprachenerwerb unter natürlichen Bedingungen.

Hakuta, K. (1974)   A Preliminary Report on the Development of Grammatical Morphemes in a Japanese Girl learning English as a Second Language. Working Papers on Bilingualism No.3. Ontario Institute for Studies in Education. Toronto.

Huang, J. (1971)   A Chinese Child's Acquisition of English Syntax. M.A. Thesis UCLA.

McNeill, D. (1965)   Some Thoughts on First and Second Language Acquisition. Manuscript.

McNeill, D. (1970)   The Acquisition of Language: the Study of Developmental Psycholinguistics. Harper and Row, New York.

Nemser, W. (1971)   Aproximative Systems of Foreign Language Learners. IRAL IX/2.   115-123.

Park, T.Z. (1974)   A study of German Language Development. Manuscript. Bern,Switzerland.

Ravem, R. (1974)   Second Language Acquisition.   Dissertation. Essex University.

Roeper, T. (1973)   Connecting Children's Language and Linguistic Theory. In T. Moore (ed.) Cognitive Development and the Acquisition of Language. Academic Press, New York.

Selinker, L. (1972)   Interlanguage. IRAL X/3.   209-231.

Author Index

Subject Index